Didacti

Theo Hug (Ed.)

Didactics of Microlearning

Concepts, Discourses and Examples

Waxmann 2007
Münster / New York / München / Berlin

Bibliographic information published by Die Deutsche Bibliothek
Die Deutsche Bibliothek lists this publication in the
Deutsche Nationalbibliografie; detailed bibliographic data
are available in the internet at http://dnb.d-nb.de

Printed with support from the
Federal Ministry for Science and Research, Vienna (Austria)
and the University of Innsbruck (Austria)

BM.W_Fª

ISBN 978-3-8309-1869-1

© Waxmann Verlag GmbH, 2007
Postfach 8603, 48046 Münster, Germany
Waxmann Publishing Co.
P. O. Box 1318, New York, NY 10028, U. S. A.

www.waxmann.com
info@waxmann.com

Cover Design: Christian Averbeck, Münster
Print: Hubert und Co., Göttingen
Printed on age-resistant paper, DIN 6738

Contents

Acknowledgements 9

Introduction
Didactics of Microlearning – Introductory Note
Theo Hug 10

Outline of a Microlearning Agenda
Theo Hug & Norm Friesen.. 15

I Media, Knowledge & Learning: Exploring the Field
From Meno to Microlearning: A Historical Survey
Helmwart Hierdeis 35

Connectivism: Creating a Learning Ecology in Distributed Environments
George Siemens 53

Order from Intermediality. An Outline of a Model of Knowledge Production
and Knowledge Reception
Monika Seidl & Klaus Puhl.. 69

II Microdidactics & Microlearning
(Micro-)Didactics: A Tale of two Traditions
Norm Friesen 83

Microlearning as a Challenge for Instructional Design
Michael Kerres 98

How "Micro" Can Learning Be? A Neuropsychological Perspective on Microlearning
Franziska Scherer & Martin Scherer 110

What Size is Micro? – Using a Didactical Approach Based on Learning Objectives to
Define Granularity
Thomas Eibl 125

Thinking About the 'm' in Mobile Learning
Gunther Kress & Norbert Pachler 139

Lurking as Microlearning in Virtual Communities. An Explorative Analysis
of Changing Information Behavior
Nina Kahnwald 155

III Towards new Learning Spaces: Educational Technology, Games
& Playful Approaches

Learning: The Creative Application of Illusions
Peter Krieg 171

Blogs and Chats: Some Critical Remarks on Electronic Communication
Karl Leidlmair 187

Playing History: Reflections on Mobile and Location-Based Learning
Joost Raessens 200

When Remix Culture Meets Microlearning
Ravi Purushotma 218

The *Doctor Who* Principle: Microlearning and the episodic nature of almost everything
Kendal Newman & Robert Grigg 236

Storytelling as a Motivational Tool in Digital Learning Games
Matthias Bopp 250

Experiences in Setting up a Virtual Learning Game Project
Pasi Mattila, Jukka Miettunen & Tony Manninen 267

IV Connecting Micro Steps

Providing Macrostructure for Microlearning
Bernhard Ertl & Heinz Mandl 283

From Double-Loop Learning to Triple-Loop Learning. Profound Change, Individual
Cultivation, and the Role of Wisdom in the Context of the Microlearning Approach
Markus F. Peschl 292

Small Steps Towards a Culture of Deliberative Learning:
Media Supported Pyramid Discussions
Christiane Schmidt 313

RTFM! Teach Yourself Culture in Open Source Software Projects
Mirko Tobias Schäfer & Patrick Kranzlmüller 324

V Microlearning & Higher Education

Web-based Video Conferencing in Transnational Higher Education:
Pedagogies and Good Practice
Stylianos Hatzipanagos, Raphael Commins & Anthony 'Skip' Basiel 341

Contents

On the Relationship of Didactical Characteristics and the Use of ICT
Sigrid Blömeke & Christiane Müller 355

What is Quality University Learning and How Might Microlearning Help to Achieve it?
Beverley Oliver 365

VI Evaluation, Implementation & Quality Management
A Generative Model for Evaluation of Microlearning Processes
Wolfgang Hagleitner & Theo Hug 381

Quality Management for the Implementation of E-learning
Susanne Kinnebrock, Berit Baeßler & Patrick Rössler 398

About the Contributors 417

Acknowledgements

This book is about microlearning – exploring examples, defining concepts and developing didactical approaches apposite to this emergent learning form. On the one hand, it revisits old pedagogical and philosophical questions concerning the design of learning environments and resources; and on the other, it deals with new learning contexts and phenomena as these appear on various micro-levels in our media-saturated society. Obviously, a book covering so many aspects of such a broad topic can only be the result of many people working together. I would like to thank all the contributors for their immense commitment, patience, and cooperation. It has been a pleasure to work together fruitfully with such a range of individuals from many different disciplines and nationalities, and to sound out important concerns related to microlearning, and finally, to turn these discussions and ideas into book form.

I would particularly like to thank Sarah Winkler for her careful layout, Gerhard Ortner for feeding final corrections, Barbara Simler for her diligent proofreading, and also Norm Friesen for always being there to discuss the many translation questions which inevitably come up in a project like this. We were fortunate to have Beate Plugge and Melanie Völker from Waxmann publishers to support us. Finally, my thanks go to the Federal Ministry of Science and Research (bm:wf⁺), Austria, and to the University of Innsbruck, Austria, for their funding of the printing costs.

August 2007

Theo Hug

Didactics of Microlearning – Introductory Note

Theo Hug

Learning is vital to human life and indispensable to education. Both the possibility and necessity of learning and unlearning can be taken as markers of the *conditio humana*, no matter how we characterize societies and lifeworlds we may be asked to consider. Imagine trying to get along with the demands of everyday life simply on the basis of instincts! Learning is necessary because we have to change ourselves in changing environments, and we have to empower ourselves to change these environments as well (cf. Göhlich & Zirfas, 2007, p. 7). Of course, countless ways of conceptualizing and thematizing learning have been developed throughout history – and they are no less in number than the ways of understanding teaching, educating, upbringing, socializing, knowing, thinking, acting, feeling, doing, and behaving. Significantly, practical and theoretical perspectives on learning seem to act as kinds of nexus-points where individual, organizational, institutional, societal, medial, and historical plans intersect (cf. Göhlich et al., 2007; Schunk, 2007).

Many aspects of learning have been described on micro- as well as on meso- or macro-levels. Astonishingly, microlearning as an area of explicit emphasis is rather new, though it is related to phenomena such as implicit, informal, and incidental forms of learning that have been on the agenda for many years. Being involved in discussions and exchanges at various conferences in different countries over last five years, I have gradually developed the impression that the question of a "microlearning agenda" and its urgency is variously understood: some tend to think that it is too late for micro-learning, for example because it has already been an implicit part of microteaching dis-courses for decades. Although we can continue to learn a great deal from the collegial and reflective models typical of microteaching, it would be a mistake to reduce micro-learning simply to a sub-type or derivative form of microteaching activity. Doing so would seriously shortchange the importance of recent developments in digital media, and the improvisatory forms and the participatory cultures that they enable. Other voices in my wide-ranging discussions drew attention to economic forms which have gained precedence not only over politics but also over processes of education and re-search. The foci of our teaching and research, they would argue, persist ultimately be-cause of economic imperatives; because of their economic utility. But even if we were to agree that knowledge has been largely instrumentalized, and that the pedagogic sphere has been thoroughly contaminated with commercial interest, we cannot ignore the intentions and will of individual learners, the limits of calculability itself, and *eigenvalues* (Heinz von Foerster) of educational systems. These and other factors con-stantly undo even the best-laid plans to reduce education to simple economic expe-diency and procedural efficiency.

There are also those who thought that it might be too early for a volume such as this, arguing that new forms of microlearning are still evolving. The implication is that this continuing change would necessitate a volume focusing on a few very specific, isolated learning cultures, and that extrapolating from these would produce a distorted "bigger picture" of microlearning. I disagree. In my view, this collection on the *Didactics of Microlearning* is very timely. New technical and institutional forms are indeed transforming the structures and dynamics of the production and distribution of knowledge, and the acquisition of skills and competencies. As social and mediatic forms change, so does learning itself. It is incumbent upon us to challenge ourselves in this regard, to explore and experiment with the educational possibilities and limitations of these new spaces and places of learning.

The contributors to this volume have accepted this challenge and undertaken these explorations, employing a range of strategies and points of departure. Apart from the introductory chapter providing an "Outline of a Microlearning Agenda" (Theo Hug & Norm Friesen), the collection is structured into six sections. In the first section on *Media, Knowledge & Learning*, the field is explored in terms of a brief history of microlearning by Helmwart Hierdeis, a connectivist approach "Creating a Learning Ecology in Distributed Environments," by George Siemens, and an "Outline of a Model of Knowledge Production and Knowledge Reception." In the latter, Klaus Puhl and Monika Seidl explain micro-macro-relations in terms of Wittgenstein's concept of "perspicuous representations," and use the informative example of the "invention" of hysteria as an "illness of the soul" by Jean-Martin Charcot in the 19th century in Paris at the Salpêtrière.

Section II on *Microdidactics & Microlearning* starts with a re-examination and re-thinking of conceptions and traditions underlying didactic and instructional theory. Norm Friesen explores the possibilities for such a re-thinking by discussing the different approaches of Anglo-American didactic (instructional) theory on the one hand, and German and northern-European Didaktik on the other. Michael Kerres also refers to these two traditions. He advocates their integration and argues that instructional design does not become dispensable, but rather, even more important, complex and challenging in the context of "web 2.0" developments. Franziska and Martin Scherer explore the size and granularity implied in microlearning from a neuropsychological perspective, while Thomas Eibl outlines a didactic approach for microlearning based on learning objectives. Further contributions focus on integration of digital technologies into social and cultural practices. Nina Kahnwald considers "lurking" as a form of microlearning in virtual communities, while Gunther Kress and Norbert Pachler raise crucial issues regarding 'mobile learning' generally, and bring these into relationship with questions of affordances, and of the pace and the dialectic of our adaptation to technologies and our adoption of technologies for our own purposes.

Section III, *Towards New Learning Spaces,* offers a wide range of conceptual considerations and practical examples concerning *Educational Technology,* and *Games and*

Playful Approaches. Peter Krieg introduces a radical "relationist" vision of learning and knowledge. He sees microlearning as an emerging application of relational and generative concepts of learning with the help of new and emerging technologies, such as neural networks and generative computer games. Karl Leidlmair investigates the role of situated knowledge for establishing and understanding well-grounded meaning. Looking at examples provided by blogs and chat forums, he explores the transparency of background knowledge through reference to Heideggerian notions of intentionality. Joost Raessens analyses the ways in which mobile and location-based technologies can be used as microlearning tools. He focuses on *Frequency 1550*, a situated exploration of historical urban environments that was developed by the Dutch Waag Society in Amsterdam in 2005, and summarizes provisional pedagogical outcomes and plans for the future. Ravi Purushotma's chapter identifies different methods employed by those involved in "mash-ups," manipulations and remixes of popular media. Furthermore, curriculum designers are encouraged to make use of some of these same techniques in order to create "natural hooks" where they can connect microlearning content directly with popular media content. Ken Newman and Robert Grigg start from the assumption that learning and microlearning are "inherently episodic." They articulate a *"Dr. Who* principle" of narrative or content arrangement, and consider its application in the context of microlearning. Similarly, Matthias Bopp provides a theoretical framework for the use of storytelling in educational digital games as a motivational tool. And Pasi Mattila, Jukka Miettunen, and Tony Manninen describe two exemplary projects aiming at the creation of a virtual space designed to enhance learning.

Section IV on *Connecting Micro Steps* presents a selection of ways in which the association of microlearning elements can be conceptualized and linked to form comprehensive models. Bernhard Ertl and Heinz Mandl show four learning environments corresponding to different communication scenarios—involving asynchronous discussion boards, computer chat, videoconferencing and co-present computer use. After highlighting differences between these scenarios, they illustrate the need for applying advanced instructional designs for such environments and their interrelated aspects. Markus Peschl takes a rather different tack, calling for "profound change, individual cultivation, and the role of wisdom in the context of the microlearning approach." He develops a typology of knowledge and an epistemological framework with reference to a *triple-loop learning strategy* and a *U-theory* (C. O. Scharmer). These constructs act as ways of integrating various types of (existential) knowledge and epistemological processes (e.g., suspending, redirecting, presencing, etc.) with the technologies typical of the microlearning approach. Christiane Schmidt explains the basic idea of deliberative didactic, intended to improve decision-making competency in discussion and research. She illustrates the potentials of this approach using a specific method of deliberation: namely, the "pyramid discussion," which enables experiences to be described and considered in small steps towards the deliberative managment of knowledge in virtual teams. Mirko Schäfer and Patrick Kranzlmüller take the everyday problem of simple questions from new users of software who refer to documentation in ReadMe files and the "Frequently Asked Questions" documents. They demonstrate how the gap between advanced and novice users could be bridged through "better co-operation between developers and end-users, facilitated by suitable integration of microlearning-steps and a dynamic information system." (ibd.)

Section V focuses on concepts and examples in the field of *Microlearning & Higher Education*. Stylianos Hatzipanagos, Raphael Commins and Anthony 'Skip' Basiel argue for the use of synchronous web-based videoconferencing (WVC) as an innovative model of delivery for tutorial support and communication in a transnational higher education context. They discuss the notion of WVC as a microlearning environment, examining two illustrative case studies in an instructional setting. They also offer best-practice guidelines that emphasize the relationship between the pedagogical focus and technological developments in WVC in higher education. Sigrid Blömeke and Christiane Müller present the core findings of an exploratory video study on teaching with information and communication technologies in Mathematics, Computer Science and German. Their data show that it is possible to identify three teaching patterns: "an 'innovative ICT teaching script,' a 'traditional ICT teaching script' and a 'modern traditional ICT teaching script'" (ibd.). Additionally, they distinguish between "'linear-directive teaching' with a use of comprehensive ICT tools versus 'student- and problem-centered teaching' with a more flexible use of microlearning tools" (ibd.). Beverly Oliver focuses on the decisive issues of quality university learning and how it might be achieved with microlearning. She argues that the key generic outcomes of a university education at all levels can be incorporated in the achievement of advanced information literacy. She explores how microlearning "enables more text-free and interactive digital environments in which to engage the mobile and connected Net Generation undergraduate" (ibd.), and she concludes the chapter with a rather provocative illustration.

The last section VI on *Evaluation & Quality Management* contains two contributions. Wolfgang Hagleitner and I present a generative model for the evaluation of microlearning processes in which qualitative and quantitative data as well as login statistics are triangulated using multiple methods. Although this generative evaluation model (GEM) is being introduced in conjunction with Knowledge Pulse® (KP), a special microlearning technology we have developed in Innsbruck (Austria), GEM can be put to use in a great variety of areas. Last, but not least, Susanne Kinnebrock, Berit Baeßler and Patrick Rössler focus on the organizational dimensions of e-learning by merging the concept of quality management and the process of implementation. They suggest an eight-phase circular model to structure the entire process of developing, producing and implementing e-learning systems in public institutions. In this model, every phase of implementation is evaluated on a micro-level. Altogether, micro-level data are mainly used "to modify the process of further development and implementation" (ibd.), and are thus clearly applicable to meso- or even macro-level problems.

In the end, this collection does not aim at a single, substantial and final definition of microlearning. The contributors discuss a variety of microlearning issues as they relate to diverse domains. In so doing, they reference a wide range of phenomena. These include not only didactic and pedagogical phenomena, but also socio-cultural, institutional, technological, economical, situational and contextual issues. On the whole, however, the authors discuss concepts, examples, and other issues as they relate to microlearning. Furthermore, it is also analyzed in terms of *how* we talk about microlearning on meta-theoretical levels (cf. Schmidt 2005, pp. 24f.). However, this collection on *Didactics of Microlearning* is not meant to serve as a set of FAQ's or how-to's for immediate application. Its many approaches and perspectives are offered to show to readers the state of the art but not the end of the road.

References

Göhlich, M. & Zirfas, J. (2007) *Lernen. Ein pädagogischer Grundbegriff.* Stuttgart: Kohlhammer.

Göhlich, M., Wulf, C. & Zirfas, J. eds. (2007) *Pädagogische Theorien des Lernens.* Weinheim/Basel: Beltz.

Schmidt, S. J. (2005) *Lernen, Wissen, Kompetenz, Kultur. Vorschläge zur Bestimmung von vier Unbekannten.* Heidelberg: Carl-Auer-Systeme.

Schunk, D. H. (2007) *Learning Theories: An Educational Perspective.* 5th edition. Upper Saddle River, N.J.: Pearson/Merrill/Prentice Hall.

Outline of a Microlearning Agenda

Theo Hug & Norm Friesen

In the rapidly-changing world of the Internet and the Web, theory and research frequently struggle to catch up to developments, interactions and permutations in technology and the social forms and practices evolving with it. Although the acuity of this situation may be new, the notion of the cultural forms of research (and society in general) lagging behind technological developments is not novel. As early as the 1920's, William Ogburn's theory of social change (1950) identified cultural lags as being an important part of the social dynamics associated with technological innovation. Even though we have much more complex conceptions of interdependent dimensions of social, cultural and medial change and the analysis of multiplex systems (cf. Rusch et al., 2007) today, challenges for timeliness and topicality of theory remain.

In the social sciences generally, Internet and Web Studies have emerged to address this lag between Internet practices and corresponding theories by developing and adapting ethnographic, social-psychological, linguistic, critical and other methodologies. These now serve as ways of investigating new online manifestations of identity, language use, and other cultural, commercial and technical forms – from blogging through YouTube. In educational research, a similar proliferation of novel practices, applications, and forms – from online educational games to learning objects, from bulletin boards to wikis – have come to be addressed under rubrics such as "e-learning," "distributed education," or "networked learning." Naturally, a number of more specific catchphrases and terms have been circulating to label, categorize and also promote more particular practices, ideas and forms. These include e-learning 2.0, personal learning environments, game-based learning, and more.

Together, these terms and rubrics help to map out an emerging sociotechnical landscape. However, this terrain is itself shifting and changing, constantly underscoring the provisional and negotiable nature of terms and labels. In many cases, terms attempt to stake out terrain that is as of yet emerging, sometimes going too far off the mark, and (less frequently), being too conservative in their estimation of the richness or extent of the territory identified.

With this in mind, this introduction to this collection on the *Didactics of Microlearning* will begin by mapping the changing but ultimately convergent definitions of the term "microlearning" as they have emerged and developed over the past five years or more. It will also explore how this term and its dynamics help to organize and order a set of pedagogical and technological phenomena and concepts in new and interesting ways. This introduction will also examine how the emergence and development of the term "microlearning" presents lessons for a range of interrelated concerns that continue to proliferate at the intersection of the social, technical and educational.

This chapter begins with an overview of the definitional issues related to micro-learning. It then presents a brief review of the research and informal literatures that have quickly been amassed in this new field. From this overview, it develops the thesis that the "microlearning agenda" – as an explicit emphasis on the minute and particular in teaching, learning and technology – presents valuable lessons for research into technology and media in education generally. Microlearning is revealed in these contexts not simply as one approach among many, but as a perspective that applies to many aspects of education, as something that goes on continuously, whether it is an explicit focus for research and technology development or not. As such, the lessons gained through microlearning are shown to have a generalized applicability to the studies of media and technology in education in the broadest possible sense. We conclude our discussion of concepts, didactics, politics and structures of microlearning by presenting some microlearning lessons. These lessons focus on the constraints and freedoms for learners and the pedagogical responsibility of teachers.

1   Definition and Context

As indicated earlier, in contrast to microteaching (cf. Dwight & Ryan, 1969) and also to other terms such as microphysics or microbiology, microlearning is a rather new expression. Similar to related expressions like microcontent or micromedia, it has been in use only since about 2002, though many aspects of learning, didactics and education have, of course been addressed on what can be called a "micro" level for centuries.

The discourse, or rather, multiple discourses that have emerged and developed around microlearning are above all polyvocal and international. In addition to a strong central-european presence, a glance at the tables of contents of the published collections in microlearning (from Innsbruck University Press) reveals contributions from North America, Asia, Australia, as well as other parts of Europe. Such cultural, geographic and linguistic heterogeneity underscores the fact that the technology central to micro-learning – like any technologies or technical systems – are not constituted in isolation, producing the same results in different institutional, social and cultural contexts. Instead, this technology and these systems are inextricably intertwined, and this embedding of the technical in the social and cultural is given expression in this introduction by referring to the "socio-technical" (e.g., see Hughes, 2001).

The heterogeneity of the contexts, cultures and ultimately, meanings associated with the term microlearning is further compounded by heterogeneity of the term learning itself. For example, learning can be conceptualized as a process of building up and organizing knowledge. But it can also refer to the change of behaviour, of attitudes, of values, of mental abilities, of task performance of cognitive structures, of emotional reactions, of action patterns or of social dynamics. No matter how learning is conceptualized, in all cases there is the possibility of considering it in terms of micro, meso and macro aspects or levels (cf. Hug 2005, p.4). As a result, microlearning can be understood in manifold ways which can refer to micro aspects of a variety of phenomena including learning models and concepts.

Along with that, the corresponding levels of meso learning or macro learning can refer to different areas, too (see figure 1).

	Example 1 *Semiotics*	Example 2 *Language learning*	Example 3 *Learning contents*	Example 4 *Course structure*	Example 5 *Competency classification*	Example 6 *Sociology*
micro level	single letters	vocables, phrases, sentences	learning objects, micro content	learning objects	competencies of learners or teachers	individual-ized learning
meso level	words, letter-figure combi-nations, sentences	situations, episodes	sub areas, narrow themes	topics, lessons	designing a lecture	group learning or organizatio-nal learning
macro level	texts, conver-sation, lingui-stic communi-cation	socio-cultural specifics, complex semantics	topics, subjects	courses, curricular structures	designing a curriculum	learning of generations, learning of societies

Figure 1. Microlearning – mesolearning – macrolearning (cf. Hug, 2005, p. 3).

These kinds of illustrative distinctions help to show the many ways in which microlearning can be understood. Depending on frames of reference and economies of scale, micro, meso and macro aspects vary. They are relational rather than "absolute." For example, in the context of language learning, one might think of micro aspects in terms of vocabularies, phrases, sentences, and distinguish them from situations and episodes (as meso aspects) and socio-cultural specifics or complex semantics (as macro aspects). In a more general discourse on learning, one might differentiate between learning on individual, group, or very broad social and/or generational levels. But whether "microlearning" is defined in terms of content, processes, technologies, competencies or learner groups, the key, of course is that which is occurring at the most minute of levels – as opposed to the meso or macro: minutes or seconds of time are relevant instead of hours, days or months; sentences, headlines, or clips are the focus rather than paragraphs, articles, programs or presentations; and portable technologies, loosely-coupled distributed environments are of interest rather than monolithic or integrated turnkey systems.

A second and broader context for the definitions of microlearning is provided by characteristics and dynamics associated with "knowledge economies." These characteristics include, of course, an increasing economic dependence on the generation, circulation and utilization of productive knowledge, and attendant pressures for instant access, workforce retraining and lifelong learning. Generally speaking, these factors are seen to involve increasing nomadicity of those generating and using knowledge, and also decreasing longevity and even coherence of knowledge itself:

> Microlearning as a term reflects the emerging reality of the ever-increasing fragmentation of both information sources and information units used for learning, especially in fast-moving areas which see rapid development and a constantly high degree of change. (Langreiter & Bolka, 2006, p. 79)

These processes are also linked with changing media industries. The diffusion of technological innovation necessitates the transformation or renewal of value propositions and business models. Making explicit reference to "micromedia," Umair Haque (2005) describes some of the conditions necessitating this transformation as follows:

> Micromedia is media produced by prosumers (or amateurs; sometimes, it's called 'consumer-generated content'). Micromedia differs fundamentally from mass media. First, it's usually microchunked. Second, because it's microchunked, it's plastic. Third, micromedia is liquid: prosumers can trade info about it via ratings, reviews, tags, comments, playlists, or a plethora of others. These are also micromedia; micromedia whose economic value lies in its complementarity with other micromedia. (2005)

Apart from other complementarities with meso- or macromedia (cf. Rusch et al., 2007, p. 13), it is important to realize that this discussion is rather about complex interrelations and new dynamics than just about small screen sizes or the nomadicity implied in handheld devices. Although the absolute novelty of the current situation – and the absolute centrality of knowledge in it – are subject to debate (e.g., Seidensticker, 2006; Friesen, 2006), it is difficult to dispute that the increasing speed, fragmentation and mobility of information production and consumption presents a new milieu for media production and forms.

Whether our focus is on learning tasks and processes, products and outcomes, it is important to avoid definitions of microlearning that lack discriminating or differentiating power. If microlearning is simply equated with informal learning, lifelong learning, or being "bathed in bits" in the digital mediasphere (see Tapscott, 1999), we end up in a night in which all cows are black. If *everything* is microlearning, *nothing* of it is to be considered of special importance. Consequently, we advocate speaking of microlearning in terms of special moments or episodes of learning while dealing with specific tasks or content, and engaging in small but conscious steps. These moments, episodes and processes may vary depending on the pedagogies and media involved, but the measures of scale of the amount of time and content involved can be made fairly constant. For example, microlearning can involve the use of different media technologies – book printing, radio, film, TV, computer, Internet and others. It can be utilized with a range of pedagogies, including, reflective, pragmatist, conceptionalist, constructivist, connectivist, or behaviourist learning, or action-, task-, exercise-, goal- or problem-oriented learning. It can be designed for classroom learning as well as for corporate learning or continuing education, entailing *processes* that may be separate or concurrent, situated or integrated into other activities. It may follow iterative methods, networked patterns or certain modes of attention management entailing different degrees of awareness. Finally, the *form* of a final microlearning product may have characteristics of fragments, facets, episodes, skill elements, discrete tasks, etc. But while it is amenable to all of these forms, contexts, technologies and combinations, in terms of its temporality and substance, microlearning carries some relatively simple markers: In terms of *time* microlearning is related to relatively short efforts and low degrees of time consumption. And in terms of *content* microlearning deals with small or very small units and rather narrow topics, even though aspects of literacy and multimodality (cf. Kress, 2003, pp. 35-59) may play a complex role.

2   Didactics of Microlearning

As to *didactics* of microlearning, it is important to be aware of different cultural and academic traditions. In the French speaking cultural area "didactique" also means a literary genre, and in German traditions we find a variety of concepts, models and understandings. By way of contrast, Anglo-American discussions on didactics mainly focus on instructional design or theory (see Friesen in this volume). Attempting to straddle these different traditions, this introduction uses the terms "didactics" to designate very generally processes of design and reflection related to teaching and learning. Depending on the level of reflection and theoretical or practical demands, didactics can also be seen to refer to concepts, approaches, models, theories, experiences, or technologies, or to questions of an art of teaching and learning. Furthermore, these considerations may focus on subjects (who), contents and skills (what), methods and technologies (how), reasons, purposes, and goals (why and what for), as well as on social relations, institutional and societal conditions, settings and arrangements, learning ecologies and cultures, media environments, power and control, or valuation and assessment. Also, we can distinguish between explicit and implicit didactics, as we do for forms and processes of knowledge generally.

In the context of wide-spread media effects such as "dumbing-down" or "data smog," microlearning and associated pedagogies may be seen by some simply as contributing to these undesirable trends. Although we believe that learning can be playful, entertaining and even joyful, we do not maintain that microlearning is simply a question of dressing up and manipulating avatars, or tinkering with bits and "pieces loosely joined" (D. Weinberger). It is easy to argue that neither differentiated knowledge and critical thinking nor social and moral competence necessarily emerge, simply because somebody may have learned to make use of RSS-feeds, wikis or weblogs. But which didactical principles and which educational experiences promote these qualities and competencies and what was and what is the role of educational systems in this respect?

Critical discussions about traditional schooling and hidden curricula, school influences, and governmentality (Weber & Maurer, 2006) in educational contexts have shown ambivalent results. In our view, microlearning always has played a role also in institutional learning contexts (cf. Hierdeis in this volume). The question is rather, *how* micro steps and short-term learning activities are positioned, situated, contextualized, valued, combined, complemented, contrasted, counterpointed, etc. and which forces are at work in institutional contexts and elsewhere. Generally speaking, besides incidental and unavoidable modes of punctuating and foregrounding single learning steps in flows of work and everyday life, there are many ways how the association of microlearning aspects can be conceptualized and linked to comprehensive models. Here are some examples:

- In the *multicomponent model* micro aspects or contents are combined more or less systematically – either in advance or on the fly – in sequences, linear, recursive and/or branching, relating to each other as separate components (e.g., Swertz, 2006).

- In the *aggregation model* microlearning elements that are fundamentally *similar* are bundled or combined as a relatively unstructured entity or homogenous mass ("aggregate").

- In the *conglomerate model* diverse micro elements are arrayed as a kind of assortment or "bouquet" of learning products and processes.

- In the *emergence model* new phenomena, coherent structures and qualities evolve from and between microlearning elements themselves. These novel patterns or properties cannot be attributed to any single element. Instead, they arise out of a multiplicity of relatively simple interactions or steps in dynamic process of self-organization.

- According to Luhmann's *medium/form distinction* (1997, pp. 190-201) learning results can be understood as *form* in a *medium* of loosely coupled elements. Because any given form can act as medium on another level, layers and layers of distinctions can be described. For example, we can create words in the medium of letters, sentences in the medium of words, and thoughts in the medium of sentences.

- In the model of *exemplification,* micro aspects of learning appear as prototypical examples which allow the explication of larger complex structures, connections and relations. Holographic depictions can be taken as special cases of exemplification.

- Furthermore, micro-macro-relations in learning processes also can be described and analyzed in terms of "perspicuous representations" *sensu* Wittgenstein (see Puhl & Seidl in this volume).

In relationship to these and other models, and also given the wide range of didactical theories and models (cf. Blankertz, 2000; Heitkämper, 2000) it becomes obvious that there are many different ways of conceptualizing, analyzing and designing didactics of microlearning. However, this variety of means also brings with it a range of implications in other spheres of value and activity. One of these that has emerged in discussions of microlearning is the sphere of politics, and it has become manifest above all in terms of network design and architecture.

3   Politics of Microlearning

Speaking of network openness, Mitch Kapor, the inventor of Lotus 1-2-3, insightfully observed in 1991 that "architecture is politics." "The structure of a network itself, more than the regulations which govern its use," Kapor argued (and has argued since), "significantly determines what people can and cannot do" using that same network (Kapor, 2006). Think, for example, of diagrams emphasizing the the distributed nature of the Internet, with multiple nodes or routing locations connected in multiple ways with others, and with any one capable of routing additional network traffic should a neighboring node become unavailable. This is typically presented as opposed to centralized networks, such as those represented by the telephone system, with a single central node.

As it has developed, microlearning can be said to have brought with it a kind of political awareness and partly a politics which is nowhere easier to trace than in architectures proposed for its technologies and applications. This politics, moreover, is primarily a politics of the institution versus the individual. Certainly there are a significant number of contributions to the microlearning discussion that emphasize its relevance to existing educational institutions and practices, or that focus on applications or studies situated within given institutional boundaries (e.g., Newman & Grigg and Oliver in this volume; Schachtner, 2006). But these are outweighed by contributions critical of existing and traditional educational institutions and practices. This is evident in calls to go beyond "the institutional shackles of today's state education systems" (Krieg, in this volume), the questioning of the "sustainability of traditional models" (Fiedler & Kieslinger) or the outright rejection of "traditional pedagogies, frameworks and roles" as "ineffective" (Molnar, 2006).

But revolutionary rhetoric aside, diagrams such as those provided by Fiedler and Kieslinger (2006), Downes (2006) and Wilson before him (2005) make clear the difference between traditional and microlearning visions. The first diagram adapted from Fiedler and Kieslinger, (see Figure 2) for example, is illustrative of architectures associated with conventional "institutional" settings.

The diagram shows "participants" (the white circles on the right) as connecting to "forum," "calendar," and "content" tools or functions, which are supplied by a single, centralized Learning Management System (LMS). The diagram could just as well have shown these same participants as similarly connecting to the "email," "conferencing," and other communications tools. Additionally, it could have also shown all of these tools or functions as associated with a single Learning Management System, combining both content, calendaring and communication functions in a single, integrated suite of tools. All communication or connection between these participants, moreover, is ultimately mediated through these centralized systems.

This is precisely what the leading Web-based learning and teaching environments – WebCT, Blackboard and Moodle – accomplish. And they do so in such a way that they allow for the surveillance of online student activities in a manner that has been described as "panoptic" (cf. Rybas, 2007). As is the case in Bentham's prison design, these learning management systems allow the behaviours of students to be visible to the teacher in individual and aggregate form, while the actions of the teacher are in no way open to such scrutiny (Land, 2004). In addition, the roles and actions that students and teachers are actually able to undertake are similarly constrained and standardized. "Bricks-and-mortar" institutions, like any other organizations, are "full of heterogeneous actors, with complex identities" (Pollock & Cornford, 2000). These are also developed, changed and improvised as necessary: students may lead a class, and may evaluate themselves and others. However, in learning management systems and organizational information systems generally, "everyone and everything is formalised, represented in a standardised form, with certain roles and responsibilities towards the system." The result with such systems is that "we risk destroying or submerging those interactions that are tacit, informal, flexible" (Pollock & Cornford, 2000). Teachers are not learners, and learners do not teach; instructors or automated systems evaluate students rather than students evaluating themselves, and all actions remain inauthentically isolated from real-world with a password-protected "garden wall."

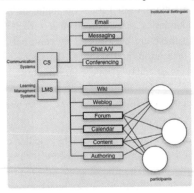 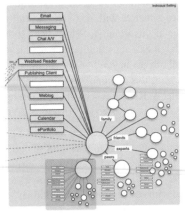

Figure 2. "Institutional Setting"   Figure 3. "Individual Setting"
(cf. Fiedler & Kieslinger, 2006, p. 80)   (cf. Fiedler & Kieslinger, 2006, p. 81)

The diagram showing the "individual setting," (Figure 3) on the other hand, shows a single participant at the centre, and a wide range of entities arrayed around him or her. These entities include not only the familiar institutional functions or tools for email, messaging, calendaring, etc.; they also include those sociotechnical developments most closely associated with microlearning, such as Weblogs, ePortfolios, RSS readers, etc. Significantly, many of these tools in this diagram are shown to be connected to related tools offered through a different "institutional setting" and the central participant in this diagram is also shown as connecting directly to other services or tools offered by this same institution (these connections are indicated by the dashed lines extending on the left of the figure; the entities to which they ultimately connect have been cropped in this version of the diagram). In addition to these tools (which are presumably still offered and centralized in a given institutional setting) the participant is shown as having direct contact with other "participants" – labelled as "family," "friends," "experts" and "peers" – outside of the institution, and involving no mediation by its systems or tools. These, in turn, are connected to further individuals, who bring along their own array of institutional tools and connections (as indicated by columns of institutional services or tools arrayed towards the bottom of the diagram). Of course, the politics of this second diagram are not those of institutional control, but of individual autonomy and self-direction. Specifically interrogating issues associated with the adult or "life-long" learner, Fiedler and Kieslinger describe a "technologically emancipated" education:

> Do we expect adult students merely to adapt to centrally hosted and controlled landscapes of tools and services? Or do we rather maintain a perspective of (technological) emancipation, which suggests that adults should also control, at least partially, the tools and services that they integrate into their personal workflows? (2006, p. 85)

This is perhaps even more explicit in the descriptions and the diagram of the "Personal Learning Environment," provided by Downes and mentioned earlier. The diagram in question, although not reproduced here, does not even provide a single institutional frame of reference. Instead it shows a central environment (a "Virtual Learning Environment" or a "Personal Learning Environment") as connecting to some half dozen services and technologies, with institutions such as "Learndirect" or the Bolton Institute having the same diagrammatic status as Flickr or del.icio.us: "It becomes," as Downes explains, "not an institutional or corporate application, but a personal learning center, where content is reused and remixed according to the student's own needs and interests." Writing elsewhere, Downes is even more explicit:

> It's just you, your community, and the web, an environment where you are the centre and where your teachers – if there are any – are your peers. It is, I believe, the future – and where, one day, the next generation of Blackboards and WebCTs and Moodles and Sakais will make their mark. (2006a)

Assuming that these kinds of statements take into account the complexity of the relationships between the technological and educational, it would be too easy to dismiss
their substance as the product of either romanticism or desperation. The kind of eman-
cipation-through-technology envisioned by Downes and others underplays the dependence of these activities on carriers, providers, division managers, infrastructures and
more. Control of these infrastructures and services presupposes a significant level of
economic enfranchisement and social integration, and technical and communicative
competency. There are a large number of factors, in other words, that exist externally
to the Internet, and that play a decisive role in determining the presence or absence.
Assuming that all of these conditions are in place, the learner in his "personal learning
environment" is still encumbered by various issues: How many bright bloggers, productive second lifers and erudite podcasters are there who have not been recruited to
media industries, or would struggle to survive on their "virtual" incomes? What of
creators and providers of quality content which is prevented from having its educational value realized due to regionalized educational policy? The mass use of social
software, the dynamics of amateur content production and consumption, and the business models that have been developing along with them require in-depth investigation
rather than continued celebration. Such investigation would require research into
macro-level considerations (e.g., see: "Parameters of the New Global Public Sphere;"
Volkmer, 1999), into the meso-levels of institutional decision-making, and down to the
micro-levels of individual mouse clicks and attention management. We are far away
from conciliation of the heterogeneous desires of consumer and participatory cultures,
wealth generation and employability in its neoliberal or critical versions, or the just
distribution of recognition and educational opportunity. Neither self-referential blogging nor unquestioning implementation of institution-wide "Blackboardization"[1] present viable solutions. We would argue that we face better chances of success (or survival) if we at least partially abandon battles for attention or rankings for the sake of
cultures of deliberative learning (cf. Schmidt in this volume) and encouragement of
phronesis (Aristotle). By this, we refer to practical, situated and flexible knowledges
and ways of acting: ones that are sensitive to context, and are able to change in keeping with changing circumstances, able also to take and support the appropriate actions
and developments at the right time and place.

The discourses and diagrams of microlearning, however, have provided a place for
articulating and sketching out visions of a politically progressive, post-institutional
education. Ways and means of learning are envisioned as being freed – at least to various degrees – from the old ways, forms, structures and limitations. One potential
challenge that arises from these developments, though, is that they blur the distinctions
separating education from more generic information and service provision, creation

---

1   "Blackboardization" is used as an idiom for processes of norming learning cultures, trivialization
     of complex issues, misleading of trustful users, selling an e-learning approach as mother-of-all
     e-education, normalization of restraints, and implementation of structural bondages by asserting
     one Learning Content Management system as proprietary solution of priority.

and consumption. For it is in some ways the "bundling" of communication, content provision and other functions and tools that characterizes their current educational use. And, more importantly, it is the embedding of this use with institutional supports and funding, with communities of teachers and researchers, and with curricular structures and organization that distinguishes it from more generic communication and information access. To be fair, the authors cited above would likely counter that these are precisely the traditional limitations from which education needs to be freed. However, the tensions and issues that would be implied in such a debate might become clearer when they are considered further below, in the light of another important theme in the microlearning literature, pedagogy.

4   Microlearning Morphology

The pedagogy associated with microlearning spans a wide range of possible approaches, from emphases on its inherently "unstructurable" and improvisatory nature (Friesen, 2006) to approaches involving the specification of actions and activities from moment-to-moment. One striking example of the latter is by the relatively early contribution to a didactics of microlearning developed by Swertz (2006), and earlier, by his supervisor, Meder (2006). Going by the name of "Web Didactics," this is an eclectic pedagogy, defined in terms of navigation, sequencing, and particular content types:

> Web-Didactics does not offer a single instructional design model (e.g., Problem Based Learning, Tasks Oriented Learning) but a choice of didactical models, that were approved in the educational tradition. These models were specified concerning the granularity of the computer screen. (2006, p. 56)

Swertz explains that the granularity of content called for by the computer screen is relatively small, and that contents at this level of granularity need to be disaggregated ("decontextualized") to form general knowledge bases, in which these contents are labelled according to specific knowledge types. These types include "receptive," "interactive," and "cooperative knowledge" (ibid., pp. 58-62), in which "receptive knowledge" is subdivided into "orientational," "explanational," "instructional," and "source knowledge." Swertz reasons that each of these types can be sequenced (generally in linear fashion) according to a number of "micro models," including models he identifies as "abstracting," "concretizing," "theory-driven" and "problem-based." Abstracting involves a progression from text through drawing and animation to video, with concretizing reversing this order. Omitting some intermediate stages, the problem-based model involves progressive moves from task and content through explanation and example to an activity and overview.

This overall approach – re-arranging small, recombinant resources to constitute given instructional sequences – will likely sound familiar to anyone who has been exposed to learning objects and technical e-learning standards. For similar processes have been envisioned as occurring with learning objects as they are "packaged," "sequenced," or "scripted" in linear, hierarchical and/or recursive order.

A similar emphasis on structure is evident in the development of applications for the integration of microlearning activities in workflows and everyday life stream as done in Innsbruck (Austria).[2] Based on the principle of making use of the use of media, time slots for small learning steps are created according to the individual use of technical devices and learning needs. There is, for example, a cell phone application usable for second language acquisition, designed to prompt the user at pre-determined (and also customizable) intervals with questions concerning vocabulary, grammar, phrases and basic comprehension in a foreign language. These intervals can be tracked to ensure that they are optimized in accordance with psychological studies in memory and retention. The result is a product which has shown some promise in early studies (Hagleitner, Drexler & Hug, 2006), and which can be integrated in new and interesting ways into everyday practices and routines. This is described as occurring almost "interstitially," under the aegis of "integrated microlearning" (cf. Gassler, 2004; Hug, 2005; Gstrein & Hug 2006), a model which tries to cope with paradoxical demands: it is open, flexible and modular and – at the same time – allows the use of learning management functions, and it enables concomitant learning embedded in workflows together with the development of knowledge architectures.

The level of pedagogical structuring entailed in this kind of interstitial, integrated microlearning is broadly comparable to a rather different pedagogy for microlearning articulated under the title: "The *Dr. Who* principle" (Newman & Grigg in this volume). Starting from the assumption that learning and microlearning are "inherently episodic," the authors point to the narrative structure of the 30 minute *Dr. Who* episodes broadcast by the BBC from the 60's to the 1980's as exemplary for microlearning. The two key characteristics they identify are 1) The structuring of "content to fit the episode (and every episode with a cliff-hanger)" and 2) The delivery of "the episodes in appropriate time intervals." Of course, the second point is reminiscent of the mnemonically optimized intervals utilized in integrated microlearning; and the episodic, narrative structure suggested in the first point, is at least morphologically similar to the short sequences suggested in the "Web Didaktik" of Meder (2006) and Swertz (2006).

If these organizational and broadly didactic strategies can be considered as at least a "partially structured" pedagogy for microlearning, they serve as a transition to those pedagogies which advocate an abandonment of structure and regulation, and an

---

2   In the context of a collaboration of the Institute of Educational Sciences, University of Innsbruck, with the Research Studios Austria, a division of the Austrian Reseach Centers GmbH, a server-client application and prototypical PC and cell phone applications particularly with regard to second language acquisition have been developed during 2003-2006. The applications research at the Research Studio eLearning Environments was supported by the Federal Ministry of Economy and Employment and the Tyrolean Future Foundation. Information on further basic and use-inspired research as well as on development of novel microlearning applications is available at http://www.hug-web.at.

autonomous role for the learner. This is described widely in terms of "learner-centered" didactic and especially in constructivist discourse of learning (cf. Kösel 2003; Reich 2006). Also Downes clearly votes for learner- or student-centered pedagogy, requiring above all "the placing of the control of learning itself into the hands of the learner." It is well represented by the likes of Freire and Papert, with Downes citing one of the latter's statements on "game-based learning" (Downes, 2005) as follows:

> The most important learning skills that I see children getting from games are those that support the empowering sense of taking charge of their own learning. And the learner taking charge of learning is antithetical to the dominant ideology of curriculum design. (Papert, 1998)

Any explicit structure applying to this "self-directed" learning is minimal: "insofar as there is structure, it is more likely to resemble a language or a conversation rather than a book or a manual," as Downes explains (Downes, 2005). The learner directs and decides the affiliations, links, contents, forms of guidance and direction (if any) that will be constitutive of the learning process – in some cases creating these him or herself. There is no pre-ordained structure, curricular, sequential or otherwise.

5   Microlearning Lessons

We argue that the as of yet inconclusive and polyvocal nature of microlearning discourse is a good thing, and should be cultivated and encouraged. Indeed, this openness and heterogeneity may well be, counterintuitively, the agenda of microlearning in the present age. Given the developing and decentralized nature of the technologies and architectures that are associated with microlearning, it seems unlikely that any kind of definitive consensus on microlearning theory and technology is likely to emerge. At the same time, the emphasis on moments, interstices, snippets, and fragments that is obvious in microlearning discourses generally is likely to remain important. It is the fragment rather than the Wagnerian *Gesamtkunstwerk* that is most suited to the Web, to the cell phone and to various forms of ubiquitous and mobile computing – and to the dispositions and pacing of 21st century life.

Similarly, the architectural politics and the various pedagogies articulated in the microlearning discourse also manifest productive tension and difference. Vital issues and questions about the institutions, traditions and practices of education are kept alive and open through this heterogeneity. It is in terms of this final issue of the political and pedagogical that this paper makes one final point. This is to argue for a preservation of institutional and structured pedagogies that are generally critiqued in microlearning. To argue for a completely "emancipated," user- or learner-controlled educational architecture and politics as does Downes and Molnar (and to a lesser extent, Fiedler and Kieslinger) is to misapprehend the multiplicity of roles of the educational institution.

And invoking questions about the feasibility of educational institutions is not anything new.

Let us reference a 1958 essay entitled "The Crisis in Education" to make both of these points. In this piece, philosopher Hannah Arendt argues explicitly against the notion that public educational institutions are to be understood simply in terms of their overt educational functions – whether these are sufficiently student-centered, or up to the challenges of the present age. Schools and universities are not simply about their overt educational functions. People do not simply become effective knowledge workers or even autonomous individuals there. Instead, the school is also where society repro-duces itself, where one generation takes over for another. Learners (above all children) are introduced into a world that is environmentally and politically broken, and for which their teachers, the generation handing it over, must be held responsible. Arendt argues that

> In education this responsibility for the world takes the form of authority. The authority of the educator and the qualifications of the teacher are not the same thing. Although a measure of qualification is indispensable for authority, the highest possible qualification can never by itself beget authority. The teacher's qualification consists in knowing the world and being able to instruct others about it, but his authority rests on his assumption of responsibility for that world. Vis-a-vis the child it is as though he were a representative of all adult inhabitants, pointing out the details and saying to the child: This is our world. (1958)

This responsibility also exists in the undergraduate classroom and in the dissertation supervisor's office: We are obligated to say that this is the past of education and this is its present. Using a different frame of reference, this responsibility is also palpable in terms of the "big spike" and "long tail" that governs the world of the blogosphere. It is the burden imposed by the arbitrary way that things have worked out, or not worked out. It is sometimes called history or tradition. As Arendt argues, it takes the form of the authority that is embodied, however, poorly, in curriculum structure and that con-strains the freedom of the student a pedagogical responsibility. It is this ongoing dy-namic of history, rather than simply historical inertia or the arbitrary authority that will prevent the most radical versions of "personal" and personalized learning from being realized. The impulse to conceive of microlearning and education generally that is freed from these constraints is important and valuable, but it exists only to counterbal-ance the recognition of the inescapability of this ongoing predicament or crisis.

References

Arendt, H. (1958) The crisis in education. *Partisan Review* 25, pp. 493–513. Available from: <http://www.eco.utexas.edu/Homepages/Faculty/Cleaver/350kPEEArendtCrisisInEdTable.pdf> [Accessed 12 August 2006].

Blankertz, H. (2000) *Theorien und Modelle der Didaktik.* 14th ed. Weinheim/München: Juventa.

Downes, S. (2006) *Learning Networks and Connective Knowledge. Instructional Technology Forum.* Available from: <http://it.coe.uga.edu/itforum/paper92/paper92.html> [Accessed 12 August 2006].

Downes, S. (2006a) *EduRSS 2.0.* Available from: <http://www.downes.ca/cgi-bin/page.cgi?post=33125> [Accessed 12 August 2006].

Downes, S. (2005) *E-learning 2.0. eLearn Magazine. October 16.* <http://elearnmag.org/subpage.cfm?section=articles&article=29-1> [Accessed 12 August 2006].

Dwight, A. & Ryan, K. (1969) *Microteaching.* Reading, Mass.: Addison-Wesley.

Fiedler, S. & Kieslinger, B. (2006) Adapting to changing landscapes in education. *Micromedia & e-Learning 2.0: Gaining the Big Picture. Proceedings of Microlearning Conference 2006.* Innsbruck: Innsbruck UP, pp. 78–89.

Friesen, N. (2006) Microlearning and (micro)didaktik. In: T. Hug, M. Lindner, & P. A. Bruck eds. *Micromedia & e-Learning 2.0: Gaining the Big Picture. Proceedings of Microlearning Conference 2006.* Innsbruck: Innsbruck UP, pp. 41–61.

Gassler, G. (2004) *Integriertes Mikrolernen.* MPhil. thesis, University of Innsbruck (Austria).

Gstrein, S. & Hug, T. (2006) Integrated micro learning during access delays: a new approach to second-language learning. In: Zaphiris, Panayiotis ed.; *User-Centered Computer Aided Language Learning.* Hershey/PA: Idea Group Publishing, pp. 152–175.

Hagleitner, W., Drexler, A. & Hug, T. (2006) Evaluation of a prototypic version of Knowledge Pulse in the context of a management course. Paper presented at the MApEC (Multimedia Applications in Education Conference) 2006, September 4-6.

Haque, U. (2005) *Media 2.0.* Available from: <http://www.bubblegeneration.com/2005/11/media-2.cfm> [Accessed 12 August 2006].

Heitkämper, P. (2000) *Die Kunst erfolgreichen Lernens. Handbuch kreativer Lehr- und Lernformen. Ein Didaktiken-Lexikon.* Paderborn: Junfermann.

Hug, Theo (2005) Micro learning and narration. Exploring possibilities of utilization of narrations and storytelling for the designing of "micro units" and didactical micro-learning arrangements. In: *Online proceedings of the International Conference "Media in Transition 4: The Work of Stories" at the M.I.T. in Cambridge (MA), USA, May 6-8, 2005,* available at: http://web.mit.edu/comm-forum/mit4/papers/hug.pdf, 2005.

Hug, T., Linder, M. & Bruck, P. A. eds. (2006) *Microlearning 2005: Learning & Working in New Media Environments. Proceedings of the International Conference on Microlearning 2005, June 23-24, 2005.* Innsbruck: Innsbruck University Press, 2006. Available online at: http://www.microlearning.org/micropapers/microlearning2005_proceedings_digitalversion.pdf.

Hug, T., Linder, M. & Bruck, P. A. eds. (2006) *Micromedia & e-Learning 2.0: Gaining the Big Picture Proceedings of Microlearning Conference 2006.* Innsbruck: Innsbruck Uni-

versity Press, 2006 Available online at: http://www.microlearning.org/MicroConf_2006/
Microlearning_06_final.pdf.

Hughes, T. P. (2001) Through a glass, darkly: anticipating the future of technology-enabled
education. *Educause Review*, 36(4), pp. 16–26.

Kapor, M. (2006) *Architecture is Politics (and Politics is Architecture)*. *Mitch Kapor's Blog*.
Available online at: <http://blog.kapor.com/?p=29> [Accessed 12 August 2006].

Kösel, E. (1997) *Die Modellierung von Lernwelten. Ein Handbuch zur Subjektiven Didaktik*.
3rd ed., Elztal-Dallau: Laub.

Kress, G. (2003) *Literacy in the New Media Age*. London & New York: Routledge.

Langreiter, C. & Bolka, A. (2006) Snips & spaces: managing microlearning. *Micromedia & e-
Learning 2.0: Gaining the Big Picture. Proceedings of Microlearning Conference 2006*.
Innsbruck: Innsbruck UP, pp. 79–97.

Luhmann, N. (1997) *Die Gesellschaft der Gesellschaft*. Bd. 1, Frankfurt/M.: Suhrkamp.

Meder, N. (2006) *Web-Didaktik. Eine neue Didaktik webbasierten, vernetzten Lernens*.
Bielefeld: Bertelsmann.

Molnar, D. (2006) Where do we go now? Possible new directions for e-learning 2.0. In: T.
Hug, M. Lindner, & P. A. Bruck eds.; *Micromedia & e-Learning 2.0: Gaining the Big
Picture. Proceedings of Microlearning Conference 2006* Innsbruck: Innsbruck UP.

Ogburn, W. F. (1950) *Social Change With Respect to Culture and Original Nature*. New
York: Viking Press.

Papert, S. (1998) Does easy do it? Children, games, and learning. *Game Developer*. Available
from: <http://www.papert.org/articles/Doeseasydoit.html> [Accessed 12 August 2006].

Pollock, N. & Cornford, J. (2000) *Theory and practice of the virtual university. Ariadne, 24*.
Available from: <http://www.ariadne.ac.uk/issue24/virtual-universities/> [Accessed 21
August 2007].

Reich, K. (2004) *Konstruktivistische Didaktik. Lehren und Lernen aus interaktionistischer
Sicht*. 2nd ed., Weinheim/Basel: Beltz.

Rusch, G.; Schanze, H. & Schwering, G. eds. (2007) *Mediendynamik*. Marburg: Schüren.

Rybas, S. (2007) Contesting the panopticon metaphor: online education and subjectivation of
the online user. Paper given at the International Conference on "Creating Communication:
Content, Control and Critique" of the International Communication Association (ICA) in
San Francisco, May 24-28, 2007.

Schachtner, C. (2006) Precise and succinct yet interlinked: requirements for e-learning in the
workplace. In: T. Hug, M. Lindner, & P. A. Bruck eds.; *Microlearning: Emerging Concepts, Practices and Technologies after e-Learning. Proceedings of Microlearning 2005.
Learning & Working in New Media*. Innsbruck: Innsbruck UP, pp. 71–78.

Seidensticker, R. B. (2006) *Future Hype: The Myths of Technology Change*. San Francisco,
CA: Berrett-Koehler Publishers.

Swertz, C. (2006) Customized Learning Sequences (CLS) by metadata. In: T. Hug, M.
Lindner, & P. A. Bruck eds.; *Microlearning: Emerging Concepts, Practices and Techno-
logies after e-Learning. Proceedings of Microlearning 2005. Learning & Working in New
Media*. Innsbruck: Innsbruck UP, pp. 55–70.

Tapscott, D. (1997) *Growing Up Digital: The Rise of the Net Generation*. New York:
McGraw-Hill.

Volkmer, I. (1999) *International Communication Theory in Transition: Parameters of the New Global Public Sphere*. Available from: <http://web.mit.edu/comm-forum/papers/volkmer.html> [Accessed 12 August 2006].

Weber, S. M. & Maurer, S. (2006) *Gouvernementalität und Erziehungswissenschaft*. Wiesbaden: VS Verlag.

Wilson, S. (2005) *Future VLE – The Visual Version. Scott's Workblog*. Available from: <http://www.cetis.ac.uk/members/scott/blogview?entry=20050125170206> [Accessed 12 August 2006].

I Media, Knowledge & Learning: Exploring the Field

From Meno to Microlearning: A Historical Survey

Helmwart Hierdeis

> *"And how will you enquire, Socrates,*
> *into that which you do not know?"*
> Plato: Meno Dialogue

1 Introduction

The question of the plausible historical reconstruction of microlearning, or better, the search for the historical traces that lead to it, would be much easier to answer or accomplish if the aim of the endeavor were clearly outlined. But this is definitely not the case (cf. Hug et al. 2006a and 2006b; http://www.weiterbildungsblog.de; Micro-wiki). Thus, for example, the term "microlearning" must repeatedly compete with that of "e-learning." Indeed, given the present upsurge of technological possibilities, ideas for application, attempts at constructing theories, and didactic considerations, it is perhaps still too early to establish microlearning's most relevant distinguishing features. At any rate, the discussion is open-ended, and it should not be burdened by polemics on terminology and on its epistemological implications.[1]

In spite of microlearning's lack of sharp focus, a number of discussions about it thus far provide some of its characteristics. Thus, Theo Hug considers microlearning the expression of a specific perspective which, in contrast to meso and macro aspects, is directed towards relatively small and time-restricted learning units and activities. What is to be learned using microlearning is left open. Furthermore, microlearning can refer to knowledge, behavior, attitudes, values, mental abilities, and cognitive structures as well as to emotional expressions, action patterns, and forms of social competence (Hug et al. 2006a and 2006b).

In dealing with the issue of learning, there is nothing particularly revolutionary in looking at the distinction between aspects of varying ranges. Two hundred years ago, for example, this distinction was made under the guise of other terminology. What *is* new is the role attributed to the media. The advent of digital media in didactics has opened up a new field of observation, description, analysis, and practical instruction. A few questions posed by the current discussion can highlight what I mean:

---

1 See http://en.wikipedia.org/wiki/Microlearning

- How can small learning units be planned and carried out using digital media such that students can cope with them? In other words, what exactly are appropriate subjects for this type of learning? Which steps should be taken, and what are suitable time units?
- How can small learning units be joined so as to build larger units?
- What are the goals and what are the particularities of interactions between teachers and students, as well as among the group of students?
- Which contexts make individual learning more appropriate than group learning?
- How can students' skills be enhanced to allow them to break down more complex subjects?
- How can knowledge be generated – whether by individual students, or among the group of students, or in cooperation with the teacher? What is guided or independent, formal or informal, and institutionalized or private learning in the context of microlearning? What is the connection between technological know-how and microlearning's yield?
- How can digital media support communication among the participants in the learning process?
- How can extra-medial learning spheres be linked with medial ones (learning environments, learning platforms …)?
- How can criteria be elaborated to assess medially relayed information, so that (young) students will not be diverted from the intended learning goals by the lure of "push technology" and "push media"? And so on.

I repeat: if we are concerned with history, then we realize that what may be useful in the discourse can also impede the search. Moreover, many of the above-raised questions have been dealt with in their specific historical context (e.g., history of learning, of the school, of didactics, the media, the pedagogic interpersonal relationship, enculturation, knowledge, and technology).

In light of the discussion at hand, I would first like to emphasize a few differences between microlearning and other (traditional) forms of learning, especially those forms which to this day have been practiced in school: that is, a learning institution that reaches all members of society.

Theo Dietrich, an educational scientist, poses in his *Introduction to Pedagogic Thinking* (*Einführung in pädagogisches Denken*), inter alia, the question whether teachers should impart learning according to the "theory of the small steps" or to the "theory of the learning of structures" (Dietrich, 1984, p. 184). Predictably, Dietrich does not mean to exclude either of the alternatives. Rather, he is interested in finding a meaningful and reciprocal complement, suitable to the subject as well as to the student:

These two methods can be distinguished essentially as well as structurally as regards their aims and their foundations. It is through *teaching* that information (*Wissen*) should primarily be imparted and knowledge (*Kenntnisse*) assimilated. With the help of 'small steps,' elements of knowledge are to be strung together, as it were, and connected. In so doing, associations will be established: in other words, links between elements of information and thought are subsequently 'made or joined into larger structures. The *teaching of structures* ... puts elaboration – that is, autonomous thinking and acting – at the core of the instruction. It aims primarily at obtaining or permitting the obtaining of insight and awareness. However, in each of these two basic methods the germ of the opposite method is also present. Learning in small steps or by association does not prevent the development of insight. The learning of structures, that is, the elaboration of insight, may take place in the course of learning by association. The difference between these two basic methods, in other words, lies mainly in the fact that in the first model, it is the teacher who 'raises' the students to the insight and, as a rule, imbues them with knowledge they are as yet unacquainted with. In the second model, it is the students who succeed in arriving at the insight based on their own experiences and analysis thereof (ibid., p. 186).

Apart from pointing out the complementariness of both learning models, Dietrich here is indicating, if indirectly, some of the conditions by which learning takes place:

– A student's acquisition of knowledge is dependent on teachers: on their presence, their planning, and their activities.
– The process of learning is therefore contingent on location and space.
– Consequently, it is incumbent upon the teachers to bring to school the "world," which they do with narratives, texts, images, models, and sounds.
– Ultimately, teachers convert the "world" into the student's knowledge, insight, judgment, and action competencies by means of shared transformation processes.

Microlearning does not entirely override these conditions, but it does imply a shift in emphasis. Here are a few general observations:

– Although similar to traditional forms of "learning by small steps," microlearning occurs exclusively by means of digital media. It presupposes a practical competence in dealing with these media which until now has not been necessary.
– The capacity to handle digital media is often acquired outside educational institutions.
– The ubiquitousness of digital media in the private sphere and its manageability allow it to be used practically everywhere. Thus microlearning is independent of institutions as well as locations of learning.

- The private/individual availability of digital media frees microlearning from limiting conditions as regards content, time, and structure, which are intrinsic to educational institutions (e.g., institution-wide educational plans, curricula, teaching units, timetables).
- What was until recently a main feature of educational institutions – that is, involuntary face-to-face situations (teacher-student relationships, student-student relationships) with their distinctive asymmetries and dynamics – is replaced by an exchange with virtual or medially relayed interactive partners.
- Together with the increase in technological know-how on the part of the students and their capacity for autonomous organizing in procuring and processing information, the role of the person who, up to now, organized their learning and conveyed knowledge changes: the teacher becomes either a mentor and accompanier to the student, or else superfluous.
- Digital media makes accessible more topical information than traditional media. It likewise allows for quicker access to more dated information.
- The digital world is a "thought-up world" (Fassler, 2005). This means that it is a world made up exclusively of signs, symbols, and images: it is a world of limited accountability. Microlearning thereby radicalizes a development that began with the introduction of books and images to the school.
- Microlearning creates loopholes in the learning processes in educational institutions, since the acquisition of information can occur without pre-established aims, without outside control and evaluation. Moreover, the acquisition of information is highly emotionally charged. Students can experience themselves "as subjects, as creators of their own life and learning history" (Meyer & Reinartz, 1998, p. 10).

2   Historical References

2.1 In my view, microlearning marks a provisional endpoint both of a long history of the imparting and acquiring of civilization skills and of the comparatively shorter history of the media. This holds true also if, as I see it in accordance with Manfred Fassler, the latter emerged some tens of thousands of years ago, when human beings scratched signs into bone, stone, and wood and created thereby a "non-biological memory" (Fassler, 2005, p. 29). Today, the discussion on the character and effect of the media is pursued in numerous disciplines (including anthropology, philosophy, sociology, communication sciences, and neurosciences; media sciences is considered an interdisciplinary field). Naturally, it is educational scientists who are posing the question of its influence on the next generation and of its use in learning. This is also the case as regards digital media, in as much as it constitutes the technological precondition for learning. Examining microlearning from a history of education viewpoint, therefore, means searching for pieces of evidence on "learning in small steps" and inquiring how media comes into play as a stimulator and supporter of such learning.

2.2 If, in accordance with the ethology of civilization, I describe human history as a history of learning (see Liedtke, 1991), then I take as my starting point the visible evidence of cultural transfer (the creation of traditions with regard to technologies, social forms, language, symbols, rituals and so forth), and ask about their inception and functions in that part of the evolution of civilization that cannot be documented. I must conclude, using analogy, that the securing of a minimal existence was based on knowledge of food, on skills to protect oneself from the elements and enemies, and on the development of some social competencies. On the level of plausibility, I then develop a hypothesis on how the acquisition and the inter-generational transfer of this knowledge and these skills may have taken place. I arrive at two forms of learning: learning by trial and error, and learning by imitation. The pressure of survival or selection made sure that the learning time had to be short. One can only speculate whether this implied learning-by-steps or by structuring processes. At any rate, it is remarkable that when characters and the earliest writing schools were first established (in Sumer, starting in 3000 B.C.E.), there was already a recognizable and differentiated mathematical, astronomical, and musical civilization. This can only be explained by complex forms of learning that long preceded this civilization.

2.3 With the spread of scripture, not only civilization, as such is passed on by this means (and more reliably than oral tradition), but also the quantity of evidence for the type of cultural transmission increases. On the one hand, we find that the Sumerian-Babylonian sciences emerge in the canon of Greek schools (expanded with grammar, rhetoric, dialectics, and geometry). On the other hand, we learn that these disciplines, during the 5th and 4th centuries B.C.E., represented the basis of knowledge for the education of future Athenian citizens and that these disciplines were taught by specialists: the Sophists. Only those who could read, write, and compute were allowed to participate in the courses (see Lenk, 1998, 31f.). Although the subdivision of knowledge into disciplines does not, as such, reveal how knowledge was transmitted, there is sufficient evidence to suggest that the method practiced by the teachers was that of the small steps (see Marrou, 1957). After all, indications of relevant Sophist teaching practices are handed down in the polemics of Socrates (approx. 470-399 B.C.E.) as rendered by Plato (428-348 B.C.E.). What Socrates stated as his own method is not simply the opposite of that of his adversaries (they teach – he questions; they permit themselves to be called teachers – he rejects this designation). Indeed, nothing can be learned from Socrates in the sense of an assimilation of knowledge and its application (see Jäger, 1959). Although Socrates did also proceed step-by-step, he was gradually spelling out ideas and concepts by means of a dialogic process, whereby he first unsettled his interlocutors' self-assurance, before he would subsequently help build it up again both psychologically and cognitively.

A well-known case that exemplifies this is the "Meno" dialogue, which is concerned with the question of whether virtue is teachable. Socrates' interlocutor, Meno, had learned from the Sophist Gorgias an entire catalogue of virtues, but he was baffled when the philosopher asked what all virtues had in common. Meno admitted to being stumped and compared Socrates to a torpedo, which made everyone who approached become rigid. Socrates responded:

> ... if the torpedo is torpid as well as the cause of torpidity in others, then indeed I am a torpedo ... for I perplex others, not because I am clear, but because I am utterly perplexed myself. And now I know not what virtue is ... However I have no objection to join you in the inquiry (Plato, 1892, p. 80).

What is specific about Socrates' relationship here is that he as the "teacher" does not stand over the "student," but rather on his side, supporting him. His superiority consists in the art of questioning, until it dawns on both of them where the truth might lie. After an encounter with Socrates, people should not take with them a certain knowledge; rather people should become able to query, to see through pretences of knowledge, and not fall prey to false certainties (Hierdeis, 1983, p. 57).

Contrary to Theo Dietrich, I do not think that Socrates can be claimed unreservedly as "representing the method of 'comprehension and inference of structures,' of 'autonomous activity of elaboration,' and for the searching and finding of insights" (Dietrich, p. 188), and even less so, if this is meant to be in opposition to the "method of small steps." This is because, on the one hand, the student in Socrates' method is not strictly autonomous; rather, he is firmly led along his path of thinking. And on the other hand, at the end of the dialogue there is only one provisional determination of a position, which necessitates further clarification. Notice how Socrates takes leave of Meno after conversing about virtue:

> But we shall never know the certain truth until, before asking how virtue is given, we enquire into the actual nature of virtue (Plato, 1892, p. 100).

The "Socratic method," however, cannot be transferred without qualifications to teaching, and those educators of the eighteenth century, who believed it possible to apply Socrates' "maieutics" as a result-oriented teacher-student-dialogue to reach one's teaching aims, failed to grasp what this type of "midwifery" meant (Böhm, 1966). The philosopher wanted to demonstrate through his method that already beforehand, human beings are endowed with knowledge as an idea, and that in such directed conversations, what is at stake is evoking this knowledge so that it becomes conscious. Socrates' successor, Plato, assumed from him the idea that the development of the human being depends less on obtaining useable knowledge (whose necessity in social life Plato did not deny) than on the "unflagging methodical learning of truth" (von Hentig, 1966, p. 1). Whatever people learn and however they learn it, be it synthetically or analytically, guided or autonomous, the meaning of all learning lies not primarily in coping with life, but in the process of approaching Truth. In the twentieth century, Donald Winnicott would see the meaning of psychoanalytic enlightenment in removing the "veil of our phantasms" from reality (Winnicott, 2002). This "macroperspective," which today is considered the key to "education," was not lost on the pedagogics of subsequent times – it had taken effect, at least as an idea, since the neo-humanism of the early nineteenth century.

2.4 Nevertheless, it is the structuring of knowledge, its distribution into courses, and its imparting through instruction that has become the formula for success for all organized learning. This is demonstrated by the entire history of schooling. At a rather early stage, the receptivity of students began to be considered, and this rendered a new quality to the transmission of knowledge. As St. Thomas Aquinas (1225-1274), the theologian and philosopher of the Middle Ages, wrote in his Prologue to *Summa Theologica*, which was the most comprehensive theological treatment of his time, he had the instruction of beginners in mind when writing this opus. Beginners, according to Aquinas' observation, were constantly hampered by the "multiplication of useless questions, articles and arguments," and "the frequent repetition brought weariness and confusion" to them (Aquinas, 1920). Aquinas's intention, as he himself asserted, was to present God's teaching "briefly and clearly" – as far as the matter itself allowed.

The entire host of questions (Quaestiones), which Aquinas introduces "briefly and clearly," are all based on the same schema: a list of arguments from other authors to each question, and then a systematic treatise followed by a confirmation or refutation of the arguments cited at the beginning. The teacher demonstrates to his students in written form as well as in a lecture that elucidates what was written – in his view, in the smallest possible steps – a pattern of argumentation that also in the oral disputes between them and himself must be strictly upheld. The subjects of the conversations, by the way, are never real-world experiences, but exclusively the statements of others. Thinking means using the thoughts of others as ingredients and comparing them. Research means the study of books. Referring to one's own thoughts is considered presumptuous (see Garin, 1971, p. 21ff.). This would remain the state-of-the-art until early modern times.

2.5 When Johann Amos Comenius (1592-1670), the "Great Didactic" of the seventeenth century, published his ideas of a life-long school to be carried out in progressive stages (in printed form, by the way, since printing had by then been around for over 200 years), he began it with an attack against the scholastic method which, because of its rigidity, one would "do better to call a disease" (cited by Garin, 1964, p. 36). Comenius' theological idea – that all persons are created by God and should return to their maker, but are unable to do this based on their own efforts – had a pedagogic consequence. All people – independent of class, sex, or talent – must be assisted by the appropriate school to reach this goal. What Comenius meant by "school," however, comprised the care provided by the parents, adult self-education up until death, as well as the stages of formal education in infancy, childhood, adolescence, and early adulthood (Comenius 1992; Hoffmann, 1998, p. 38ff.). The appropriate school proceeded slowly, step-by-step, and progressed from easy tasks to difficult ones. It well considered age and the child's level of knowledge; it assisted the weak; it made use of sensual perception; it linked singular pieces of knowledge to greater contexts; and it paid attention to developing a sense of community (Comenius, 1977). Adding to these also Comenius' call for a school for everyone, these were truly unheard-of innovations for his time. But as strong as his aversion against the scholastic method may have been, he hardly extricated himself from the tradition that held that learning must primarily occur through representations of the world in books (Mollenhauer, 1986). What Comenius understood as a "sensual" experience in school was not a direct confrontation with nature and civilization. Rather, it was contact with the illustrated world, which would be elucidated by texts (Comenius, 1977). Equally in keeping with tradition, the teacher filled a central role, even if it was now endowed with a new ethos. The first and final image of Comenius' *Orbis Sensualium Pictus*, an illustrated textbook, which depicted both the perceptible and the "sacred" world, demonstrates this point most clearly:

Figure 1. "Come Boy! learn to be wise" (Comenius 1685, A1)

In an introductory dialogue, the teacher explains to the student exactly what is required in order to be "wise." When the student asked him, "Who will teach me this?" he answered: "I, by God's help." (Comenius, 1777). The student could do no more than agree: "See, here I am. Lead me, in the name of God!" (ibid.). After the last image, the teacher offered the young one advice as he departed: "Go forward and read attentively other good books, so that you will be educated, wise, and pious" (ibid.). In other words, learning was not about keeping one's eyes open and having experiences, but about using pictures and texts to understand "the world." If the boy fails to follow this advice and falls short of becoming "educated, wise, and pious," it is not the books that are to be blamed. From this point on, books shaped the school to such an extent that their critics, eighteenth-century Philanthropists as well as twentieth-century reform pedagogues, included the term "Buchschule" (book school) as a curse word into their vocabulary of polemics (Hierdeis, 1992, p. 169ff.).

2.6 It took another two hundred years until Jean-Jacques Rousseau (1712-1778) would initiate a pedagogic development, whose consequences on didactics would also be felt in the twentieth century. Indeed, these consequences are significant in spite of the fact that Rousseau hardly had experience as an educator and that his pedagogic ideas were expressed in the guise of a novel (*Émile*).

Rousseau, as is well-known, was among the most sharp-tongued Enlightenment critics of civilization and society. In the opening line of *Émile: or On Education*, Rousseau writes: "Everything is good as it leaves the hands of the Author of things; everything degenerates in the hands of man" (Rousseau, 1911/2007). He thus revealed the role he attributed to education: It should do no less than halt the general decline of humanity. Pedagogy, as practiced until then, was of no use, because it was corrupted by society. By contrast, what was needed was a type of education that lay outside of the up-to-then prevailing institutions, and an educator who should no longer represent society but become the child's advocate. He had to see to it that justice was done to the child's own nature. In other words, children should be allowed to be themselves. In this way, the educator stops being a teacher and becomes the child's escort. If he takes seriously this principle that the child should find his or her own self – because only then will he get hold of his or her true nature – then he must allow for time and renounce every type of direct influence:

> The first education ought thus to be purely negative. It consists not at all in teaching virtue or truth, but in preserving the heart from vice and the mind from error. If you could do nothing and let nothing be done, if you could bring your pupil healthy and robust to the age of twelve without knowing how to distinguish his right hand from his left, the eyes of his understanding would be open to reason as soon as you began to teach him … Since they want their child to be a doctor instead of a child, fathers and teachers think it never too soon to scold, correct, reprimand, flatter, threaten, promise, instruct, and reason … Let childhood to ripen in children. Has some lesson finally become necessary? Beware of giving it to them today if it can be put off without danger until tomorrow (Rousseau, 1911/2007).

Naturally the child learns something – but not what adults consider important. Rather, the child follows his or her own curiosity, confronting neither images nor books, but regarding the actual things themselves and learning to orient his or her behavior to their laws. The educator, in turn, neither teaches nor presents the world. S/he rather withdraws behind the objects (Rang, 1965, p. 373), observes the child's development, and carefully harmonizes the environment to this development. Only when the child reaches youth does the educator assume a more active role and begin to intentionally guide and teach the student, and to present him or herself as a role model.

While one may well criticize Rousseau's concept of nature, his unilaterally negative understanding of civilization and, from today's perspective, his developmental psychology and anthropology, this criticism does not affect his discovery and promotion of childhood as an independent phase. Indeed, it took almost 150 years to see their effects on pedagogic praxis. In the reform pedagogic movement in the first decades of the twentieth century, the principles of teaching "proximity to real life," "autonomous activity," and the "free mental school work" were discussed and put into practice under the motto of "starting from the child" (Hierdeis, 1971). In spite of these claims, however, the principle of instruction still retained its predominance, as it could draw upon centuries of tradition. In addition, the exponential increases of knowledge, together with the growing importance of economic interests in learning, have determined a type of legitimacy in the educational system that has been quite hard to shake off.

2.7 As previously mentioned, reform pedagogy's critique of the school system already reaches back to a long tradition. For some time, however, the focus of this criticism has not been on "scholastic" instruction any more and instead turned to a teaching system which had been founded in the early nineteenth century by Johann Friedrich Herbart (1776-1841), but became formalized only by his successors (especially Tuiskon Ziller and Wilhelm Rein) who transformed it into "a pedantically practiced template" (Asmus, 1970, p. 481). This later development should not prevent us from considering its origins.

Herbart was the first to draft a theory of instruction that described synthetic and analytic approaches and that postulated their reciprocal complementarities. A "synthetic procedure for instruction" means that instruction begins with the collection of elementary experiences and observations. As individual fields are introduced and developed (Herbart mentions, for example, mathematics, language, history, and physical science), the starting point is at their smallest elements. Even though children also acquire knowledge from their singular surroundings, scientifically trained teachers know, according to Herbart, the children's needs and level of development and are thus able to provide their school environment with appropriate learning objects in incomparably more stimulating ways. This, however, should be initiated at a much earlier age, even against the resistances of various know-it-alls:

> As for the model triangles, I had suggested putting them on a board, highlighted by shiny nails, and placed constantly in front of the child in the cradle. People ridiculed my idea. And let them laugh some more! Because my idea was to put rods and balls beside the board, covered with all sorts of colors. I very diligently move, combine, and vary these rods and later also plants and all sorts of the child's toys; I bring a small organ into the children's room and let simple sounds and intervals ring for several minutes; I add a pendulum ... in order to observe the rhythmic conditions; in addition, I train the sensitivity of the child to distinguish between hot and cold by using a thermometer and to determine the measures of heaviness through weight as well .... Indeed, who knows whether I might not even ornate the walls of the children's room with very large colorful letters of the alphabet? All this is based on the simple idea that surreptitious and tedious impressions, which one calls learning by heart, will either not be necessary or else be very easy, if early enough the elements of the synthesis are made part of the child's daily experience (Herbart, 1806, p. 100).

To familiarize the child with images, objects, and trappings that later appear in the instruction, and to train the child's senses was something that Herbart's contemporary,

Friedrich Fröbel (1772-1852), who invented a type of institutionalized preschool education, considered just as highly as Maria Montessori (1870-1952) did at the beginning of the twentieth century. But for Herbart, the instruction has in store additional means for the "synthetic procedure": books, instruments, models, and above all illustrations (ibid., pp. 115). In order to refrain from allowing the creation in the child's mind of "any cloudy masses" (ibid., p. 73) which might result from all of these comings and goings, the objects, which might supersede each other, must be organized by associative and logical combinations and ordered in rows. Even the smallest step in learning requires its own "articulation": the student is responsible for establishing "clarity," as regards the single object; he must determine through "association" what it is that links this object with other ones; he has to unite the linked objects into a "system," and he has to ensure that the previous path of insight is correct ("method"). In this process, a constant change between "scrutiny" and "contemplation" must occur. Herbart calls "scrutiny" the concentration on the single object or on the class to which it belongs. In this context, "clarity" and "association" represent the steps that belong to it (ibid., p. 70). "Contemplation" means "a structuring or systematizing of one's own experience, which is open for future experiences, corrections, extensions and new systemizations …" (Benner, 1986, p. 115). It encompasses the steps of "system" and "method" and should lead to the growing up person reaching an autonomous judgment and a consciousness of self.

The scattered impressions and pieces of information, which are present at the beginning of all learning processes, are to be observed more closely; they are also to be ordered. This is the primary task of the school. With the increase of cognitive skills, the "synthetic process of instruction" lessens in importance compared to the analytic method, without ever becoming entirely insignificant, however (Herbart, 1806, p. 109). For analysis, the same steps of articulation apply all the way up to the level of self-reflection. It uses the same means and media, and it has the same goal: "morality's strength of character" (ibid., pp. 58, 134). Thus, for Herbart, all instruction is "educating instruction" (ibid., p. 25), which should be emphasized once more only in as much as he did not expect educational effects coming from appeals and lectures. Rather, Herbart viewed these effects as the result of the instruction's unvarying strict articulation, of the obligation to clarify the objects of the instruction, and to position oneself to the objects into a contemplative relationship. Ultimately, he saw it as the result of the interpersonal contact with a teacher who himself practices this type of mental acquisition of the world, of arriving at informed judgments, and of self-reflection (ibid., p. 33).

In his theory of instruction, Herbart applied the school's media repertoire rather casually. He did not develop a theory on the means of instruction and work. His followers ("Herbartians"), too, who dominated the doctrine of teaching in Germany until the end of the nineteenth century, did not alter anything in this regard. Likewise, they changed very little of the spectrum of the existing media of instruction itself.

2.8 After the turn of the twentieth century, a rapid change initiated – both as regards the extent and quality of the media, and its integration into the instruction and the understanding of instruction methods. First, there were the movies, whose potential for stimulating and illustrating animated considerations on media didactics, particularly in the context of the reform pedagogic idea of autonomous activity (Austermann, 1989, p. 1039f.). In the 1930s, with the advent of instructive movies, a special medium developed for schools. Moving pictures were used to evoke interest in the subjects taught, to transform themes into actions, to magnify and to shrink objects, and to repeat essential contents as often as may be considered desirable. The more feature films were present in everyday life (especially after World War II), the more distrustful pedagogics became towards it; there was a fear that movies might divert the youth, confront them with inappropriate topics, overtax their faculty of judgment, and jeopardize them morally. An analogous tendency could be observed in the 1960s, when television brought moving pictures into people's homes. Consumers could now choose for themselves topics and time-frames. At the outset, media pedagogics sensed here, too, more danger than opportunity. On the other hand, TV channels (as earlier with the school's radio programs) developed with school television a didactic support for learning. Its attractiveness for stimulating motivation, its visual capacity, its development of suspense, level of language, and structuring of themes, left teachers hard put to compete. Motion and voiceless media now remained largely unused in the arsenals of teaching material.

The stormy arrival of audio-visual media in everyday life, as well as in the school, has forced didactics to react. It has become aware of the failure of making moralistic attempts to preserve the old ways, and it has discovered media's wide range of potentials for the learning process. Moreover, it has recognized the possibility that those learning, in the course of dealing reflectively with the media in lessons, may transfer this acquired criteria to their extracurricular media consumtion. With regards to school instruction, since Paul Heimann formulated his conception in 1962, the finding has gained general acceptance that all decisions relevant for teaching are also decisions about the media used in teaching (Heimann, 1962, p. 407ff.). Consensus on this point has opened the way for describing their varying functions and for practical guidelines. For Wolfgang Schulz, for example, media is either "*aids for communication* about intentions and subjects, about initial positions and controls on success, about procedural conditions and methods ... or the media is autodidactic: that is, *it objectifies teachers' functions or those of other participants in the learning process*" (Schulz, 1991, p. 76). In this way, teaching is implemented such that

– the media in the teaching is not an isolated means of acquiring and processing information; rather, it has to submit to two central functions of teaching: namely, instruction and communication
– its language must not erect any learning barriers

- its inherent goals, principles of constructions and means of being effective must be made transparent
- it has to be examined with regard to the potentials of self-instruction, of individual and cooperative problem-solving, and of the self-control it opens up, in order to prevent students from being reduced to a passive role (Schulz, 1991, p. 76f.; Adl-Amini, 1994, p. 11ff.).

The new reflection about media also signals a new understanding of methods. For Herbart, for the Herbartians, and for their followers in the twentieth century, the methods of instruction are based on the students' path of learning, which is to be planned and controlled by the teachers. In this perspective, the students' activities are always seen as a consequence of their teachers' activities. The students must proceed, spoon-fed with their teachers' intensions, to their desired result (teaching goal = learning goal). Such a conception has always been favored by the school's organizational and curricular conditions: that is, by the way society likes to see the learning in subsequent generations organized. This, however, corresponds to neither the demands of learning that should be as comprehensive and sustainable as possible, nor the pedagogic idea of self-determination, nor the teachers' implicit teaching theories, nor the actual non-linearity of what happens during learning and teaching (Altrichter, Posch & Welte, 1997, p. 1484). If the prevailing tendency (in theory) currently points towards connecting the methodological activity of the teacher with his or her pre-professional experiences (Altrichter & Posch, 1990) and towards declaring it "the intelligent tinkering with known and novel didactic forms and objects" (Hiller, 1991, p. 137), then synthetic and analytic methods ("small steps" vs. "structure"), too, may be released from their corsets. In this way, none of the Herbartian elements loses its weight (any teaching whatsoever, in the absence of factual clarification, linking, order, and reflection, would lose its justification). And yet "levels" become instruments with which those participating in the learning process may get down to their problem-solving, either together or with divided tasks.

2.9 In the heyday of audiovisual media, a didactic-medial renovation coincided with the emergence of "programmed learning," which had begun in the United States in the 1920s, and in the 1950s been given a new foundation within the framework of learning theory by B.F. Skinner. In retrospect, this can be seen as an attempt to perfect the traditional small-step method: it offered the learners information from a teaching program and provided them with tasks and feedback on the success or failure of any given step. The program was presented in textbooks, as well as in mechanical devices, language labs, and computers. The basis for this is provided for by discoveries on the fostering effect of intrinsic motivation, of positive reinforcements, of taking into account an individual's learning speed, of learning sequences that build on one another (hierarchy of content), of the reduction of irrelevant stimuli, and of clearly defined tasks and controllable goals (Skinner, 1965a, p. 72ff.; Skowronek, 1970, p. 491ff.). If, in the early stages of this development, Skinner placed his bets on specific teaching machines, which mechanically relayed to students whether their solution was accurate (subsequent pieces of information could not be retrieved until the previous answer was correct), then his two most important claims on their quality, at any rate, also apply to other programs of this type: 1) The student should formulate his or her own answers alone and not choose from a list of available possibilities, because the capacity to re-produce from one's memory is to be valued higher than the mere recognition of infor-mation; 2) "to acquire complex behavior, the student must go through a carefully de-signed sequence of steps ... Every step must be small enough to be executed in any case, but with every step the student must slightly advance to the complete goal be-havior. The machine [the program – H.H.] must guarantee that these steps are carried out in a carefully predetermined and sequential order" (Skinner, 1965b, p. 41f.). Both requirements apply to linear programs (one-way programs), which foresee only one type of learning path and which can effect an individualization of the time used for learning, as well as to ramified programs, which adapt to the individual student (adap-tive programs) and thereby enable an individualization of the learning path (Zifreund, 1970, p. 350).

Teaching machines are hardly used outside of the United States, and other forms of programmed learning have not as yet gained general acceptance, either. On the one hand, it is acknowledged that programmed learning offers the opportunity to individu-alize learning under competition-oriented group conditions, to bring students who have slower learning speeds, extended absences from school, or those who have made ca-reer changes up to a given school class level, to stimulate students, to structure target-oriented lessons, and to lessen the teacher's burden. But apart from the problem of the rigidity of teaching institutions and of teachers' education, it turns out to be difficult to construct learning programs in such a way as to correspond to the didactic structures of a given subject: namely programs that would organize appropriately the learning steps and would structure the material so that no achievement is demanded from the student which had not already been introduced in all of its components (Skowronek, 1970, p. 492). Moreover, also in view of a situation where the student would be forced into a reactive and isolated role, the idea of replacing teaching to a large extent with learning programs clearly has to be ruled out (Schröder, 1978, p. 645f.). That these programs also might stimulate productive and creative capacities in students remains at this point more of an expectation and a hope.

3   Conclusion

3.1 Learning by small units in small steps has a tradition, which reaches beyond the documented development of civilization. One may presume that this type of "step-by-step learning" made cultural evolution possible. With the "invention" of the school, it became the practice of enculturation. Reflection on it and its first intentional applica-tion in teaching probably began in the Middle Ages. In the nineteenth century, this became a psychologically and didactically based "synthetic" method of teaching. Programmed learning in the twentieth century led to a more precise conception of the learning steps and to an individualization of learning speed and paths. Since the 1980s, the computer has superseded previous media in use as an instrument of comprehensive cultural knowledge and didactic "can-do-everything." On the one hand, this is because computers can take over presentation functions more quickly, with more diversification and with less energy. On the other hand, it vastly outperforms them as regards access to information in general, to linking information, and to simulation capacities. The computer allows the method of small steps, as well as the analysis of more complex realities, to be perfected. Herbart had already seen the danger that learning in small steps could only lead to an aggregation of isolated pieces of information. Based on his theory of articulation, the following reservations regarding microlearning may be deduced:

- Acquiring a piece of information does not mean understanding it.
- Understanding a piece of information does not mean being able to contextualize it.
- Creating a context for that piece of information does not mean being aware of its personal significance.
- Awareness of its personal significance does not mean that the individual will know its relevance for practical, social, or moral action.

3.2 Civilization generates technologies, social forms, systems of knowledge, and ideas that cannot solely be understood as effects of learning in small steps. It can be assumed that early on, synthetic learning connected with analytic learning. In addition, with the advent of a reflective culture (religion, philosophy), humans became aware that the mere securing of survival and alleviation of living conditions might not constitute the entire meaning of "being human." Out of ideal conceptions of the human being, specific "ideas of education" developed according to which the realization of a "higher" human existence was considered a learning task. Starting from the Greek antiquities to the present, the essential criteria for what should constitute the human being are so formulated: Truth/truthfulness (Socrates, Plato), transcendental orientation (St. Thomas Aquinas, Comenius), autonomy in the face of societal infringement (Rousseau), and intellectual order/self-reflection/character (Herbart). Today, one would add solidarity and the capacity for political action. If learning (which includes microlearning) is to be understood not only as the training for specific qualifications, but also as a moment of educational processes, then it finds in these criteria its reflective counterpart. That is the one side of the coin. The other side consists in the fact that the user of digital media, more than the user of earlier media, enters the "areas of the artificial, the inanimate, and the fictitious life contexts" (Fassler, 2005, p. 125), and that there exists the danger that because of their attraction, the individual fails to develop a capacity to distinguish between both worlds (real and virtual). Hence, perhaps, certain effects of training and acquiring information are not impeded, but there nonetheless remain fewer opportunities for those skills to develop which are needed for

- "... observing and evaluating cultural frames of existence and action,
- outlining new variants of language, communication, action, and shaping
- or even inventing 'comprehensive' or 'transcending' orders and processes and 'ascribing' meaning to them" (Fassler, 2005, p. 338).

4   Epilogue

The main question of the future is not how to teach better with computers, but what is left for us to teach, if we have such powerful assistants ...? (www.weiterbildungsblog.de: e-learning 2.0 Archives).

Should it be that the author of this question, Hermann Maurer, did not simply submit himself to the temptation of a smart formulation, it would behoove us to pose the response – following the motto of this paper – with Plato's Meno:

And how will you enquire, Socrates, into that which you do not know? What will you put forth as the subject of enquiry? And if you find what you want, how will you ever know that this is the thing which you did not know? (Plato, 1892, p. 80).

References

Adl-Amini, B. (1994) *Medien und Methoden des Unterrichts.* Donauwörth: Auer.

Altrichter, H. & Posch, P. (1990) *Lehrer erforschen ihren Unterricht. Eine Einführung in die Aktionsforschung für Lehrer.* Bad Heilbrunn: Klinkhardt.

Altrichter, H., Posch, P. & Welte, H. (1997) Unterrichtsmethode. In: Hierdeis, H. & Hug, T. eds.: *Taschenbuch der Pädagogik, Vol. IV.* Baltmannsweiler: Schneider.

Aquinas, T. (1920) The Summa Theologica of St. Thomas Aquinas. Available from <http://www.newadvent.org/summa> [Accessed 12 April 2007]

Asmus, W. (1970) Formalstufen. In: *Lexikon der Pädagogik, Vol. I.* Freiburg: Herder, p. 481.

Austermann, A. (1989) Medienpädagogik. In: D. Lenzen (ed) *Pädagogische Grundbegriffe, Vol. II.* Reinbek: Rowohlt, p. 1035.

Benner, D. (1986) *Die Pädagogik Herbarts. Eine problemgeschichtliche Einführung in die Systematik neuzeitlicher Pädagogik.* München: Juventa.

Böhm, B. (1966) *Sokrates im 18. Jahrhundert.* Schwabach: Wachtholz.

Comenius, Johann Amos (1685) *Orbis sensualium pictus quadrilinguis.* Leutschoviae: Typis Samuelis Brewer.

Comenius, J. (1777) *Joh. Amo. Comenius's Visible World: or A Nomenclature, and Pictures, of all the Chief Things that are in the World and of Men's Employment Therein. The World of Things Obvious to the Senses, Drawn in Pictures,* translated by Charles Hoole. 12th ed. corrected and enlarged, London 1777. Available from <http://books.google.com/books?vid=OCLC27390661&id=pxkaVd0-bpgC&pg=RA3-PA1&lpg=RA3-PA1&dq=inauthor:Comenius&_as_brr=1#PPA193,M1> [Accessed 12 April 2007].

Comenius, J. A. (1997) *Didactica Magna (1657) Große Didaktik. Die vollständige Kunst, alle Menschen alles zu lehren.* Stuttgart: Klett-Cotta.

Dietrich, T. (1984) *Zeit- und Grundfragen der Pädagogik. Eine Einführung in pädagogisches Denken.* Bad Heilbrunn: Klinkhardt.

Fassler, M. (2005) *Erdachte Welten. Die mediale Evolution globaler Kulturen.* New York: Springer.

Garin, E. (1964) Von der Reformation bis John Locke. In: Raith, W. (ed.) *Erziehung – Anspruch – Wirklichkeit. Geschichte und Dokumente abendländischer Pädagogik, Vol. III.* Reinbek: Rowohlt.

Garin, E. (1971) Europäische Erziehung im Mittelalter. In: Raith, W. (ed.) *Erziehung – Anspruch – Wirklichkeit. Geschichte und Dokumente abendländischer Pädagogik, Vol. I: Von der antiken Tradition bis ins Mittelalter.* Starnberg: Raith.

Heimann, P. (1962) Didaktik als Theorie und Lehre. In: *Die Deutsche Schule,* p. 407.

von Hentig, H. (1966) *Platonisches Lehren, Vol. I.* Stuttgart: Klett-Cotta.

Herbart, J. F. (1806) *Allgemeine Pädagogik aus dem Zweck der Erziehung abgeleitet.* Bochum: Kamps.

Hiller, G. G. (1991) Ebenen der Unterrichtsvorbereitung. In: Adl-Amini, B. & Künzli, R. (ed.) *Didaktische Modelle und Unterrichtsplanung.* München und Weinheim: Juventa, p. 119.

Hierdeis, H. (1971) Kritik und Erneuerung. Reformpädagogik 1900 – 1933. In: Raith, W. (ed.) *Erziehung – Anspruch – Wirklichkeit. Geschichte und Dokumente abendländischer Pädagogik, Vol. VI.* Stamberg: Raith.

Hierdeis, H. (1983) Der pädagogische Bezug zwischen Lehrer und Schüler in der Vergangenheit. Konzepte und Fakten. In: Schnitzer, A. (ed.) *Der pädagogische Bezug. Grundprobleme schulischer Erziehung.* München: Oldenbourg, p. 53.

Hierdeis, H. (1992) "Die Reisen der Salzmannischen Zöglinge." Bemerkungen über Verstand, Sinne und Exkursionen nach drinnen und draußen. In: Hierdeis, H. & Schratz, M. (eds.) *Mit den Sinnen begreifen. 10 Anregungen zu einer erfahrungsorientierten Pädagogik.* Innsbruck: Österreichischer Studienverlag, p. 169.

Hoffmann, A. (1998) Die Didaktik des Johann Amos Comenius. Bildungsgang mit Blick auf das ewige Leben. In: Meyer, M. & Reinartz, A. (ed.) *Bildungsgangdidaktik. Denkanstöße für pädagogische Forschung und schulische Praxis.* Opladen: Leske & Budrich, p. 38.

Hug, Th., Lindner, M. & Bruck, P. A. eds. (2006a) *Microlearning. Emerging concepts, practices and technologies. Learning and working in new media environments. Proceedings of microlearning conference.* Innsbruck: Innsbruck University Press.

Hug, Th., Lindner, M. & Bruck, P. A. eds. (2006b) *Micromedia & e-learning 2.0: gaining the big picture. Proceedings of Microlearning Conference.* Innsbruck: Innsbruck University Press.

Jäger, W. (1959) *Paideia. Die Formung des griechischen Menschen.* Berlin: deGruyter.

Lenk, R. (1998) Die Enkyklios Paideia. In: Meyer, M. & Reinartz, A. (eds.) *Bildungsgangdidaktik. Denkanstöße für pädagogische Forschung und schulische Praxis.* Opladen: Leske & Budrich.

Liedtke, M. (1991) *Evolution und Erziehung. Ein Beitrag zur integrativen Pädagogischen Anthropologie.* Göttingen: Vandenhoeck & Ruprecht.

Marrou, H. (1957) *Geschichte der Erziehung im klassischen Altertum.* Freiburg: Alber.

Maurer, H. (01. 03. 07) www.weiterbildungsblog.de: e-learning 2.0 Archives

Mollenhauer, K. (1985) *Vergessene Zusammenhänge. Über Kultur und Erziehung.* München: Juventa.

Plato (1892) *The dialogues of Plato*, translated from the Greek by Jowett B., Vol II. London: Oxford University Press. Available from <http://oll.libertyfund.org/Home3/HTML.php? recordID=0403> [Accessed 10 April 2007].

Rang, M. (1965) *Rousseaus Lehre vom Menschen.* Göttingen: Vandenhoeck & Ruprecht.

Rousseau, J.J. (1911/2007) *Emile, or On Education.* Translated from the French by Roosevelt, G. with Foxley, B. Everyman's Library collection. London: J.M. Dent and Sons Ltd (London) and New York: E. P. Basic Books; Available from: <http://projects.ilt.columbia.edu/pedagogies/rousseau/> [Accessed 12 April 2007].

Schröder, H. (1978) Programmierter Unterricht. In: Hierdeis, H. (ed.) *Taschenbuch der Pädagogik, Vol. II.* Baltmannsweiler: Schneider.

Schulz, W. (1991) Ein Hamburger Modell der Unterrichtsplanung – seine Funktionen in der Alltagspraxis. In: Adl-Amini, B. & Künzli, R. (eds.) *Didaktische Modelle und Unterrichtsplanung.* Weinheim/ München: Juventa, p. 49.

Skinner, B. F. (1965a) Die Wissenschaft vom Lernen und die Kunst des Lehrens. In: Correll, W. (ed.) *Programmiertes Lernen und Lehrmaschinen.* Braunschweig: Westermann, pp. 66.

Skinner B. F. (1965b) Lehrmaschinen. In: Correll, W. (ed.) *Programmiertes Lernen und Lehrmaschinen.* Braunschweig: Westermann, p. 37.

Skowronek, H. (1972) Lehrmittel und Lernleistung. In: Roth, H. (ed.) *Begabung und Lernen. Ergebnisse und Folgerungen neuer Forschungen.* Stuttgart: Klett, p. 491.

Winnicott, D. (2002) Objektwerdung und Identifizierung. In: Winnicott, D. *Vom Spiel zur Realität.* Stuttgart: Klett-Cotta.

Zifreund, W. (1970) Programmierter Unterricht. In: *Lexikon der Pädagogik, Vol. III.* Freiburg: Herder, p. 350.

Connectivism: Creating a Learning Ecology in Distributed Environments

George Siemens

Over the last decade, substantial changes with global connectivity and technology have been shifting the relationship between theory and practice. Today, educational theory trails the activities of educators with access to decentralized, distributed Web-based technologies: blogs, wikis, podcasts, and emerging technology are creating a landscape where learning is no longer controlled and managed. Theories of learning today need to account for the rich, dynamic, interconnected, and complex systems in which knowledge is created and shared. Metaphors of "learning ecologies" and "learning networks" provide the basis for future educational models, more tightly aligned with the context and characteristics of knowledge today – chaotic, cross-discipline, and emergent, not hierarchical as reflected in the current approach to course and curriculum design.

1   Introduction

Education exhibits a substantial dichotomy: the manner in which learning is created and designed does not align with how learning occurs. Carefully crafted, sequenced learning resources – hierarchically classified – belie the more chaotic traits of learning itself. To address the tension in academic design and the manner in which learning actually occurs, alternatives are emerging, with microlearning holding a promising position on which to build future models of education.

Microlearning focuses on the "micro-perspectives in the context of learning, education and training" and "deals with relatively small learning units and short-term learning activities" (Wikipedia, 2007). As the elements of learning content "break down" into smaller components – evidenced in mainstream media and entertainment; individual songs replace CDs, articles (or blog posts) replace newspapers, five minute YouTube videos provide an alternative to half-hour sitcoms – the process of creating learning content and learning experiences require restructuring.

Specifically, the restructuring of education today requires consideration of two aspects:

1. The spaces of learning (a move from classrooms to ecologies)
2. The structures of learning (from hierarchical content to networked content).

This paper will explore networks and ecologies as the basis for conceptualizing education in complex, technology-mediated environments. Theo Hug (2005) offers numerous dimensions which are impacted by microlearning: time, content, curriculum, form, process, mediality, and learning type. These multiple dimensions and interactions between them, as well as the myriad of options generated in the recombination of different dimensions, are fully to consider in the dual model of networks and ecologies.

Abundance

The abundant, and rapidly growing global knowledge base is the primary change driver in the shift from classrooms to ecologies. A research project at the University of California at Berkeley (2003) stated that the global information base grew 75% from 2000 to 2002. A recent IDC (2007) report predicts a six-fold increase in digital information between 2006 and 2010. Classroom-centric learning models, coupled with instructional design models which function as if knowledge were an object, are no longer capable of providing for learner needs.

Steven Johnson terms the rapid growth of information as a "crisis of overload" requiring "new tools to manage the glut, tools that eliminate the need for centralized archivists and editors, tools that lean on the entire community ... for their problem-solving" (2001, p. 218). Networks form the basis or structure of a) how learning content is organized, b) how connections are formed to facilitate discussion of content and creation of new content, c) how conversations and content flow in an environment of information abundance.

Ecologies, on the other hand, provide the space or context in which networks function. An ideal learning ecology is one in which:

- learner's access to information is not hampered (through corporate restrictions, government policy, or lack of resources)
- experiments and failures are tolerated (even encouraged) as part of the process of innovation
- knowledge is shared and transparent, allowing for co-creation and re-creation by others.

The joint adoption of networks and ecologies provides the basis for continued growth of education. Tomorrow's academic systems, whether public or corporate, must possess three critical traits: they must be 1) connected to real life, that is, relevant for the learner at the point of need and application; 2) capable of adjusting and adapting to rapidly changing environments; and 3) capable of filtering the overwhelming quantity of information. In essence, the primary shift necessitates that we move from seeing knowledge as an object or product to seeing it instead as a process or state of flow (Siemens, 2006a, p. 53). Carl Bereiter (2002, p. 183) extends the "knowledge as process," declaring that knowledge is not only something we share through conversation, but is actually created as a result of the conversation. This emphasis on co-creation aligns with Seymour Papert's constructionist view of learning, and is evident in the prominence of user-generated content in sites like YouTube (www.youtube.com) or Wikipedia (www.wikipedia.org).

As knowledge becomes less a constant state and more a constant process, we require different models for direct interaction. What may previously have been the goal of educators, that is, getting knowledge into the heads of learners, quickly shifts to a goal of actively engaging learners with the subject matter through the process of creating diverse networks possessing: a) diversity, b) autonomy, c) interactivity, and d) openness (Downes, 2006).

The capacity for these networks to exist requires a space that is conducive to their formation. The World Wide Web was adopted on an unprecedented global scale (and in an extremely short period of time) largely because it was an ecology which permitted innovation to emerge due to lack of onerous control. The adoption of standards provided the structure of innovation. Simple protocols of communication (HTTP, HTML, URL) provided the structure needed to create diverse types of networks. Instead of proprietary, closed standards, the openness of the Web enabled end users to create and innovate. Had the initial conception of the Web been more structured and controlled, it is likely that adoption levels would have trailed.

2   Presenting Connectivism

Connectivism posits that learning occurs through the creation of networks (Siemens, 2003, 2005a, 2005b, Downes, 2007). Knowledge is an entity, existing in a distributed manner, much like cognition (Edwin Hutchins' notion of distributed cognition), the World Wide Web, or the human brain (Dayan & Abbott, 2001, p. 276). No one node comprises, reflects, or represents the whole; rather, the aggregation and interoperation of the entire network represents the whole.

Several factors are involved in a connectivist view of learning:

1.   The internal act of learning (the formation of neural networks) is reflective, at a biochemical level, of the external act of learning through network formation. While too early to declare confidently, it seems that the insight of neuroscience into how the human brain learns, remembers, and functions in general may provide a model for how we learn and hold knowledge in a distributed manner with our external networks.

2.   Externally, learning occurs through the creation of networks (with people and information sources mediated and enhanced by technology). Overall understanding is reflected by the patterns that emerge as a result of the network (information is being considered, filtered, or discarded).

3.   External networks are formed to:
     a. Manage overwhelming levels of information

     b. Filter information according to trusted nodes

    c. Ensure existing information is current and timely

    d. Co-create new sources of information and knowledge with other network nodes

4. Information growth requires a different relationship to information than we have had in the past. In the past, when information was scarce, access became the most significant concern; now that information is overwhelmingly abundant, filtering and capturing critical components become the key challenges.

5. Context and intent determines approach and method. The type of learning required – whether at a basic level, such as memorizing a multiplication table or more advanced, such as understanding the changing global political landscape due to the growth of nations like China – influences the learning tools and manner of learning. Some types of learning are well-suited to self-directed activities. Other types require a mentor/apprentice model. Attending to the varied contexts of learning requires a shift from learning determined in advanced by established methods (e.g., a lecture) to learning reflective of the current discussion (e.g., blogs and wikis).

6. Systemic, holistic views of learning are critical in attending to numerous potential approaches. An approach to learning that works in one situation may not work in another. When learning is perceived as a system, a Web of interconnected elements, each impacting the other, the implications of choice and diversity are brought to the forefront. When learners explore a subject area from numerous viewpoints, they increase the likelihood of forming a systems view or Web of how ideas relate. Tools are required which enable the exploration of, and dialogue around, varying perspectives.

7. Grunt-cognition is performed by technology, which frees people to analyze meaning at a more rapid pace. Consider resources like tag clouds, data visualization, and social network analysis. These tools and methods perform basic data and information organization and visualization, tasks which would require significant time without technology.

How learners relate to each other and to content has changed significantly. As knowledge is subjected to accelerating change, a more adaptive model is required. Learning curriculum structured as courses and programs lack the capacity to adapt. Smaller segments of learning content, however, can be rapidly updated and integrated into curriculum. It is precisely in these rapidly changing environments that microlearning can make its greatest impact. As, according to the Microlearning 2007 Conference site, "all is falling into small digital fragments, loosely joined and permanently rearranging to form a multitude of new patterns, tasks and threads." These smaller "digital fragments" form the basis of a new model of learning and a new approach to curriculum design. Microlearning shifts the focus of instructional design, as will be explored shortly in relation to learning ecologies, from one of designing the learning content to designing the spaces in which the learning content is rearranged in new patterns.

3 Externalizing the Internal

Prior to exploring networks and ecologies, a brief detour is required to explore humanity's quest to externalize knowledge and share meaning. In order for a knowledge element to be accessible by a network, it must first be made transparent. When knowledge is seen only as an object, sharing is fairly simple and involves the use of services like archives, libraries, or museums. Most courses and learning experiences are built around object-centric views – textbooks, videos, magazines, articles, or other learning artifacts. For centuries this model was effective; however, the content-centric view of learning loses effectiveness in quickly changing environments. When information growth is abundant and rapid, the *process of content creation* (conversation), not *content as an object*, becomes the key consideration.

Conversation, in contrast with content, is fluid and continual – a key distinction in the many emerging social software tools. Language, media, symbols, and technology, which will be explored in greater detail shortly, aid in externalizing our understanding. As our capacity to externalize ideas and concepts in public forums (such as offered by blogs, wikis, and podcasts) becomes more common, content itself becomes less rigid (greater dialogue fosters increased presentations of perspectives), further shifting the body of knowledge from content to conversation.

Educationally, this shift is becoming more pronounced. Instead of emphasizing memorization of knowledge elements, educators are seeking more holistic structures to improve learning. Bransford, Brown, and Cocking (eds) (1999) emphasize the movement from basic understanding of a discipline or subject, to advanced, integrated understanding:

> Yet it is the network, the connections among objectives, that is important. This is the kind of knowledge that characterizes expertise … Stress on isolated parts can train students in a series of routines without educating them to understand an overall picture that will ensure the development of integrated knowledge structures and information about conditions of applicability.

Language

Language, as the cornerstone of conversation and dialogue, is in itself transformative. Postman (1995) asserted that we use language to transform the world, but we are then in turn transformed by our invention (p. 87). Alex Kozulin expresses a similar concept in his foreword to Vygotsky's (1986) *Thought and Language*; he writes that "abstract categories and word meanings dominated situational experience and restructured it"

(p. xl). Language is a conduit, a medium through which individuals are able to create shared meanings or interpretations of concepts.

Deriving or assigning this shared or externalized meaning as a cognitive process has historically been detailed in two regards: (a) images, as assigned to and shaped by words, are crucial in creating meaning (Bloor, 1983, p. 7); and (b) the symbol or image is rooted in the intent of the speaker – a "conscious orientation – actively directed at its object. The symbol is 'meant' a certain way, as its correct application is governed by an 'intention'" (p. 8).

According to Ludwig Wittgenstein (as cited in Bloor, 1983), the role of externalization is an attempt to replace "internal, mental constructions" with external and "non-mental" constructs (p. 10). The intent of externalization is to eliminate the hidden power, or in Wittgenstein's terminology, the "occult character" (p. 10) of an image, permitting greater clarity in discussions. Wittgenstein (as cited in Bloor, 1983) explores the private and public nature of meaning, arriving at the view that the "systematic pattern of usage" (p. 19) is the primary expression of meaning. The patterns of usage are public and external, not private and internal as mental image or act theorists detailed.

Wittgenstein presented right and wrong as "public standards, and their authority comes from their being collectively held." Per Bloor, Émile Durkheim, and Wittgenstein pursued a differing view of objectivity than is normally associated with learning. Their source of objectivity resides outside of the mind and in society as a whole (p. 58). The statement that there can be no private language assaults the notion of individual subjectivity (p. 60):

> The point is that even introspective discourse is a public institution which depends on conventions and hence on training. We have no immediate self-knowledge and no resources for constructing any significant account of a realm of purely private objects and experiences. (p. 64)

Vygotsky (1986), like Wittgenstein, attached a certain element of externality to thought: "The meaning of a word represents such a close amalgam of thought and language that it is hard to tell whether it is a phenomenon of speech or a phenomenon of thought" (p. 212). Vygotsky then extrapolated the thought/word connection by asserting that thoughts do not come into existence unless expressed in words (p. 218).

Vygotsky (1986) stated his interest in language as a means to ensure complete understanding of a concept:

> Psychology, which aims at a study of complex holistic systems, must replace the method of analysis into elements with the method of analysis into units …We believe that such a unit can be found in the internal aspect of the word, in *word meaning* (p. 5).

The interplay of language, symbols, ideas, cognition, meaning, and learning are not clearly defined. Pietroski (2004) stated the challenge:

If theories of meaning are theories of understanding, and these turn out [to] be theories of mental faculty that associates linguistic signals with meanings in constrained ways, then we should figure out (in light of the constraints) what this faculty associates signals with.

To extend Pietroski's argument, the concerns go beyond simply determining constraints. The challenge involves acquiring a common language of meaning that relates to learning and knowledge, and explores how supporting processes (cognition and emotions) are influenced not only by communication models (linguistics) but also by the conduits that deliver information and knowledge (technology), as well as philosophical views of learning (truth, objectivity, subjectivity, epistemology).

Media, Symbols, and Technology

Media, language, technology, and symbols are devices that provide humans with the capacity to externalize the nebulous elements of private thought. Albert Bandura (1986) stated, "power of thought resides in the human capability to represent events and their interrelatedness in symbolic form" (p. 455). It is important to consider the externalization of thought in light of traditional theories of learning, which largely emphasize knowledge construction and cognition as primarily internal events (in the mind of individuals).

Education, as a process, has its origin in the earliest recordings of human activity. It is believed that foundational elements of communication or knowledge transmission had their origin in pictograms (Bowen, 1972a, p. 7), the attempt of people to express thought in physical form. Pictograms developed in complexity as *determinatives* were added to clarify ideas and eliminate ambiguity. Even in early recordings of thought and reasoning, the notion of ambiguity influenced activities of communicators. The potential that one concept may be represented or interpreted in various ways is a foundational challenge that continues to drive attempts to communicate and share knowledge. Perspective and subjectivity add complexity to dialogue-based processes like learning.

The attempt to communicate also presented the continuing challenge of the imperfect nature of physical tools to express mental thought. Writing and visuals are conduits only partly able to properly reflect intended meanings and understandings held in the minds of individuals. Through symbols, we desire clarification: "The world of our experience must be enormously simplified and generalized before it is possible to make a symbolic inventory of all our experiences" (Sapir, as cited in Vygotsky, 1986).

The act of externalizing thought and images as symbols and language has been a key element of the cycle of understanding for much of recorded history. More recently, media and technology have begun to play a central role in creating the constructs of understanding that house shared conceptions and experiences of individuals. McLuhan (1967) suggested that "societies have always been shaped more by the nature of the media by which men communicate than by the content of the communication" (p. 8). The rapid growth of social-based technology tools creates an unprecedented opportunity for anyone with a computer and Internet access to play the role of journalist, artist, producer, and publisher. If media truly does shape humanity, the changed nature of dialogue and information exposure created by the Internet will have greater implications to our future than the nature of the content currently being explored. Much like tools shape potential tasks, the Internet shapes opportunities for dialogue – outside of space and time – that were not available only a generation ago.

4   Networks of Learning

Why this attention to externalization? What is externalized can be connected. What we externalize can be shared and subject to the continual process of *creation, co-creation, and re-creation*. *Time Magazine*'s recent declaration (2006) of "You" as the person of the year, reflects the culture of creation and co-creation. Our artifacts, whether video, text, audio, or software code, are often created in a collaborative manner. Once created, the openness of these artifacts results in others re-creating newer artifacts based on what was generated by others. In order for this approach to knowledge-sharing and meaning-making to work, resources must exist in a networked manner.

The value of networks resides in their simplicity. Barabasi claims that "networks are everywhere. All we need is an eye for them" (2002, p. 7). The many forms of networks have gained attention in the five years. Terrorist networks possess, structurally at least, similar attributes to food webs, transportation, sexual contact, or the spread of tuberculosis.

Networks can be reduced to two primary elements: *nodes* and *connections*. Additional characteristics emerge within networks over time – hubs, connectors, power laws, and others – but for this brief exploration of networks, we will remain centered on the simple attributes of networks.

From the simple building blocks of nodes and connections arises the remarkable complexity of our world. In his intriguing re-conceptualization of economics as complexity-based systems, Beinhocker (2006, p. 149) explores the tremendous impact of connections in Boolean networks. The Human Genome Project revealed only 30,000 genes, far less than the 100,000 originally anticipated. In contrast, a roundworm has 19,000 genes. Beinhocker suggests that the increased complexity of humans in comparison with roundworms may stem from the scaling and attendant affordances of Boolean networks.

Valdis Krebs, of Orgnet (www.orgnet.com), reveals the numerous insights available in graphically representing connections between voters, books by political affiliation, or interactions within a workplace. Complex interactions, when visually represented, form insightful patterns. Rob Cross (2004, p. 131) connects networks with organizational effectiveness and innovation. Networks, according to Cross, represent an organization's "relational capital." Through network analysis, key organizational value points can be identified, or such desired networks can be created through planned design.

Watts (2003, p. 273) recognizes the importance of networks as a means of coping with "complex problems in ambiguous environments." Ambiguity requires communication (or the formation of networks). Complexity is managed, in part, in a distributed manner where many nodes carry the burden.

When we transfer the principles of networks to learning, we see benefits similar to those that result when they are applied to the management of complexity and ambiguity, innovation, or the creation of adaptive systems and structures. As previously detailed, learning networks can be conceived of in two broad categories:

1. Internal – the actual structure of the human mind – how concepts are held in a distributed manner across neurons

2. External – the creation of external networks to assist in managing information across distributed structures, and the use of numerous sources to serve a filtering function in coping with abundance

Our consideration of learning networks will rest exclusively in the second category.

External networks mimic the Web. Millions of servers and billions of individuals are able to interact due to the simple node/connection structure discussed previously. The incredible growth of information requires us to adopt different techniques of coping. Most knowledge fields are becoming progressively specialized. No one individual is capable of possessing the knowledge required to perform complex tasks. The field of medicine, for example, is increasingly specialized due to advancements in research and technology. The "general practitioner" of decades past has been replaced with a model of connected specialists.

This same splintering into specialties is replicated in all aspects of society. Complexity and abundance requires the adoption of approaches that scale and adapt. Traditional hierarchical, taxonomic, tree-like representations of knowledge, while loosely based on node/connection models, fail to adequately display and show connections between sources and different types of knowledge. Interconnections between numerous, separate elements reveal the weaknesses of traditional conceptions of knowledge. Networks enable individual nodes (or sequences of nodes) to grow and develop, and provide value to the balance of the network as a result of their growth. When one node grows, the network grows. Hierarchies, often better suited to representations of stable knowledge, like Aristotle's encyclopedia of Greek knowledge, rely strongly on central, critical nodes. Networks rely on distributed representations, enabling complex processing and scaling (much like the Web reveals).

To learn then, in the extrinsic aspect presented earlier, involves the creation of networks which filter information, present patterns of potential meaning, and provide a structure for currency of information. The creation and navigation of learning networks, with increased understanding generated as the network evolves in complexity and richness, provides the foundation of working in a knowledge-intensive environment.

The sheer abundance of, and access to, information today requires an approach different from the one education has traditionally defined. The use of search tools such as Google[1], the increased reliance on social filtering,[2] information visualization such as IBM's Many Eyes,[3] and rich media tools like online video[4] and podcasting create a new climate in which:

- Knowing "where" to find information is more important than what is already known
- Specialized nodes are used to filter abundant information
- Information structures become more important than what the structure itself distributes
- Content becomes a conduit to conversation and connections, not an entity pursued for its own sake
- Learning is a two-way flow process
- Expertise is defined by connectedness to, and awareness of, a particular discipline. A robust network
- Knowledge, and as a result, learning, is seen as nuanced, multi-faceted, multi-domain and highly dependant on context

5   Ecologies of Learning

Elaborating on John Seely Brown's (2000) listing of attributes of an ecology – an open system, dynamic and interdependent, diverse, partially self-organizing, adaptive, and fragile – and David Solomon's (2000) definition of ecologies as a "vast and intricate network of systems," Siemens (2006a, p. 89) presents numerous aspects of ecologies:

1. Supports and fosters learning – the ecology is structured to serve a particular aim. Learning ecologies are

2. Adaptive, dynamic, and responsive – the ecology enables (or more specifically, fosters) adaptation to the needs of agents within the space. If agents (or nodes) require greater autonomy to function, the ecology itself is capable of reacting and responding.

3. Chaotic – diversity generates chaos. The chaos which is created in dynamic environments and systems

---

1   www.google.com
2   www.technorati.com or http://del.icio.us
3   services.alphaworks.ibm.com/manyeyes/home
4   www.youtube.com

4. Self-organizing and individually directed – the ecology is self-organizing (an at-
    tribute found in emergent systems), and under the direction of individual nodes.
    Organization, however, is not mandated by an external authority or key entity in
    the ecology. Organization occurs through the ongoing interactions of elements
    within the ecology.
5. Alive – continual changes, newness, activity
6. Diverse – multiple viewpoints and nodes (often contradictory) exist. The widest
    possible range of perceptions exists.
7. Structured informality – the ecology has limited structure, much like the Web is
    moderated through simple protocols in open spaces. The ecology is largely in-
    formal, with structure enabling ongoing diversity of openness, not restricting
    development. The minimum control required to function, but no more.
8. Emerging – the space itself is evolving and adaptive. As the ecology itself
    changes and evolves, these changes create an emerging ecology, where the
    space itself changes to what the space is becoming (and what the space en-
    ables). Emergent systems "get their smarts from below ... they are complex
    adaptive systems that display emergent behaviour" (Johnson, p. 18).

A learning ecology is simply the space in which learning occurs. A classroom is an
ecology. So is the Internet. Or a business. Different ecologies possess different traits
and properties that make them suitable for different purposes. For instance, a jungle is
well suited for abundant plant, animal, and insect life. Cold arctic regions provide an
ecology to which animals and plants must similarly adapt in order to survive. The
characteristics of an ecology determine what can exist within it. In a microlearning
context, the learning ecology is the space that permits (even fosters) the formulation of
learning content in new patterns. The process of formulating content at a micro-level
permits the context of the ecology to be embedded into the newly formed content.
While the network activity of formulating new content and emergent meaning based
on how nodes (in this case, micro-content) are connected, the ecology in which the
network forms is contextually reflected in the new structure. The psychological notion
of *situated cognition* (namely, that our learning takes place in a particular ecology,
space or situation) reflects the overlay of context, almost like meta-data, contributing
to the overall meaning created by the formation of a network of micro-sized learning
content.

In terms of knowledge and learning, an ecology sets the basis for what can exist and
the likelihood of various elements forming connections. A restrictive ecology (due to
corporate policy or government interference) reduces the opportunity for forming connections (or relationships). An ecology of this nature presents additional challenges.

Ecologies are dynamic, living, and evolving states. Knowledge or learning ecologies
should have the following components (Siemens, 2003); specifically, they should be:

- Informal, not structured. The system should not define the learning and discussion that happens. The system should be flexible enough to allow participants to create according to their needs.
- Tool-rich. Many opportunities for users to dialogue and connect.
- Consistent and timely. New communities, projects and ideas start with much hype and promotion ... and then slowly fade. To create a knowledge sharing ecology, participants need to see a consistently evolving environment.
- Trustworthy. High, social contact (face to face or online) is needed to foster a sense of trust and comfort. Secure and safe environments are critical for trust to develop.
- Simple. Other characteristics need to be balanced with the need for simplicity. Great ideas fail because of complexity. Simple, social approaches work most effectively. The selection of tools and the creation of the community structure should reflect this need for simplicity.
- Decentralized, fostered, connected ... as compared to centralized, managed, and isolated.
- Highly tolerant of experimentation and failure

Much like physical ecologies are defined and enabled by elements like soil, temperature, moisture, and so on, learning ecologies are enabled by policies, available tools, freedom and opportunities, and the spirit of the space. Policies provide the formal rules of a space, typically mandated from a node "higher up" in a hierarchy. These rules strongly influence the actions of agents. The policies may establish a goal to which all agents must aspire (such as quarterly sales targets), guidelines of conduct (harassment policies), or procedures for navigating information flow and ensuring all needed areas are attended to (such as developing a new course in a university, or hiring a new employee). Organizational policies are influenced by "meta-policies" mandated by government or other ruling agencies. Policies of an excessively restrictive nature negatively impact the self-organizing dynamics of an ecology.

Tools enable functionality. The intentions of a space determine the types of tools required. Managing the security of learners, for example, requires clearly established policies and centralized tools. If, however, the intent of a space is to provide innovation and exploration (as in a learning environment), tools should enable openness, dialogue, co-creation, and the ability to connect disparate resources and ideas. Healthy ecologies provide the tools required to achieve the aims of the ecology. Within academic settings, the use of Learning Management Systems can hamper the intentions of exploratory, learner-driven learning (Siemens, 2006b).

Freedom and opportunities provide a large opportunity for all agents to have equal possibility of success. When predetermined metrics are established, politics can begin to play an unwelcome role. Consider an organization where the ideas of those who are politically astute rise to greater prominence, without careful consideration of their merit. In an ideal ecology, all elements are given equal possibility for success, based on how they contribute to the larger structure and provide value to other agents.

The spirit of an ecology evolves out of the policies, tools, and freedoms available to all agents. If the ecology is tolerant of failure, innovation may be a natural by-product; innovation, after all, flows from experimentation, which in turn requires numerous failures. Organizations possess a climate or spirit. Apple (www.apple.com), Google (www.google.com), and Microsoft (www.microsoft.com) each possess a certain organizational spirit. The critical challenge for any corporation or institution is how well their organizational spirit aligns with the types of problems they wish to solve. Microsoft may be comfortable with the spirit of a "business" ecology due to its heavy presence in corporate computing. Similarly, Apple and Google may be satisfied with their innovative products and easy-to-use features, due to their prominence in consumer markets.

6   Skills Required

What types of skills are required for learners to function in the spaces and structures of ecologies and networks? The American Library Association provides a broad overview of information literacy competency standards (2000). An individual who is information literate is able to (p.2)

– Determine information needed
– Access needed information
– Evaluate information and sources critically
– Incorporate information into own knowledge network
– Use information to achieve an intended purpose
– Understand issues surrounding use of information (economic, legal, social)

These skills set the foundation of interacting with information in a digital age. Of equal importance are the skills required for individuals to co-create content, that is, collaborate. The ability not only to access and assess but also to dialogue about information shifts the learner presence from consumer to active agent who connects, forms, and creates a personal knowledge and learning network.

7   Types of Tools

The tools required for the creation of learning ecologies and networks are already largely in place: blogs, wikis, podcasts, content feeds (RSS), aggregators, and video logs. The tools themselves, however, are not the key point to consider. Within a few years' time, blogs may no longer exist as a unique or meaningful term. Technology and society move too quickly for any single tool to retain a lofty position of distinction. (At the time of this writing, newer microblogging tools enabling persistent presence, like Tumblr (www.tumblr.net) and Twitter (www.twitter.com), are gaining attention).

The challenges of information abundance and complex, interdependent environments in which information occurs have been modeled in the technology industry for several decades. Many of the original search tools (Alta Vista, Google, Yahoo) gained prominence in helping technically skilled professionals and researchers "make sense" of the information being published online (Battelle, 2005). Wider indexing, combined with innovative search approaches like Google's Page Rank, assisted researches in navigating and prioritizing information. As the information base increased, methods of filtering, sharing, and commenting became important.

Tim Berners-Lee's goal with the Web was centered on connections, information availability, and access:

> ... anything being potentially connected with anything. It is a vision that provides us with new freedom, and allows us to grow faster than we ever could when we were fettered by the hierarchical classification systems into which we bound ourselves. It leaves the entirety of our previous ways of working as just one tool among many. It leaves our previous fears for the future as one set among many. And it brings the workings of society closer to the workings of our minds. (1999, p. 2)

Berners-Lee's conception of the Web of constant connections has created an ecology of information abundance, to the point of being overwhelming. The involvement of many individuals as filters or organizing agents has assigned order based on the networks created. As people create networks of personal, trusted sources, they tame the abundance of the Web to something more relevant and meaningful (or at a minimum, contextually appropriate). The informal, self-organized nature of "folksonomies" and tagging (end user classification approaches) have provided additional filters based on the aggregated actions of the many.

8   Conclusion

Future models of education face the difficult task of embracing the fluid nature of rapidly changing knowledge, while simultaneously attending to the political and organizational structures created to capture and solidify knowledge. Organizations aspire toward certainty. Whether in the creation of shareholder value, new curriculum, new models of education, or serving the needs of a specialized community, the organization of activities to achieve a primary aim is a key managerial task. The metrics of success in these instances are generally clearly defined. Education, knowledge, and learning are less bounded than the organizations seeking to use them in the service of established aims. By nature, knowledge is about growth and expanded boundaries. In contrast, organizations seek to bound knowledge to make it manageable and useful.

Today's challenges arise due to the unprecedented growth in information, conversations, and connectivity. Our models of learning were created to mirror the certainty desired by organizations. Instead, information abundance is returning education and learning to the roots of ancient Greece – climates of learning as exploration and dialogue, and not as replication and distribution of what is already known. Flanking the explosive information growth, are technology trends, new tools, increased access to content and conversation for virtually everyone, and the increased capacity to form connections with individuals from around the world. Traditional curriculum and learning design seem woefully inadequate in contrast to the tumultuous changes influencing society. In this ethos of change, adaptability and flexibility are key. Networks and ecologies form the spaces and structures of the required adaptive learning cycle. Microlearning provides the conceptual overview for a model and process of education which reflects the needs of today's learners, educators, and organizations.

References

American Library Association (2000) *Information literacy competency standards for higher education.* The Association of Colleges and Research Libraries. Available from: <http://www.ala.org/ala/acrl/acrlstandards/standards.pdf> [Accessed 7 April 2007].

Bandura, A. (1986) *Social foundations of thought and action: a social cognitive theory.* Englewood Cliffs: Prentice-Hall.

Barabási, A. (2002) *Linked: the new science of networks.* Cambridge: Perseus Publishing.

Battelle, J. (2005) *The Search: How Google and its rivals rewrote the rules of business and transformed our culture.* New York: Penguin Group.

Beinhocker, E. (2006) *The origin of wealth.* Boston: Harvard Business School Press.

Bereiter, C. (2002) *Education and mind in the knowledge age.* Mahwah: Lawrence Erlbaum Associates.

Berners-Lee, T. (1999) *Weaving the Web: the original design and ultimate destiny of the World Wide Web.* New York: HaperCollins.

Bloor, D. (1983) *Wittgenstein: a social theory of knowledge.* London: MacMillan Press.

Bowen, J. (1972a) *A history of western education.* (Vol. 1.) New York: Routledge.

Bransford, J.D., Brown, A. L., & Cocking, R. R. eds. (1999) *How people learn: brain, mind, experience, and school.* Available from: <http://books.nap.edu/html/howpeople1/ch6.html> [Accessed 7 April 2007].

Brown, J. S. (2000) *Learning, working, and playing in the digital age.* Available from: <http://serendip.brynmawr.edu/sci_edu/seelybrown> [Accessed 7 April 2007].

Cross, R. (2004) *The hidden power of social networks.* Boston: Harvard Business School Press.

Dayan, P. & Abbott, L. (2001) *Theoretical neuroscience: computational mathematical modeling of neural systems.* Cambridge: MIT Press.

Downes, S. (2006) *Learning networks and connective knowledge.* Instructional Technology Forum. Available from: <http://it.coe.uga.edu/itforum/paper92/paper92.html> [Accessed 7 April 2007].

Downes, S. (2007) *What connectivism is.* Half an Hour. Available from: <http://halfanhour.blogspot.com/2007/02/what-connectivism-is.html> [Accessed 7 April 2007].

Grossman, L. (2006) Time's person of the year: you. *Time Magazine*. Available from: <http://www.time.com/time/magazine/article/0,9171,1569514,00.html> [Accessed 7 April 2007].

Hug, T. (2005) *Microlearning and Narration. Exploring possibilities of utilization of narrations and storytelling for the designing of "micro units" and didactical microlearning arrangements*. Paper presented at the fourth Media in Transition conference, May 6-8, 2005, Massachusetts, USA.

IDC, (2007) *The expanding digital universe: a forecast of worldwide information growth through 2010*. Available from: <http://www.emc.com/about/destination/digital_universe> [Accessed 7 April 2007].

Johnson, S. (2001) *Emergence*. New York: Scribner.

McLuhan, M. (1967) *The medium is the massage: an inventory of effects*. Corte Madera: Gingko Press.

Pietroski, P. (2004) *Character before content*. University of Maryland. Available from: <http://www.wam.umd.edu/~pietro/research/papers/cbc.pdf> [Accessed 7 April 2007].

Postman, N. (1995) *The end of education: redefining the value of school*. New York: Alfred A. Knoff.

Siemens, G. (2003) *Learning ecology, communities, and networks: extending the classroom*. Available from: <http://www.elearnspace.org/Articles/learning_communities.htm> [Accessed 7 April 2007].

Siemens, G. (2005a) Connectivism: a learning theory for a digital age. *International Journal of Instructional Technology and Distance Learning*. Available from: <http://itdl.org/Journal/Jan_05/article01.htm> [Accessed 7 April 2007].

Siemens, G. (2005b) *Learning as network creation*. Learning Circuits. Available from: <http://www.learningcircuits.org/2005/nov2005/seimens.htm> [Accessed 7 April 2007].

Siemens, G. (2006a) *Knowing knowledge*. Lulu Press. Available from: <http://knowingknowledge.com> [Accessed 12 August 2007].

Siemens, G. (2006b) *Learning or management system?* University of Manitoba. Available from: <http://ltc.umanitoba.ca/wordpress/wp-content/uploads/2006/10/learning-or-management -system-with-reference-list.doc> [Accessed 7 April 2007].

Solomon, D. (2000). *Philosophy and the learning ecology*. Learning Development Institute. Available from: <http://www.learndev.org/dl/DenverSolomon.PDF> [Accessed 7 April 2007].

University of California, Berkeley. (2003) *How Much Information 2003*. Available from: <http://www.sims.berkeley.edu:8000/research/projects/how-much-info-003/execsum.htm> [Accessed 7 April 2007].

Vygotsky, L. (1986) *Thought and language*. Cambridge, MIT Press.

Watts, D. (2003) *Six degrees: the science of a connected age*. New York: W. W. Norton.

Wikipedia. (2007) *Microlearning*. Available from: <http://wikipedia.org/wiki/Microlearning> [Accessed 7 April 2007].

Order from Intermediality. An Outline of a Model of Knowledge Production and Knowledge Reception

Monika Seidl & Klaus Puhl

Looking at a famous example of a power/knowledge formation, we argue that objects of knowledge not only are constructed or constituted in the process of their medialisation, but that medialisation also allows them to be learned and appropriated in student-teacher contexts. The example chosen is the "invention" of hysteria as an illness of the soul by Jean-Martin Charcot in the 19th century in Paris at the Salpêtrière.

We demonstrate that what Charcot managed to achieve is best understood as creating a complex overview from incoherent and confusing symptoms and data. This overview resembles the "perspicuous overview" ("übersichtliche Darstellung"), as defined by the philosopher Ludwig Wittgenstein. By constructing perspicuous representations, that is, an intermedial order of texts, pictures, photos, performances, etc., Charcot turns a situation of fragmentation, of information overflow and of cognitive-emotional confusion into a meaningful and informative configuration.

We connect this to the question of micro-macrolearning on several levels. First, we show that Charcot was in a similar situation to people today who are confronted with information overflow. It was only by creatively connecting all the differing micro-aspects of hysteria onto the macro-level of a perspicuous representation that the micro-aspects could be understood, and, hence, be learned. To be able to learn and understand effectively, learners today not only have to reduce information to smaller units, but – like Charcot – learners also have to "find and invent connections" (Wittgenstein) between these units in order to integrate them into a bigger picture. Secondly, we argue that Charcot's macro representation of hysteria is itself, on a micro-level, an example for a successful perspicuous representation, which in a teacher-learner context can be used to learn what it means to successfully connect. Thirdly, our example might, furthermore, help to develop a perspicuous representation of the different discourses and practices of the micro-macro-learning debate itself.

Tracing Hysteria

To begin with, we turn to hysteria before Jean-Martin Charcot (1825-93) entered the stage. Relying on work done by Michel Foucault, G. F. Drinka, Elaine Showalter et al., we give a survey of the incoherent symptoms and the inconclusive data that Charcot managed to turn into a coherent and conclusive formation. From the age of Plato to the 19th century, hysteria and hypochondria, unlike other forms of madness, like mania or melancholy, were named as such, but could not be conclusively identified with coherent symptoms and characteristics. While hysteria was linked only with women, hypochondria allegedly affected mostly men. The problem hysteria especially posed was how to account for an illness that could not only affect any part of the body from head to toes, but also affect them in completely different ways, such as nervous fits, panic attacks, convulsions, tremors, vomiting, blindness, paralyses, catalepsy, sleeplessness or incoherent movements. Michel Foucault writes about this instability and elusiveness of hysteria in *Madness and Civilization*, quoting from George Cheyne's eminent book on melancholy, published in 1733, *The English Malady*:

> According to Cheyne, the disease maintains its unity only in an abstract manner; its symptoms are dispersed into different qualitative regions and attributed to mechanisms that belong to each of these regions in its own right. All symptoms of spasm, cramp, and convulsion derive from a pathology of heat symbolized by 'harmful, bitter, or acrimonious vapors.' On the contrary, all psychological or organic signs of weakness – 'depression, syncopes, inactivity of the mind, lethargic torpor, melancholia, and sadness' - manifest a condition of fibers which have become too humid (…) As for paralyses, they signify both a chilling and an immobilization of the fibers (...).

> It was difficult for the phenomenon of hysteria and hypochondria to find a place within the compass of qualities as it was easy for mania and melancholia to be established there. (Foucault, 1965, pp. 140-1)

From the age of Plato up to the end of the eighteenth century, this evasive mobility of hysteria was believed to be caused by the womb, either by its unpredictable movements through a women's body, or after it was realised that the womb was fixed, by spontaneous vibrations sent out by the womb to other organs of the body, especially the brain. The seat of hypochondria was also localized in the lower area of the body, the stomach, liver and pancreas. In the seventeenth century, these vibrations were understood in terms of fluids, and, later, in terms of life-spirits, which both moved freely through the body and could cause any organ to *simulate* its own illness. The organ inflicted would then imitate the disorder specific to its nature. For instance, hysteria affecting the colon would cause a pain in this region which resembles the pain usually caused by a spinal infection or injury. When the spirits move to the brain, they cause vomiting and other symptoms which are very similar to the ones caused by meningitis. The body becomes the stage of hysteria:

> Each part of the body determines in its own right and by its own nature the form of the symptom produced. Hysteria thus appeared as the most real and the most deceptive of diseases; real because it is based upon a movement of the animal spirits; illusory as well, because it generates symptoms that seem provoked by a disorder inherent in the organs (...). Actually suffering from the disordered and excessive movements of spirits, the organ imitates its own illness. (Foucault, 1965, p. 148)

That more women suffered from hysteria than men from hypochondria (the male hysteria), was explained by the fact that the female body was seen as being more easily penetrated than the male body, which was thought to be more solid and dense. The more robust and mentally strong a person was, the less the spirits were allegedly able to move through someone's body and have an effect on someone's nerves. The concept of life-spirits slowly lost authority and was gradually replaced by the emerging idea that the nerves themselves and the condition they were in held responsibility for various symptoms. Hysteria and hypochondria thus turns into an illness of the nervous system, which is thought of as a complex system of irritability and resonance. Hysteria is now caused by too much sensitivity, like too much sympathy with other people, and, in general, by overstimulation and irritation from the outer world. Hysteria has become the illness of the-too-much. The hysteric suffers from too much sympathy with his/her environment. Any object of desire can cause hysteria, but only by overindulging. The patient's mind reacts to too much irritation by becoming insensitive, numb, blind, petrified, in short, by becoming mad. This idea of overload associated with hysteria shows similarities to the issue of information overload identified in pedagogy. In both cases, it is a situation of excess and too-much that needs to be coped with.

At the time when hysteria turns into an illness of the nervous system caused by excess, the discourse about hysteria turns into a *moral* discourse about the patient's character and behaviour. In most cases, the patient is now gendered as a woman who has to undergo an ethical valuation of her nervous sensibility. The patient becomes responsible for her own illness; her madness results from her being morally deficient. "(...) everything to which one was attached in the world, the life one had led, the affections one had had, the passions and the imaginations one had cultivated too complacently – all combined in the irritation of the nerves, finding there both their natural effect and their moral punishment" (Foucault, 1965, p. 157).

For our purposes, it is important to note that all the explanations offered during the history of hysteria attempted to account for the fact that hysteria (and its counterpart hypochondria) could not be identified with a field of consistent symptoms and characteristics, or as Foucault describes this predicament:

> It was not so much a question of escaping the old localization in the uterus, but of discovering the principle and the pathway of a diverse, polymorphous disease dispersed throughout the entire body. A disease was to be accounted for (...) that traversed corporeal space so rapidly and so ingeniously that it was virtually present throughout the entire body. (Foucault, 1965, p. 145-46)

The travelling and vibrating womb, the fluids going up and down the body, the life-spirits which moved freely everywhere in the body and caused the organs to simulate their own illnesses, the irritable nervous system, which could affect any organ or body part, were in fact desperate attempts to come to terms with the multiple and unrelated symptoms of hysteria. And morally blaming the patient for her illness is perhaps the admission of having been unable to come up with a unified medical explanation of hysteria. In terms of micro-macrolearning the situation could be described as one in which, because of the abundance of more or less unrelated information, it was almost impossible for medical students and physicians, at any stage of history, to learn about the diagnosis and treatment of hysteria in a systematic way.

Staging Hysteria

This was the situation when Charcot, the founder of neurology, entered the stage. Charcot was in a situation similar to somebody today who needs to cope with big amounts of information, fragmented and unconnected, and who needs not only to reduce the overflow of information into smaller units, but also to make the right connections, in order to "get the whole picture." To get at what he thought was the nature of hysteria, Charcot used and creatively adapted, in a very contemporary way, the different media of his time. He treated hysteria as a mental and not an organic disorder, and also diagnosed it in men. In 1862, Charcot became senior consultant and in 1872, Professor of Pathological Anatomy at the Salpêtrière in Paris, which, since the Revolution, had served as an insane asylum and a hospital for women, "a nightmare in the midst of Paris' *Belle Epoque*, 'the Versailles of pain,' with more than 4000 women, prostitutes, epileptics, 'decrepit and demented women'" (Didi-Huberman, 2003, p. xi & 15). Charcot started working on hysteria in 1870, which he in fact rediscovered in the Salpêtrière, in the sense that before Charcot, apparently none of the patients were labelled as hysterical. Charcot isolated hysterics from epileptics and other cases of "insanity," and later also treated men for traumatic hysteria, demonstrating the similarity of the latter to classical hysteria.

Cases of traumatic neuroses, or hysteria, started to turn up in the nineteenth century among war-traumatized soldiers and male workers as a result of factory and railway accidents. People who suffered these traumas were bodily unharmed, or only slightly injured, but developed symptoms that were not connected to the physical injuries suffered and that were similar to symptoms known from classic hysteria. Charcot stressed the psychological, that is, the non-organic nature of bodily symptoms linked to hysteria. Following the principle of good science of his time, which ruled that once there is a symptom, there had to be a lesion, he had in vain attempted to find a lesion in patients who were diagnosed with hysteria, as he had in cases of multiple sclerosis. The only bodily condition he conceded in hysterics was a hereditary weakness of the nervous system. Nevertheless, hysteria in its different forms was a real illness, Charcot claimed, which was caused by emotions beyond a subject's control. His main reason for this claim was that, apart from traumatic hysteria, the fact that he got patients to have hysterical fits, either by pressing a so-called hysterogenic spot on the patient's body, or by hypnotizing them. For Charcot, and also for Pierre Janet and many other neurologists and psychologists at the time, only hysterics could be hypnotized.

Charcot was a master of the media. During his famous Tuesday lectures, Charcot staged a true spectacle of hysteria by getting his female patients to perform, under hypnoses, hysterical poses and other deeds, like behaving like a dog or rocking a hat like a baby (Didi-Huberman, 2003, p. 227). This performance was usually rounded off by the performance of "the great hysterical attack," also called "hystero-epilepsy," which developed in four stages: the *epileptoid* phase, so called because it "copied" an epileptic fit, *clownism*, the phase of contortions and big movements, reminiscent of Yoga poses, then the phase of *passionate,* theatrical postures, and, finally, the painful stage of *delirium*, during which the patients started to talk and had to be woken up. The phases of the *great attack*, which Charcot compared with the four acts of a drama, were partly matched by stages of the *great hypnotism,* the *cataleptic*, the *lethargic* state, and the state of *somnambulism*. Some of Charcot's Tuesday models became quite famous, like Blanche Wittman, "the queen of hysterics," and also one of the attractions of the Salpêtrière's annual "Bal des Folles," or Augustine, the most famous of his photo models. In his Tuesday lectures, Charcot also used multimedia aids, like drawings, diagrams, coloured chalk, models, plates, statuettes, photos and, quite uncommonly at the time, projectors and slides.

The Tuesday performance was part of Charcot's method, a mix of medical theory, experiment and aesthetics, or as Claude Bernard, a major influence on Charcot, put it, "the art of obtaining facts and putting them to work," (Didi-Huberman, 2003, p. 19) that is to say, of making hysteria visible in a regulated way by provoking the pathological nervous system to manifest itself in bodily symptoms. As Sigmund Freud, who had studied with Charcot in 1885-86, stressed, Charcot was a visual type who

used to look again and again at things he did not understand (…) he was not a reflective man, not a thinker: he had the nature of an artist – he was, as he himself said a "visual," a man who sees (…) the apparent chaos presented by the continual repetition of the same symptoms then gave way to order: the new nosological picture emerged, characterized by the constant combination of certain groups of symptoms. (Quoted in Didi-Huberman, 2003, p. 26)

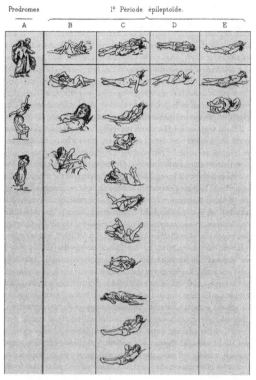

Figure 1. Paul Richer, "perspicuous overview" of the great hysterical attack, in: Richer (1881).

Paul Richer, Charcot's collegue, co-author of *Les démoniaques dans l'art*,(1887), and professor of artistic anatomy, created a synoptic table or tableau with eighty-two figures (exclusively of women) of the "complete and great hysterical attack," showing its different stages. The typical positions were given in only twelve figures on the horizontal line and the variations on the vertical line. Richer's chart presented hysteria in a way which allowed it to be taken in at one glance, and set the standard for other work done on hysteria.

Charcot also had a photo studio installed at the Salpêtrière and employed two photographers, first Paul Régnard and then Albert Londe. Eventually, there was set-up a glass-walled studio with beds, screens, platforms, gallows to suspend patients, backdrops in different colours, a darkroom, artificial lightening, and cameras with multiple lenses, in order to shot sequential photo series of the hysterical poses. In short, what happened at the Salpêtrière was the most extensive medical use of photography at the time. "(…) photography, for Charcot was simultaneously an experimental procedure (a laboratory tool), a museological procedure (scientific archive), and a teaching procedure (a tool of transmission)" (Didi-Huberman, 2003, p. 30). The photos were published under Charcot's auspices by Bourneville and Régnard in the now famous three volumes of *Iconographie photographique de la Salpêtrière*. The first volume of *Nouvelle Iconographie de la Salpêtrière*, by Londe, Richer and de la Tourette, appeared in 1888.

Figure 2. Paul Richer, "perspicuous overview" of the great hysterical attack (1881).

The whole setup Charcot put to work, impressive as it was, looks highly artificial and constructed to our eyes. It happened that only certain female hysterics were used as models to be photographed again and again, the most famous being Augustine, and, as mentioned above, Blanche Wittmann, the star of the Tuesday lecture. Especially the *passionate* poses looked very similar to the classical acting poses of the French theatre at the time and to poses in 19th century paintings. There are also striking similarities in the first phase of the *great attack* to an epileptic fit, which seemed to result from the fact that the female hysterics lived in the same wing of the Salpêtrière as the epileptics did, and had to look after them. Furthermore, Charcot's medical colleagues outside the Salpêtrière failed to reproduce the great attack with their patients, and thus it was suggested by some that the women's hysterical fits were the result of unconscious suggestion or imitation, in order to please Charcot and to keep the special treatment they enjoyed as his models. There was, also, a remarkable increase of hysteria diagnosed at the Salpêtrière during Charcot's time.

Charcot and Londe, however, like most of their contemporaries, believed in the realistic powers, and the neutrality and immediate objectivity of photography. Thus, whatever looks artificial and constructed to us was a true representation of reality to them. The photographic image, "the pencil of nature" (Didi-Huberman, 2003, p. 32), seemed to guarantee the reality of the object pictured, freeing scientific knowledge from its dependence on language and drawings, and pushing it in new directions. Londe stated "the photographic plate is the scientist's true retina" (Didi-Huberman, 2003, p. 35), also stressing the particular sensitivity of the photographic plate compared to the sensitivity of the human eye. And because the nature of hysteria has always been linked with simulation and imitation of other illnesses, the similarity of the hysterical poses to epilepsy, theatrical poses, etc., was, for Charcot, not a contradiction to the genuine nature of the poses. Also, Charcot was apparently not very aware of the "group dynamics" at his institution between doctors and patients, especially the possibility that the performances of his patients were partly the result of suggestion, imitation and of the training they had by his assistants. This is Charcot, answering his critics in one of his lectures, even confessing rather naively to a denial of theory:

> Behold the truth (…). I am not in the habit of advancing things that aren't experimentally demonstrable. You know that my principle is to give no weight to theory, and leave aside all prejudice: if you want to see clearly, you must take things as they are. It would seem that hystéro-épilepsy exists only in France and only, I might say, as it is sometimes said, at the Salpêtrière (…). But, truth to tell, in this I am nothing more than a photographer; I inscribe what I see (…). (Didi-Huberman, 2003, p. 29)

The important point to note, is how Charcot, by creatively using all the media of his time, constructed, or in his words "inscribed" hysteria as a unified illness and thus created a clearly demarcated point of reference for the medical and psychiatric discourses about it. Hysteria, in the complete and reproducible form of "the great attack," appeared at the intersection of medical texts, of Richer's tableaus, the hypnotic performances at the Tuesday lectures, the sequential photo images, the charts and diagrams and of classical paintings depicting the obsessed. At the same time, the many hetero-dox micro-forms of hysteria could now be reproduced under hypnoses and could, therefore, be more easily and more effectively learned and studied because they were structured and connected into the synoptic, macro-level configuration of "the great attack" and its different variations.

Teaching Hysteria

In the part that follows, we argue that Charcot's macro representation of hysteria is itself, on a micro-level, an example of what the philosopher Ludwig Wittgenstein called a *perspicuous representation* (*übersichtliche Darstellung*) or *synoptic overview*, the art of "finding and inventing connections" between puzzle cases and things we already know or only have to remember. In a pedagogic context, Charcot's representation of hysteria provides an instructive example, on the micro-level, of a successful perspicuous representation, of how to connect well, of how to use creatively every media at one's disposal.

Wittgenstein developed the art or method of perspicuous overview in order to find a way out of philosophical problems. Perspicuous overview, then, works on a macro-level, enabling the understanding of diverse phenomena, which cannot be understood on their own, by connecting and arranging them in such a way that the interconnections between them become visible.

In *Philosophical Investigations* §§ 122-3, Wittgenstein writes:

> A perspicuous representation produces [...] that understanding which consists in 'seeing connections.' Hence the importance of finding and inventing intermediate cases.
> The concept of a perspicuous representation is of fundamental significance for us. It earmarks the form of account we give, the way we look at things. [...]
> A philosophical problem has the form: 'I don't know my way about.'

Wittgenstein's model can be useful for the question of micro- macrolearning. He developed it in the context of his language-games, which again are first introduced in the context of teaching practices on a micro-level as "primitive forms of language," "forms of language with which a child begins to make use of words" (BB, p. 17). Examples of the "countless kinds" of language-games are: "giving orders and obeying them, describing the appearance of an object, or giving its measurement, constructing an object from a description (a drawing), reporting an event, speculating about an event, forming and testing an hypotheses, (...) asking, thanking, cursing, greeting, praying" (PI §23). Wittgenstein's point is, that how we learn and teach the use of words in language-games sheds light on what they mean, for instance, in the case of words for sensations. The philosophical problem of meaning, the relation between language and world, becomes closely linked to the question of teaching and learning. Any philosophical theory which cannot explain how the *concepts* it is talking about are *learned* and *taught* must be incoherent. About the language-games with psychological concepts Wittgenstein writes:

> But how is the connection between the name and a thing set up? The question is the same as: how does a human being learn the meaning of the names of sensations? – of the word "pain" for example. Here is one possibility: words are connected with the primitive, the natural, expression of the sensation and used in their place. (PI § 244)

As to psychological or mental states, Wittgenstein rejects theories which pretend to explain the meaning of psychological terms by their connection with private objects like sensations, experiences and thoughts. Such a theory cannot explain how the meaning of those terms can be learned and taught. The private objects would have to be accessible, say for the child, in order to be learned as the meaning of the relevant terms. However, as no one else can have my sensations and thoughts, no one else could learn what I mean by "pain" for instance. By the same token, I could not have learned what someone else means by "pain," because his or her inner sensation is not accessible to me.

Philosophical problems which result from ignorance of the set up and rules of particular language games can be solved or even resolved on the micro-level by drawing attention to the particular language-games involved. But even this level is dependent on a more comprehensive macro-level, as individual language-games are connected to each other in a particular language which again belongs to a "form of life": "Here the term 'language-*game*' is meant to bring into prominence the fact that the *speaking* of a language is part of an activity, or of a form of life." (PI § 23)

Another form of problems is caused by conflating *different* language games, especially from using the words of one language game according to the rules of another, for instance, using the rules of physical or causal descriptions for talking about mental states, or using the rules of physics to talk about psychology. This conflation, and the resulting "failure to understand," has its main source not on a micro-, but on a macro-level, that is, in the fact "that we do not command a clear view of the use of our words. – Our grammar is lacking in perspicuity ("Übersichtlichkeit")." (PI §122) And because of this muddled view, the relevant philosophical differences can, again, neither be taught nor learned. A perspicuous representation provides the perspicuity lacking and allows it to identify, solve or even dissolve the problem in question, and to understand it eventually. And only what we understand, we can learn and teach.

Another important feature of perspicuous representations is their locality and purpose-relativity and, closely connected, their dependence on *being acknowledged* by the person addressed by it, or by the one who creates it – as something which makes things clear and satisfies her. Being perspicuous is not an intrinsic property of a representation, or of the object represented, but rather related to certain disquieting or puzzling aspects of a specific situation on the side of the subject. It does not abstract from the particular (contextual, historical, or psychological) relations the subject has to its object, but tries to make this relation clear, in order to show how the way the object is represented is constituted by this particular relation. Perspicuous representations are thus geared to the particular situation of individual learners in which they have to make the right connections between the many micro-units, in order to "get the picture."

What motivates constructing a perspicuous overview is marked by a (philosophical) problem in the form of "I don't know my way about" (PI §123), or by a feeling of "a vague mental uneasiness," or intellectual discomfort. Its subject-matter can be some puzzling aspect of the use of certain words, mathematical proofs, magical rites, religious ceremonies, and dreams (as in Wittgenstein's reading of James Frazer's *The Golden Bough* and Sigmund Freud's *Interpretation of Dreams*). In the case of Charcot, it was the mysterious puzzle of hysteria, an illness without an organic cause, and incoherent symptoms, which he hoped to get into a unified picture.

A perspicuous representation proceeds by finding intermediate cases (*Zwischenglieder*) so far unnoticed, or by *inventing* them. It follows the slogan "only connect," either by "seeing" connections already there, or by coming up with new ones. As for Charcot, it is not easily seen what he actually found and what he invented by connecting hysteria with hypnoses and by closely linking the nature of the illness with what could be made visible, that is, photographed and repeatedly performed. According to today's commentators like Georges Didi-Huberman, George Drinka or Elaine Showalter, Charcot more or less invented hysteria, giving an impressive example of constituting a scientific object by creating a multi-media discourse about it.

Being perspicuous is not an intrinsic property of a representation, but rather dependent on *being acknowledged* by the person addressed by it – as something which makes things clear and satisfies her. As regards this respect, Wittgenstein compares his method to psychoanalysis and to aesthetic explanations. As to justification, perspicuous representations are on *the same level* as the puzzle cases they make perspicuous. They show other contrasting, but coherent, ways of seeing things and *thereby* make one realize that one has always been dealing with forms of representing things and not the things themselves. The subjective aspects of perspicuous representations, their dependence on our acceptance and whether they satisfy us, do not allow for separating the phenomenon made perspicuous and its representation. A perspicuous representation not only comes later than what it represents, but also constitutes its meaning and identity (Puhl, 2006).

Prima facie, the subjective aspects of perspicuous representations contradict the scientific-objectivist ambitions of Charcot and his denial of theory, as quoted above: "But, truth to tell, in this I am nothing more than a photographer; I inscribe what I see." Of course, nobody today believes that Charcot only humbly described an independently existing illness called "hysteria." Since the early twentieth century, the number of cases diagnosed as hysteria has sharply declined, and today it is no longer recognized as an illness. There is also the highly constructivist nature of Charcot's project, his theatrical staging of hysteria, the *reality effect* he produced by constructing photographic images of the "great attack." In the light of all this, what Charcot, in fact, did is better understood as not just to unveil hysteria as it is, but to establish a new and systematic *way of representing* the data, a multi-medial scheme for ordering and hence teaching them, that is, a perspicuous representation as outlined by Wittgenstein.

Inventing the object of hysteria by creating its perspicuous representation is, of course, situated on a bigger scale than being in the situation of an individual learner who, say, wants to find his or her way through the complexity of information offered by the Internet. However, both cognitive situations are structurally similar, as Charcot and today's learners have to find and invent the right connections, "right" not meaning here connections how they can be found in the things themselves, but as they make up a perspicuous synopsis, that is, how they fit the specific interests, experiences, habits and needs of the learner and further his or her goal to learn better and more effectively.

Hysteria as a perspicuous representation not only provides an example of the dependence of the micro- on the macro-level. In a teaching and learner's context, hysteria provides also an instructive example, this time on the micro-level, of a successful perspicuous representation, of how to connect well, to use creatively every medium at one's disposal and to be a skilful bricoleur. It could also help to develop a perspicuous representation of the "bits and pieces" from different discourses and practices of the micro-macro-learning debate.

Klaus Puhl wishes to express his gratitude to the Deutsche Forschungsgemeinschaft (DFG) for generously funding a research project which has fed into this article.

References

Didi-Huberman, G. (2003) *Invention of Hysteria. Charcot and the Photographic Iconography of the Salpêtrière*. Cambridge Mass.: MIT Press.

Drinka, G. F. (1984) *The Birth of Neurosis. Myth, Malady, and the Victorians*. New York: Simon and Schuster.

Foucault, M. (1965) *Madness and Civilization. A History of Insanity in the Age of Reason*. New York: Random House.

Puhl, K. (2006) "Only connect ... perspicuous representation and the logic of Nachträglichkeit. In: *Grazer Philosophische Studien*, 71, pp. 23–38.

Richer, P. (1881) *Etudes cliniques sur l'hystéro-épilepsie ou grande hystérie. Avec une préface du J. M. Charcot*. Paris: Adrien Delahaye et Emile Lecrosnier.

Showalter, E. (1987) *The Female Malady. Women, Madness, and English Culture, 1830-1980*. London: Virago.

Wittgenstein, L. (1953) *Philosophical Investigations*. Oxford: Basil Blackwell (PI).

Wittgenstein, L. (1958) *The Blue and Brown Book*. Oxford: Basil Blackwell, (BB).

II Microdidactics & Microlearning

(Micro-)Didactics: A Tale of two Traditions

Norm Friesen

The instructional or didactic principles associated with the practices and technologies of microlearning present significant challenges to conventional notions of system, planning, and design that tend to operate most meaningfully on a pedagogical macro-level. As a result, microlearning in general invites a radical re-examination and re-thinking of conceptions and traditions underlying didactic and instructional theory. This paper explores the possibilities for such a re-thinking that are presented by con-sidering the divergent and convergent paths of Anglo-American didactic (instruc-tional) theory on the one hand, and German and northern-European Didaktik on the other. After an historical overview of the common concept "didactic," this paper fo-cuses on two areas of recent convergence in these traditions that are of direct signifi-cance to microlearning: Contemporary attempts to address emerging conceptions of educational content management presented by the Web, and recent emphases in both instructional and didaktik theory on situated action.

1   Introduction

The term "didactic," used in the title of this collection *Didactics of Microlearning*, brings with it a particular cross-cultural complexity and ambiguity that has challenged scholarship in the past (e.g., Holmberg, 2004). "Didactic" and its German cognate "Didaktik" point not only to a common Greek root, *didaktikos* ("apt at teaching"), but also bring with them varied and often significant and surprising histories and associa-tions. These are the subject of the first part of this paper.

The term "didactic" has an ambivalent and largely colloquial history in the English language. But it is marked by a very lively and scholarly history in German. (Its equivalents in the Nordic and Flemish languages have enjoyed similarly significant histories and academic associations.) The academic and theoretical significance of the term "didactic" in German-speaking countries is only infrequently mentioned in Eng-lish; but there have recently been signs of growing interest, especially in the area of curriculum studies (e.g., Gundem & Hopmann, 1998; Hudson et al., 1999; Westbury, Hopmann, & Riquarts, 2000; Kertz-Welzel, 2004; Nordkvelle, 2004).

2   Didaktik, Bildung, Geisteswissenschaften

In the German-speaking world, "Didaktik" designates a sub-discipline of Pedagogy (*Pädagogik*) that is concerned with the theory of instruction, and more broadly, with the theory and practice of learning and teaching (e.g., Weniger, 2000, p. 113). Present-ed in these very general terms Didaktik does not appear in any obvious way to delimit an area of scholarship that is not already covered by fields in English-language scholarship such as instructional design, curriculum, and perhaps especially, educational psychology.

However, the relationship between Didaktik and what would be its English-language equivalents is orthogonal and disjointed, not simply opposed on some points and in agreement on others. What differentiates Didaktik is not so much any formal definition, but the overall orientation of the field, its interrelationship with other disciplines, and the organization of its subordinate specializations. As a result, even the simplest introduction cannot help but highlight differences in cultures and in ways of thinking that are perhaps too easily papered over in discussions about technologies and pedagogies in English-dominated e-learning research. In itself, the relationship between Didaktik and its Anglo-American counterpart(s) also provides important evidence of the heterogeneous and culturally-determined nature of education and of understandings of learning and development generally – presenting a significant counter-argument to the ongoing redefinition of these phenomena in terms of a-historical, natural-scientific paradigms (e.g. brain-, learning-, or cognitive-science).

The relationship between Didaktik and English-language "instruction" or "education" involves not only cultural, but also linguistic differences:

> many of the meaning-conveying educational concepts, terms and words of the German-Scandinavian language area [related to education and Didaktik] lack counterparts in English – and resist exact translation. Indeed the term Didaktik itself with its comprehensive intertwining of action and reflection, practice and theory, is one such untranslatable concept. (Gundem & Hoppman, 1998, p. 2)

Two further, untranslatable yet indispensable terms are *Bildung* and *Geisteswissenschaft*. Both underscore the overall philosophical and humanistic orientation of Didaktik. Bildung, on the one hand, designates "the character-forming surplus beyond mere knowledge and skills that is at the centre of didaktik" (Künzli, as quoted in Westbury, 1998, p. 60). The term denotes an excess or a remainder that is not captured by standardized testing, performance measures or learning outcomes. Its meaning may most readily find illustration in the word *Bildungsroman*. This imported literary term refers to the novel of education or formation – of which *The Adventures of Huckleberry Finn* or *To Kill A Mockingbird* are prominent English-language examples. As the themes and developments in each of these novels suggests, Bildung refers to a dialectical process of becoming an individual (on the one hand), and becoming part of a society and culture (on the other): It designates, in other words, the accomplishment of "reasonable self-determination, which presupposes and includes emancipation from determination by others" (Klafki, 2000, p. 87). Following Kant's famous definition of enlightenment as the "emergence from one's self-incurred … intellectual dependency" (Kant, 1784), Bildung is understood as a development in which becoming one's self and gaining one's voice and identity is also and simultaneously the way in which one becomes a full member of society. Some recent scholars of Bildung describe such a broad, dialectical process in terms that come close to notions of "socialization" or "social reproduction" articulated in anthropological and critical-theoretical studies of education in English (e.g., Apple, 1982). Weniger, Mollenhauer, and Klafki, for example, all speak of education in terms of "intellectual encounters" between generations, or the identification and representation of aspects of one's culture for the purposes of intergenerational mediation (Weniger, as cited in Künzli, 2000, p. 46; Mollenhauer, 2003, p. 17-18; Klafki, 1986).

Geisteswissenschaft, literally the science of the mind or spirit, has served as academic nomenclature in German-speaking countries to designate what in English is commonly referred to as the "humanities." Although this designation is gradually giving way to terms reflecting more Anglo-American orientations, such as "Kulturwissenschaften" or even the imported term "Cultural Studies," some implications of Geisteswissenschaften as a category remain important. For example, the Geisteswissenschaften have traditionally included psychology, linguistics, and importantly, *education*. Thus grouped together with humanistic and cultural subject areas, education in German-speaking countries has, for example, remained untouched by the successive waves of scientifically-oriented behaviourism and cognitivism that have washed over English-language educational theory. Also consistent with this "humanistic" emphasis, German research in Didaktik has given consistent emphasis to dialectical and normative or explicitly ethical approaches, and to anthropological and even aesthetic understandings, whereas these generally remain on the margins of English-language educational discourses.

3 Didactic in English: Dewey's Loss and Thorndike's Gain

The ambivalent and freighted character of the English term "didactic" is evident not only from colloquial uses, but is also illustrated by the multiple definitions it receives in dictionary entries. At best, the term is taken to refer to instruction (rather than more substantial processes such as "education" or "development"), and it often applies to kinds of moral instruction that accompany entertainment (for example, a fable, or a song with a moral). It also carries a strong, negative, secondary significance, variously characterized as "making moral observations" or as being "excessively instructive" (e.g., Merriam-Webster, 2006; WordNet, 2006).

But at the same time, it is apparent that the term was not always understood so narrowly. The late 19[th-] and early 20th centuries represented a period of remarkable contiguity between the German and Anglo-American traditions. For example, John Dewey wrote favourably about didactics in the *Cyclopedia of Education* (1911), and was an enthusiastic reader of didactic theorists such as Herbart and Lotze – names long since forgotten in the annals of English-language research.

What led to this forgetting? One American observer has a simple answer: "One cannot understand the history of education in the United States unless one realizes that

Edward L. Thorndike won and John Dewey lost" (Lagemann, 1989, p. 185). The implications of this statement are easily illustrated by considering the legacy of these two figures: Thorndike studied animal behaviour as a way of understanding human learning, and his work anticipated both Skinner on operant conditioning and current connectionist research in neuroscience and cognitive psychology. To him, we owe the now familiar terms "mental map" and "learning curve."

Dewey, on the other hand, has been ascribed the role of the "patron saint" of American education, a title that – when compared to Thorndike's substantial legacy – appears more honorific than substantive. According to Langemann, "Thorndike's thought" has ended up becoming "more influential" than Dewey's, being now "more significant in shaping both "public school practice as well as scholarship about education" (Langemann, 1989, p. 185).

Correspondingly, Dewey's work receives relatively little attention in educational technology research. And where it *has* been referenced, the implications of his humanist and pragmatic philosophy are generally ignored. However, as the final part of this paper will show, these two traditions, which have been divergent in many respects since Dewey, have recently begun to converge at points of direct relevance to the latest developments in education and the Internet.

4   Didaktik Technology

Having explicated the different understandings associated with the term "Didaktik," I will now explore their relationship to Internet and Web technologies in general, and microlearning in particular. The two diagrams provided below serve as starting points for such an exploration. The first, from Morrison, Kemp and Ross (2001), shows the steps for designing instruction and instructional content. These steps are often utilized in the development and implementation of educational technologies, and identical or similar diagrams are to be found in instructional and curriculum design textbooks. The second is a particular version of the "didactic triangle," variations of which can be found in almost any German-language introduction to the subject (e.g., see Meyer, 1988, p. 132). The version shown here specifically reflects didactic conceptions developed in Cohn's "theme centered interaction" (as outlined in Schenk & Schwabe, 2000), which give special emphasis to group learning, and also implies a broadly Freudian psychological frame of reference.

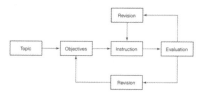

Figure 1. "A Typical Instructional
Design Model"

Figure 2. The Didactic Triangle (based on
Cohn's theme-centered interaction)

Like the empirical English-language and dialectical, continental traditions from which they respectively originate, the two diagrams relate to one another orthogonally, but a number of differences in overall emphasis are clear: The "instructional design model" emphasizes a goal-oriented instructional development process, with clear, functional, systemic and procedural steps. In keeping with Thorndike's work on behavioural conditioning and cognitivist connectionism, the objectives, instruction and evaluation that are a part of this model are most often associated with either clearly behavioural or explicitly cognitive goals, strategies and metrics. Significantly, the purpose of the process depicted in this diagram is the revision or adjustment of instruction and objectives for an objectively "given" content or topic. It is also significant that the "topic" component in this diagram is not subject to feedback from any other components in the system, and that it could, in theory, be operationalized as any kind of content or subject. The model, in other words, is intended to be content-neutral. Also, in principle, the instructional "output" of this process is ultimately perfectible: Once instruction and objectives for a given topic are revised to maximize the results of evaluation, a stable end-state may be reached. Finally, as the arrows in the diagram indicate, the relationships between each of these steps are all reducible purely to function, that is, in terms of inputs and outputs. This model, like many North American instructional approaches, strives to be "teacher-proof" (Westbury, 1998, p. 53), and subordinates the individual, group and subject to the *system* (Westbury, 1998, p. 21; although instructional designers would likely object that the system serves the *user* and her requirements as captured through initial or iterative needs analyses).

Regardless of the variations and interpretations applicable to such a diagram, it remains a system whose ultimate goal, *qua* system, is its final outputs, and its own equilibrium. On the other hand, the didactic triangle can be said to be defined by relations whose dynamics are dependent on tension and contradiction, rather than equilibrium or entropy:

> It is not to be regarded as a technological model of interaction, in which individual factors can be meticulously calculated. Rather, theme-centered interaction [from which this model is derived] is to be understood as a collaborative-pedagogical concept in the tradition of humanistic psychology, which begins

with human values, emphasizing growth, authenticity, self-actualization, and responsibility. (Hug, 1994, p. 50)

In this sense, the Didaktik triangle does not schematize a process or set of relationships that are somehow perfectible. Instead, in keeping with Dewey, and his pragmatic and "experiential" philosophy, this diagram also implies a significant, qualitative experiential emphasis – ascribing more importance to the vicissitudes of undergoing a learning process than the quantitative alignment of inputs and outputs. It describes a process that has been characterized as dynamic, dialectical and conversational (e.g. see: Meyer, 1988; Klingberg, 1982; Klafki, 1973). Dialectically, through the dynamic of thesis, antithesis and synthesis, the tensions between contradictory aspects of the three elements can be integrated to arrive at a position which supersedes the two. (So, for example, the position of an "I" [person], versus that of the "we" [group] or larger, surrounding "global" society can be overcome through the development of a self whose independence is realized explicitly *within* the context of social participation.) The conversational dynamic to be found in the relationships in this diagram is understood both figuratively and literally. It is generally seen as a kind of interaction or dialogue between an "I" and a group or even a thing, text or theme. In this dialogical interrelationship, the differences between self (I) and other (whether "we" or "it") are simultaneously respected and addressed. Didaktik scholars such as Klafki highlight in this connection understandings of conversation articulated by the likes of Martin Buber and Hans-Georg Gadamer – both of whom emphasize the irreducibility of conversation to predictive logic or, indeed, to the control or intentions of either conversant:

> We say that we "conduct" a conversation; but the more genuine the conversation is, the less its conduct lies within the will of either partner. Thus, a genuine conversation is never the one that we wanted to conduct. Rather, it is generally more correct to say that we fall into conversation, or that we become involved in it. No one knows in advance what will "come out" of a conversation. (Gadamer, 1989, p. 383)

Given this and the other differences that separate the "instructional design model" from the "Didaktik triangle," it is not surprising that each also entails a very different relationship to computer or Internet technologies or media. Specifically, the functionally-oriented instructional design model can be said to open up nearly every aspect of the instructional process to technological intervention or mediation, while the other model only admits of specific *points of contact* with technology. For example, just as the instructional design model is open to any type of content, it is also described as being capable of working with any kinds of media or technology, creating instructional processes that can be delivered over the Internet, using text, multimedia or other combinations of technologies (Morrison, Kemp & Ross, 2001). The question of "automating instructional design," of subjecting each step in the instructional design model to computerization, has also been a popular focus in research and development (e.g., Tennyson & Baron, 1995). Despite the thorough interpenetration of this model by technology, and its ostensible content- and instructional-neutrality, problems appear when its potential for microlearning and other technology-intensive approaches are considered. These will be discussed further below.

The points of contact with technology admitted by the Didaktik model, on the other hand, are indicated by the dialogical relationships between the elements of "I," "we" and "it." Some adaptations of this diagram have connected "media" or "Internet" technologies to all three relationships or elements in the triangle, indicating that these media or technologies can "help" with or support in the relationships between each (e.g. Boeckmann & Heymen, 1990). Indeed, it is relatively easy to think of examples in which media or technology is able to facilitate communication between an "I" (whether teacher or student) and "we" (e.g., online conference, chat or email systems, voice-over IP). It also requires no stretch of the imagination to see a similar facilitation as occurring in interactions of such an "I" or "we" with the "it" represented by the topic or material at hand (e.g., simulations, multimedia and interactive hypermedia). Naturally, there are also many applications (and ways of understanding them) that simultaneously address all three types of relationship, from course management systems supporting interactive course materials and teacher-student/student-student communication, to audio/video teleconferencing systems allowing for simultaneous application sharing (e.g., see Anderson's triangular diagram of technologically-mediated interaction types: Anderson, 2003).

5   Didaktik/Instructional Designs for Microlearning

When applied to the technologies and practices of microlearning, both Didaktik and instructional design approaches encounter similar problems and challenges. Both approaches, it appears, are too closely wed to concerns of the macro-level – the level of full courses, of general instructional programs, or even of individual lesson-plans – to be readily or directly applicable to the particularities and vicissitudes of the micro. In fact, the original move to learning objects (small chunks of learning content related in many ways to conceptions of microlearning and micro-content) began in the mid-1990's, in response to complaints of the unsuitability of macro-level design and development conceptions for educational practice. (For example, Roschelle and Kaput promoted the use of object-oriented "component software" back in 1996 by arguing "that stand-alone applications are incompatible with typical production, distribution, and usage patterns for educational software.") However, what has become apparent in the intervening decade since the introduction of component or object models is that didactic and instructional theories have not been able to "catch up" and to be modified to easily and adequately address issues of design and management on the micro-level. Speaking specifically of German-language pedagogical and didactic approaches, Baumgartner puts it rather forcefully:

A big problem ... is that traditional pedagogical-didactic models either are too coarse-grained or that they have no direct relationship to the possibilities of new, interactive media. Only very recently have there been attempts to flesh out the characteristics of didactic scenarios that are relevant to Web-based learning. Representative of such attempts is work by Meder and Schulmeister. (Baumgartner, 2004, p. 319)

Also representative of these attempts are those of a scholar who has worked closely with Meder, Christian Swertz. Swertz has proposed a "Web Didactics" specifically for "microlearning" (microlearning text) and for the "micro"-level of granularity suited to computer and browser-based interfaces (German). Emphasizing the importance of retaining and adapting traditional didactic approaches for finely-grained designs and resources, Swertz observes:

> Computer technology naturally brings changes with it. That does not mean, however, that all didactic traditions simply loose their value. Web Didactics combines this realization with an emphasis on the individualization of instruction. [The aim of Web Didactics] is a systematic and therefore clearly structured knowledge base or form of navigation that takes into account different didactic models, while simultaneously facilitating individual learning processes. (Swertz, 2005, p. 5)

Swertz goes on to explain how these fundamental goals can be realized through processes of *decontextualization* and *recontextualization*: Decontextualization represents the systematization and structuring of granular resources according to media type and knowledge type in large knowledge bases; recontextualization occurs subsequently through the reorganization and recombination of these carefully catalogued resources in hyperlinked or sequenced form, according to similarly classified and stored didactic models. Thus, according to Swertz, an example of such a sequence specifically for problem-based learning would begin with an appropriate "problem task" resource, followed by appropriate resources classified as "explanations," "overviews," "planned cooperation," and "sources," respectively (2005, p. 18). Such a sequence would end, according to Swertz, with a resource listing "sources." Swertz provides further examples utilizing models from the German Didaktik tradition and containing other media and resource types. (He does not explain, however, how his approach would work in the context of more complex and more explicitly humanistic didactic models, such as the "theme-centred interaction" model described earlier.)

This overall approach – re-arranging small, recombinant resources to constitute given instructional sequences – will likely sound familiar to anyone who has been exposed to educational technology standards and specifications, which have recently received much attention in Anglo-American research. These standards and specifications include Learning Object Metadata (IEEE, 2002), Simple Sequencing (IMS, 2003a), Learning Design (IMS, 2003b) and the integration of multiple specifications in SCORM (ADL, 2006). All of these standards and specifications (often working together) seek to facilitate the systematic description, management, sequencing, and interaction of "Web-based learning content" (ADL, 2006) and of structured "instructional strategies" (IMS, 2003b). Using Swertz' terms, one could describe the role of Learning Object Metadata (and other specifications, such as Digital Repository Interoperability [IMS, 2003c] and Content Packaging [IMS, 2003d]) as enabling the "decontextualization" of granular learning resources in structured repositories or knowledge bases. Simple Sequencing and Learning Design (along with certain components of the SCORM) are correspondingly designed to facilitate the "recontextualization" of such resources according to instructional or didactic models. In fact, millions of pounds, dollars and euros have been spent on building infrastructures to support the use of these standards in different parts of the world, and to realize the effective decontextualization and instructional recontextualization of granular contents for millions of learners.

The similarity of standardization and learning object approaches on the one hand, and Web Didactics and related approaches (e.g., Heyer & Nowaczyk, 2005) on the other, could be said to mark a notable convergence in German-language and Anglo-American traditions. Both approaches have been motivated by the proliferation of content and possibilities presented by the Web, and both have sought to apply didactic and instructional insights drawn from their respective pedagogical traditions to the use and organization of this content.

But as indicated earlier, this common approach of linking modular materials to didactic/instructional models presents significant challenges. The large sums invested in different nations in learning object projects have not yet resulted in the predicted returns. The instructional or didaktik issues associated with these difficulties are given pointed expression in a well-known paradox associated with the design of learning objects – David Wiley's "Reusability Paradox":

> Instructional designers of learning objects problematically focus on removing as much context as possible in order to maximize the reuse of the learning objects they create. A paradox arises because modern learning theorists are increasingly emphasizing the preeminence of context in learning, using language such as "social context" (Vygotsky, 1981); "cultural, historical, and institutional setting" (e.g., Wertsch, 1991), and "situatedness" (e.g., Lave & Wenger, 1990; Jonassen, 1991).

It is this kind of language and this theoretical emphasis that poses the most significant challenge for Swertz and for learning object approaches generally. For the language and theorists listed by Wiley articulate notions of context and setting that are qualitatively different from what can be addressed through the recontextualization provided by hypertext navigation, simple Didaktik sequencing or structured instructional strategies. For example, the Lave and Wenger source cited by Wiley emphasizes that learning is "integral," to its context, and that the relationship between learning and context involves "generative" and "emergent processes which cannot be reduced to general-

ized structures" (Lave & Wenger, 1990, pp. 16, 35). In other words, learning displays
a contextual and organizational complexity that is irreducible to the "generalized structures" of pre-defined classifications and sequences. And this becomes even more em-
phatically the case on the "micro" level of individual activities, and very granular
components.

It is not by chance that these characterizations of learning as irreducible to structure
and design are similar to what was said earlier in this paper about the conversational,
dialogical dynamic characterizing the Didaktik triangle. Both of these views ultimately
derive from common sources: Marxist sociology, and the philosophy of Heidegger and
Husserl (e.g., see the diagram of philosophical influences on learning theories provided in Stahl, 2003 and reproduced in Allert, 2004). The similarity of these sources
and of the ultimate implications of these orientations represents a second, conspicuous
and relatively recent convergence of German-language and Anglo-American instructional theory. Both emphasize that learning is something that escapes any predictive
logic and cannot be easily or completely contained within prescribed structures and
sequences. But it is a moment of contiguity that is obviously opposed to the similarly
recent, common emphasis of both on the combination of Web-based materials with
instructional/didactic structures, sequences or strategies.

This second point of convergence is manifest in many remarkable resonances in research on both sides of the Atlantic. For example, Hans-Georg Gadamer (who supplied
the earlier description of the irreducibility of conversational logic) emphasizes that the
improvisational characteristics of conversation are not restricted to dialogue, communication or "interaction," but to human activity in general:

> As a rule, we experience the course of events as something that continually
> changes our plans and expectations. Someone who tries to stick to his plans
> discovers precisely how powerless his reason is. There are odd occasions
> when everything happens, as it were, to its own accord, ie. events seem to be
> automatically in accord with our plans and wishes. On these we can say that
> everything is going according to plan. But to apply this experience to the
> whole of history is to undertake a great extrapolation that entirely contradicts
> our experience. (Gadamer, 1989, p. 372).

Gadamer's insights on this matter find remarkable, and likely also independent, confirmation in the work of a former colleague of Lave and Wenger, Lucy Suchman, in
her book-length study, *Plans and situated actions: The problem of human machine
communication* (1987). Suchman's essential argument is that the titular categories of
"plan" and "situated action" need to be reconsidered, and that the rationally "'planned'
character of our actions is not ... inherent [in these actions] but is demonstrably
achieved." What Suchman means by this is that plans serve only as rough guidelines
for activities, and that they gain their full meaning only after they are realized in action. In her own words, Suchman's "primary concern in [the book is] to suggest a
"shift in the status of plans from ... control structures that universally precede and de-

termine actions, to discursive resources produced and used within the course of certain forms of human activity" (2003, p. 299).

Sadly, the *radical* implications of Suchman's, Gadamer's and Lave and Wenger's insights into the unplannable and irreducibly situated character of learning and activity generally have not been emphasized in Anglo-American instructional theory or even psychology (e.g. Lynch & Bogen, 2005; one exception is Streibel, 1995). There is also little evidence of this lesson being integrated in the application of Didaktik theory to the Internet and the Web. However, it is arguably the most important lesson for both Didaktik *and* instructional theory and practice in microlearning. And the fact that it finds articulation in both German- and English-language instructional theory underscores this.

6   Conclusion: Towards a Microdidaktik

What precisely are the implications of this lesson for microlearning? Just as plans change in their status when they are viewed in terms of the particularity and variability of situated action, Didaktik and instructional plans, structures and patterns acquire a new status when the focus is on the micro-level (or indeed, on the component or object level, too). The improvisatory, situation-dependent character of learning on this level makes the use of rigid, detailed plans and designs as structures for controlling, determining or confining behaviour not just difficult, but in all likelihood counter-productive. If plans are just discursive resources or *a posteriori* descriptions of what occurs in situated experience, conversation and action, it then follows that instructional and Didaktik objectives, patterns and sequences need to be seen also as resources or heuristics, to be put to use or set aside as the situation demands. It is the intelligence of the user and of the manifest constraints or opportunities offered by the given situation that are of greater importance –rather than what can be provided through pre-ordained classifications, and *a priori* structures or plans. To use Swertz's own terminology, micro-contents cannot be *recontextualized* simply in accordance with the established sequences of a given Web Didactics. What is important instead, is that these same contents should not be so completely *de*-contextualized that they cannot be recognized as relevant and put to use in highly contextualized circumstances.

Certain characteristics then become desirable when both micro-structures and micro-contents are thus re-defined as *contingent* resources: Their actual or potential function and purpose should be immediately recognizable. This could be what makes Wikipedia entries and definitions (at least potentially) valuable to teachers and students alike. These entries and definitions are seen to represent "consensus knowledge" in either the established "nano" format of the definition or the conventional "micro" format of an encyclopaedia article. Also, the relationship of micro-resources to the macro, and especially the meso levels or contexts should be readily graspable. For example, a short chat exchange or a computer conference posting, viewed as micro-content, should be easy to re-situate in the flow of conversation or messages from which it is derived. (Such a broadly dialogical flow is also a good example of the kind of irreducible context emphasized in Lave and Wenger, and elsewhere.) As yet another illustration, mobile phones become more effective not by specifically supporting the micro-structures of conversational interaction, but by providing affordances to support situated and improvisational action that are part of conversation. So, even though people have been shown to begin mobile phone calls with short exchanges that display remarkable structural similarity (e.g., Arminen, 2005), it is not these "micro-structures" that have proven important in the further development of this technology. Instead, what has emerged as important has been affordances and modalities that provide greater communicative flexibility, for example, hands-free operation, SMS, e-mail, photos, video and other communicative possibilities.

The solution to Wiley's instructional paradox, after all, is a matter of balance, of finding a kind of Aristotelian golden mean between context, granularity and abstracted decontextualization. Only by seeking out this mean, through the continuation and permutation of what has been already accomplished in established micro-genres and resource types, and by navigating a careful path between the Scylla of inclusion and the Charybdis of isolation, can didatics and applications of microlearning develop successfully.

References

ADL (2006) *SCORM® 2004 3rd Edition Overview*. Available from:
   <http://www.adlnet.gov/scorm/20043ED.cfm> [Accessed 1 September 2006].
Allert, H. (2004) Coherent social systems for learning: an approach for contextualized and community-centered metadata. In: *Journal of Interactive Media in Education*, 2004 (2). Available from: <http://www.jime.open.ac.uk/2004/2/allert-2004-2-disc-03.html#2> [Accessed 10 September 2006].
Anderson, T. (2003) Getting the mix right again: an updated and theoretical rationale for interaction. In: *The International Review of Research in Open and Distance Learning* 4 (2). Available from: <http://www.irrodl.org/index.php/irrodl/article/view/149/230> [Accessed 1 September 2006].
Apple, M.W. (1982) *Education and Power*. Boston: Routledge & Kegan Paul.
Arminen, I. (2005) Sequential order and sequence structure: the case of incommensurable studies on mobile phone calls. In: *Discourse Studies* 7, pp. 649–662.
Baumgartner, P. (2004) Didaktik und reusable learning objects (RLO's). In: *Campus 2004 – Kommen die digitalen Medien an den Hochschulen in die Jahre?* Münster: Waxmann, pp. 309–325.
Boeckmann, K. & Heymen N. (1990) *Unterrichtsmedien selbst gestalten. Handbuch für Schule und Unterrichtspraxis*. Berlin: Luchterhand.
Gadamer, H. G. (1989) *Truth and method* (2nd Revised Edition). New York: Crossroad.
Gundem, B.B. & Hopmann, S. eds. (1999) *Didaktik and/or curriculum: an international dialogue*. New York: Peter Lang.

Gundem, B.B. & Hopmann, S. (1999) Introduction: Didaktik meets curriculum. In Gundem, B.B. & Hopmann, S. eds.: *Didaktik and/or Curriculum: An International Dialogue.* New York: Peter Lang.

Heyer, S. & Nowaczyk, O. (2005) *Übertragung der didaktischen Modelle Flechsigs auf E-Learning. Forschungsbericht für das Projekt CampusContent.* (Forschungsbericht im Fachbereich Elektrotechnik und Informationstechnik der FernUniversität in Hagen.) Available from: <http://www.fernuni-hagen.de/etit/fachbereich/forschung/ Forschungsbericht_10_2005.pdf [Accessed 1 September 2006].

Holmberg, B (2004) *Theory of Distance Education Based on Empathy.* Available from: <http://info.umuc.edu/mde/Misc/Holmberg-transcript.doc> [Accessed 1 September 2006].

Hug, T. (1995). Zeitgemäßes Unterrichten und lebendiges Lernen: Neue Wege von Interaktion und Kommunikation in der Klasse. In: Verband Bildung und Erziehung, ed. Bildung als Beruf – pädagogische Professionalität heute. VBE – Dokumentation des 13. Deutschen Lehrertags am 12.11.1994 in Aschaffenburg. Bonn: VBE, pp. 47–54.

IEEE (2002) *Draft standard for Learning Object Metadata.* Available from: <http://ltsc.ieee.org/doc/wg12/LOM_WD6_4.pdf> [Accessed 1 September 2006].

IMS (2003a) *IMS Simple Sequencing Specification.* Available from: <http://www.imsglobal.org/simplesequencing> [Accessed 1 September 2006].

IMS (2003b) *Learning Design Specification.* Available from: <http://www.imsglobal.org/learningdesign> [Accessed 1 September 2006].

IMS (2003c) *Digital Repositories Specification.* Available from: <http://www.imsglobal.org/ digitalrepositories> [Accessed 1 September 2006].

IMS (2003d) Content Packaging Specification. Available from: <http://www.imsglobal.org/content> [Accessed 1 September 2006].

Kant, E. (1784) *Beantwortung der Frage: Was ist Aufklärung?* Available from: <http://www.digbib.org/Immanuel_Kant_1724/Was_ist_Aufklaerung> [Accessed 1 September 2006].

Kemp, J. E., Morrison, G. R., & Ross, S. M. (1998*) Designing Effective Instruction* (2nd Edition). Upper Saddle River, NJ: Prentice-Hall.

Kertz-Welzel, A. (2004) Didaktik of music: a german concept and its comparison to american music pedagogy. In: *International Journal of Music Education 22*, pp. 277–286.

Klafki, W. (1973) Dialogik und Dialektik in der gegenwärtigen Erziehungswissenschaft. In: Kluge, N. ed.: *Das pädagogische Verhältnis.* Darmstadt: Wissenschaftliche Buchgesellschaft, pp. 344–377.

Klafki, W. (1996) *Neue Studien zur Bildungstheorie und Didaktik: Zeitgemäße Allgemeinbildung und kritisch-konstruktive Didaktik.* Weinheim & Basel: Beltz.

Klafki, W. (2000) The significance of classical theories of Bildung for a contemorary concept of Allgemeinbildung. In: Westbury, I., Hopmann, S. & Riquarts K. eds.: *Teaching as a Reflective Practice: The German Didaktik Tradition.* Mahwah, NJ: Lawrence Erlbaum, pp. 307–330.

Klingberg, L. (1982) *Einführung in die allgemeine Didaktik.* Frankfurt am Main: Athenäum Fischer.

Langemann, E.C. (1989) The plural worlds of educational research. In: *History of Education Quarterly*, 29 (2), pp. 185–214.

Lave, J. & Wenger, E. (1991) *Situated Learning: Legitimate Peripheral Participation.* Cambridge, UK: Cambridge University Press.

Lave, J. (1996) Situating learning in communities of practice. In: L.B. Resnik, J.M. Levine & S.D. Teasley eds.: *Perspectives on Socially Shared Cognition*. Washington: American Psychological Association.

Lynch, M. & Bogen, D. (2005) "My memory has been shredded": a non-cognitivist investigation of "mental" phenomena. In: H. te Molder and J. Potter eds.: *Conversation and Cognition: Discourse, Mind and Social Interaction*, pp. 226–240. Cambridge: Cambridge University Press.

Martinez, M. (2001) Using learning orientations to design instruction with learning objects. In: Wiley, D. ed.: *Instructional Use of Learning Objects. Association for Educational Communications & Technology*. Available from: <http://www.reusability.org/read/chapters/martinez.doc> [Accessed 1 September 2006].

Meder, N. (2000) Didaktische Ontologien. In: Ohly, H.P., Rahmstorf, G., & Sigel, A., eds.: Globalisierung und Wissensorganisation: Neue Aspekte für Wissen, Wissenschaft und Informationssysteme. Würzburg: Ergon, pp. 401–416.

Meyer, H. (1988) *Unterrichtsmethoden 1: Theorieband*. Berlin: Cornelson.

Mollenhauer, K. (2003) *Vergessene Zusammenhänge: Über Kultur und Erziehung*. Munich: Juventa.

Nordkvelle, Y. (2004) Technology and didactics: historical mediations of a relation. In: *Journal of Curriculum Studies 36* (4), pp. 427–444.

Schenk, B., & Schwabe, G., (2000) "Auf dem Weg zu einer Groupware-Didaktik" In: Reichwald, R. & Schlichter, J. eds.: *Verteiltes Arbeiten – Arbeit der Zukunft – Tagungs-band der Deutsche Computer-Supported Cooperative Work Konferenz*. Available from: <http://www.ifi.unizh.ch/im/imrg/fileadmin/publications/Auf_dem_Weg_zu_einer_Group ware_-_Didaktik_-_Erfahrungen_und_ Konzepte_aus_den_Schulungen_in_Cuparla.pdf> [Accessed 1 September 2006].

Stadtfeld, P. (2004) *Allgemeine Didaktik und Neue Medien: Der Einfluß der Neuen Medien auf didaktische Theorie und Praxis*. Bald Heilbrunn: Klinkhardt.

Stahl, G. (2003). Meaning and interpretation in collaboration. In Wasson, B., Ludvigsen S., & Hoppe, U. eds.: *Designing For Change in Networked Learning Environments*. Dordrecht: Kluwer, pp. 523–532.

Streibel, M.J. (1989) Instructional plans and situated learning: the challenge of Suchman's Theory of Situated Action for Instructional Designers and Instructional Systems. In: *Journal of Visual Literacy* 9 (2), p. 834.

Suchman, L. (1987) *Plans and situated actions: The problem of human machine communication*. Cambridge: Cambridge University Press.

Suchman, L. (2003) Writing and reading: a response to comments on plans and situated actions. *Journal of the Learning Sciences 12* (2), pp. 299–306.

Swertz, C. (2005) Web-Didaktik. Eine didaktische Ontologie in der Praxis. In: *MedienPädagogik. 4* (2), pp. 1–24. Available from: <http://www.medienpaed.com/04-2/swertz04-2.pdf> [Accessed 1 September 2006].

Swertz, C. (2006) Customized learning sequences (CLS) by metadata. In: Hug, T., Lindner, M., & Bruck, P.A. eds.: *Microlearning: Emerging Concepts, Practice and Technologies: Proceedings of Microlearning 2005: Learning and Working in new Media Environments*. Innsbruck: Innsbruck University Press, pp. 55–70.

Tennyson, R.D. & Baron, A.E. (1995) *Automating instructional design: computer-based development and delivery Tools*. New York: Springer-Verlag.

Weniger, E. (2000) Didaktik as a theory of education. In: Westbury, I., Hopmann, S., & Riquarts, K. eds.: *Teaching as a Reflective Practice: The German Didaktik Tradition.* Mahwah, NJ: Lawrence Erlbaum, pp. 111–128.

Westbury, I. (1999) Didaktik and curriculum studies. In: Gundem, B.B., & Hopmann, B.B., eds.: *Didakik and/or Curriculum.* New York: Peter Lang.

Westbury, I., Hopmann, S., & Riquarts, K. eds. (2000) *Teaching as a Reflective Practice: The German Didaktik Tradition.* Mahwah, NJ: Lawrence Erlbaum.

Wiley, D. (2004) *The Reusability Paradox.* Available from: <http://cnx.org/content/m11898/latest/> [Accessed 1 September 2006].

WordNet. (2006) *WordNet Search.* Available from:
<http://wordnet.princeton.edu/perl/webwn2.1> [Accessed 1 September 2006].

Microlearning as a Challenge for Instructional Design

Michael Kerres

Traditionally, models of instructional design presume that (e)learning is organized as lessons or courses. But with the growing importance of microcontent and e-learning scenarios labeled as "web 2.0," this assumption of models of instructional design is challenged. If users arrange their personal learning environments themselves by aggregating microcontent, why would we need (models of) instructional design?

The following chapter discusses the role of instructional design in these scenarios. It presents different views on instructional design: the American tradition which views instructional design as an engineering task (which eventually can be delegated to a computer algorithm), the German tradition of Didaktik which emphasizes the situative and emergent properties of instruction and the "Hypertext-Wiki" paradigm, which focuses on learning as a user-generated activity. In an e-learning scenario that follows a "web 2.0" approach, instructional design has to integrate these perspectives. It therefore puts forward the argument that in the future, instructional design even will be more complex and challenging than before.

1   Learning with Small Units

When we think of instructional design, we think of lessons lasting 45 minutes or more, of courses consisting of several lessons over some weeks, or of curricula for classes or schools. Current theories of instructional design typically distinguish between the *micro level* of instructional design that relates to the structure of a single lesson, the *meso level* which describes a course structure and the *macro level,* the curriculum of a program or a school. However, small chunks of "microcontent" for learning and new technologies for distribution and aggregating these contents over the Internet are becoming increasingly available. Microcontent relates to a single Internet resource, which can be referenced directly by a URL, and may consist, for example, of a slide of a presentation, parts of an animation sequence, an interview, a test question ... These contents all relate to entities *below* the course or lesson level.

Also, an e-learning lesson and course typically does have some kind of temporal dramaturgy; it consists of, for example, an opening, a presentation, a section for exercises and a closing. Instructional design models discuss the sequencing of "elements" within a lesson and present guidelines on how to arrange lessons for courses. "Nine events of instruction" from Gagné (1985; Gagné, Briggs & Wager, 1988) is such a model for sequencing instruction that has gained much attention in teacher education as well as in the realm of e-learning. Essentially, these models assume that "good" instruction has to follow a certain temporal dramaturgy. Merrill (1994) elaborated and applied these concepts to computer based instruction. His early "component display theory" relies on the idea that the optimal sequence for instruction primarily depends on the type of content you want to teach: The teaching of facts, concepts, procedures or principals requires different types of instructional elements and lesson sequences. They mainly differ with respect to the amount and timing of abstract vs. concrete information and teacher vs. student led activities.

Now, when a (e-learning) lesson is split up into smaller units of segments of, for example, 5-15 minutes of learning time, we abandon the lesson dramaturgy and have the basic elements (also called "assets") that had been assembled into a course beforehand by the instructional designer or teacher. These elements could consist, for example, of a single presentation (slide?), an exercise sheet (or a single exercise?), a case study or a short test. If they shall be delivered for use as *stand-alone* learning units, it is obvious that they must be organized differently and we arrive at the question: What actually would be instructional design on the level of microcontent? And: what happens to instructional design if we move below the unit of a lesson? Does it become obsolete because the learner him-/herself will choose and arrange the elements and thus construct the sequence of a "lesson design"?

2   Instructional Design: An Engineering Approach to E-Learning

To answer these questions, we will first look at features of planning and designing e-learning applications. Compared to traditional FTF-teaching, e-learning products need very precise planning. If some unexpected problem occurs during learning (the "delivery"), it is difficult and costly to modify learning materials after they have been implemented. In contrast, a teacher (hopefully) can adapt to situational demands in a classroom more easily and will be able to change a teaching strategy within seconds if the situation requires it. In spite of all efforts of "artificial intelligence," technology based learning applications still are far less diagnostic than teachers in FTF scenarios. The instructional designer of an online learning environment might receive usage statistics and evaluation results, but typically does not experience the immediacy of responses from human learners in a FTF-situation, when they, e.g., complain about materials – and even if s/he had a direct relation with learners, it typically will not be possible to modify e-learning materials and lessons instantly.

Traditional theories of instructional design reflect this clear distinction between instructional designers, on the one hand, and the learner/the teacher, on the other hand (figure 1). It is the instructional designer who selects learning materials and defines sequences through lessons and courses – after analyzing learners and contents and defining the conditions of learning, e.g., the learning objectives.

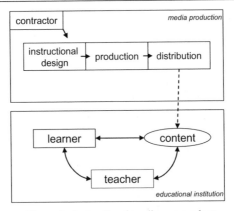

Figure 1. Instructional media as a product

E-learning products, then, are solutions for a certain context and a certain instructional goal, for example, a computer based training program for teaching Business English for a certain group of adult learners in further education. Instructional design models describe analytic procedures to unravel the didactical structure of such an "instructional problem" and they provide "blueprints" for selecting an appropriate instructional approach (or "instructional method") based on these analyses. Typical procedures are, for example, target group and learner analysis, task or content analyses (Jonassen, Hannum, & Tessmer, 1989). These analytical procedures provide the "toolbox" for instructional design and constitute the professional competence of instructional designers, to a major extent.

Models and procedures of instructional design are based on the idea that instructional decisions must rest on an analysis of the context and its constraints: the learners, the learning situation, the institutional and cultural context. Instruction should be planned to exactly fit these conditions.

Consequently, instructional design theories guide instructional designers to select and elaborate instructional materials and lessons. According to Reigeluth (1998), instructional design theories comprise of the following elements:

– Instructional conditions: What is to be learned? Who is the learner? What are situational/developmental constraints (time, money, resources)?
– Desired instructional outcomes: What are the desired levels of appeal, effectiveness and efficiency?
– Instructional methods: Given certain instructional conditions, what are appropriate instructional methods to reach the desired instructional outcomes?

"Problem based learning," for example, is an instructional method that has attracted much research and discussion. But as Reigeluth (1998) points out, PBL is not an instructional design model in itself: it can be an *element* of an instructional design model, that describes when this method will result in certain defined outcomes and how it should be implemented to reach these results.

Hence, *instructional design* is being conceptualized similar to an engineering approach. In its most general sense, an engineering approach relates to a transformation of a given state into a desired state with instruments and means grounded in scientific methodology. Similarly, the instructional designer is finding a solution that helps a learner to acquire certain knowledge.

With the rise of constructivism in instructional science in the early 1990s, instructional design models have been questioned quite fundamentally (Jonassen, 1990; Merrill, 1991; Tripp & Bichelmeyer, 1990). When learners themselves are acknowledged as constructers of their learning, what is the role of "instructional design" then? Does it become obsolete, or do we need alternative models? Some proponents of instructional design, like David Merrill, do not see a necessity for a fundamental change. According to Merrill, the basic design issues and analytical procedures are the same, no matter what instructional approach or method one prefers. The critics argue, on the other hand, that – with the new view to learning - traditional linear models of instructional design should be abandoned (Braden, 1996), because they essentially rely on the asymmetry between learners and instructional designers. Alternative models, based on current approaches of (software) engineering, like rapid prototyping, participatory design, or usability engineering, give the voice of users a more prominent role in the development process and therefore reduce the asymmetry between learners and designers.

It is, however, interesting to note that the "classic" approaches to instructional design, so far, have not been abandoned and without much refinement are still being published and taught quite vividly. This might be attributed to the fact that the classical models can be taken up rather intuitively by students of instructional design. But it also might be an indication that the essential elements of instructional design are still valid.

3   Computer Algorithms for Instructional Design Decisions

Since the early days of computer based learning, this model of producing instructional materials has always been criticized as being expensive, and soon the idea came up that materials should be produced for reuse in several applications. A "handcrafted" e-learning application exactly tailored to the needs of a single group of learners in a single institution at a single point in time obviously in many cases is too expensive to produce. Why not let the *computer* select and sequence instruction instead of the (expensive) instructional designer?

An e-learning course could be broken up into smaller units that can be reused in other courses and reassembled into new sequences with a high degree of flexibility. If certain information about these units is provided, then the computer could select the appropriate units for the learner, and thus produce the learning sequence.

It is interesting to note that the problem of reusability actually has been discussed ever since computers have been used for teaching. The idea of a computer algorithm that sequences learning material on the basis of some metadata (e.g., degree of difficulty) was already outlined and implemented by Helmar Frank, then at the University of Education in Berlin, in the 1960s (Frank, 1969; Frank & Graf, 1967). In the 1980s, intelligent tutoring systems were another attempt to let the computer sequence learning elements at runtime and depending on the progress of the learner. In the 1990s, this line of discussion was continued with approaches to "automating instructional design" (Tennyson & Barron, 1995) which eventually leads to the current discussion about "reusable learning objects."

These approaches are built on the assumption that the computer should select and sequence instruction based on small units of learning materials. The sequence should be generated by the computer; either based on data the computer would interfere from analyzing user inputs (according to the vision of "artificial intelligence"), or based on metadata the author provided before. After many years of research, it must be acknowledged that both approaches have not solved the problem of reusability in the practical field yet. It has turned out that implementing procedures to analyze learners while working on learning applications in most cases is far too complicated. Eventually, they fail to provide the necessary information for computer algorithms to sequence "intelligent" instruction.

On the other side, it has turned out that the standardization of metadata for describing learning elements is very difficult to accomplish, due to cultural and contextual differences between different languages and meanings. We are still lacking accepted standards for metadata to describe learning elements, such as "level of difficulty" or features of a "target group." Furthermore, authors are quite reluctant to provide metadata and "obey" to standards they feel compelled to use. They do not experience the added value of this additional work, which makes the production of learning materials even more expensive.

After all, the question arises if the selection and sequencing of learning materials might not be easier done by learners themselves – instead of instructional designers or computers? In the early 1990s researches in the field of computer based learning were faced with the sudden success of hypertext for learning. Before this, it was always taken for granted that a didactically sound CBT application would provide paths that guide learners. It was assumed that by providing and keeping learners on a certain track, they would reach a specified learning objective more reliably. This assumption, however, is being questioned – at least for learners that are willing and are able to find their way for acquiring knowledge.

There has been much discussion if and when learners are able to successfully learn with open hypertexts that do not force users to follow a certain sequential sequence of text and assignments. The discussion also points out that even if learners are not – yet

– able to learn in such open environments, they should (supported to) acquire the competency to use such environments appropriately.

Recently, this line of reasoning has been reinforced with the discussion about "Wikis" as tools for the collaborative production of contents. Now, users not only generate their own *sequences* through given materials, they have a very easy tool to actively participate in the *production* of such materials for learning.

4   Didaktik: Less Planning for Better Instruction?

Instructional design has been described as an engineering approach to selecting and sequencing instructional elements. With "learning objects," these decisions eventually could be delegated to a computer algorithm.

The German tradition of Didaktik presents a different, rather opposite view to the "design" of instruction: The fundamental assumption in this line of reasoning is: instruction cannot be planned, instruction can only be prepared. Instruction, that enables learners to acquire a level of education that can be qualified as "Bildung," must allow for a high flexibility in a lesson or course structure. Some authors even see interruptions and interferences as "the" fertile moments that allow for Bildung. Figure 2 presents a basic model of didactical design that relates to the German tradition of Didaktik and to the work of Heimann, Schulz & Otto (1965), that is being discussed in more detail by Norm Friesen in this book.

Figure 2. A basic model of didactical design

Though it is acknowledged that a learner can be "taught" and "trained" to some extent, the tradition of Didaktik emphasizes that a certain level of education can only be reached by the learner her-/himself. A teacher should even be cautious to not "disturb" the learner by some highly "over"-planned lesson design. Bildung can (!) emerge, if teachers offer themselves as a person to truly interact with the learner and therefore permit encounters from person to person. The concept of "interaction" here can be related to the tradition of *symbolic interactionism* by Herbert Blumer and Georg Herbert Mead that emphasize the mutual exchange of meaning, which is different than the idea of a transmission of knowledge from one person to another. It also can be related to the person-centered approach of Carl Rogers (1961) and the humanistic psychology movement. Teachers, then, should be open to the situational demands and to the emergent process of interaction between persons.

The work of a teacher is to be seen more as a service, where the learner is supported to co-produce a certain (learning) result by him-/herself. It becomes obvious that this line of reasoning is rather skeptical of approaches of "rigorous" planning of instructional settings. Consequently, also the analytical procedures that instructional design models suggest are questioned. They are being criticized as methods that do not help teachers much, but might even narrow their views and interfere with the ability to really "interact" with learners.

If we apply this approach to e-learning, this would mean that an instructional designer should be very careful not to "over-plan" learning by defining strict paths through a learning environment that consists of technical artifacts and to restrict the use of learning tools unnecessarily. The approach of Didaktik points out to the limits of learning with "materials" and emphasizes the social nature of ambitious learning (= for "Bildung"). It therefore provides a theoretical foundation for using "social software" in e-learning that enhances the interchange between humans while working on tasks or discussing topics with sophisticated technological means.

If we follow this argument, we would consider learning materials as starting points for individual reflections, as well as discussions with others. In this view, the instructional designers provide materials and tools for learning and arrange them in a learning environment that encourages individual and social activities. Furthermore, teachers should be available as tutors that should support and encourage learners to direct their learning activities.

5   Instructional Design and Web 2.0

Currently, the Internet is going through an interesting metamorphosis, which is indicated by the somewhat vague term "Web 2.0." This development can be interpreted as a technological innovation that refers to social software, weblogs, user-generated content and tagging. But more importantly, it implies a different view of the web. The Internet gradually becomes ubiquitous and a part of life. Borders that existed before tend to vanish and users develop a different use of the Internet:

(a) The boundary between users and authors dissolves: there used to be a clear distinction between authors and users of a web page. Now, user-generated content is recognized as a very valuable source, and thus, users become authors.

(b) The boundary between local and remote is disappearing. My data and my tools increasingly are going "into" the web, whereas my local computer becomes part of the Internet and can act as a public server.

(c) The boundary between "public" and "private" is changing: More of my private data move into the web. Weblogs, shared photos, or bookmarks, for example, are made available on the Internet and disclose formerly private information.

These changes have implications for the design of e-learning environments. Consequently, Stephan Downes uses the term "E-Learning 2.0" to refer to the transition computer based learning is currently undergoing. In this perspective, users will learn in an environment that provides a lot of content for learning and tools to work on these materials individually, with others, or with the guide of a tutor. For the user, this "personal learning environment" is not a separate space on the Internet, it is an essential part of the users workspace. It should be highly integrated with the user's framework of tools for his/her personal use of the Internet. An instructional designer would arrange some of the materials and tools the learner will work on, but would also arrange the environment to be open to the vast sources and tools the Internet provide, thus providing a soft transition between the learning environment and the "other" Internet.

The border between the inside and the outside of the learning environment becomes permeable: content is being aggregated outside of the learning environment and is made available for the learner. Contents created by the learners are made accessible for the outside world. All this is accomplished by using the mechanism of XML-feeds with varying degree of complexity. These feeds provide a solution to link a learning environment with the "outside."

The growing interest towards "microcontent" for learning can be related to this line of discussion. The learners themselves are gaining competencies to construct their personal environments where they select and sequence contents available on the Internet. Then, the Internet, with its vast resources, itself becomes the primary "knowledge base" that is transformed to "learning material" not by instructional designers or computer algorithms, but the learner him-/herself.

Obviously, this scenario is different from e-learning scenarios typically used today. They rely on learning platforms that for the most part are being used to distribute or download documents. These platforms essentially are based on the assumption that all learning contents and activities should be brought onto the learning platform. With this, they are islands on the Internet without many connections to other resources or tools. They force the author/teacher to import all materials into the learning environment, they constrain learners to the tools the platform provides – many of them less capable and appealing than other tools available on the Net. And they prevent contents that are being generated during the learning process to be fed to other applications to the Net. Certainly, learning platforms will soon deliver new versions of their software that might include some of these features. But the question remains, why we would need learning platforms at all? A Web 2.0 approach to e-learning would argue that the "personal learning environment" should be arranged on top of the personal workspace of Internet users and should rely on mechanisms the Internet provides for sharing information and tools on the Net.

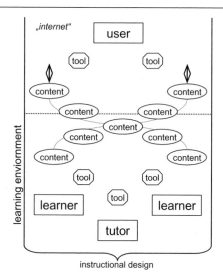

Figure 3. Instructional design for Web 2.0-environments

In such a scenario, the task of instructional design would imply to provide an arrangement of contents and tools that can be intrinsically interwoven with the personal workspace of the learner. The following paragraphs present aspects for designing e-learning environments that follow principles of web 2.0.

Guidelines for an E-learning Scenario Following a "Web 2.0" Approach

1. An e-learning environment should be perceived as a "gate" to the Internet with paths to existing materials and contents on the net as well as materials that have been developed/assembled/uploaded just for this environment (especially assignments for learning).

2. The learning portal aggregates contents from the Net and integrates them as an integral part of the learning environment. These materials typically consist of a low complexity ("microcontent") and are fetched by XML-feeds from other sites.

3. Complex materials can be integrated as learning objects that contain learning materials, as well as metadata describing the content, e.g., sequences for delivering the content.

4. Materials that are being produced within the learning environment should be offered as feeds for reuse at other sites on the net, e.g., for delivery on mobile devices.

5. Learners and teachers / authors use the same tools for working with contents of various kinds, for editing and sharing documents, like weblogs, wikis, forum, pictures, calendars. Teachers and learners actively participate in developing the

learning environment – with small differences regarding administrative rights to the learning environment.

6. In order to find information and to share it with others teachers, as well as learners, use free tags or tags from a taxonomy to describe this information.

7. As far as possible, users can use tools of their choice to produce and work on content. Learners are encouraged to arrange their own digital work space and to integrate existing tools to construct and share documents.

8. There is a smooth transition between the personal learning environment and the environment people use for their work and other personal activities on the Net. Teaching means observing, participating and evaluating the individual and social learning activities within the learning environment.

9. The environment supports social group processes by making visible what tools the users prefer and providing direct access to these tools (e.g., furl or del.icio.us). This does also relate to the use of communication tools. Users should be free to use those tools they prefer. The learning environment simply presents which tool a user prefers to be reached on the Net (e.g., ICQ, Yahoo, Skype). Furthermore, it displays if the user currently is available with one of these tools.

10. The system supports community building by presenting who the members of the group are (background, interests, competencies …), how they have contributed so far, and how often these contributions have been accessed and evaluated by others. Thus, the system publishes the degree of personal engagement of each user.

11. It should be attractive to become a member of the community. Registered users and members of learning groups should enjoy certain privileges. They have access to more information and gain more rights, e.g., to promote information to the front page and to comment immediately).

12. The environment documents the learning activities and results automatically. Contributions become visible to other learners and the teacher, and they can be included directly into an e-portfolio of the user (and the institution).

13. Learners are encouraged to reflect their learning activities (Did I set appropriate goals? Did I make a sufficient progress?), for example, with a Weblog.

14. An e-learning provider generates an added value to customers by supplying
    –   new and re-arranged (sequenced) (micro-)contents for the learning environment,
    –   assignments that structure the learning process and
    –   different variants of tutorial support (including examination and certification).

15. Teachers provide a role model. They are actively engaged and show their presence in the learning environment, e.g., by using the tools the environment offers,

by supplying personal information, by supplying materials and participating in discussions, and by using a weblog and working on wikis. They react to feedback and error messages immediately.

This short description of an e-learning scenario that follows a "web 2.0" approach outlines some of the tasks instructional design has to address to develop such a scenario. It demonstrates that this design task, to some extent, relates to *all* four views on instructional design presented before:

- Instructional design as an engineering task (sensu Gagné): Materials and tools must be developed to fit the situational demands of the learning context. They must be based on a precise analysis of didactical variables: task analysis, learning objectives, target group characteristics or didactical methods.
- Instructional design can be delegated to a computer algorithm (the "learning object" approach): Reusable learning objects can be integrated that present a certain sequence depending on parameters the learning environment provides.
- Instructional design as a situational, emergent action (the Didaktik tradition): The learning process can be prepared, but not completely prearranged. The environment should support "real" interactions between learners and tutors.
- Instructional design as a user-generated activity (the "Hypertext + Wiki"-Paradigm): The environment should encourage learners to develop exploratory search and learning strategies. It should provide tools to support learners to actively (co-)produce contents (not only assignments and documents, but also comments, images, bookmarks, etc.)

Therefore, we can conclude that with "web 2.0," instructional design definitely is changing. Our analysis of a typical e-learning scenario that follows a "web 2.0" approach demonstrates that instructional design is not dispensable, but even becomes more complex. It does not imply a completely new approach, but should integrate the various views to instructional design developed in different theoretical traditions. A successful strategy for implementing e-learning still relies on a sound and professional concept of instructional design. With this, instructional design will even become more challenging.

References

Banathy, B.H. (1987) Instructional systems design. In: R.M. Gagné ed. *Instructional Technology: Foundations*, pp. 85–112. Hillsdale, NJ: Lawrence Erlbaum.

Braden, R. A. (1996) The case for linear instructional design and development: a commentary on models, challenges, and myths. *Educational Technology,* 3, pp. 5–23.

Dick, W., & Carey, L.M. (1996) *The Systematic Design of Instruction.* 4 ed. New York: Harper Collins.

Frank, H. (1969) Prinzipien der objektivierten Formaldidaktik 'Alskindi.' *Grundlagenstudien aus Kybernetik und Geisteswissenschaft*, 10, pp. 2328.

Frank, H., & Graf, K.D. (1967) ALZUDI – Beispiel einer formalisierten Didaktik. *Grundlagenstudien aus Kybernetik und Geisteswissenschaft*, 8, pp. 27–34.

Gagné, R. M. (1963) Military training and principles of learning. *American Psychologist*, 17, pp. 83–91.

Gagné, R.M. (1985) *The conditions of learning and theory of instruction*. New York: CBS College Publishing.

Gagné, R.M., Briggs, L. ., & Wager, W.W. (1988) *Principles of Instructional Design*. 3rd ed. New York: Holt, Rinehart & Winston.

Heimann, P., Schulz, W., & Otto, G. (1965) *Unterricht – Analyse und Planung*. Hannover: Schroedel.

Jonassen, D.H. (1990) Thinking Technology. Chaos in instructional design. *Educational Technology, 30*, pp. 32–34.

Jonassen, D.H., Hannum, W.H., & Tessmer, M. (1989) *Handbook of Task Analysis Procedures*. New York: Preager.

Kemp, J. E. (1985) *The Instructional Design Process*. New York: Harper & Row.

Kerres, M. (2001) *Multimediale und telemediale Lernumgebungen. Konzeption und Entwicklung*. 2nd ed. München: R. Oldenbourg.

Merrill, M.D. (1991) Constructivism and instructional design. *Educational Technology, 31* (5), pp. 45–53.

Merrill, M.D. (1994) *Instructional Design Theory*. Englewood Cliffs, NJ: Educational Technology Publications.

Reigeluth, C. ed. (1998) *Instructional-Design Theories and Models. A New Paradigm of Instructional Theory, Vol. 2*. Hillsdale: LEA.

Rogers, C. (1961) *On Becoming a Person*. Boston: Houghton Mifflin.

Schiffman, S.S. (1991) Instructional systems design. Five views of the field. In: G.J. Anglin ed. *Instructional Technology: Past, Present, and Future*. Englewood, CO: Libraries Unlimited.

Tennyson, R.D., & Barron, A.E. eds. (1995) *Automating Instructional Design: Computer-based Development and Delivery Tools (NATO ASI Series F. 140)*. New York: Springer.

Tripp, S.D., & Bichelmeyer, B. (1990) Rapid prototyping: an alternative instructional design strategy. *Educational Technology: Research and Development*, 38, pp. 31–44.

How "Micro" Can Learning Be? A Neuropsychological Perspective on Microlearning

Franziska Scherer & Martin Scherer

1   Introduction

A wide range of explanations can be found when exploring the web (see reference "MicroWiki") for a definition of microlearning: "short interaction with a learning matter", "small bits of content" and "multitasking" – highly relevant terms in the current discussion of neuroscience. The neuropsychology of learning deals with psychological and physiological principles of information acquisition.

This article transfers these findings to the context of microlearning. In this, we follow the path each fragment of a learning matter has to undergo – from perception through various forms of processing and stages of memorisation to what is called knowledge.

At first, an overview about perception, memory, and emotion in terms of neuropsychological processes is given. In a second step, we try to answer questions regarding the key characteristics of microlearning: How small may the bits of content be? How short may the interaction with a learning matter be? And how much multitasking is possible? Finally we conclude and focus on implications for further research.

2   Neuropsychological Background

2.1   Perception

For anyone dealing with learning environments it is important to realize that processes of perception are complex. Perception is the starting point of every contact with a learning matter. It is the connection between the physical reality and a representation in our mind. Although all senses are involved in learning, visual and auditive perception play an important role in artificial learning environments, as learning matters are mostly presented through print, pictures, voice and sounds. Detailed information on the neurobiology of perception can be found in current literature (e.g., Kandel, Schwartz & Jessel, 2000). To be memorized, a physical stimulus has to undergo several levels of processing. The visual perception system is focused on to demonstrate the complexity of these processes.

For a long time, contradictory theories of light (Newton's particle theory and Huygens' wave theory) have strongly influenced the theories of light perception (Gregory, 2001). At a physiological level it is crucial to know which aspects of the physical reality are caught by the receptive cells.

Visual perception can be divided into an early sequence, in which forms and objects are extracted from the visual scenery, and a late phase in which forms and objects are perceived. Light travels through the lens and the vitreous body and then falls on the retina (figure 1). The light sensitive cells of the retina (photoreceptors) set off a photochemical process that transforms light into neuronal activity.

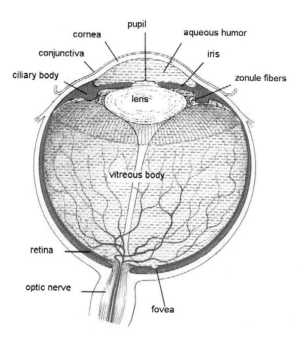

Figure 1. The human eye (Adapted from Gregory, 2001)

There are two different types of light photoreceptors in the retina: rods and cones. The cones react on different wavelengths and are thus responsible for seeing colours. Some are more sensitive to long wave (red) middle wave (yellow) or short wave (blue) light, which are the prime colours that all other colours are made of. The rods are much more sensitive to light than the cones. However, their resolution and sharpness is lower. They are responsible for black- and white seeing, even when the light intensity is low, as we experience at night. A very high number of cones are assembled in a small area of the retina, called fovea. If we fixate on an object, we move our eyes in a way that the object of interest falls on the fovea to enable the reception of fine details. The rest of the visual field is responsible for more global information and the perception of movement. The rods and cones see a picture only as a field of unrelated points of light, darkness and colour.

The photoreceptors are linked to ganglion nerve cells responsible for long-distance information transmission. Some of these cells also summarize and structure information about light intensity. Their neuronal signals are sent through the optical nerve on the back of the eyes to brain areas where the further processing takes place. Every nerve cell in the optical nerve encodes the sum of stimulation of a small retinal region. The optical nerves of both eyes meet at the *optical chiasma*, where the nerves of the nasal side of the retina cross over and go to the opposite side of the brain, whereas the nerves of the outside retina go to the same side of the brain (figure 2). This means that the right halves of both retinas are processed in the right brain side, whereas the left halves of both retinas are processed in the left brain side. Since light from the left visual field falls on the right half of the retina, and is thus processed in the right cerebral hemisphere, it is also true for visual perception that the hemispheres process information about the opposite side of the world (Anderson, 1996).

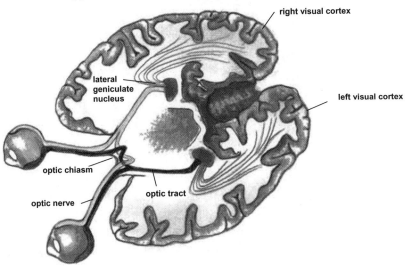

Figure 2. Primary visual pathway

The primary visual pathway is arranged in such a way that visual structures contain an organized map of the opposite visual field. After passing the lateral geniculate nuclei of the thalamus, visual information is projected to the back side of the brain, called the visual cortex. The incoming signals are distributed to at least thirty different brain areas specialised on movement, colour, spatial detail, form, size, direction, and many other features.

Some axons bypass the lateral geniculate regions and terminate in the optic tectum of the midbrain. This so-called tectopulvinar system is an evolutionarily primitive visual system, which does not reach awareness. It can be thought of as a "reflex" system that controls eye (and head) movements in response to visual stimuli. Thus, it makes us look towards what is interesting. It helps us to focus on a picture rather than the white wall, the pencil, if we need one, or a car that is racing towards us.

Cells in the visual cortex behave in a much more complex way than cells at the lower levels. For example, they can detect edges or beams, specific to position, direction and spatial expansion. A small area in visual space is related to a set of cortical neurons that are specialized on processing the properties of the stimulus. Next, the brain has to decide where in the three-dimensional environment those edges and beams belong. Processes in the striate cortex combine information from both eyes to enable depth perception. Additional cues like texture and movement help to build a three dimensional representation of the environment. The visual cortex enables us to combine visual messages with other sensory messages and earlier experiences.

At this point, information is still fragmented. To build a coherent picture, the brain has to know exactly which lines, edges and beams belong together. The Gestalt approach (see Murray, 1994, for a review) states that objects are perceived as organized patterns rather than separate components. According to this approach, we do not see fractional particles in chaos. Instead, we notice larger areas with defined shapes and patterns. The main point of Gestalt theory is the idea of grouping objects to facilitate the interpretation of a visual field. The four factors that determine grouping are:

1. proximity – elements tend to be grouped together according to their nearness,

2. similarity – similar items tend to be grouped together,

3. closure – items are grouped together if they complete some entity, and

4. simplicity – items will be organized into simple figures according to symmetry, regularity, and smoothness.

Following these rules, even unknown stimuli have a tendency to be united.

At this point of visual information processing we can dissect the visual world into objects. Yet, we are still far from seeing the world, because we still have to identify the objects. In a next step, those unknown objects have to be analyzed. Each stimulus is seen as a combination of elemental features like horizontal or vertical lines, beams and areas. Even complex objects can be understood as a known configuration of simple components.

Yet, we can perceive a seamless picture only if the parts of the puzzle are fit together again. This process starts in associated brain areas that add data about the "where" and "what" of an object. Colour, texture and form are processed by the temporal cortex, whereas the parietal cortex is responsible for details. These areas project their results to the frontal cortex. Only at this point we get aware that we sit in a room and look at black letters on a white background, called a text.

The physical stimulus to be recognized is not the only information we have, because objects appear in contexts. These contexts can be helpful, but also distorting. If the stimulus is ambivalent, contextual information makes one or the other interpretation more probable. For example, a small cloud at the horizon may be just a natural phenomenon to someone who does not know the industrial area located in that area. Although both persons see the same cloud, contextual knowledge changes the interpretation of the stimulus. According to Anderson (1996) perception is a process that is highly dependent on probability calculations.

Higher regions of the brain can send visual input back to the neurons in the lower areas of the visual cortex. This feedback system helps the brain to filter inputs that are redundant or should be ignored. For example, higher brain areas help to focus on the pencil we forgot in the library without analysing every book in every bookshelf we come across. Without this filtering mechanism, our perception would be chaotic and disorganized.

To take the short cut, these exemplary neurophysiological processes show that perception is complex and easily deceived by ambivalent stimuli. To facilitate perception it is fundamental to avoid ambiguous stimuli by making them clear and rich in contrast. In the case of microlearning, the fact that our eyes automatically focus on what is deemed interesting implies, for example, that the information device should not be more interesting than the display. When we consider "mobile learning", the learner should be made aware that his or her eyes may be distracted by too many alternative stimuli, for example if learning on a train, during a lunch break or on a crowded desk. Yet, the level of optimal perceptual stimulation is highly individual.

> Visual perception can be divided into an early sequence, in which forms and objects are extracted from the visual scenery, and a late phase in which forms and objects are perceived trough a complex neuronal network.

2.2   Memory

Memory is a form of information processing. It can be seen as the ability to encode, consolidate, maintain and recall information that has been perceived. In many ways, our everyday knowledge of the brain and its functions is still stamped by historical concepts. According to Wolpaw (2002), the view of memory as a "storehouse" of information has emerged through the history of psychology. Although concepts like "storehouse of information" are helpful in every day life and in the study of behaviour, they are not adequate at the level of brain functioning. According to Wolpaw, in the nervous system, "the plasticity produced by a learning experience comprises a shifting set of effects at a shifting set of sites and contributes to a shifting set of behaviours." Thus, in current neuropsychology, the brain is seen as a vast communication network, where some neurons serve as transmitters, firing off messages to other neurons that act as receivers. All of this data exchange occurs across synapses.

2.2.1   Learning at the Cellular Level

Plasticity refers to lasting changes in the nervous system. Our brains have a stunning ability to adapt to changing circumstances and acquire new information. On the cellular level, *synaptic plasticity* is the ability of neuronal connections to change in strength. These synaptical changes depend on various neurochemical and electrophysiological mechanisms (Kandel, et al., 2000, Walkowiak, 2001). Changes in the strength of a neuron's response depend on the number of receptors. More receptors on the post-synaptic (information receiving) neuron, lead to a stronger transmission. This strengthening of connections between neurons, which can last hours or even days, is known as *long-term potentiation* (LTP). It is assumed to be the cellular basis for memory (Anderson, 1996). In other words, the more one neuron activates another neuron, the stronger the connection between them grows. Long-lasting changes in synaptic connectivity between two neurons can involve the making, but also the breaking of synaptic contacts.

Long-term potentiation does not occur at every synapse (a small gap between neurons) on a given cell, but only on activated synapses. This feature of LTP is important, because activation of one set of synapses selectively enhances particular sets of inputs. A weak stimulation of a pathway may not by itself trigger LTP. Yet, if one pathway is weakly activated and an adjacent pathway onto the same cell is strongly activated at the same time, both pathways undergo LTP. This means that conjointly activated sets of synaptic input are enhanced. Some authors (e.g., Blakemore & Frith, 2005) consider this a cellular analogy of classical conditioning. More generally, neuronal *associativity* is always expected if one set of information is linked with another.

Although the interrelationship between LTP and behavioral plasticity is not yet fully understood, synaptic plasticity provides a plausible neural mechanism for long-lasting changes on a cellular level.

The weakening of a neuronal synapse is called *long-term depression* (LTD). It may play a role in clearing the memory from old information. Various feedback mechanisms help to maintain the attained changes. For example, if a cell has been affected by a lot of plasticity in the past, future plasticity is made less effective to avoid overwriting.

> The strengthening of neuronal connections is called *long-term potentiation*, while *long-term depression* the weakening of a neuronal synapse.

2.2.2   Memory Systems

There are several possible ways of classifying memory systems, but only some appear to be biologically reasonable (Kalat, 1995). Different parts of the brain contribute to different aspects of memory, but they do not have exclusive relationships with certain memory types. Thus, such classifications should not be mistaken for theories

(Robertson & Cohen, 2006). Memories can be classified by duration of retention, temporal direction, and type of information encoded.

2.2.3   Classification by Duration of Retention

Sensory memory is the ability to retain sensory information, even after the stimulus has ended. A sensory memory exists for every sensory channel: *iconic memory* for visual stimuli, *echoic memory* for auditive stimuli and *haptic memory* for touch. Information cannot be kept for very long (less than 1/2 second for vision; about 3 seconds for hearing), because new impressions come in every second. At this point of information processing, *Attention* plays an important role.

Information being attended to is passed from sensory memory into *short-term memory*. Only stimuli of interest are filtered from the sensory channels. The capacity of short-term memory has a span of about seven elements, called "chunks" of information. A "chunk" is a piece of information such as digits, letters, words, or other units. Thus, the short-term memory span as can be increased by increasing the number of items in each chunk. Information from short-term memory has a higher probability of being stored in long-term memory if the information is rehearsed or repeated. According to Mayer (2003) three basic learning processes can be distinguished: *Selection:* Attention is focused on relevant stimuli; *Organization:* incoming information is structured; *Integration:* Incoming information and old memories are combined.

A part of short term memory – referred to as *working memory* – can be used for performing mental manipulations. It has been conceptualized to be the system that enables us to hold information "online" for a short time, even if we are occupied by something else. Thus, working memory is responsible for multitasking. The *articulatory loop* refreshes the auditory information in a rehearsal loop and thereby prevents them from fading. For example, you can maintain a phone number for as long as you repeat it to yourself loudly or silently. The other system, the *visuo-spatial sketch pad*, stores visual and spatial information. It can be used, for example, for constructing and manipulating images and maps. Areas in the prefrontal cortex are considered to be central to working memory. As the prefrontal cortex develops throughout childhood and adolescence, children and young adults may not be capable of very much multitasking. This is important to keep in mind when designing learning environments for different age groups.

Of all the information encountered every day, only a small fraction becomes an available in the *long-term memory*. "Long-term" implicates any time span from 30 seconds to a lifetime.

Consolidation is the process by which recent memories are transformed to longer-lasting memories, thereby stabilizing or enhancing preexisting knowledge. At a cellular level, short-term memory is a temporary potentiation of neural connections that can become long-term memory through the process of long-term potentiation. As mentioned above, LTP is achieved through rehearsal and meaningful association. Consolidation does not only "store" new information, it can also produce a qualitative change in the execution of a task. As Robertson and Cohen (2006) point out, memories are processed "offline", i.e. without awareness, before they are being used at retrieval. In many cases, a phase of reconsolidation (e.g., exercising dance steps, telling stories of former times, etc.) helps to maintain a memory for another time span. Different processes are engaged during those stages.

Memories may consist of multiple components and can be encoded in distinct neural networks. Frequently, skill improvements are associated with practice, but they can also be supported by sleep. This may be due to a passive mechanism, in which sleep prevents memories from being disrupted. Additionally, there may also be an active mechanism in which the so-called "sleep architecture" (in this case, phases of REM or NREM sleep) plays an important role. Each component of a memory may undergo consolidation at different times. Rehearsal is one diurnal technique that is known to improve long-term maintenance. For example, if you repeat a word in a foreign language often enough, you may remember that word at a test or even years later. On the other hand, the more meaningful an event is to you, the faster and more strongly you consolidate a memory of it. If someone gave you a ticket for a concert you always wanted to go to, you would not need to hear the sentence twice to store it in your memory. Exciting experiences arouse the sympathetic nervous system, increasing the secretion of epinephrine. If an optimum of activation is reached (too much epinephrine induces fear and reduces the ability to fine tune cognitive processes), the level of glucose in the blood raises. Glucose is the brain's "fuel" and thereby enhances cognitive processes.

Consolidation is also enhanced if an item is related to other items that are already known, which gives the item meaning. According to Robertson and Cohen, consolidation provides an opportunity for past experiences to be processed from different angles than at the actual moment of encoding. As long-term memory is subject to fading ("forgetting"), several retrievals may be needed for long-term memories to last for years. This can happen through reflection or recall, dependent on the perceived importance of the material.

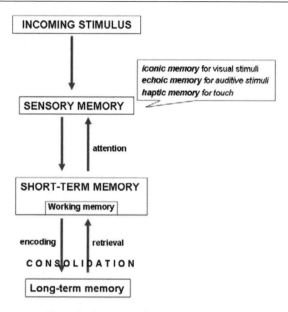

Figure 3. Sequence of memorization

Consolidation is not just a matter of time, but of organizing complex information before it can be transferred to long term memory. As is described in the third chapter, meaningfulness and emotional content play an important role in the process of organization.

2.2.4   Temporal Direction

In contrast to memories referring to knowledge or skills acquired in the past, *prospective memory* is dedicated to future intentions. If we are involved in one activity (like reading this article) we often have to remember to do something in the future (e.g., buying a birthday present). This ability is associated to the anterior prefrontal cortex that is especially well-developed in humans, compared to other primates. Thus, prospective memory is probably unique to humans (Blakemore & Frith, 2005). Nevertheless, bearing in mind an intention to do something in the future may interfere with the task you are doing and slows you down.

2.2.5   Information Type

Implicit learning occurs when an individual gains knowledge (e.g. riding a bicycle) without awareness. It is associated to areas in the basal ganglia and the cerebellum, both very deep and evolutionary old structures of the brain (Kalat, 1995). *Implicit memory* is typically encountered when something seems familiar or strange to us

(Blakemore & Frith, 2005). For example, as familiar objects are often preferred over unfamiliar objects, you rather pick a familiar piece of chocolate from the chocolate box.

Skills may also be learned intentionally and with an individual's awareness, which defines *explicit learning*. *Explicit memory* is the conscious use of memory to recall information. The hippocampus is fundamental for processing explicit memories. Analogous to a library's catalogue, hippocampal damage makes it difficult to store new memories, but it does not impair old memories.

Priming is a very basic implicit memory phenomenon. It means that a memory content is recalled faster (or even automatically) if related or associated cognitive contents have been actualized before. In a neurological view, priming can be seen as the activation of clusters of neurons. If one cluster is activated, for example by the input of sensory neurons, activation spreads to interconnected clusters. In an experiment by Bargh and Chartrand (1999), participants primed with a list of words relating to the "elderly" stereotype, walked down a hallway more slowly than participants primed with age-neutral words. If primed with words like dirt, smell, waste, etc., participants are more likely to complete the word stem gar___ with "garbage" than, e.g., with "garden".

Another basic type of implicit memory is called *conditioned response*. It is a new response to a stimulus that has once had a different meaning or no meaning at all. Two well known conditioned responses are feeling ill at the smell of food that has made you sick a long time ago and army veterans who may still feel panic at the sound of sirens.

Another useful memory distinction is between is between things of which we know and things we know how to do. Instead of the explicit-implicit distinction, you can also distinguish between *declarative* and *procedural memory*. While procedural memories consist of movements and motor skills (like walking, braiding, or riding a bicycle), declarative memories consist of facts and events that be talked about. Thus, declarative memories are mostly explicit, and procedural memories are mostly implicit, but the terms do not match exactly. Frequently, behaviours have multiple components and are not purely procedural or declarative. This is apparent when motor skills are taught. Trainers have to translate their own procedural skills into a sequence of declarative facts to pass on their knowledge.

Declarative memory can be subdivided into a memory for events (*episodic memory*) and a memory for meanings (*semantic memory*). Episodic memory helps us to encode and recall memories of particular events that have occurred in a certain time and place. The frontal cortex and the hippocampus are involved in processing episodic information. Episodic memory also tells us when and how we have acquired information and keeps track of what we say or do. Thus, it prevents us from repeating ourselves. Since hippocampus starts to mature from late infancy, we experience "childhood amnesia" before about three years of age. Semantic memory is responsible for categorical contents like the meaning of words, names, numbers, symbolic descriptions, etc. Thus, it has little to do with personal experiences (Ratey, 2003).

2.3   Emotion and Meaning

If you try to recall childhood memories, you will probably encounter the most meaningful events. Meaning is always coupled with emotion, so that our most vivid memories tend to be of emotional events. The actual function of our memories is to enable us to show adequate behaviour in the future (Wolpaw, 2002). Through evolution, the various memory systems developed the ability to retain events that are relevant for survival, which are typically those associated with strong emotions and motivational goals. Thus, the experience of our ancestors is the filter through which we see the world.

Each emotion leads to a survival strategy, relating to basic needs like the need for food, warmth, partnership, social contacts, or the avoidance of pain. Learning is only meaningful if there is a certain probability that the learning contents will help us in future situations (Arnold, 2002).

The emotional value ("good or bad") of a stimulus is encoded very early in the perceptional process, within the first 100-300 ms after the appearance of a stimulus (Compton, 2003). During perception, a subcortical circuit (involving the amygdala) evaluates the emotional significance. Emotional arousal leads to a narrowing of attention, so that emotionally significant stimuli are given priority in the competition for selective attention.

Emotion is also important for long-term retention. A memory may be stored in long-term memory or successively fade, depending on its emotional value. This is why we can easily memorize information in an area of interest but have difficulty memorizing uninteresting topics. If a daily memory (like slicing bread) does not have a strong good or bad emotional value (like cutting your finger), it is faded out. Although the brain will memorize unemotional information with frequent repetition or constant use, the memory will fade away as soon as is not used anymore.

The amygdala (a structure belonging to the limbic system) and prefrontal cortex, as well as their striatal and thalamic connections, are involved in processing emotions, and also participate in the complex neural processing responsible for what we consider rational thinking and decision making. Decision making needs a fast evaluation of positive or negative outcomes. The emotional valences of the anticipated consequences help to identify favourable or unfavourable outcomes.

Maybe you remember the state of anticipation before unpacking a birthday present or before solving a puzzle. Our brains are equipped with search systems that strive to fill information gaps and to make sense of incoming information. The neurotransmitter dopamine plays an important role in learning reward-directed behaviours (Berridge & Robinson, 1998). The pleasure of being rewarded then reduces the activity of the seeking system. For example, the feeling of anticipation gives way to happiness after you know what was inside the gift wrapping. The sequence of anticipation and rewarding applies to all kinds of information gaps. This is why learning is self-rewarding if you have expectancies and questions of your own. Obviously, satisfaction is strongly associated with motivation, since behaviours associated with satisfaction will be repeated again and again. Curiosity can be considered as a motivational drive. Thus, novelty in the learning environment is probably an important element in motivation.

As you can see, emotional systems take part in the encoding of new information, because emotional states are connected to values and priorities. Even though living in highly engineered surroundings, humans are still driven by instinct, and cognitions and culture have only limited influence.

3 The Neuropsychology of Microlearning

Techniques for passing along information have changed rapidly since the first book press. In contrast, our brains have evolved rather slowly and are physiologically still the same as before the invention of computers. What happens if the evolutionary old brain meets new information devices? The neuropsychological findings help to answer the questions posed in the introductory chapter.

3.1 How Small May the Bits of Content Be?

In microlearning, contents are small or very small units and narrow topics. As already discussed above, there is basically no downward limitation concerning the amount of information. As in implicit learning, the learning matter does not even have to be conscious. It seems that size and form are no suitable terms to describe the minimum size of learning contents. Consolidation occurs if information is meaningful to the learner. Thus, ways must be found to make small units relevant and meaningful enough to enable the transfer to long-term memory. In the case of fragmented information, it is a special challenge to provide a context meaningful to the individual learner. Questions like "why are you doing this?" or "does this learning matter match with your values and goals?" could explore the learner's motivation. Since meaning is highly individual, the smallest possible learning unit depends on each person's interests, values, goals and past experiences.

> As long as the bits of content are considered meaningful, their size does not matter.

3.2   How Short May the Interaction with the Learning Matter Be?

Microlearning aims at being efficient and using very little time. Whereas conscious learning of a single semantic item can be accomplished in less than a second, implicit learning may be even faster (Blakemore & Frith, 2005). Anything perceived consciously or unconsciously may become a memory. What may be problematic about little time is not perception or short term maintenance, but the transmission to long term memory.

Information with little emotional colouring needs lots of repetitions to be consolidated. In contrast, emotionally significant events are maintained effortlessly and virtually forever with no repetition needed. In large part, consolidation (and therefore full understanding) does not occur during a learning unit, but hours, weeks or months later. To make consolidation likely, the context has to be designed properly. It should incorporate reflection and metacognitions to help learners creatively evaluate the facts, skills, or experiences.

The use of formerly wasted time (due to a lack of technical devices) is a big advantage of micro media. Inter time, the time span between activities, may be used to learn with micromedia and should satisfy the need for efficiency. Yet, there are certain limitations to the use of inter time. The preliminaries for the optimum of memory use are "relaxed alertness" and the absence of fear, stress, helplessness, tiredness and exhaustion (Arnold, 2002). What is referred to as unused time may often be a time of recreation or adjustment to the next task. Inter time cannot be used effectively if the learner is tired or distraught. To avoid feelings of helplessness, the learner should be able to handle the medium with ease. However, if learners are free to choose time, place and pace of their occupation with the medium, they will probably choose a setting that meets most of the above requirements.

> The time needed to memorize a learning matter depends on its emotional impact.

3.3   To What Extent is Multitasking Possible?

From a biological perspective, the whole nervous system is a multitask system. Even the simplest memory involves multiple events at multiple locations (Wolpaw, 2002). Starting from perception, all senses provide information that is filtered for meaningful content at the same time.

The prefrontal cortex mediates a person's ability to depart from a main task to pursue alternative tasks and then return to the main task. This complex mental activity is called prospective memory. Multitasking implies that several tasks are pursued consecutively by switching from one task to another. In both cases, speed and accuracy of completion may suffer. The capacity of working memory is the needle's eye for multitasking. If too many things have to be done simultaneously or worried about in the future, the processing speed decreases.

For microlearning this implies that learning materials should be interesting enough to compete with the vast number of other incoming stimuli. Although time spans may be short, the learning environment should be free of distracting tasks. As capacities are limited, priority should be given to the task of learning.

If multiple tasks have to be executed, processing speed may decrease.

4   Conclusions and Implications for Further Research

Are there really new forms of living, learning and knowledge, as some developers of e-learning devices want to make us believe?

From a neuropsychological perspective, microlearning is not a new invention. Our brains have always been equipped to make sense of fragments and to integrate pieces of information into contexts. As the brain is very efficient, it primarily memorizes issues important for future situations. Inconveniently, individual meaningfulness is unpredictable.

At the same time, micro media can enhance the acquisition of knowledge through multi-sensory, reflective, naturalistic environments unconstrained by time, place and formal restrictions. This circumstance may encourage curiosity and accommodate our seeking systems. The significance of microlearning lies in the ability to be interactive, and to immediately satisfy the need to fill information gaps.

As you can infer from the past sections on perception and memory, neuronal processes that lead to the memorisation of a perceived element are very complex and not yet fully understood. Learning depends on genetic predispositions, past experiences, current mood, hormonal status, physiological needs, individual values and many other variables. It is impossible to predict if, and for how long, a fragment of information is memorized. The only way to find out is by systematic observation. As frequently in cognitive neuroscience, input and output are the only assessable variables. To find out if microlearning is effective, outcomes should be subject to systematic research.

References

Anderson, J.R. (1996) *Kognitive Psychologie.* Heidelberg/Berlin/Oxford: Spektrum.

Arnold, M. (2002) *Aspekte einer modernen Neurodidaktik. Emotionen und Kognitionen im Lernprozess.* München: Verlag Ernst Vögel.

Bargh, J.A. & Chartrand, T.L. (1999) The Unbearable Automaticity of Being. In: *American Psychologist* 54 (7), pp. 462–479.

Blakemore, S.-J. & Frith, U. (2005) *The Learning Brain. Lessons for Education.* Malden/Oxford/Carlton: Blackwell Publishing.

Berridge, K.C. & Robinson, T.E. (1998) What is the role of dopamine in reward: hedonic impact, reward learning, or incentive salience? In: *Brain research. Brain research reviews* 28(3), pp. 309–369.

Compton, R. J. (2003) The Interface Between Emotion and Attention: A Review of Evidence From Psychology and Neuroscience. In: *Behavioral and Cognitive Neuroscience Reviews* 2 (2), pp. 115–129.

Gregory, R.L. (2001) *Auge und Gehirn. Psychologie des Sehens.* Reinbek: Rowohlt.

Kalat, J.W. (1995) *Biological Psychology.* Pacific Grove: Brooks/Cole Publishing.

Kandel, E.R., Schwartz, J.H. & Jessell T.M. (2000) *Principles of Neural Science*, 4th ed., New York: McGraw-Hill.

Mayer, R.E. (2003) (Ed.) *Cambridge Handbook of Multimedia Learning.* Cambridge, UK: Cambridge University Press.

Studio eLearning Environments (2005) *MicroWiki.* Available from: <http://www.microlearning.org/MicroWiki.html> [Accessed 2006-8-30]

Murray, D. (1994) *Gestalt Psychology and the Cognitive Revolution.* New Jersey: Prentice-Hall.

Ratey, J.J. (2003) *Das menschliche Gehirn. Eine Gebrauchsanweisung.* München: Piper.

Robertson, E.M. & Cohen, D.A. (2006) Understanding consolidation through the Architecture of Memories. In: *The Neuroscientist* 12 (3), pp. 261–271.

Walkowiak, W. (2001) Neurobiologie des Lernens. In: Schmidt, S.J. ed.: *Lernen im Zeitalter des Internets. Grundlagen, Probleme, Perspektiven.* Pädagogisches Institut für die deutsche Sprachgruppe, Bozen, pp. 45–66.

Wolpaw, J.T. (2002) Memory in Neuroscience: Rhetoric Versus Reality. In: *Behavioral and Cognitive Neuroscience Reviews* 1 (2), pp. 130–163.

What Size is Micro? – Using a Didactical Approach Based on Learning Objectives to Define Granularity

Thomas Eibl

1   New Challenges for Learning and Teaching

Microlearning is a new and also an overdue concept. It is new, because the technologies used are modern and themselves in a continuing elaboration and development process, and it is overdue, because it provides answers to some pressing tasks of facing today's learning and teaching. The so-called modernity is driven by the pursuit for changes. New variations, new forms, new processes are established to overcome old, reputedly outdated perspectives. At the end of the 20th century, philosophic discussion showed that this belief in constant and endless modernization is stuck in a crisis and is the cause of several paradoxes in all sections of our societies. Whatever the overall (re-)solution may be in the long run – to redeem the "project of modernity" as proclaimed by Habermas (See Habermas, 1984 and 1992) or to abandon it, in order to accept the concept of postmodernism as stated by Lyotard (see Lyotard, 1984) – microlearning is likely to provide solutions for some paradoxes concerning our handling of knowledge, our learning and knowledge management.

Out of the five paradoxes, described by Geißler & Kutscha (1992), in the modernization of vocational education, the following three are of utmost interest in the context of microlearning:

1.   The completion of vocational education releases the student into lifelong learning. Obtaining a degree or achieving graduation is no longer a terminus, but a starting point for more, for lifelong learning; the end of institutionalised education marks also the beginning of further training. In this transition, the direct guidance and control from institutions decreases and the indirect regulation by inherent necessities and market forces increases. This implies also an increasing responsibility on the part of the learner.

2.   Learning has to be regarded as an accelerated process of invalidation. The knowledge acquired during education and training expires faster and faster; the half-life of knowledge becomes shorter and shorter. The time slot between the acquisition of qualification and the invalidation of qualification diminishes increasingly rapidly. This implies that a good part of our learning is a re-learning, which includes the erasure of outdated information.

3.   Congestion, hold up, is regarded as a mean of acceleration. Education and training react to the dynamics of social and cultural changes, but are also used in an attempt to control these dynamics. Training activities are regarded as breaks in the everyday working process. Through these training activities, it is intended

that the trainees acquire the ability to support the acceleration processes, to keep up-to-date. So the congestion caused by the separation of the trainee from the working process is necessary for the acceleration. Necessarily, the training phases become shorter and shorter and consequently, the alternation between learning, working and leisure becomes quicker, the dividing lines between these domains dissolve. This process enables, even enforces, new scopes of training and learning designs. With blurred borders existing between various spheres of their lives, individuals increase their options, but also their own personal responsibility. Geißler & Kutscha stated that, due to these processes, the opportunities offered by "Kurzzeitpädagogik" (1992, p. 23) – i.e. a short-term education or training – have to be explored in order to cope with discontinuous and cavernous educational processes.

Learning is on its way to becoming a highly important and constant, even a habitual, task in individual schedules; in the so-called information society, learning is acknowledged as being a lifelong process. In 1992, when Geißler & Kutscha described the paradoxes of vocational education, the digital media were clearly on their way to infiltrating the working and private lives of citizens of industrial nations, but the full impact of the "digital revolution" is being experienced right now. As a matter of fact, the increasing use of digital tools, means of communication and entertainment technologies intensifies the three paradoxes and accelerates the ongoing processes even more:

1. As long as digital means and tools advance at the current pace, the worker is forced to adapt to the ongoing changes, i.e. workers are repeatedly forced to learn the handling of digital media, lifelong. Every certification a worker receives after completion of a software training is the starting point for new training in regard to updates and even newer developments. The faster these updates and new releases progress, the higher the learning frequency will become. On the other hand, the responsibility of keeping up-to-date is shifted more and more towards the employees.

2. Especially in the field of digital means and tools, acquired knowledge expires very rapidly. When new software demands new skills, the knowledge of how outdated software is handled becomes irrelevant, even disturbing. The half-life of knowledge in handling digital media is directly linked to the innovation rate.

3. The digital media increasingly blur the dividing line between working time and private life. On one hand, the same technologies are employed in business and during leisure. On the other hand, this mixture enables the emerging "knowledge worker" to do his or her job whenever and wherever he or she is needed. The congestions, the interruptions caused by learning, have to occur in quicker succession, but also have to become shorter and shorter. So, with the dissolution of borders between the working and private environments, with the use of laptop computers and mobile phones, mobile computing devices and

wireless high-speed data transfer, working, learning and entertainment will increasingly blend together.

All these developments emphasize the necessity to discuss "Kurzzeitpädagogik" as Geißler & Kutscha put it, to discuss short-term education and training. Brought to the context of digital media, using means of digital communication, this is a concept of microlearning. In the following, an approach for vocational training shall be described and will include an exemplary focus on military and aviation training. Although this approach contains aspects which can be transferred to other sectors of teaching and learning, a corresponding revision of the described approach has not yet been performed and is still to come.

2   Microlearning

In his introductory note for the Microlearning Conference 2005, titled "Microlearning: A New Pedagogical Challenge," Theo Hug wrote:

> It's not a well designed paradigm we have as starting point – it's rather bits and pieces from different discourses and practices we are starting from. (Hug, 2005a, p. 2)

So, to ask for a definition would be the wrong way to approach this concept; it is much more fruitful to ask for features and characteristics of microlearning. Emerging from (post-)modern times, they reflect the necessity for a revised approach for learning as implied in the descriptions above.

> Microlearning deals with relatively small learning units and short-term-focused activities. (Hug, 2005b, p. 0)

This short statement gets directly to the point of what the essence of microlearning is and shows how it reflects the aspects of short-term education. Describing a tool for microlearning, Theo Hug explains that microlearning features can augment learning processes by

> [...] making use of the everyday use of information and communication technologies for didactical purposes. (Hug, 2005b, p. 5)

With borders dissolving between the different aspects of life, with digital technologies and communication means as links, as constants in our daily lives, this approach, once thought through, seems obvious, almost indispensable.

Microlearning "[...] makes us go step by step in the right direction" (Eichenauer, 2005, p. 1), applying microlearning principles "[...] information is broken down into smaller units[...]" (Bruck, 2005, p. 2). The learning itself is split "[...] into small activities embedded in everyday life." (Hug, 2005b, p. 6) which implies, in times which demand high mobility, "[...] anytime-anywhere access to learning resources[...]" (Gabrielli, Kimani & Catarci, 2005, p. 1).

The features and characteristics of microlearning, as briefly exemplified by citations, answer to the paradoxes of (post-)modern education and training. The concept of short-term education and the new digital communication media are merged, are blended together to enable step-by-step learning in short time slots, anywhere and anytime. So, one focus of the considerations necessary to promote microlearning lies in the breakdown into single units of learning representing the steps of the learning process.

3   Granularity

Microlearning aims at small and dissected learning units, but how small can these units be? How can the learning content be dissected into these units? Microlearning aims at a step-by-step approach, but what is the size of these steps and how can we assure that the steps carry the learner in the right direction? Although not new to didactical considerations, these questions obtain additional relevance in the concept of microlearning.

As starting point, it shall be declared axiomatically for vocational training: a planned and designed teaching-learning process is to be purposeful and objective-oriented. Based on a detected or experienced need, an objective is defined for the instruction process, in order to fulfil this need. If a company is compelled to buy new machinery due to economic demands, the ability of the workers to handle this new machinery efficiently is experienced as such a need. So, from this detected need, the objective for the training process can be derived. The task of the training (teaching) is to guide the trainee (learner) to this objective, i.e. the training has to provide an environment which is conducive to the formation of appropriate knowledge by the trainee. This environment may include the presentation of multimodal and multicodal information (Weidenmann, 2002), the stimulation of interaction, assistance through measurement of results, and so on. The size of the steps towards the objective is highly dependent upon the target group and also upon the content to be learned.

As a second axiom, it shall be stated that microlearning, in the sense of a planned, designed and purposeful teaching-learning process, can be applied to a manifold of teaching purposes on a wide variety of different aspects of life. So, with this huge variety of possible training needs, learning objectives and content, it is not possible to define the size of the single units for all conceivable microlearning processes. Nevertheless, it is possible to establish a tool for the definition of the unit size, the granularity of single, concrete microlearning projects, which can be used for most training needs.

The single units of a defined microlearning process, which aim for the fulfilment of a learning objective, have to fulfil two demands: firstly, they have to be self-explanatory and self-contained in order to be recognized as autonomous units; they have to make sense to the trainee, to provide sense and to communicate sense. This comprises the demand to provide a story for the trainee. This last statement may, at first, seem contradictory to the postulation of brevity implied in microlearning. But stories do not necessarily call for several text-pages of information. Stories can be told using a single picture, a short animation, or just a few words (see also Hug, 2005b, pp. 9-11). Secondly, the units have to be objective-oriented, they have to lead the trainee step by step towards the fulfilment of the overall learning objective derived from the recognized training need.

So, on the one hand, the units have to be short to reduce complexity and to fit into a small timeslot, in order to be incorporated into everyday life. On the other hand, they have to be big enough to fulfil objectives themselves and thereby bring the trainee further in his or her learning task. On the one hand, the single units have to be self-contained and autonomous, on the other hand, they have to be a part of a larger whole, providing a step towards an overall objective. The single units can be described as "holons," a term coined by Arthur Koestler (1967) to label entities which are a whole in themselves and at the same time parts of a greater whole. Single parts of a whole system of holons influence one another and the whole system; the system influences the single holons.

Although confronted with a single piece at a time, with many small units of learning content, the trainee must not get the impression to deal with desultory fragments. Objective-orientation avoids this impression. The defined overall learning objective is analysed, it is dissected into sub-ordinate objectives on different hierarchic levels, or, defining holons, levels of a holarchy. In this process the granularity is defined.

4   A Didactical Approach Based on Learning Objectives

How to define learning objectives, how to break down overall objectives and how to build up curricula, in other words, how to deal with a hierarchy (holarchy) of learning objectives, is the main focus of a didactical theory which will gain new significance with the emerging new learning and teaching concepts. This approach, based on learning objectives, this curricular didactic shall help with the adequate description and organisation of learning objectives, the analysis of the content of learning objectives and the definition and the operationalisation of learning objectives (von Martial, 2002, p. 231). A learning objective-based didactical approach aims for a change in the cognitive structures of the trainee, which can be evaluated using empirical methods; the learning environment provided shall stimulate a change in the (potential) behaviour of the trainee. The assumed correlation between the outcome of the learning process and a change in the potential behaviour determines the analysis and the formulation of learning objectives. Learning objectives are to be formulated in a manner that renders the desired change in the cognitive structures identifiable.

It has already been stated above that a designed learning process has to be objective oriented, i.e. the learning has to strive for an overall objective, a focal objective. As long as this focal objective can be evaluated by monitoring observable behaviour, a didactical approach based on learning objectives can be applied. The focal objective, the focal point of the learning, has to be formulated in an abstract way, comprising a large variety of learning content relevant for the fulfilment of the objective. To fulfil an exemplary focal objective, "The trainee shall be able to create a web site using HTML," obviously a wide variety of behaviour, i.e. a concretion of knowledge, of cognitive structures, has to be shown. In this example, the trainee has to know how to format text elements, how to insert pictures into web pages, how to establish links between the pages and so on. These parts of the content to be learned can be defined as coarse objectives; they build the second level of the holarchy. To get to the actual steps of learning, the actual learning units, a further analysis dissects the coarse objectives into fine objectives. These fine objectives define the single microunits, the holons, and have to fulfil the demands stated above. The fine objectives have to be small enough to break down the complexity into chunks of information which can be cognitively handled by the trainee in a relatively short time, and at the same time big enough to serve a definable learning object and guide the trainee noticeably on his or her way to the focal objective. The fine objectives have to be self-contained and autonomous.

Learning objectives are formulated containing a "behaviour part" and a "content part," stating what a trainee has "to do" with regard to a specific content of the training. "Know the HTML tag for bold text formation," as an exemplary fine learning objective, is composed of the behaviour part "Know..." and the content part "... the HTML tag for bold text formation." Whether the objective is fulfilled after the training, or not, i.e. whether the trainee knows the appropriate HTML tag or not, can be evaluated by tests such as multiple choice questionnaires. If the learning process is to be designed using a step-by-step approach, the formulation of the fine objectives has to reflect this approach. Methods of constructing such learning objectives were investigated by Benjamin S. Bloom and his group, beginning in 1948, resulting in a well-defined taxonomy to describe the behaviour part of the learning objectives and provide a bottom-up approach for teaching. The steps for cognitive learning, in accordance with Bloom's taxonomy, are: knowledge, comprehension, application, analysis, synthesis and evaluation (Bloom, 1975). These steps represent different cognitive and intellectual capabilities which build up on each other. With each step in this learning process, the complexity of the necessary cognitive operations and the demands on the trainee increase. The learning process begins with rather simple objectives, which aim for a mere knowledge of facts and can end with learning objectives which aim for complex problem solving strategies (evaluation). After the trainee has learnt to recognize the notation of HTML tags (knowledge), he or she can learn to understand the principles of the HTML tags (comprehension) and then to use these tags to format text (application).

The work of Bloom and his group was performed with regard to childhood learning in school. So, before actual learning objectives can be defined, the given taxonomy must be adapted to reflect the necessities of the instruction process. One possibility is to project the given taxonomy onto the content to be trained, to reveal inappropriate parts (for further details on this approach applied during an actual project, refer to Eibl, 2006). These parts are deleted, e.g., the levels analysis, synthesis and evaluation, which would not be applicable for a HTML basic course, amended, e.g., by new cognitive levels expressing specialities of the learning content or the target group and redefined. Redefining in this context also includes the definition of a selected set of verbs to formulate the behaviour part of the learning objectives. To guarantee a consistent build-up, a coherent courseware and – for larger projects – to guarantee that each member of the project team has the same understanding, for each applicable cognitive level, appropriate verbs have to be defined in detail, to clearly state their meaning with regard to the learning process. The adaptation of the taxonomy should be designed as a hermeneutic circle. Once the taxonomy has been adapted to the actual project, its fitness has to be evaluated. It has to be projected onto the content, i.e. exemplary parts of the content are translated into learning objectives with the use of the new taxonomy and the result is checked. It is likely that the process "redefinition-evaluation" will have to be executed several times, which may seem time-consuming and uneconomic. On the other hand, it is important to build a solid base for the courseware to be designed, to avoid reworking afterwards.

In order to actually formulate learning objectives, not only the learning content has to be considered, but also other relevant components. The traditional "didactical triangle" is comprised of the three components "learner, teacher and learning content" and no longer matches current considerations about learning processes. Using digital technologies to promote learning, an appropriate theoretical concept has to be used. The "Universal Constructive Instructional Theory" (UCIT) represents such a concept (Schott, Grzondziel & Hillebrandt, 2002). UCIT amends and modifies the didactical triangle, resulting in the four components "learner, learning content, learning environment and frame of reference." The learning environment is defined as representation of the aspects of learning which can be arranged intentionally, such as media, communication systems, and schedules, but also the help from tutors and the assistance from co-learners. By the frame of reference, all aspects are addressed which cannot be influenced, but affect the learner and the learning process and have, therefore, to be considered. All four components are interconnected; each component is interrelated with the others. For each project, the four components have to be analysed together with their interdependencies.

The learning objective, comprising behaviour and content part, has to serve three purposes. Firstly, it defines the objective, the aim of the actual learning unit, what the learner has to be capable of, after the unit has been worked through. Secondly, it provides the headline under which the learning unit can be addressed in the holarchy. And thirdly, it defines the content mediated by the learning unit. Using a didactical approach based on clearly defined learning objectives, the outcome of the learning process shall be evaluated, i.e. the outcome of each microunit shall be evaluated. Therefore, tests have to be provided. Of course, multimedia test methods, using the same digital environment as that used by the mediation of the learning content, can be used, but only to a certain extent. Knowledge can be evaluated using multiple choice tests, fill-in questions, etc., with high reliability and validity. For the higher cognitive levels such as comprehension and application, these methods are not appropriate. For learning objectives relating to these higher levels, other test methods have to be found, such as evaluation by tutors. For each learning objective, it has to be analysed how the fulfilment of the objective can be evaluated and to which extent the learning environment can be used for this task.

Keeping all the above statements in mind, a project concerning the production of courseware on the basis of well-defined learning objectives contains the following steps:

1. Directly derived from the needs assessment, the focal objective is formulated. This focal objective defines the desired outcome of the complete learning process and is the focal point, the highest hierarchical level of the holarchy.
2. The four components, as described by the UCIT, are analysed together with their interdependencies.
3. The taxonomy to be applied for the formulation of the learning objectives is elaborated on the basis of the analysis performed in step two. The resulting taxonomy provides the frame for the holarchy of learning objectives.
4. The elaborated taxonomy is evaluated and adapted in a hermeneutic process.
5. The actual learning objectives are developed, projecting the well-defined taxonomy onto the content to be learned. The microunits are created and the frame of the holarchy is filled with actual learning objectives.
6. The resulting holarchy is evaluated for consistency and for its capability to establish a learning flow.
7. Appropriate tests are elaborated for the microunits, to evaluate whether the learning process has been successful or not.

In step five of the project sequence described above, the granularity of the courseware is established. The expert performing the translation of the learning content into actual learning objectives can establish the granularity by deciding which single steps can be grouped under one objective, or have to build one objective on their own. Between different learning environments, large discrepancies in granularity can be seen, or as Theo Hug put it:

"In terms of time, the range goes from less than a second up to more than one hour." (2005b, p. 3).

Defining the granularity, the interdependencies between the single components of the learning process become obvious. The learning environment, the media to be used, affects the learning content of the single microunits and vice versa. If the defined communication tools are mobile devices, the learning content has to be split up into very small single units, which fit on small screens. This decision, of course, directly affects the granularity. Mobile phones and PDAs with limited displays demand learning atoms, while laptop computers with larger displays can handle learning molecules. So, three possibilities emerge: Firstly, the distribution device is predetermined, which means that the learning content and the sizes of the microunits have to be adapted to the device. Secondly, the learning content and the size of its units cannot be adapted, so the distribution device, the learning environment, has to be chosen according to the demands of the content. Thirdly, the learning content has to be split into units of different sizes, demanding different distribution media. Then, the content itself has to be distributed over a range of output devices, using, e.g., mobile phones for atomic units and laptop or desktop computers to provide larger units, i.e. to establish a kind of blended learning.

The didactical approach based on learning objectives dissects the learning content into learning objectives, into single units. In this process the granularity is established. The question "how small can the units get?" cannot be answered apodicticly for all possible projects. Following the explanations above, with the definition of the learning objectives, the granularity, i.e. the size of the single units, can be determined. The size of the microunits can vary, even within one project, one designed learning environment. Atomic units, e.g., a single word of a foreign language learned using a mobile device, can be summed up through the learning process, can be one small step in the holarchy and thereby serve as basis for larger learning units at a higher level of the holarchy, e.g., complete paragraphs of text for grammar lessons, learned using desktop computers.

An actual project concerning training for work on and operation of a new, high tech military helicopter shall serve as an example to show how the size of microunits can be defined. The target group for this training is comprised of already experienced personnel, so the trainees do not need information on the basics of aviation, but have to learn, in a so-called "conversion to type" training, what is new about this aircraft, and what are the changes in comparison to the helicopter types with which they were previously acquainted. The high complexity of the training content demands a reduction of complexity of the associated instruction material in order for this training content to be manageable during the learning process. The content has to be broken down into chunks of information, which can be cognitively handled by the trainee and learned. This implies a modular approach towards the training, a step-by-step structure, which corresponds to the principles of the learning-objective-based didactical model.

After all tasks relevant for the training were detected during a training need analysis, an appropriate taxonomy was defined by close collaboration between subject matter experts and experts for instructional design and didactics. The verbs "describe" and "state" were defined for the cognitive level "knowledge," the verbs "explain" and "identify" for "comprehension" and the verbs "use" and "apply" for "application." The definition of the verb "identify" reads as follows:

> The trainee shall acquire the ability to clearly recognize a given item, sub-system or component and explain the relevant environment. Furthermore the characteristics of the respective item, sub-system or component (which make it unique) have to be explained.

This definition aims at the special needs of aviation training and gives a clear understanding of a verb, which otherwise would imply a variety of connotations. The defined verbs of the taxonomy shall lead the trainee step by step through the training.

In the next step, the tasks were translated into actual learning objectives. During this process, the size of the individual objectives, of the individual microunits, was defined and established. The framework for this definition is given by the elaborated taxonomy for the formulation of learning objectives. To establish the size of the units within this framework, the logic of the subject to be trained and the psycho-logic of the trainees had to be observed and respected. The training need analysis showed that the task "Replace the fuel pump of tank 1" has to be trained. The complete replacement procedure includes many single steps to be performed, more than could be handled cognitively for learning purposes. While defining the learning objective, a way had to be found to keep the learning content for a single objective in manageable limits, to keep single microunits as small as possible, but as extensive as necessary. The psycho-logic, the way the trainees think and use their cognitive structures after several years of maintaining helicopters and the inherent logic of the procedure itself had to be evaluated and showed that the whole replacement procedure could be dissected into three self-contained parts with the result that the task "replace" was split into the sub-tasks "remove," "install" and "test." This led to a manageable and learnable amount of information for each new sub-task. Combined with the established taxonomy, each of the learning objectives "Apply the fuel pump removal procedure," "Apply the fuel pump installation procedure" and "Apply the fuel pump test procedure" was formulated to build one microunit of learning content. These three objectives lead, step by step, to the objective "Apply the fuel pump replacement procedure" on a meso level; the learning objective on the meso level brings together the three objectives of the micro level and guarantees the connection of the constructed knowledge.

To establish the granularity, the restraints from the inherent logic of the subject to be trained and the psycho-logic of the trainee have to be analysed and evaluated together with their interdependencies. The single steps of a procedure have to be trained in their context and cannot be separated randomly. On the other hand, the trainees need a reduction of the complexity of the procedures and a structure of the learning content which gives connection points to already constructed knowledge. Both demands led to the size of the various individual microunits.

The different cognitive levels described in this example imply a blended learning setting. While it is possible to evaluate whether learning objectives at knowledge level, formulated with the verbs "describe" and "state," are fulfilled by means of multimedia tests, it is not possible to evaluate the fulfilment of the learning objective "Apply the fuel pump removal procedure" using such methods. The multimedia environment can only provide simulated controls and displays, i.e. haptic and psycho-motorical aspects cannot be mediated. Thus a valid test of the abilities concerning the application level can only be performed using training devices, including hardware rebuilds of the actual aircraft or using the aircraft itself. The use of a learning objective oriented didactical approach makes it easy to set up blended learning environments. The individual microunits, corresponding to the individual learning objectives, can be assigned to a training media appropriate for the mediation and the testing of the learning content. Thereby again, a step-by-step training approach is established. The training is split into several parts on the meso level and distributed over a set of devices, which guarantees a successful training at the best cost-performance ratio. The trainees will start with Computer Based Training, before using their constructed knowledge to handle so-called "light training devices" such as Virtual Maintenance Trainers, Training Rigs or Cockpit Procedure Trainers and can then train using Full Flight Simulators and the actual aircraft.

With considerable breaks between the different learning steps, and the processing of the single microunits by the learner, the learning process is likely to appear as fragmented, insular. This impression could increase if the learning process is spread over several media. In order to guarantee that the single fragments can be summed up into a larger whole, the learner has to experience a learning flow, a noticeable flow towards an aim. Especially for this task, the learning-objective-based didactical approach has proven valuable. As long as the fine and the coarse objectives are made transparent to the learner, as long as the learner knows what are the detailed objectives of the learning steps, the direction of his or her learning becomes clear. The step-by-step build-up of the learning process, as represented by the single objectives, leads to the knowledge of "where I am" within the process and of "where I have to go." Giving the learner this information means involving him or her on a meta level.

To return to the example: The build-up of the learning objectives for the different systems of the aircraft, such as fuel system, flight control system, communication system and so on, follows an identical structure. After the trainee has learned to "describe" the system, its sub-systems and components and to "state" the limitations and safety requirements, he or she will learn to "explain" the principles of operation and the architecture of the system, to "identify" parts within the architecture and then the "use" of controls and displays and to "apply" the control actions. The build-up leads the trainees through the different cognitive levels defined for the training. During the learning process, the trainees become more and more accustomed to this build-up, and they notice to which aim the single steps lead, and thereby experience a learning flow, i.e. the learning is not experienced as fragmented and incoherent, but as a successional, coherent flow leading through more and more sophisticated and challenging training devices to the focal objective. The target group consists of highly motivated trainees and it can be assumed that they personally identify with the focal objective, to be able to handle the new aircraft. This motivation is essential for the flow experience in this training project: the individual, small and manageable steps lead the trainees towards their goal and as long as it is obvious at which point in the progress they are, what already has been achieved by them and where they are heading, the intrinsic motivation, together with an appropriate representation of the training path, as provided by computer based Learning Management Systems, lead to the experience of a learning flow.

The didactical approach based on well-defined learning objectives, focuses clearly on prescribed learning objectives. The step-by-step approach makes it mandatory to work through the learning content as predefined by the instructor; possibilities for a self-dependent choice of learning objectives are limited to the decision on skipping single objectives. Nevertheless, the organisation of the content in microunits provides the trainees with the opportunity to work through the individual units as often as they wish and to branch back to already learned units whenever they need to. This possibility, it has to be emphasized, does not qualify this didactical approach as "hypertext learning" although the use of hyperlinks in a learning-objective-based multimedia learning environment could lead to this impression: the learner cannot choose his or her path through the learning content freely with the possibility of choosing at his or her own discretion but has to fulfil predefined objectives. This may seem to be inopportune or out-of-time teaching and learning, but is still of high validity and importance, especially for vocational training, and is clearly appropriate and indispensable for military and aviation training.

5   Conclusion

Microlearning, as a new emerging field for the design of learning processes and courseware, provides answers to pressing questions posed by the (post-)modern information society and provides solutions to the paradoxes of the (post-)modern vocational training. Particularly "knowledge workers" are compelled to update their knowledge in constantly accelerating succession, while the borders between working, learning and relaxing become blurred. Providing short-term training and courseware which promote learning whenever and wherever a small timeslot can be found, microlearning will surely become an important concept in the near future. A didactical approach, based on well-defined learning objectives, although not a new approach, fits in very well to this evolving concept. Although allowing the learning content to be split up into single microunits, which are self-contained and autonomous, it guarantees the consistency of the training and involves the trainee in the learning flow.

The size of the single learning units has to be determined case by case. The learning-objective-based approach provides the designer of the courseware with the tools to determine the appropriate size. The analysis of the relevant components of the learning process, together with a well-defined taxonomy, establishes the granularity. The courseware is arranged as a holarchy, a hierarchical, interdependent structure of single holons breaking down and organising the learning objectives, from the focal objective, via coarse objectives, to fine objectives, each representing a step in the learning process.

This concept of microlearning on the basis of well-defined learning objectives addresses experienced learners and is intended for vocational training. Although originally developed with regard to childhood learning in school, the implementation of a learning-objective-based didactical approach to computer based microlearning and blended learning settings requires motivation on the part of the learner and the ability to orientate oneself in modular learning environments. With the necessary fragmentation of the learning process, the provision of structure becomes increasingly important. The defined learning objectives and the consistency of the used taxonomy enable the trainee to find orientation within the process, revealing which level has already been reached and what has to be learned next.

The didactical approach, based on learning objectives, has already been used in large scale projects; the described procedure for the development of courseware has proven reliable. Nevertheless, a further elaboration of this approach with regard to future microlearning applications and the detailed adaptation to new emerging distribution technologies, is still to come.

References

Bloom, B.S. (1975) *Taxonomy of Educational Objectives. Handbook 1: Cognitive Domain.* New York: David McKay Company.

Bruck, P.A. (2005) *Microlearning as Strategic Research Field: An Invitation to Collaborate.* Available from <http://www.microlearning.org/micropapers/ MLproc_2005_bruck.pdf> [Accessed 21 April 2006].

Eibl, T. (2006) Training objectives in computer based training for highly structured technological learning content. In: *Proceedings of the 1st International Conference on Digital Media and Learning, March 13-14, 2006.* Bangkok Thailand: Tana Press, pp. 117–122.

Eichenauer, R. (2005) *The Complementary Character of Microlearning.* Available from <http://www.microlearning.org/micropapers/MLproc_2005_eichenauer.pdf> [Accessed 24 April 2006].

Gabrielli, S., Kimani, S. & Catarci, T. (2005) *The Design of Microlearning Experiences: A Research Agenda.* Available from: <http://www.microlearning.org/micropapers/ MLproc_2005_gabrielli.pdf> [Accessed 22 April 2006].

Geißler, K.A. & Kutscha, G. (1992) Modernisierung der Berufsbildung – Paradoxien und Paradontosen. In: Czycholl, R. et al. eds.: *Paradoxien in der beruflichen Aus- und Weiterbildung.* Frankfurt, pp. 13–33.

Habermas, J. (1984) *The Philosophical Discourse of Modernity.* Cambridge: Polity.

Habermas, J. (1992) *Postmetaphysical Thinking.* Cambridge: Polity.

Hug, T. (2005a) *Microlearning: A New Pedagogical Challenge.* Available from: <http://www.microlearning.org/micropapers/MLproc_2005_hug.doc> [Accessed 6 March 2006].

Hug, T. (2005b) *Microlearning and Narration.* Available from: <http://web.mit.edu/ comm.-forum/mit4/papers/hug.pdf> [Accessed 10 April 2006].

Koestler, A. (1967) *The Ghost in the Machine.* London: Hutchinson.

Lyotard, J.-F. (1984) *The Postmodern Condition.* Manchester: Manchester University Press.

Schott, F., Grzondziel, H. & Hillebrandt, D. (2002) UCIT – instruktionstheoretische Aspekte zur Gestaltung und Evaluation von Lern- und Informationsumgebungen. In: Issing, J.I. & Klimsa, P. eds. *Information und Lernen mit Multimedia und Internet.* Weinheim: Beltz, pp. 179–195.

von Martial, I. (2002) *Einführung in didaktische Modelle.* Baltmannsweiler: Schneider Verlag Hohengehren.

Weidenmann, B. (2002) Multicodierung und Multimodalität im Lernprozess. In: Issing, J.I. & Klimsa, P. eds. *Information und Lernen mit Multimedia und Internet.* Weinheim: Beltz, pp. 45–62.

Thinking About the 'm' in Mobile Learning

Gunther Kress & Norbert Pachler

Contemporary Environments of Learning

There is, in educational contexts, a justified intensity of interest around the effects of digital, in particular portable, technologies in all manner of ways. There is a promise of greater 'reach,' of more and easier access, of a kind of democratization of education, a sense not just of a transformation, but a revolution of wide- and far-reaching areas of the educational world. The emergence of these technologies is accompanied by economic, political and social changes, which are related and connected everywhere, and, if anything, more profound in their effects; this heightens both the effects and the expectations. At the same time, social, political and economic changes are coming together with pedagogic changes at a breathtaking pace, and so it is, maybe, little wonder that the responses are equally breathless.

The social, political and economic effects are often gathered under the banner of 'globalization'; they are multiple, often contradictory, or at least in tension with each other, difficult to untangle, and seemingly impossible to control. In this chapter we want to show some of their effects on and in education in order to set the ground for a discussion around technologies and education. In any one locality – and for the purposes of our discussion here – we might say that together they amount to a transfer of power from state to market, so much so that in some places – the UK being one such – the state seems to have the role of being that of servant of the market. State and market once had quite different aims and goals, and, therefore, as far as the education 'system' was concerned, profoundly different effects. The (19th century) nation-state, in Europe at least, needed the education system to produce 'citizens' for the purposes of the state, and a labour-force for the national economy. We will not attempt to sketch the meanings and values promulgated in such education systems, nor their effects; suffice it to say that they aimed at a kind of homogeneity through the notion of the citizen, and were in many ways similar to the values held as essential for the labour-force.

The market differs profoundly in both respects; it has no interest in the production of a labour-force: it needs consumers; and where the state wanted – for its own reasons – a high degree of homogeneity, the market in its contemporary form is interested in a high degree of differentiation. This process, which promotes micromarket developments, is also linked with new media via the new notion of 'micromedia.'

In this context, Umair Haque (2005) asks: "To what extent are microplatforms, micromedia, and aggregators and reconstructors a substitute or a complement for production, publishing/marketing, and distribution in my value chain? ... To what extent is increased micromedia penetration likely to erode the power of publishers, distributors, and marketers in my value chain, and shift value to the edges?"[1]

Such multiple processes of differentiation have profound effects for education. Our case here is that any assessment of the effects of technologies on education have to be set in this frame, for they set the foundations of the environments of education in which technologies can become active, and in which their use is shaped. With the market as the ruling, dominant social model, identity is shaped through consumption, rather than through the achievement of a place in a social structure and a place in the labour-force. Agency is exercised as choice from commodities provided by the market. These factors become naturalized as the ruling social model and, once naturalized, become the dominant effects and forces in education, itself now experienced and lived in terms of the market.

In an educational context, the model of choice in the market makes learners into consumers, and all that pertains to the structures and experiences of consumption now becomes a feature of educational processes. The move from teaching to learning, from the authority of the teacher to the agency of the learner, is the effect of the naturalization of the market model in the domain of education. Teachers held scarce resources, and had the authority to dispense them. The contemporary form of the market does not know scarcity, whatever the commodity; rather it poses the problem of choice. In marketized education *learning* is *consumption*. Now all the emphasis is on the agency that attaches to choice, on the agency of the learner as consumer rather than the authority of the teacher.

In this context, digital technologies hold out the promise of unlimited access to educational commodities and of the consumer-learner's sovereignty of choice. But, of course, the perspective of the learner/chooser is not the only one. The state as the servant of the market is highly interested in speeding a development which seems to hold the promise of significant saving in resources. That phenomenon, too, is not limited to education: in all social domains, the neo-liberal state attempts to reduce its commitments: whether in social services, pensions, health, whatever, increasingly the requirement on individuals is that they should assume responsibility for their own affairs.

In other words, the centrality of 'learning' is everywhere entrenched as a part of contemporary social/political trends; the digital technologies offer the seemingly best chance to achieve much of this in the domain of education. Our chapter attempts to examine what actually is entailed in this, as an advance or a benefit; or what might be surface, glass beads offered to the natives, glitter without substance. We take the case of mobile-learning as our example, though we believe that it can stand in for many, most or maybe all others.

---

1   Source: http://www.bubblegeneration.com/2005/11/media-2.cfm; see also:
    http://www.bubblegeneration.com/resources/mediaeconomics.ppt

The Question of Affordances: Characteristics and Potential of Digital Technologies

The intensity of interest in digital technologies is also to a large extent motivated by a certain fascination, even fetishisation, of technology by parts of society, in particular policy makers. Perpetual developments in technology, coupled with its continued reduction in size, have resulted in an unabated integration of technology into social and cultural practices, for example leading to the possession of technological gadgetry as a status symbol.

In the literature this fetishisation of (digital) technology, depending on the author's point of view, is often conceptualised either as technological versus social determinism or as utopia versus dystopia.

Bruce and Hogan (1998) rightly point out that technologies should be viewed as ideological tools which embody social values and that they are organic "because they merge with our social, physical, and social beings." The question for them is one of how technologies are realized in particular settings and whether they become so embedded and integrated in our lives, discourses and activities that they become invisible. Bruce and Hogan also point out that effective use of technologies becomes the norm and a lack of an ability to use them can become a (negative) social and cultural marker. This consequence represents a particular danger of the **'disappearance' of technology** and is inherent in its increasing integration of digital artefacts in the 'ecology' of everyday life.

They conclude that it is less useful to focus on the technical attributes per se, instead there is the need to understand the ways in which ideology is embedded within technology.

> To understand what a technology means, we must examine how it is designed, interpreted, employed, constructed, and reconstructed through value-laden daily practices. (Bruce and Hogan, 1998)

This recommendation notwithstanding, and despite questioning of the usefulness of the notion of 'affordance' as a metaphor (Oliver, 2005), we want to examine, albeit briefly, some of the characteristics, properties, potentials and implications of digital technologies here.

Recent years have seen a growth in the social networking capability of web-based services, known as 'Semantic Web' or 'Web 2.0.' These terms refer to online collaboration tools, such as photo and video sharing services, pod- and video casting, weblogs, wikis, social bookmarking, syndication of site content, etc., which facilitate the sharing of content by users. In other words, they characterise a fundamental **shift in agency** from broadcast to content generation, a decentralisation of resource provision and, as the Wikipedia entry on Web 2, dated March 23, 2007 suggests (http://en.wikipedia.org /wiki/Web_2), an enhanced organisation and categorisation of content with an emphasis on 'deeplinking.' The shift in agency is also one of user-led media content consumption, for example, with users increasingly selecting what information to access and what music and films to watch and when.

New generation digital technologies can also be characterised by a **new breed of users**. Bruns (2007, p. 3) refers to them as 'Generation C,' which, according to him, is best understood as a loose grouping of participants who share a set of common aims and practices around user-led content creation communities. They 'occupy a hybrid, user-*and*-producer position which can be described usefully as that of a *produser'* which can be seen to be characterised by the following:

Community-Based – produsage proceeds from the assumption that the community as a whole, if sufficiently large and varied, can contribute more than a closed team of producers, however qualified they may be.

-   Fluid Roles – produsers participate as is appropriate to their personal skills, interests, and knowledges; this changes as the produsage project proceeds.
-   Unfinished Artefacts – content artefacts in produsage projects are continually under development, and therefore always unfinished; their development follows evolutionary, iterative, palimpsestic paths.
-   Common Property, Individual Merit – contributors permit (non-commercial) community use, adaptation, and further development of their intellectual property, and are rewarded by the status capital they gain through this process. (Bruns, 2007, p. 4)

In short, the characteristics of (the effective use of) new digital technologies revolve around a combination of technology- and user-related factors. They all bring with them challenges for users in general, and those in educational contexts, be they formal or informal. One such challenge, for example, surrounds the physicality of the devices: due to their small size, the amount of data that can be displayed at any one time and the ease with which it can be manipulated is limited. They include:

Flexibility and portability: digital technologies are characterised by their relatively small size which makes them readily portable and, therefore, usable anywhere anytime. Increasingly, they offer connectivity and networking. Being digital, they allow resources to be easily modified, presented and re-presented according to changing needs and user groups.

Multifunctionality: mobile devices now normally feature more than one function. Whereas, only recently, separate devices were needed to listen to music, look at images and watch video, maintain a calendar and contact list, view computer files created by different software packages, read e-mails, view webpages etc., these functions are now readily available at affordable prices as single small devices. This characteristic includes availability on demand, as well as the creation of content 'on the fly,' i.e. in real time.

Multimodality: digital technologies allow content to be presented using a diverse range of systems of representation and a combination of different semiotic means of meaning-making. Digital video, for example, allows learners to create representations of themselves and the way they see and interact with the world, for example in the form of narratives or documentaries that are not based on traditional notions of textuality.

Nonlinearity: hyperlinking, i.e. the ability to break up sequential ordering of information/pages/screens and allow lateral connections intra- and intertextually, between related as well as unrelated documents/artefacts, allows for unprecedented levels of interconnectedness and possible synergies.

Interactivity and communicative potential: mobile devices allow for new forms of creative relations between people on the basis of reciprocity and negotiation, in writing and in speech, in real time (synchronously) or delayed (asynchronously). Exchanges can be recorded, stored and analysed post hoc; overcoming the ephemerality hitherto of spoken interactions. Communication between a number of interlocutors can occur concurrently and multi-directionally, with different conversational fragments being interwoven.

There are larger level social consequences. Digital technologies and their affordance have a significant socio-cultural impact which we want to allude to by raising some questions even if we do not provide answers to them here. In particular, the question needs to be asked to what extent they can, or already have, become a prosthesis for some users and what their impact is on notions of the self and society. To what extent do, can and should they govern the way in which we perceive and apperceive the world around us? What is the impact of the (seeming?) fracturing of the self into multiple identities as well as the membership of a wide range of user groups and communities of practice? How important for notions of society is the lack of shared cultural experiences as a consequence of a move away from a centrally determined broadcast contents and media of transmission and the move towards a 'distributed' culture and a model of knowledge assembly? What of the increased fragmentation of mainstream culture into scenes, and the sub-cultures of life styles, each with their own practices? Or what of the individualisation of social and cultural experiences on the basis of the principles of bricolage?

Here we mention just two such issues:

(Meta-)Collaboration: closely related to the communicative potential of digital technologies is the capability of collaboration with others across traditional barriers of place, peer/age/interest/professional groups, social strata etc. 'Meta-collaboration,' understood as effective and successful membership of 'Generation C' (Bruns, 2007, p. 8), includes the knowledge when, where, and with whom (not) to collaborate and to understand its consequences. This, Bruns (2007, p. 7), points out, requires a critical stance both towards potential collaborators and their output as well as towards one's own abilities and work.

Virtuality and hyper-reality: widely used metaphors in the discussion of ubiquitous technology are 'virtuality' and 'hyper-reality'; yet, their use is rarely problematised and their meanings seldom defined. A narrow dictionary definition of 'virtual' with reference to computing is 'not physically existing'; in the main, virtuality is normally used as a parallel reality to the physical world. In an interesting think-piece, McFarlane (2003) posits the following five 'rules' of virtuality:

– the uptake and use of new technologies depend crucially on local social contexts;
– the fears and risks associated with new technology are unevenly socially distributed;
– virtual technology supplements rather than substitutes for real activities;
– the more virtual, the more real; and
– the more global, the more local.

In short, notions of virtual realities are problematical and can't be seen as existing divorced from the here and now. The use of digital technologies does not transport oneself into another world, rather it affects the world in which we live, work, learn, shop, seek entertainment, etc. Price (2007) expresses the potential of digital technologies to link to and interact with the physical world as 'augmentation.'

Beyond the Surface: What *Is* Learning?

At the moment, the list of prefixes available for the word 'learning' is a near endless one and it grows by the day: e-, m-, online-, ubiquitous-, life-long-, life-wide-, personalized-, virtual- etc. learning. The question is: why this sudden explosion of kinds of learning, what is it about? Many of the prefixes point to technology, whether as m- or as e-, as virtual- or online-. In view of the numerous characteristics discussed above, it might be good to ask whether any of these point to different *kinds* of learning? In the case of *life-wide* and *lifelong learning*, the prefix indicates sites and temporal extent; and with *ubiquitous* there seems the idea that conditions and opportunities for learning are boundless. It seems, in other words, that the issue is not a difference in *kinds* of learning, but in *conditions* and *environments*.

In this perspective, microlearning, the central issue in this volume, can be seen in a number of distinct ways. It links with our focus here on 'mobile learning,' in a focus on individuals and learning, on individual moments of learning – rather than a focus on larger environments of learning, or on policies and larger level practices around learning. And it links as dispersed learning activity in fast moving conditions and in mediated environments.

Learning, on the one hand, always occurs as a set of short-term learning activities and micro steps. On the other hand, the relations of these activities and their integration into patterns or schematas may be simple or complex, loosely structured or dense, with single- or multiple-loop characteristics, dealing with "pieces loosely joined" (D. Weinberger) always needing and producing meaningful contexts. Means for the creation of context (Sinnzusammenhang) and punctuation (Interpunktion) make a difference: we may speak of microlearning in the sense of a dispersed, concomitant learning process leading to all kinds of low level framing competence – or in the sense of new forms of aggregation or emergence of patterns, etc. (leading to new forms of high level framing competence).

Where in this do we also fit all the 'e-forms' in their various guises? Is there a difference in kind between *on-line* and *e-learning*? Or, a slightly different question: what exactly is 'virtual' about *virtual learning*? Are all these in fact descriptions of conditions and environments in which learning takes place, environments distinct enough to suggest a significant difference in the experience of learning, even if not a difference of kind?

One way to start may be to ask the simple question: 'so what *is* learning'? In answering, our approach is a semiotic one. That is, we see a very close connection between *meaning-making* and *learning*, in semiotic terms between the *making of signs* and the *making of concepts*. For us, both are the result of semiotic work: that is, purposive work with meaning-resources. Semiotic work produces change; change in semiotic resources produces meaning; so semiotic work produces meaning. Semiotic work changes the tools – the semiotic resources; it changes that which is worked on; and it changes the worker.

In the example just below (figures 1 and 2), we show two three-and-a-half year-old girls trying their hand at writing.

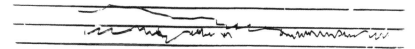

Figure 1. Alphabetic script

We think that each of the two examples is the result of semiotic work. Each is the result of an engagement with a salient aspect of the cultures of the two young writers. The contrast between the two shows that their 'writing' is a principled attempt – that is, an engagement on the basis of discernible principles – to understand the bases of the script systems of their cultures. Neither is mere scribbling, or simply incompetent imitation. In the case of 1 a) (some) of the principles might be: the elements of the script system are simple; they seem at times to be repeated; they are linked; they are produced in sequence; they are displayed on a line. In the case of the other, the principles might be: the elements of the script system are complex; they are not repeated, each differs from the other; they are not linked; they are produced in sequence; they are displayed on a line.

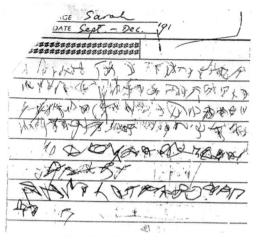

Figure 2. Character-based script

Our assumption is that the graphic work here represents meaning, in the way we have described it; the 'inner' resources of each of the two are changed as a result of this work (the evidence for that lies in the gradual change that can be discerned from this to the next instance, over time); the semiotic/conceptual resources of each of the makers of these signs is changed. In their work they have learned something about the script system of their culture: they have changed; and the resources they have for dealing with their cultural work also have changed.

In this view learning is change; it produces both a transformation of that which was encountered and of the learner; it is an augmentation of inner (conceptual) and outer semiotic resources.

Given our focus on conditions and environments of learning, we might ask a number of further questions, such as: *whose attention* was at issue here? That is, who decided that this should be attended to? *What* has been framed? *Who* has framed the world to be engaged with? In school, traditionally, the answer would be "well, the teacher has directed the attention of the children to this phenomenon." Out of school, the answer is "the children's own *interest* directed their attention." Teachers are likely to answer the question "what has been framed?" differently to children – in one case it would be an answer to a curricular question "what has been framed is the script system of the two cultures", "learning of writing", "a question of literacy." In the other, it is a question about fun, pleasure, genuine curiosity and puzzlement. Neither of the children might be aware of adult criteria: it is quite likely that both thought they were "drawing writing." In one case power is at the base of attention and framing, in the other case it is interest and pleasure. Agency, in one case, is that of the two three-and-a-half year olds; in the other case, agency is complex and mediated, from curricular authority to teacher to children. Of course, each has their own interpretation of their agency, and therefore each acts in distinct ways.

The question of "whose power is at issue?" seems one necessary starting point. It also provides a crucial point of 'completion,' in the sense of evaluation and assessment. Where official power of curricular authority is at issue, the principles of evaluation will be those of that authority. Relative degrees of success or failure will be assessed/measured in terms of the criteria of that authority. If the learners' power, their own interest is the starting point, then the principles of evaluation will be those of the learner. If that which has been made/drawn/written by each of them satisfies them, then their aim has been achieved. Official pedagogy (and its deeply entrenched common-sense derivatives) might not recognize that learning has taken place here: it is unlikely to have apt principles of recognition.

Here is one crucial point of attention for a general account of learning: the frame of institutional pedagogy is neither necessary nor necessarily most efficacious for learning. Institutional pedagogy has its special and important frames and contents, and principles of recognition of learning – or at least of behaviours which might be efficient in simulating what is expected as learning. In all learning these are the central issues: whose agenda is at work, with what power, with what principles of recognition of learning. How is that agenda presented and is it accepted or recognized by those who are potential learners. As 'learning' escapes the frames of institutional pedagogy – a matter in which the e-technologies are deeply implicated – these are questions of increasing importance.

We might note, in passing, that our assessment of the children's writing had been on the basis of *their* attention, *their* framing; and that our assessment of their learning had focussed on the principles which seemed at work in their engagement with the world.

The questions of "what is to be learned," "whose framing?," "whose power?," will increasingly come to the fore. The forces of the market push in the direction of individual agency in the choice of commodities – pedagogic or other. The current trend toward "personalized learning" is, of course, just one further response to that. We might note, simply in passing, that some of the inherent facilities/affordances of the e-technologies entirely support and sustain and even accelerate this trend.

Contemporary Environments of Learning and the Dilemma of the School

We might also note in passing that three questions might be useful to pose, in relation to current interests in learning: "what stays?", "what changes?" and "why?"

The dilemma for the school arises out of specific mixes of the factors we have so far mentioned. They are culture, technology, environments and (conceptions of) learning. Culture cannot be thought about other than in the presence of power, that is, in social environments. What society expects of 'its' education system of course shapes what 'the school' can and must do – at the moment at least, though that, as we pointed out, is changing. If the school has had the task of putting forward certain forms of knowledge and kinds of value, as the servant of the state and its economy, then there is now a clear disjunction between school and state, state and market, and market and school. No new accommodation is as yet in sight. The state pursues policies to favour the neo-liberal market, which pushes the school beyond its control. At the same time, the state attempts to use the school – as one of the remaining instruments under its control, to promulgate traditional values – relation to nationality/culture/ethnicity/ethics. The school has lost its two major supports: the unquestioned support of the state, and the promise of the reward of a (relatively) secure place in the productive economy.

All the time, digital technologies, which dominate the cultural and economic domain, urgently suggest the same potential for action as those of the market. If technologies are – in the end – culturally shaped tools to manage the world, then there is a close homology at the moment between the facilities offered by these technologies and the promises of the market. Dominant models of learning are provided by the seductive model of the freedom of the consumer in the market – unfettered up to the moment of truth at the checkout of the super-market. Yet there is also truth in the model, for those, at least, who are in possession of the necessary wherewithal at the checkout. The two lies of the model – one, the harsh reality of the checkout and the other, the less obtrusive reality of the near invisible limitations of the offer of commodities in the supermarket – "you may have everything you may wish for - from the things we make available to you" – do not deny or undercut agency: they simply confine it. If consumption is identity, then you may become any identity that combines the resources of the supermarket (of course constrained one more time by 'fashion,' the naturalization of convention). And if consumption is learning, then you may, as learner, engage with everything available to you *here*.

What this model does not supply is 'navigational aids,' that is, resources for making sense of this world of choice. What the model also does not supply is *knowledge*: it supplies 'stuff,' which individuals assemble in relation to their interests. This adds another point, the final one that we wish to make at this time, to notions of learning, and environments of learning and their effects. In the not-so-distant past the school had provided a curriculum which was much more than a set of things to learn, but was a set of tools which had utility in relation to the problems encountered in the social and economic world. It provided a curriculum of knowledge and of skills – that is, of tools for dealing with problems in a known world. As the world around the school has changed, so this curriculum has lost its utility: the world to which the school could provide answers is a world with different demands.

Learning and Technologies of Text-Making

Where before 'learning' had as one of its meanings 'the acquisition of knowledge relevant to issues encountered in the world,' now the individual is asked to shape *their* knowledge out of *their* own sense of *their* world:

> Information is material which is selected by individuals to be transformed by them into knowledge to solve a problem in their life-world. (Böck, 2004)

The demand made of individuals in the market-dominated society is nothing short of that of developing a new habitus of learning. What it amounts to is constantly to see the life-world of the individual framed both as challenge and as an environment and a potential resource for learning. In the article from which we have taken the quote just above, the author speaks of a fundamental change in what she calls 'information habitus,' that is, from a habitus where the individual could rely on 'authorities' of the relevant kind to bring information and knowledge to them (what she terms '*Bring-schuld,*' that is, the authority had the responsibility to bring knowledge to the individual), to one in which the individual is now responsible for obtaining and shaping that knowledge for themselves (what she terms 'Hol-schuld,' that is, an obligation resting with the individual to obtain information/knowledge for themselves). Her concepts are based on an extensive and detailed ethnographic account of a geographically marginal community in Upper Austria, where she found a distinct difference in terms of this habitus. Importantly, the difference was not so much one that could readily be described in larger level terms such as *class* or *generation*; rather these were *dispositional* differences which could only be tracked through micro-historical accounts of the individuals concerned.

These differences are apparent in forms of texts and in modes of text-production, themselves related to the factors so far mentioned, though also, importantly, to technologies of text-making and to technologies of (text) dissemination.

The point can best be made through examples. Figures 3 and 4 show book pages from a book first published in 1926 (*The Boy Electrician)* and one from the later 1990s (a Dorling & Kindersley book *Fossils,* Taylor, 2000) respectively, that is, a change in the form and meaning of pages over a period of eighty years, in which one settled form of representation has been definitively overtaken by a new, deeply different one. It is also the period during which the social and economic changes we have been describing have been taking place.

Figure 3. The boy electrician

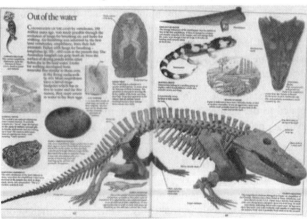

Figure 4. Eyewitness: Fossils

There are two points that we wish to make in relation to these texts: one is around the relation of *author and reader*, and the other is around the issue of *medium and 'site of display.'* Other factors – such as the shifts over the more recent decade in use of image and writing – have a fundamental effect, though we will not discuss that here. In the first example, we have a clear example of 'Bring-schuld': the author has assembled 'knowledge' about electricity, which will be interesting and above all helpful to young boys in experimenting with the kinds of things they make.

That is the author's task; the reader's task is to follow the *order* of the author's setting out of this knowledge. *Order* – as *reading path* – is designed into the text: the order of reading, from line, to syntax, to paragraph, to chapter. *Reading against* the order designed into the text is not possible, unless one has no interest in understanding the text the author produced. The '*site of display*' does not seem to be an issue; though when we turn to the Dorling & Kindersley book it becomes clear what the issue is: the double-page spread determines not just the layout but the content of this book-segment (not now a chapter). That is, a matter of display affects a matter of content. With the book from the 1920s, it is the other way around: content determines length of chapter, as well as the distribution of images within the written text. The profound change illustrated here, in the Dorling & Kindersley text, is that of a change in *order* and in *who determines order*. Here the reading path is not firmly fixed, indeed really not fixed at all. It is the reader's interest which determines the order in which the page will be engaged with; 'read.' In effect, readers design their own ordering of the page; and to the extent that readers' interests differ, the page offers the potential of different distinct 'designs' – e.g., writing first, image second; or, large image first, smaller images second; or, etc.

What we have here is a transition from a stable, settled world, of knowledge produced by authority/authors, to a world of instability, flux, of knowledge produced by the individual in her or his life world, out of resources available to her or him, and in relation to both needs and interests that come from the reader's life-world.

From the perspective of 'mobility,' we might say that the former world was *im*mobile – at least relatively speaking – while the present world has become highly mobile. Here *mobility* resides in respect to *who* produces knowledge and *how*. The move from *reading* to *design* is a move from a world in which the text is an authoritative source of knowledge to one in which the text is treated as a *resource*, available for the reader's production of knowledge.

From one perspective, a text had traditionally been a settled and coherent projection/account of knowledge about a framed aspect of the world, produced by the figure of the author. Contemporary forms of text, by contrast, are dynamic, fluid, and above all, *contingent*; they are ever more frequently multiply authored, with 'shared'/ distributed power and consequently *provisional*. In their form, they realize contemporary forms of social organization: of *distributed* resources, *distributed* information, *distributed* power, *distributed* across life-worlds organized as life-style. The new social arrangements find their realization in new genres we mentioned above: blogs, wikis, and so on. A world of stability has given way to a world of fluidity; a world of the power of the author has given way to a world of collaborative text-making; and a world of canonicity – whether of knowledge or of text – has given way to a world of provisionality.

That is the larger environment in which we think the issue of *mobility* has to be considered.

'*Mobile* Learning' as an Example of Digital Learning: Hunting-isms

Our discussion so far has in part been an attempt to show that *mobility* is a feature of the contemporary social, political, economic, political and *technological* world. It is by no means a feature of the latter alone; and in our view it would lead to an entirely misleading analysis of the effects of technology to think otherwise. Younger readers of printed texts treat them as resources: they take upon themselves the right to act in a highly mobile fashion in relation to them – and that applies not only to the D&K texts, but for them, to all texts. So several questions pose themselves around *mobility*: 'who is mobile?' and 'what is mobile?' If we do not see the widespread mobility every-where, we will certainly misdiagnose mobility in relation to digital media.

In 'mobile learning' we have, first of all, individuals who have the new habitus of learning (never mind the existence of devices which had provided relative mobility for learning – in museums, etc.) which we have described above. A part of the develop-ment of that habitus is that those who 'have' it are accustomed to immediate access to the world (to be) framed and that it should be ubiquitously available. *Ubiquitous access* to resources for learning assumes an attitude to the world where all of the world is always already curricularized, everywhere. The habitus has made and then left the individual constantly mobile – which does not refer, necessarily, to a physical mobility at all but to a constant expectancy, a state of *contingency*, of *incompletion*, of moving toward completion, of waiting to be met and 'made full.' The answer to 'who is mo-bile?' is therefore 'everyone who inhabits the new habitus.' Given the new learning habitus, the answer to 'what is mobile?' is then 'all the world.' All the world has be-come the curriculum; the world itself has become curricularized. The habitus of the individual for whom all the world is always already seen as a curriculum, becomes shaped by that experience and expectation: always expecting and ready to be a 'learner.'

The development of devices for 'mobile learning' rely on the existence of a habitus of mobility, provisionality, fluidity, etc. That which is 'mobile' is *not* knowledge or in-formation, but is the individual's habitus: whether I am out in the country-side, in my bed, or in a classroom is, relatively speaking, beside the point. What is NOT beside the point is the ability to bring things into conjunction which might previously have been relatively difficult to join. An instance of this might be data-logging. I take a device with me somewhere. On the device forms of information can be recorded (or it may be (pre-)specialized to the recording/coding of information). I record the information in the manner enabled by the device. The site to which I have gone has been turned from 'a field' or 'a meadow' into a science classroom. I have taken my (budding) habitus as scientist into the field together with a device that conveniently enables me to 'log' in-formation. When I left the school to go to the meadow or when I return to school, say, I have in fact not left a site of learning: I have turned the environment in which I am, whatever it may be and wherever I may be, into a site of learning

We might leave the issue there, except for one thing: to return briefly to the questions of attention, framing, engagement and of assessment. While in principle all the world may be becoming curricularized, the environments of learning will still vary from time to time, depending on the individual, their position, etc. And so the environments of/for learning will vary: from those where power is still exercised in traditional ways to those where the learner has the power to decide (and the responsibility for the effect of the decision); where framings of the world are determined by others or by oneself; curricula set by others for their purposes, and forms of assessment determined by the power of others or by the individual. For the time being, there will be a 'mixed economy' of pedagogy and learning.

A Few (and Troubling) Questions

Given the wider and dominant social conditions, digital technologies have the potential to place me, as learner, at the centre of the world. One might ask 'what gain?' and equally one might ask 'what loss?' In the societies which we have known, and which seem to be involved in a relentless process of deconstruction, a common curriculum provided one major resource for community – in part what we have described as the educational project of the nation state. When all those who attended school had access to the same knowledge, then even those who rejected it in any one of many different ways had been through a process of engagement and rejection: the curriculum had provided a common agenda of knowledge, values, skills, dispositions: the essential resources of 'community.' Personalized learning, with a personalized curriculum, can, in that context, be seen as the end-point of the neo-liberal project of the destruction of community. Of course it can also be seen as the triumph of individuality. The question is: 'what place for community?'

We might also ask about the effect on individual habitus of a curricularized world, a world seen in terms of occasions and resources for learning. Where are the sites of difference, from which entirely different perspectives open up? Where are the opportunities for (seeming) down-time? And where are the times for reflection? In the world of insistently urgent choice of a pedagogic market, where is the time to opt out? In a period of increasing speed, where is the time for slowness?

We might, in that context, wish to argue for a concern with rhythm, an alternation of pace, the slow and the speeded up, and each for its purpose. We definitely need to ask whether the task for us is that of adaptation of ourselves to technologies (including the social technologies we described earlier) or whether the urgent task is a careful consideration of the utility in a wide range of ways of our adoption of technologies for considered purposes. In a period of speed, we might wish to make a plea in praise of slowness.

References

Böck, M. (2004): Family snaps: life worlds and information habitus. *Journal of Visual Communication*, 3(3), pp. 281–293.

Bruce, B. & Hogan, M. (1998) The disappearance of technology: toward an ecological model of literacy. In: Reinking, D. et al. eds. *Handbook of literacy and technology: transformations in a post-typographic world.* Mahwah, NJ: Lawrence Erlbaum Associates, pp. 269–81. Also available from: <http://www.isrl.uiuc.edu/~chip/pubs/ disappearance.shtml> [Accessed 5 May 2007].

Bruns, A. (2007) Beyond difference: reconfiguring education for the user-led age. Paper presented at ICE3: Ideas in Cyberspace Education: Digital Difference. Ross Priory, Loch Lomond, March 21-23. Available from: <http://snurb.info/> [Accessed 5 May 2007].

McFarlane, A. (2003) *Alone together – learning in Higher Education.* Keynote given at Beyond Theory, Oxford Union Debating Chamber, April 11. Available from <http://www. oucs.ox.ac.uk/ltg/events/beyondnew/transcripts.html> [Accessed 5 May 2007].

Oliver, M. (2005) The problem with affordance. *E-learning*, 2(4), pp. 402–413.

Price, S. (2007) Ubiquitous computing: digital augmentation and learning. In: Pachler, N. ed. *M-learning: towards a research agenda.* WLE Centre Occasional Papers in Work-based Learning 1. London: Institute of Education.

Sims, J. W. (1946) *The boy Electrician.* London: Morrison & Gibb. Also available from: <http://rawfire.torche.com/~opcom/tbe/the_boy_electrician.pdf> [Accessed 5 May 2007].

Taylor, P. (2000) *Eyewitness: fossils.* London: Dorling Kindersley.

Lurking as Microlearning in Virtual Communities.
An Explorative Analysis of Changing Information Behavior

Nina Kahnwald

1   New Concepts of Networked Learning

In his paper "E-Learning 2.0," Stephen Downes claims that during the last several years, e-learning at large developed further together with the world wide web to an extent that requires new terms and models for analytical description. A closer look at discussions and publications of the last several years reveals a number of approaches and concepts that aim at modeling actual media use. Three of them will be summarized in the following chapter.

2   E-Learning 2.0

The term "E-Learning 2.0" was chosen by Downes in analogy to the buzzword "Web 2.0" that summarizes platforms, applications and services that enable users to easily create, share and connect content on the web (e.g., social networking sites, blogs, wikis,...) which is thus continually transformed from the so-called Read-Web to a Read-Write-Web. Although "Web 2.0" is about technological development, the most fundamental changes occur at the level of internet users, who as "digital natives" (Prensky, 2001) developed new approaches to learning, working and gaming online:

> They absorb information quickly, (...) from multiple sources, (...) expecting instant responses and feedback. They prefer random 'on-demand' access to media and expect to be in constant communication (...). (Prensky, 2001)

At its core, "Web 2.0" is based on participation, content-creation and personalization. Against this background, the term "E-Learning 2.0" is chosen by Downes, to adequately describe a range of analogous approaches and developments in the field of e-learning.

In contrast to the currently prevailing learning platforms with prestructured, linear learning paths, Downes anticipates the e-learning-application of the future to be a learning environment with several interoperating applications. This environment acts as a node in a web of content and supports learners by contextual collaboration with people and systems. This vision of future e-learning is, among other things, based on the learn-theoretical approach of connectivism, which is getting more and more influential since its first publication in 2004 by George Siemens.

3   Connectivism

In the article "Connectivism: A Learning Theory for the Digital Age," Siemens claims that the three main learning theories, behaviorism, cognitivism and constructivism, can no longer be used to adequately describe and analyse learning processes, or develop learning environments, considering the radical changes of the last 20 years. He emphasizes the necessity of a fundamentally new perspective on learning:

"Many important questions are raised when established learning theories are seen through technology. The natural attempt of theorists is to continue to revise and evolve theories as conditions change. At some point, however, the underlying conditions have altered so significantly, that further modification is no longer sensible. An entirely new approach is needed." (Siemens, 2004)

Technological development, that brings with it a reorganization of living, communicating and learning as well as the shrinking half-life of knowledge, leads to a change of learning processes. Some significant trends are:

- Informal learning is gaining more importance as learning occurs through communities of practice, personal networks or completion of work-related tasks;
- Technological tools are altering and shaping the way we are thinking;
- (cognitive) processes can be supported or taken over by technology;
- Know-where is getting more important than know-how or know-what.

The starting point of connectivism is the individual, but learning is no longer considered to be an internal, individualistic activity. Rather, it is becoming a core competency, to connect to specialized nodes, or information sources, when individual knowledge at the point of application is not sufficient. In this way, access to what is needed is getting more important than the knowledge currently possessed. As we can no longer personally experience and acquire all learning that is needed to act, competence has to be derived from forming connections. To facilitate continual learning, it is necessary to create and maintain multiple connections. From a connectivist point of view, learning is a process of connecting specialised nodes, or information sources, and may also reside in non-human appliances.

4   Microlearning

The term microlearning is not so much a clearly structured concept, but "a metaphor referring to a set of models of learning" (Hug, 2006, p. 3). Microlearning is understood as learning of microcontent, or acquisition of microknowledge (Langreiter & Bolka, 2005, p. 1). In contrast to connectivism, microlearning is rather an integrative perspective that concentrates on structuring and syndication of information. The focus is on the learning individual, and although microlearning includes informal learning, it has been mainly applied to model formal contexts.

The concept of microlearning is trying to provide forms of teaching and learning that comply with the demands of the information society, like highly specialized knowledge work, information-overload and lifelong learning (Bruck, 2005, p. 1), by focusing on dealing with large amounts of information and continuing integrated learning processes. Although there doesn't exist a precise definition of microlearning, its different forms can be analysed through the interaction of several dimensions (Hug, 2006, p. 3).

In the context of virtual communities, microlearning denotes spontaneous, informal and rather short learning- or information-activities, that connect to other social knowledge-sources via the Internet. The shift to microlearning is characterised by the following three aspects (Bruck, 2006, p. 15):

- Creation of new architectures of information through reduction of information abundance and complexity as well as structuring in small units.
- Reduction of information from the perspective of the individual that has to cope with large amounts of new information and wants to learn. This requires new didactic models.
- Development and use of technologies to support learners in their individual habits and needs and offer personalised services to allow individuals to chose time, place and pace of learning.

Especially for the development of better support for individual information-habits, it is necessary to analyse in a first step individual needs and behaviour. As virtual communities are recognized as social learning and information spaces to which people quickly connect on demand, they are the obvious place for an analysis under the perspectives described in this chapter. In the focus of the following chapters is the theoretical foundation of an analysis of individual information-strategies and information-networks in social learning spaces.

5 Social Learning in Virtual Communities

Since the early days of the *Internet*, even before the invention of graphical browsers, its different services have been used for communication between locally separated people. Soon, the first virtual communities developed, like "The Well" (Whole Earth 'Lectronic Link), that Howard Rheingold analyses in his book *The Virtual Community* (Rheingold, 1993), giving a first description of the phenomenon of online communities. In the following years, it was intensively discussed among experts if community can develop and exist on the *Internet* at all, a question that has been answered in the affirmative today (Matzat, 2004). At the same time, virtual communities were identified and examined as places of collaborative learning and implemented in formal and informal contexts.

Theoretical background for this research was provided by the moderately constructivist approach of situated learning, which Wenger connected to the concept of communities of practice in 1998 (Wenger, 1998).

5.1   Situated Learning

At the end of the '80s, the assumptions of cognitivism in learning-theory were fundamentally questioned. This criticism was aimed mainly at the reduction of human behavior to cognitive information processing (Kerres, 2001, p. 74) without considering the context of action. Brown, Collins and Duguid criticised, for example, the common assumption of a

> "separation between knowing and doing, treating knowledge as an integral, self-sufficient substance, theoretically independent of the situations in which it is learned and used." (Brown, Collins & Duguid, 1989, p. 32)

Although different approaches of situated learning are connected through this fundamental criticism of the cognitive point of view, there is no comprehensive theory of situated learning, but different approaches using the same concept (Clases & Wehner, 2005, p. 563).

One of the main constructivist thoughts of situated learning is that concepts are neither right nor wrong, but merely more or less functional for certain situations. Like this, knowledge is closely connected to experienced situations, it kind of indicates the situation in which it was acquired and used. The term "situated," which was already used by Mead (1934), was taken up again in the '80s in the context of artificial intelligence-research (Winograd & Flores, 1986) and then referred to situated human action (Suchman, 1987).

5.2   Communities of Practice

From a situated perspective, learning can only take place in connection to authentic action, which in this context designates that action is embedded in a culture, ("ordinary practices of the culture" Brown, Collins & Duguid, p. 34), contrary to scholarly action with symbols (Lave, 1988). Because functional knowledge can only be acquired in interaction with the social and physical context, processes of social participation have a key function for the learning process. Thus it is no surprise that already in the context of early situated approaches, learning has been understood as enculturation into a community of practitioners (Geertz, 1983), a concept that has been developed further by Wenger and Lave under the term "Communities of Practice" (Lave & Wenger 1991).

In an interview, Wenger summarizes three central elements that constitute a CoP (see De Cagna, p. 7):

1 Domain: The members must have expertise in a common area ("domain"). In contrast to teams, CoPs are defined not by a common task, but by the shared interest in a topic.

2 Community: There must be a group of people, who interact with each other, develop ideas together and exchange experiences.

3 Practice: A further important element is a shared practice of the members, that is developed over time within the community, e.g., by together finding solutions for current problems.

The process of jointly defining meaning within a CoP is described by Wenger as a combination of participation and reification (Wenger, 1998, p. 55). While participation designates the comprehensive sharing of common practice, reification represents the process of the shared formalization of experience and/or abstract knowledge into artifacts of the Community. Over time, a commonly negotiated repertoire of abstractions, stories, tools, concepts, routines and procedures develops. Although CoPs in enterprises are increasingly created from the outside, they always are self-organized systems without a teacher role. The activities and topics of a CoP reflect the understanding of the individual members of relevant topics in their daily practice. CoPs represent a place of common learning: participants exchange ideas and best practices and together generate new knowledge, which in turn improves the individual practice of the participants.

5.3   Legitimate Peripheral Participation

The Community of Practice approach is based on the concept of situated learning. In their book *Situated Learning. Legitimate Peripheral Participation*, Lave & Wenger (1991) describe learning based on anthropological research as legitimate peripheral participation (lpP) in a CoP.

At the beginning of the learning process and in the state of lpP, the novice takes up a position at the fringe of the community. Free of the responsibility that full membership would bring, he participates only partly in common practice (described as peripherality), but at the same time has full access to the common practice of community members (legitimacy). The process of situated learning leads to the expert status and a full membership within the CoP and represents thereby also a process of cultivation. LpP thus describes the relationship between experts and novices and the process of growing into the community.

Lave and Wenger indirectly take on Wygotsky's concept of support in a zone of next development: learning is being facilitated through participation in the practice of experts, who already are in an advanced zone of development.

The learning motivation of the participants arises from the desire for intensified sharing of common practice, as well as for its improvement. Only through this shared practice can learning objects become important for the individual (see Arnold, p. 80). It has to be taken into account that frequently it is not, as generally presumed, the exchange with the experts that is most efficient, but rather the exchange with other novices (Lave & Wenger, 1991, p. 93).

Naturally, the learning process is not finished after developing expertise. The introduction of novices is, as Wenger points out, only a variation of the learning process that also defines the later advancement of the shared practice by the community members (Wenger, 1998, p.102).

6   Community-Research Revisited

Wenger (2000) distinguishes five different levels of participation in communities of practice (see figure 1).

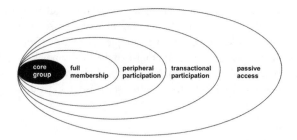

Figure 1. Participation levels (Wenger, 2000, p. 219)

Discussion of situated learning processes of enculturation described above only includes the three participation levels shown on the left side. The levels of passive access (access to artefacts produced by the community, e.g., archives) and transactional participation (outsiders who interact occasionally to receive or provide a service) are hardly ever considered, especially not in terms of learning. Even peripheral participation is not researched very often, as community-studies mostly focus on learning processes of active participants and full members.

This is why, as Stegbauer (1999) observes, community-research often provides a distorted picture of actual community use, because access by these peripheral groups constitutes a large part of community usage, but is rarely considered nor supported on this note.

6.1   Lurkers – the Neglected Majority

Those users of virtual web-based communities who read messages of other users but either do not, or rarely do post messages themselves, are commonly referred to as lurkers. Lurking-behaviour is a mass phenomenon, as lurkers are, in most cases, the majority of users in mailing lists and message boards. Estimations run up to a lurker-poster-relationship of 100:1 (Carroll & Rosson, 1996). A survey of a large business consultancy in Chicago indicated that 98% of the visitors of large online message boards (e.g., AOL and MSN) never posted any of their own ideas or messages (Katz, 1999). Other researchers found an average lurking rate of 46% in health-related boards and 82% in mailinglists about software support (Nonnecke et al., 2000), respectively a rate of 52% lurkers that read postings and 6.2 % that never read postings of active members (Soroka, 2003).

Given the prevalence of lurking in virtual communities, behavior, strategies and motivations of this user group are rather sparsely investigated. In publications about virtual communities, there are mostly only posters viewed as community-members. Lurkers are hardly ever explicitly examined, although according to the concept of legitimate peripheral participation, they are supposed to represent an especially active group where learning is concerned. This reluctance can probably at least partly be explained with methodological problems that occur when researching "invisible" lurkers. For this reason, it is mostly research about lurking in mailinglists, as in these cases it is at least possible to gain information about numbers of subscribers, which is much harder in the case of message-boards. But without analysing logfiles, it is also hard to tell whether, in mailinglists, subscribers ever read postings of others at all (Soroka, 2003).

Another problem when researching the phenomenon of lurking is that it's not easy to find a clear definition. Some authors, for instance, also define transactional (Wenger, 2000) community-members, who are posting seldom or only sporadically, as lurkers (Nonnecke, 2000; Rafaeli, 2004). This example shows that it is impossible to establish fixed classifications of lurkers and posters, as they can neither cover changes in time nor in individual behaviour in different lists. In addition, it is, in most cases, not possible to confirm if members are sending side-posts, i.e. messages directly send to other listmembers. The phenomenon of lurkers sending side-posts is described by Katz, who analyses differences between public and private reactions to his postings and articles (Katz, 1998).

6.2   Perspectives on Lurking

In many cases, lurkers are viewed in a rather depreciatory way. In a discussion about the subject in the virtual community, "The Well," which was described by Rheingold (1993), one poster claimed that lurkers should pay more for their Internet connection than active members. The appraisal expressed here, that lurkers are supplying themselves with information at the expense of the community, is expressed not only by active community members, but also regarded as reason for lurking by numerous researchers.

Schönberger (1998), for instance, holds the opinion that lurkers are merely wasting bandwidth. Furthermore, not only Kollock and Smith (1996), but also Wellman and

Gulia (1999), as well as Morris and Ogan (1996), defame lurkers as free-riders. Beside this basically rather negative view, lurking is often advised to newcomers in virtual communities, to help them get to know rules, conventions and topics of the community before actively participating themselves (see Stegbauer & Rausch, 2001, p. 49). This strategy corresponds to the concept of legitimate peripheral participation in communities of practice, according to Lave and Wenger (1991). Empirically validated was the approval of so-called educational lurking through a study, according to which 64% of the members of educational and 71.5% of health support communities are considering it important to allow and accept lurking (Abras, 2003). In addition, posters' feelings of resentment against lurkers seem to be less distinct than the above-mentioned negative connotations assume (Nonnecke, 2004).

Views on the phenomenon of lurking are ambivalent – an observation that also proves to be true for scientific discussion. Rafaeli summarizes the conflicting approaches to lurking from the perspective of the community as follows:

> On one hand lurking is a way of getting to know the community and becoming an integral part of it [...]. On the other hand lurking is seen as a negative behaviour that can jeopardize communities' existence. Free-riding can cause a "tragedy of the commons" [...]. (Rafaeli, 2004, p. 3)

It is noticeable, as already mentioned, that even in the scientific community, a negative view of lurking prevails. In this context, lurking is primarily viewed from an e-business-perspective, i.e. the perspective of community operators. Nevertheless, in recent years there has been a continual change to the perception of lurking as legitimate strategy to be taken seriously (see also Nonnecke & Preece, 2004):

> We used to think that we should encourage all community members to participate equally. But because people have different levels of interest in the community, this expectation is unrealistic. (Wenger, McDermott & Snyder, 2002, p. 55)

Despite this trend, the aim and focus of most research remains at least implicitly the process of so-called delurking, which means the development from lurker to active participant, i.e. poster (see Nonnecke, 2004). In many cases, the results are merged to recommended measures to better support the development from lurker to poster (e.g., Soroka, 2003).

The described conflicting perspectives towards lurking will, in the following, be examined closer from a pedagogical perspective. This examination is led by the assumption that through a change of perspective, the reproach of free-riding can offer an alternative view on individual strategies of informal learning of lurkers. We assume that learning activities identified in this context can be matched and explained with the concepts of networked learning introduced above.

6.2.1 Lurking as Legitimate Peripheral Participation

The notion, that lurking is an important developmental stage while integrating into a virtual community, will be designated in the following as a developing perspective.

Theoretically, it is based on the concept of situated learning through legitimate peripheral participation by Lave and Wenger. Also in the context of community-building, different development stages of the community are conceptualized according to the shift from lurker to core member on the individual level. Reichelt, for example, identifies three steps of community-development: entry, participation and emancipation. While in the first phase, input is mainly given by the operators, community-members continually learn to operate the platform themselves and begin to form a social network that leads to a self-organised community of emancipated members (Reichelt, 2004, pp. 72). The assumption that active participation in a virtual community of practice is preceded by a phase of passive observation is self-evident and it applies in many cases. But there are also findings that contradict the general applicability of this model, like a recent survey showing that a core of active community-members participates from the beginning and does not necessarily need to go through a process of activation (Zinke et.al., 2004). Soroka found that the time span of lurking prior to the first posting had no influence on users' future participation behaviour (Soroka, 2003, p. 10). Also, the analysis of Stegbauer shows that the first posting was, in most cases, sent after a relatively short period of passive membership. The likelihood for inactive participants to become active was already minimized after four months. Of the new subscribers during the period of data collection, only 30% became active posters (Stegbauer, 2000, p. 123).

It can be summarized that the concept of legitimate peripheral participation is applicable to learning processes of lurkers in virtual communities. But it cannot be used to exhaustively describe and explain the mass phenomenon of lurking, as lurking appears to be less a phenomenon of transition, but rather a durable pattern of behaviour.

6.2.2 Lurking as Microlearning

As an alternative to the developing perspective, one might re-evaluate the accusation of free-riding raised by the community to facilitate a different perspective on the lurkers' individual informational strategies. This perspective will in the following be called informational perspective. With this perspective, lurking can be seen as a legitimate and – probably – very efficient informational behaviour. As has been said earlier, this perspective is being supported in research to an increasing degree (e.g., Nonnecke & Preece, 2004). For the examination of this perspective it is not sufficient anymore to use the earlier described paradigm of enculturation, which has been transferred from offline- to online-cultures as the strategies of information enabled by digital networking seem to possess new qualities.

Concerning the reproach of free-riding, there are numerous approaches and arguments that emphasize the social function of lurking for the community, e.g., bridging to other communities in the sense of weak ties (Stegbauer, 2000, Nonnecke et al., 2000), management of resources, which means the use of archives and faqs to keep inquiries low (Madanmohan, 2004) and the avoidance of information overload, which would be the result of intense contribution by all members (Stegbauer 1999, Rafaeli, 2004). But besides that, there exist also findings on the reasons for lurking which indicate that lurking supports individual strategies of information and learning.

Asked for the reasons for lurking, 54% responding lurkers in mailinglists stated that reading/browsing was enough, 13.2% had no intention to post from the beginning and the majority was looking for answers to questions they had (62%). Although not posting, 50% of the lurkers did profit from list-membership as expected (Nonnecke & Preece 2004). In a survey about reasons for using online-communities, the reason mentioned most often was to find solutions and answers for urgent problems and questions and to receive general suggestions and tips while discussion and debate with others was no reason for community use (Zinke & Fogolin, 2004). Aviv (2003) conducted a content-analysis in an informal message-board to study processes of knowledge construction and found that only simple questions were answered and that discussions never constituted processes of negotiation of meaning.

This summary of recent results regarding reasons for lurking shows that in many cases, learning is not necessarily connected to enculturation into the community, but that users are accessing archives or even posting some messages in order to quickly find needed information. The high percentage of lurking that occurs also depends on the special conditions of virtual communities. In many cases, for instance, it is much less costly to passively access archives of a virtual community or post a single question than to find experts for a face-to-face-meeting. Furthermore, virtual communities can be, according to Wellman (1999), characterized by their network-structure: people are no longer embedded in traditional, closely knit and binding face-to-face communities, but are moving through loosely connected, less binding and often changing networks that are nevertheless still supportive and sociable.

7   Conclusions and Further Research

Drawing on existing studies about user, and especially lurking, behavior, it could be shown that established concepts of informal learning in virtual communities are not suitable to grasp user behavior in all forms.

It can be assumed from the above presented research and considerations that by visiting, using and participating in different virtual social spaces, users create and maintain their individual informational environments to which they can connect on demand if acute problems or questions arise. Thus it appears adequate to view informational- and learning-strategies in virtual communities as microlearning from a connectivist perspective.

To further analyse individual strategies and behavior, explorative qualitative studies will be conducted by the authors. By using interviews for data-collection, it will furthermore be possible to draw a more complete picture of lurking behavior in different web-based environments than existing studies that mostly focus on mailing-lists. As informal learning in virtual social spaces is becoming more important, it is necessary to gain a deeper understanding about personal strategies of learning in virtual social spaces. Based on the empirical description and awareness of changing individual information behavior, it will become easier to develop adequate supportive educational scenarios.

References

Ahmed, S. & Fortier, A.-M. (2003) Re-imagining communities. In: *International Journal of Cultural Studies*, 6, (3), pp. 251–259.

Anderson, B. (1991) *Imagined Communities. Reflections on the Origin and Spread of Nationalism* (Revised Ed.). London/New York: Verso.

Abras C., Maloney-Krichmar D. & Preece J. (2003) Evaluating an online academic community: 'purpose' is the key. In: C. Sephanidis & J. Jacko eds. *Human-Computer Interaction, Theories and Practice*. Vol. 2, HCI International, Crete pp. 829–833.

Arnold, P. (2003) *Kooperatives Lernen im Internet. Qualitative Analyse einer Community of Practice im Fernstudium*. Münster: Waxmann.

Aviv, R., Erlich, Z., Ravid, G. & Geva, A. (2003) *Network analysis of knowledge construction in asynchronous learning networks*. Available from: <http://www.ravid.org/gilad/avivHaifa.pdf> [Accessed 20 November 2006].

Brown, J. R., Collins, A. & Duguid, P. (1989) Situated cognition and the culture of learning. *Educational Researcher*, 18 (1), pp. 32–42.

Bruck, P. A. (2005) *Microlearning as strategic research field: An invitation to collaborate*. Available from: <http://www.microlearning.org/micropapers/MLproc_2005_bruck.pdf> [Accessed 20 February 2006].

Carroll, J.M. & Rosson, M.B. (1996) Developing the Blacksburg electronic village. *Communications of the ACM*, No. 39, pp. 69–74.

Clases, C. & Wehner, T. (2005) Situiertes Lernen in Praxisgemeinschaften. Ein Forschungsgegenstand. In: Rauner, F. *Handbuch Berufsbildungsforschung* Bielefeld: Bertelsmann, pp. 562–568.

De Cagna, J. (2001) Tending the garden of knowledge: A look at communities of practice with Etienne Wenger. *Information Outlook*, No. 6, pp. 6–13.

Downes, S. (2005) *Are the basics of instructional design changing?*. Available from: <http://www.downes.ca/cgi-bin/page.cgi?db=post&q=crdate=1120241890&format=full> [Accessed 10 December 2005].

Downes, S. (2005) *E-Learning 2.0*. Available from: <http://www.elearnmag.org/subpage.cfm?section=articles&article=29-1> [Accessed 22 May 2006].

Hug, T. (2005) *Microlearning: a new pedagogical challenge* (Introductory Note) Available from: <http://www.microlearning.org/micropapers/MLproc_2005_hug.pdf> [Accessed 20 February 2006].

Katz, J. (1998) *Luring the lurkers.* Available from: <http://slashdot.org/features/98/12/28/1745252.shtml> [Accessed 15 April 2006].

Kerres, M. (2001) *Multimediale und telemediale Lernumgebungen.* München: Oldenbourg Verlag.

Kollock, P. & Smith, M. (1996) Managing the virtual commons: cooperation and conflict in computer communities. In: Herring, S. ed. *Computer-Mediated Communication: Linguistic, Social, and Cross-Cultural Perspectives.* John Benjamins, Amsterdam, pp. 109–128.

Langreiter, C. & Bolka, A. (2005) Snips & spaces: managing microlearning. In: Hug, T. et al. eds. *Microlearning: Emerging Concepts, Practices and Technologies after e-Learning.* Proceedings of Microlearning 05, Innsbruck, Innsbruck University Press.

Lave, J. & Wenger, E. (1991) *Situated Learning. Legitimate Peripheral Participation.* Cambridge, Cambridge University Press.

Madanmohan, T.R. & Navelkar, S. (2004) Roles and knowledge management in online technology communities: an ethnography study. *International Journal of Web Based Communities*, No. 1, pp. 71–89.

Matzat, U. (2004) *Cooperation and community on the Internet: past issues and present perspectives for theoretical-empirical Internet research.* Available from: <http://www.tue-tm-soc.nl/users/matzat/papers.htm> [Accessed 13 April 2005].

Mead, G.H. (1934) *Mind, Self and Society. From the Standpoint of a Social Behaviorist.* Chicago: Univ. of Chicago.

Morris, M. & Ogan, C. (1996) The Internet as mass medium. In: Newhagen, J. & Rafaeli, S. eds. *Journal of Computer Mediated Communication*, 1 (4).

Nonnecke, B. (2000) *Lurking in Email-Based Discussion Lists.* London, South Bank University.

Nonnecke, B. & Preece, J. (2000). *Lurker demographics: counting the silent.* Available from: <http://www.ifsm.umbc.edu/~preece/paper/13%20Nonnecke&PreeceCHIpaper_ACMnotic e.PDF> [Accessed 07 April 2006].

Nonnecke, B., Preece, J., Andrews, D. & Voutour, R. (2004) *Online lurkers tell why.* Available from: <http://www.ecademy.ch/ecademy/ecadpubli.nsf/BD003963CF2FDDFBC 1256F100025685E/$file/SIGEBZ05-1198.pdf> [Accessed 10 April 2006].

Prensky, M. (2006) *Digital natives, digital immigrants.* Available from: <http://www.marcprensky.com/writing/Prensky%20-%20Digital%20Natives,%20Digital% 20Immigrants%20-%20Part1.pdf> [Accessed 15 December 2005].

Rafaeli, S., Ravid, G. & Soroka, V. (2004) De-lurking in virtual communities: a social communication network approach to measuring the effects of social and cultural capital. *Proceedings of the 37th Hawaii International Conference on System Sciences (HICSS).* Los Alamitos, CA: IEEE Press.

Reichelt, W. (2004) Erfolgsbedingungen virtueller Lern- und Wissensgemeinschaften. In: *Online Communities – Chancen für informelles Lernen in der Arbeit.* Bonn: Bundesinstitut für Berufsbildung, pp. 71–89.

Rheingold, H. (1993) *The virtual community.* Available from: <http://www.rheingold.com/vc/book/> [Accessed 2 May 2006].

Schönberger, K. (1998) The making of the Internet. Befunde zur Wirkung und Bedeutung medialer Internetdiskurse. In: Rössler, P. ed. *Online-Kommunikation.* Wiesbaden: Opladen, pp. 65–84.

Siemens, G. (2004) *Connectivism: A learning theory for the digital age.* Available from: <http://www.elearnspace.org/Articles/connectivism.htm> [Accessed 12 October 2005].

Soroka, V., Jacovi, M., & Ur, S. (2003) We can see you: a study of communities' invisible people through ReachOut. In: Huysman, M., Wenger, E. & Wulf, V. eds. *Proceedings of International Conference on Communities and Technologies (C&T2003).* Norwell: Kluwer Academic Publishers, pp. 65–79.

Stegbauer, C. (2000) Die Rolle der Lurker in Mailinglisten. In: Ohly, P., Rahmstorf, G. & Sigel, A. eds. *Globalisierung und Wissensorganisation: Neue Aspekte für Wissen, Wissenschaft und Informationssysteme.* Würzburg, Ergon, pp. 119–129.

Stegbauer, C. & Rausch, A. (2001) Die schweigende Mehrheit – "Lurker" in internetbasierten Diskussionsforen. *Zeitschrift für Soziologie* No. 30, pp. 47–64.

Suchman, L. (1987) *Plans and Situated Actions: The Problem of Human-Machine Communication.* Cambridge: Cambridge University Press.

Wellman, B. (1999) *Networks in the Global Village: Life in Contemporary Communities.* Boulder: Westview Press.

Wellman, B., Gulia, M. (1997) *Net-Surfers dont ride alone: virtual communities as communities.* Available from: <http://www.chass.utoronto.ca/~wellman/publications/netsurfers/netsurfers.pdf> [Accessed 23 March 2006].

Wenger, E. (1998) *Communities of Practice: Learning, Meaning, Identity, Cambridge.* Cambridge: Cambridge University Press.

Wenger, E. (2000) Communities of practice. The structure of knowledge stewarding. In: Despres, C. *Knowledge Horizons: the Present and the Promise of Knowledge Management.* Boston: Butterworth-Heinemann, pp. 205–224.

Wenger, E., McDermott, R. & Snyder, W.M. (2002) *Cultivating Communities of Practice: A Guide to Managing Knowledge.* Harvard: Harvard Business School Press.

Winograd, T., Flores, F. (1987) *Understanding Computers and Cognition.* Boston: Addison-Wesley.

Zinke, G., Fogolin, A. & Jablonka, P. (2004) *Nutzung von Online-Communities für arbeitsplatznahes, informelles Lernen. Endbericht der Online-Befragung.* Bonn, Bundesinstitut für Berufsbildung (BIBB).

III Towards New Learning Spaces: Educational Technology, Games & Playful Approaches

Learning: The Creative Application of Illusions

Peter Krieg

> *Only those questions that are in principle undecidable,*
> *we can decide.*
> Heinz von Foerster[1]

> *It is wrong to think that the task of physics is*
> *to find out how Nature is.*
> *Physics concerns what we say about Nature.*
> Niels Bohr

This paper attempts to introduce a radical "relationist" vision of learning and knowledge, It challenges some traditional views about learning and knowing by demonstrating that they are illusions, while at the same time arguing that such illusions are useful and necessary. Such a contradictory and inconsistent concept may not be considered scientific in the strict sense of the word, but it could be helpful in a more praxeological approach to learning and education. The paper also proposes to describe learning as a compositive, synthetic and ontogenetic process of constructing knowledge from simulations. Microlearning is seen as an emerging application of such relational and generative concepts of learning with the help of new and emerging technologies, like relationist computers and generative computer games.

Certainty with Uncertainty

We are living in a continuous and fundamental condition of uncertainty. Certainty describes a state where all that exists is known in all its aspects and relations. If, for example, we deal with a system that is interconnected to other systems, certainty would require that we not only know all about the system in question, but also about all the others it is connected to, and thus influenced by. We furthermore would have to know all about the knowing system itself, how it makes distinctions, creates knowledge, how it remembers what it has known before, and, if it has evolved over time, all about the historical factors of this evolution, including its beginning states, etc. And finally, certainty would require that we can order all these variables into logical (causal) relationships based on axioms – in other words, integrate them into a consistent theory.

It is quite obvious that none of these requirements can ever be met for anything, not even for mathematics, as Kurt Gödel has demonstrated. In a dynamic universe, where

---

1   Heinz von Foerster (1994) *Ethics and second-order cybernetics.* Available from:
http://www.stanford.edu/group/SHR/4-2/text/foerster.html

light travels in time, we cannot even fully observe the present; we can only look into different and distant pasts. Indeed, the condition of uncertainty is the axiomatic condition of our existence.

So much for exact knowledge, we must conclude and consequently consider all knowledge as sheer illusion: the process of learning, in the sense of building or accumulating exact knowledge or truth is principally futile. In a philosophical sense, this can hardly be denied and many religions and philosophies, from Heraclites and Buddha to Vigo, Hume and Kant, more or less explicitly say or at least imply so. Nevertheless, the very reason why we can develop religions, philosophies and scientific theories in the first place, is precisely that paradox which I shall call the 'creative application of illusions': it is *because* we cannot escape uncertainty, *because* we can never know 'for sure' and *because* we cannot build certainty in a world of uncertainty – it is *because* of these fundamentally undecidable and uncertain conditions of our existence that we can make decisions, that we can learn, can know, can create order and can make predictions. If this sounds paradoxical, it is meant to do so.

Chaos with Order

Paradoxes arise in complex systems when different frames of reference ('logics') are applied at the same time. We are, in fact, living in such a paradoxical, polylogic world, where at least three universes continually intersect: in the 'natural' universe we exist physically as living, metabolizing, moving entities. In the other 'mental' universe of intuitive knowledge we exist in a 'virtual world' of simulations generated by interacting with the first. This universe has evolved together with our abilities to develop perception, and instinct. The third, exclusively human universe, consists of descriptions and communication and is based on our unique languaging abilities.

The first universe is just as it is. Its existence is all we can assume about it, because otherwise *we* ourselves would not exist and thus could not make such assumptions. We must assume that this universe is an evolving, chaotic, dynamic and interwoven whole of relations: there are no rules, no objects, no distinctions, no order, no systems that we could independently observe. Nothing can be assumed to repeat in this universe, nothing can be the same, all appears as a constant flux of relation.

Only in the second universe does order arise. Living beings are producing such order by making distinctions, creating causalities, building up expectations and making predictions. All living things base their orders on one very shaky, and in an evolving universe quite illusionary, principle: whatever happened before will happen again. To uphold this principle requires an important first step of ordering by categorizing distinctions into groups of sameness or similarity of events. Only then can we take the next step of recognizing the same and similar events and develop expectations of reoccurrence.

In a dynamic, evolving universe, both assumptions must be considered illusions. But they are very practical and useful illusions, allowing no less than the evolution of living beings. What sets us apart from the animal world and constitutes us as human beings (at least this is the axiomatic prior distinction we base our claim of difference on) is language. This third universe of language is "what we are talking about" when we speak. It is here that we use the notions of knowledge and learning, and it is here were we fall into most traps. The most severe of these traps is the belief that the orders we create in language reflect the order of the universe itself. As a consequence, we expect that knowledge and learning can be trusted and are promptly "fooled by randomness."[2] The formal language of mathematics has greatly contributed to this error.

Causality and Logic

"The invention of the laws of numbers was made on the base of an already established error: that there exist several things that are equal (but in fact, there is nothing equal to anything); at least that there exist things (in fact there is no such thing as "a thing"). The assumption of multitude always presupposes that there exists anything, occurring in multiplicity: but already here reigns the error, already here are we fictioning beings and entities that are non-existent." (Nietzsche)[3]

Based on the illusionary concept of the reoccurrence of similar or same events, living beings develop another concept: that of causality. Events are experienced together with other events. They tend to form neighbourhood patterns, in the form of clusters and chains of correlated events. By categorizing these patterns we can develop concepts of cause and effect and eventually of rules and natural laws. In language, these concepts can be formalized in rules of logic. Logic is nothing but the formalization of categories (A=A) interacting lawfully in causal orders. Now even before we have language, we already have constructed a second universe. The main difference between the two: the first is not directly accessible but only exists in the form of changing relations in our biological system (e.g., the nervous system, but not restricted to it). We can say that we "learned" something about this first universe by developing distinctions, expectations, descriptions, theories and logic strategies of behaviour in the second universe that can be tested in interaction with the first. This is not specifically human; all organisms base their operations and evolution on this principle.

Human language uniquely enables us to include and describe ourselves in the second universe, so we become both subjects and objects of a descriptive third universe. What we describe in this universe is also not the "world as it is" but rather as we perceive and model it in the second universe of our experience. We describe our own experi-

---

2   „Fooled by Randomness" is the title of an excellent book by Nassim Nicholas Taleb, a Wall Street financial trader and philosopher who has gained deep professional and human insights into the issue.
3   Nietzsche, Menschliches, Allzumenschliches, I, 19.

ence of something we assume to be an outside world. And the rules, regularities and causalities we seem to find are in fact rules, regularities and causalities projected onto our experience. Since human beings are quite similar, apart from the fact that we are all quite different, we can agree on common experiences as long as we can induce similar results in other human beings.

Language as Simulation

Language creates such a unique new quality that we can rightfully call it a third universe, because it allows us to free ourselves in this universe from the restrictions and limitations of the first and even the second: in language we can envision and describe ourselves in ways that are completely free from our biological and physical restraints. We can imagine ourselves as birds flying through the air, as fish diving into the deep sea, as astronauts travelling to the moon, or even as time travellers going forward or back in time. Probably best of all, we can develop empathy by projecting ourselves into others and create simulations of them.

Based on these mental simulations, we eventually can develop self-consciousness, make purposeful plans, evolve variable social systems and individual concepts of living, we can build airplanes, submarines and space ships. Not all of these mental concepts will be executable; some remain, at least for the time being, in the realm of pipe dreams or science fiction. But language has the capability to mentally simulate the second universe to such a degree of realism, that it can induce the same (or similar) relational changes and activities in our cognitive and senso-motoric systems as the direct interaction with the first would: we can laugh and cry by just reading a text, or listening to music, we can get sick by looking at gruesome photos and get angry when watching an 'insulting' cartoon. Language, and only language, creates the phenomenon of self-consciousness, reason and "free will," allowing us to make decisions, to develop theories and to enact strategies towards reaching wilfully defined goals.

When we talk about learning, we mostly talk about the universe of language and linguistic explanations, although learning is always coupled to the second universe and can be tested in the first by interacting with it. In order to provide the capabilities of creating a separate universe that can simulate a "real" one, language needs to build a bridge between complexity and simplicity, between randomness and determinism, chaos and order. Language constructs models of the world as metaphors. As a system of naming, it provides building blocks for a complex relational and compositive structure of concatenations of words. These concatenations of words are synthesized into sentences, utterances, messages, arguments, statements, etc. Words and their concatenations can be combined nearly arbitrarily (in the case of poetry), guided by few and simple rules. They are generated within conversational and cultural contexts that provide meaning, thus allowing more than one interpretation of each word and applying the same term in different contexts.

This ambivalence of natural language is not a restriction, as computer scientists seem to believe, who must rely on "formal" non-ambiguous languages, but a necessary condition for building bridges not only between different contexts, but also between different speakers and their different domains of experience. Metaphors, comparisons or synonyms provide interpretation 'overlaps' which are essential for communication between different speakers. We also unconsciously learn to understand how the other partner in dialog applies language to his experience and thus how to 'reach' him or her.

Synthesis and Analysis

Learning can be described as the ability to create viable models as metaphors of operations in an environment. Viable means here that the models are developed in an interactive construction and testing process, which can be described as a cyclical triadic process of integrating non-logic processes of experiencing by inductively, as well as intuitively, synthesizing categories of sameness from multitudes of similar, but never identical, experiences with a logic-analytical process of deducting from these synthesized categories. The third step can be described as a process of testing both non-logic and logic inferences by putting them into practice in interaction with whatever the first two have decided as being the 'environment,' or 'the world.' These triadic integrated processes are operating continually on a micro-level in an interaction of the third and second with the first universe. As a result, we develop microscopic modular building blocks of relations of sameness, causality and neighbourhood. Again relating and correlating these in ever higher next orders, we synthesize, simultaneously from the bottom up and the top down, a structure of expectations and strategies we call 'knowledge.'

Human knowledge is mainly about understanding and applying patterns of such relations. These relational patterns transcend their immediate context. For example, in a family we can observe certain relational patterns which we can also find not only in other families, but in other social organizations as well. Metaphors, correlations, connections, comparisons, similes, allegories or synonyms are extensively used to describe such relational patterns by relating them to patterns of other contexts. While such patterns of relations are continuously generated in a growing associative synaptic complex network, we continuously categorize them and synthesize hypotheses in order to imply order, regularity and rules. These allow us to make logical deductions, another important part of learning. We learn to consciously learn by reflecting these processes of combination and logic, of synthesis and analysis. They are not mutually exclusive opposites, but complimentary polarities allowing us to construct and unify a *virtual* universe of objects and relations which we call 'reality.' Although the rules in science are very strict about the admissible methods (e.g., "correlation does not imply causation") we generally and intuitively ignore such formal rules and rely instead on our experiences that naturally evolve into prejudices, intuitions and preferences. Since science does not provide a formal logical method to arrive at hypotheses, even the scientist must adopt the fuzzy road instead.[4] The first step is usually made by referring to an "object."

Relations Make Objects

Physical objects are usually described as dynamic yet stable relations of smaller particles. A human body, for example, is considered a stable aggregate of cells. But when we look at these smaller particles (like cells), we can see that they are also composed of stable relations of other particles, e.g., molecules. And these, in turn, are composed of stable relations of atoms. A closer look at atoms reveals the same pattern again, and so on, until we can find only pure relations. We can assume that objects, in general, 'emerge' as stabilities in a continuous flux of relations. The search for 'elementary particles' as the finite building blocks of objects has proven quite futile, so that even in physics today, these concepts are increasingly replaced by pure relationist concepts. If we consider relation to be the primary 'object,' we can gain a new understanding of the universe as a complex network of relations. But then again, one of the cornerstones of our knowledge, the object and its ontology, becomes dynamic and even fuzzy.

Networks and Trees

Thinking in relations and in networks of relations does not make things easier for learning, however, since one of the most useful and mind-soothing achievements that comes with objects is the hierarchy in which we can order them. Non-hierarchical complex networks do not usually show much order at all: we can produce them easily by just tracing and connecting things and events, their neighbourhoods, and their relations to other events. What we get is a growing cloud of links and nodes (as patterns of relations) without any order, but with a high degree of uncertainty and ambivalence. The order of logic looks different: in a graph, logic can be expressed as a hierarchical tree. The ultimate cause (axiom, proposition, prior distinction, hypothesis, theory, etc.) forms the root of the tree, and all branches and leaves have consistent and orderly layered relations based on the rules of logic (e.g., if-then dependency). Navigation in such a tree is simple and always defined. No such navigation is possible in a complex non-hierarchical network, unless each node is self-identifying (i.e. has a unique name) and self-connecting (knows its neighbours).

Language is such a network: words are names, and we only need a few rules (and some more exceptions …) to generate neighbours from words. Neighbourhoods of words form contexts, which in turn provide the link to meaning by relating to other

---

4   This makes the scientific method principally "incomplete,", because it has no formal scientific procedure to arrive at axioms. Religion, in turn, provides such axioms through various methods. This is the reason why the two do not really overlap. This insight is missing in most current discussions about the role of science and religion, including the "Intelligent Design" debate.

contexts which serve as metaphors. Language can be described as a self-organizing complex network of names (words). This description collides, however, with current mainstream theories of language based on deductible tree structures, which once seemed very appealing to computer linguists, since hierarchical tree structures are what computers can deal with.

Learning and Doing

Learning entails being increasingly able to navigate in a complex network of relations with some degree of certainty. We can do so by adding 'order,' i.e. by generating hierarchies (as categorizations) and rules (logic), by recognizing patterns of relations (similarities) and remembering, as well as selecting, operations (adaptation). This entire highly integrated process is essentially the process of evolution (variation and selection). Learning then is a process leading to better adaptation, it is not necessarily adaptation itself. As long as we survive, we are adapted, our survival being sufficient proof of adaptation. But we are never optimally adapted, only marginally. Accidents, failure, error, losses of income, illness and even death are always around the corner. Learning enables better adaptation by building order and certainty, but since nothing repeats in the exact way we experienced before, we never stop learning and adjusting what we learned earlier.

If we consider learning to be a permanent adaptive activity not only in our second (mental) universe but also in our third (linguistic) universe, we can better escape the traps of learning as a process of accumulating knowledge about the "real world." In fact, the first universe as "real world" has nothing to do with it at all. The theories we learn about it are principally wrong, because this world cannot be described by the rules that make up a logically consistent theory. Sir Karl Popper, for good reason, therefore distinguished only between theories that have not yet been falsified and those who already have been. A universe that is not accessible must be considered uncertain, random and indescribable by logic.

Only because this is the case, we can – as paradoxical as it may sound – create theories in a world where everything is uncertain, declare identity where everything is different, distinguish objects where everything is relation, make predictions where everything is random, pretend to be able to learn where we can never hold an absolute truth. Of course, by doing so we must be prepared to look like fools most of the time. But it takes a lot of intelligence to survive as a fool!

Language enables us to consciously learn to simulate and model ourselves, our environment and our actions in the universe of descriptions. In this universe, we can define goals and develop theories of learning, experiment with different methods and evaluate what we learned even before we apply it in the 'real world.' Although learning has, necessarily, a social aspect, since we exist in a social environment, as an evolutionary mechanism of optimizing adaptation, it is always and exclusively individual. Only individuals can learn, although groups of individuals can collectively exhibit as social behavior, for example, what their individuals have learned in the field of social cooperation with others.

As an individual cognitive process, learning cannot be biologically disconnected from other operations of our body. Learning depends on, and is always integrated and embedded in, our metabolism and senso-motoric activities. This integration can be consciously applied to make learning more effective and enduring. "Learning by doing," "On the job training," or learning by playing, are just some elementary approaches making use of this effect. Individual dialog integrated with application (interaction) seems to be the optimal learning situation, because it allows for individually supporting the student, as well as immediately providing feedback both from the instructor and from the environment.

As a mental simulation in language, however, learning is an operation of self-consciousness and as such can logically be completely separated and disconnected from our biology. The body-mind dichotomy, the doctrine of free will, but also the concept of knowledge are based on this seeming paradox.

Knowing and Believing

In an evolving universe of uncertainty, there can be no absolute truth or objective knowledge. Action, however, requires at least some assumptions that appear true enough to allow the individual to act. Whether we call it belief, conviction or knowledge, we need a trustworthy basis for action. This basis serves as axiom, root, or – quite literally – 'ground.' When we walk into a new room, we need to trust that the floor will not fall down under us and the ceiling will not collapse on us. If we did not have this trust, we could hardly move at all. The same is true for operations in language. During our lifetime, we continuously build up principles, generalizations and axioms as expectations that enable us to perform deductive reasoning. Even prejudice as 'pre-judgment' serves this purpose, and often enough serves it quite well.

Without such axiomatic expectations, logic and reason would be impossible and useless. We so transform a world of uncertainty and unpredictability into a world of order and stability, where predictions can be made, operations can be planned and actions performed without fear. We should be aware, and are often enough painfully reminded, that this order is never more than a fragile and illusionary construction, but as long as it proves viable it is 'true' enough to enable adaptation and survival in a given social and natural environment. Since this construction is made individually in the universe of language and is not predetermined by genetic evolution, it has infinite variability. The objective of learning, therefore, cannot be some imaginary 'absolute truth,' but to develop every individual's ability to create, variate and test such illusions in the form of viable axiomatic assumptions.

Objectivity and Subjectivity

Aximomatic assumptions can be called objective when they are widely accepted in communication. If we use the word 'objective' in this way, we refer to the fact that a certain assumption has stood the test of time and community. It has proven to be viable beyond the subjective experience of one individual, and thus can be generally and safely applied as a rule or even as a 'law of nature.' Such natural laws are no more, but also no less, than viable, "self evident", and thus generalized assumptions based on experience. They exist only in the world of language and description and cannot be claimed as being absolute laws of the natural world. But they can be tested in interactions with the world, and if they 'hold,' we rightfully accept them as laws – until some new observation and explanation appears and the old law is replaced by a new law or theory. Natural laws are first principles, and only if we hold such first principles as "irrefutable truths" and axioms, can we in fact apply logic, reason and rationality. In this sense, they are 'objective' and whatever can be deduced from them can be called 'objective,' as well, because it is based on, and can be logically traced back to, a first principle. Again, objectivity has no basis in the "world as such," but is a precondition for constructing worlds in which we can operate and communicate. Objectivity in this understanding does not refer to the object, but rather to the stability of the relations that generate it in our minds and languages. "Anything goes," but not everything works. Our ability to create concepts in the universe of language is unlimited. But we are responsible for whatever we create in language. If post-modern thinking does not emphasize this point, it can easily fall into the traps of positivism.

Rule and Choice

The acceptance of radical constructivist assumptions of reality, truth and objectivity as human linguistic constructions, therefore, does not require throwing out logic and giving up on first principles and axiomatic truths. It only means that we must take responsibility for our constructions. Since first principles and natural laws are only ontic and objective truths in the world of language and human consciousness, they represent choices. A choice is a decision we make, consciously or unconsciously, based on a value we attribute to something. Yet even the most fundamental choices that are so self-evident that we consider them natural laws can still be challenged. A very topical example is the axiom of human 'free will':

The ability to be self-conscious and thus able to make decisions, act reasonably and rationally in our own interest and based on our own individual will, constitutes the basic distinction by which we separate ourselves from the animal kingdom. "Free will" is the constitutive axiom of mankind. It is also the logic root of our elementary social doctrines: freedom, human rights and even of the concept of property, because human rights are based on the concept of self-ownership. So are the concepts of natural law, of justice and of solidarity as voluntary social relations. By negating these axioms, we do not contradict some "absolute truth," but an elementary human doctrine. There is nothing less "true" in any other doctrine, even if it allows for considering, and eventually treating, people as "sub-human," as creatures unfit for reasoning, rationality, self-consciousness, responsibility and freedom. This doctrine, too, is quite alive and well today, and we cannot criticize it on the grounds of truth, but only on the grounds of personal preference and, perhaps, utility. We can, however, ask whether denying the fundamental axiom of "free will" is not itself an act of free will.[5]

So while the establishment and upholding of 'objective' first principles is necessary for grounding our ethics, morals and social modes of interaction, none of these principles can claim to be an absolute truth.

Prediction and Speculation

We use models for understanding complex networks of relationships and to make predictions of "what comes next" and "what to do next." They ground our principally ungroundable expectations and predictions. In this sense, they are illusions, but useful and necessary illusions. Learning to construct models from the experience is the most illusionary, and at the same time, the most useful (as well as potentially most harmful) form of learning.

In a world of flux, prediction is essentially a form of speculation. We just cannot know whether events happen again as they happened before. We cannot model the past and expect it to repeat according to that model. Mathematical models are fundamentally static: based on incidental measurements, they describe a time series of momentary snapshots, of moments in time, and then try to find transformation rules to describe the path from one snapshot to the next.

Mathematicians measure different states and invent formulas based on differential equations to describe the changes between these states, so that the model somehow matches the curve of the time series of measurements. By extrapolating these states, based on the model and its equations into the future, they make predictions. It is quite easy to see that these predictions are completely dependent on the assumption that nothing new is introduced into the formula: no factors previously not identified, no values previously not measured, no relations previously not foreseen. Models are logically closed.

It was the early economists of the 18th and 19th centuries who first understood that the mathematical approach was neither sufficient nor useful for predicting complex social systems like an economy. It was they who first tried to describe complexity:

---

5   It could be argued that because it cannot be logically challenged, the doctrin of „free will" cannot be a scientific theory. In this case, it could be the prior distinction and common ground for both science and religion.

"Assuredly the degrees of the capacity, of the probity of men, those of the energy and the power of their passions, prejudices and habits, cannot possibly be estimated in numbers. It is the same as to the degrees of influence of certain institutions, or of certain functions, of the degrees of importance of certain establishments, of the degrees of difficulty of certain discoveries, of the degrees of utility of certain inventions, or of certain processes. I know that of these quantities, truly inappreciable and innumerable in all the rigour of the word, we seek and even attain to a certain point, in determining the limits, by means of number, of the frequency and extent of their effects; but I also know that in these effects which we are obliged to sum and number together as things perfectly similar, in order to deduce results, it is almost always and I may say always impossible to unravel the alterations and variations of concurrent causes, of influencing circumstances, and of a thousand essential considerations, so that we are necessitated to arrange together as similar a multitude of things very different, to arrive only at those preparatory results which are afterwards to lead to others which cannot fail to become entirely fantastical."[6]

Yet even today, there still exist widespread misconceptions among lay people, scientists and even some mathematicians, about the problem of prognostics in complex systems. The advances of computer soft- and hardware and the success of some computer models, in particular, led them to believe that if computers are only big and fast enough, they can, in fact, precisely predict the future. They hope that new types of simulations could once and for all solve the problem of prediction.

But today's computer models are still based on mathematical and statistical rules. They still can only simulate systems provided there is no uncertainty in the system, as well as in the model. (Otherwise, the computer would never reach a result). Any description of anything in this universe, however, is principally based on uncertainty – which makes it complex in the first place. There still is no way we can ever have all the necessary information. This is true for any complex system in the universe – be it the weather, the climate, the stock market or any other social, biological or dynamic system (and if one looks at the world from a quantum theoretical and evolutionary standpoint, one cannot find a single exception).

The proper value of models and simulation is in better understanding systems, their operations, mechanics, interdependencies, variables and degrees of freedom, etc, but not in predicting their long term behavior. A prediction can only apply to next steps, to short term probabilities. Any prediction of complex systems contains uncertainty and randomness. It does not even necessarily get better if we have more data about the system: stock market predictions by experts equipped with large computers are not necessarily better than those of non-experts or even chimpanzees. Knowledge in the

---

6   Destutt de Tracy (1815). French liberal philosopher and politician (1754-1836), in: *A Treatise on Political Economy,* trans. by Thomas Jefferson (1817; rep. ed. New York: Augustus M. Kelley, 1970), p. 38.

form of a good model does not guarantee good long term predictions, but rather helps the predictor towards better long term survival.

Edward Lorenz, the meteorologist who coined the famous chaos theoretical term, 'butterfly effect,' tried, in fact, to demonstrate not so much that a butterfly flapping its wings in Brazil could predictably change the weather in China, but rather that minute differences in the variables of a computer model can dramatically change the results of the simulation. All computer models, whether they describe the weather, the climate, or the economy, necessarily must operate with incomplete values and measurements. A model is a specific theory or metaphor describing a complex system. Its usefulness for predictive purposes is utterly restricted and fragile: like with a theory, one wrong result immediately falsifies the model. The near perfect accuracy that computer models promise in producing correct results should not be interpreted as a quality of the prediction, but rather as falsification. There are good reasons why in history the people in charge of predictions have preferred a very fuzzy language: the words of the Delphi oracle or the mutterings of fortune tellers have always left plenty of room for interpretation in order to avoid falsification.

The additional problem with computer models is that currently they cannot even scale the variables they have available for computation. Since they operate in multidimensional complex networks (of nodes and relations), every time a new node is added, the relational complexity of the entire network increases exponentially. So the models either have to be severely simplified, or the computational costs go through the roof. Data driven simulations where the system is not isolated from the environment during simulation, but can continuously integrate new data and even change its model accordingly during operation (which is what living systems do!) could improve this situation somewhat, but they are not possible with the current technical approaches.

Even if new approaches currently in development could change this dramatically by operating with pure relations instead of data,[7] the fundamental problem of models would not change. The reason why this innovation is of interest in this context is because it employs an approach much closer to learning, and our brains in general. By not representing data in the system at all, but instead *assimilating* data as pure relations, this new 'relationist' approach achieves scalability which could be used for data driven simulations of scalable complexity in the future.

The concept of assimilation has been introduced into the cognitive sciences and the science of learning by Jean Piaget as part of his "genetic epistemology" of knowledge, or the way children learn by assimilating new experiences into existing internal schemas and accommodate the latter as adaptation or learning. The concept of assimilation runs counter to the input-output metaphor that has plagued our idea of communication for so long. Assimilation is not based on storing content in memory-like data on a computer disk. It is a purely relational and genetic (in the sense of generative) concept

---

7   For a more detailed introduction, see Krieg (2005) and Westphal (2006)

based on difference instead of representation: internal relations are changed and correlated with other internal relations in interactions with the environment. Once we start thinking in terms of relations, connections and relations of relations, we lose the notion of objects and of memory as a storage and retrieval device. Memories like words or images are not retrieved from some hierarchical storage device, but are generated from an interrelated and thus associative structure of relations and connections.

It can be considered one of the tragedies of computer science that the metaphor of the brain, which was used in early computer history ("mechanical brain," "electronic brain") soon was reversed and adopted by the cognitive sciences by referring to the brain as a "computing device" and to memory as a system of storing and retrieving representations of the world. The metaphor or assimilation, however, allows us to introduce and apply new concepts of associative memory and data generation in a new type of computer that does not any longer "process data" or store representations, but assimilates differences and computes in an interconnected space of relations from which data are generated dynamically like images in a computer game.

But even then, no computer model or method, not even the most adaptive and the most powerful can reliably predict the future. In a universe of uncertainty, this always will be the privilege of fortune tellers and clairvoyants (if we want to believe them). Anyone claiming that computers or models can reliably predict the future should be classified in that very same category. This applies first and foremost to the current trend in politics and the media to base political decisions and demands on the predictions of computer models. It is a sad comment on the state of science that many scientists go along and even support this trend for whatever reason. Challenging this unholy alliance between bad science and bad government is becoming increasingly difficult.[8]

Beyond Institutional Learning

"I never let my schooling interfere with my education," Mark Twain once said. Indeed, institutional learning is probably the most wasteful and ineffective of all learning environments. It is conceptually linked to the idea of learning as data storage and tends therefore to concentrate on remembering the contents of books and to disconnect the process of learning from the process of doing. The average classroom situation, – whether in school or university – where students are forced to sit passively in rows for six hours or more listening to a teacher and interacting as little as possible with their co-students, is the worst of all possible learning environments. A private teacher for every child is no viable alternative, of course, but there is a world of education to be discovered beyond the institutional shackles of today's state sponsored and controlled education systems.

---

8   A case in point is the current climate debate.

The Internet, with its global access to libraries and teaching materials, with its interactive potential and peer-to-peer networking, could spell the beginning of the end of institutional education. Through mobile communication, language based education and learning can be brought everywhere and integrated in other, private, as well as professional, activities. But these are only the first steps on the road to undermine and eventually get rid of unproductive learning approaches.

Among the most promising new learning environments are *microlearning* and *games*:

Microlearning is compact and location independent. It can be applied anywhere and anytime. Microlearning lessons can be delivered through mobile phones, the Internet, or dedicated networks. They are not tied to institutions or classrooms. Microlearning can be highly modularized and individualized as well as highly networked and social. Modularization can relate to specific contexts, while individualization can relate to specific methods of learning and degrees of knowledge. Social learning can be supported by peer networking. By itself, Microlearning is not more than a distribution platform. What could turn it into a paradigm shift is the integration of Games.

Games represent a new quality for individual and social learning and, therefore can be seen as a much deeper technical and educational innovation than even the gamer community and game industry currently recognize:

– Games are dynamic models of relationships the player can become immersed in as an actor within the model. All traditional educational tools, with the possible exception of role plays, are based on external observer perspectives.

– Games provide a new interactive man-machine interface with promises for high degrees of individual personalization, flexibility and adaptivity;

– Games are based on fluid and dynamic simulation, not on static and hierarchic data structures. This puts them in a new machine category much closer to the human users;

– Game image data are "virtual data," i.e. these data are dynamically *generated from code,* not physically stored and retrieved as static data frames. This represents an entirely new data paradigm;

– The computing space of game engines primarily is a relation space, not a data space (although traditional data are still employed, also). This points towards a new *relationist* paradigm;

– In contrast to the traditional closed Turing machine concept of computing, the game concept is interactive and open to input during operation. This is just a step away from a revolutionary extension of the Turing machine concept.

Computer games combine a new educational approach of immersive modelling or role playing with a new technical approach. While the technical innovation has been widely realized and successfully applied, the educational potential has not even been scratched yet.

Technically, the generative data approach of game images (CGI = computer generated imagery) will, in the near future, be available for any signal sequences, not just for pre-constructed images. This will allow developers not only to simulate and animate pictures, but to simulate just about anything: databases, structures, arbitrary data types, i.e. whatever can be converted to electronic signals. The implications for learning are dramatic, especially when games and microlearning are combined:

– Nearly any process can be dynamically modelled, allowing the learner to immerse himself in a role play. The human capacity for projection and empathy enables him to assume his own personal identity, or roles of other human players, but also of any other identity created by the game, however abstract.

– As a result, computers and computer driven devices in general will become simulation machines for just about everything: not only games, but also data driven simulations of our bodies, of complex systems in society and nature, etc.

– Being able to change an internal model based on external input is the basic requirement for any learning system: computers able to do such will, for the first time, become true learning machines.

– These new interactive learning machines will be able to adapt to their individual user and are no longer restricted to one static 'standard user,' thus enabling a much more individual and personal learning experience.

Conclusion

With today's games and emerging microlearning applications, we are taking just a tiny first glimpse into the future universe of ubiquitous simulation computing, but we have not even begun to explore the possibilities. When we do, we can finally say that we have left the Gutenberg galaxy, because today we have not really done so yet. In terms of data, we have not much more than an electronic extension of the old library systems – just digitally enhanced and globally networked. The post-Gutenberg era will be an era of simulation and interactive learning systems. The relationist approach philosophically opens new perspectives on knowledge and learning. It technically enables us to integrate simulation and microlearning. Together, this can liberate us from many of the restrictions of institutional learning, and eventually from the current dependency on institutional learning altogether. Not everyone will consider this a desirable option, but at least it will provide additional options and alternatives to an educational system that seems to be much in need of such alternatives.

References

Krieg, P. (2005) *Die paranoide Maschine – Computer zwischen Wahn und Sinn.* Hannover: Heise Verlag.

Krieg, P. (2006) *Die Spiele der Zukunft – Zukunft der Spiele* in Rebensburg, K. (Ed.) 2. Tagung NMI 2006, Berlin-Brandenburgische Akademie der Wissenschaften

Taleb, N. N. (2004) *Fooled by Randomness* (2nd Edition) New York, Random House

Tracy, Count Destutt de (1817) *A Treatise on Political Economy,* translated from the French by Thomas Jefferson. Quoted in: Salerno, J. (2006) *A Conspiracy of Silence on The French Liberal School.* Available from: <http://www.mises.org/story/2227> [Accessed 14 July 2006]

Westphal, R. (2006) *Freeing Data from the Silos: A Relationistic Approach to Data Processing.* Available from <http://www.pilesys.com/new/Documents/Freeingdatafromthesilos-Pileexplained.pdf> [Accessed 13 May 2006].

Blogs and Chats: Some Critical Remarks on Electronic Communication

Karl Leidlmair

Preliminary Remarks

In post-modern times, after the "End of the Great Narratives" (Lyotard, 1984), there has been a return to singularity, contextually anchored in a unique situation. In the new media, this new turn has found expression in blogs and chats. A Blog is a kind of electronic diary in which stories are told. The type of knowledge transmitted via blogs is now and then termed micro content – it contains pieces of instant knowledge like metadata (e.g., a commentary to a URL (link), an abstract of an article).

In chatrooms, it comes to an assimilation of written terms in oral speech. Performative speech acts are replaced by performative acts of writing. The culture created by electronic information and communication technologies and the Internet is therefore characterised as a juxtaposition of elements of orality and literacy. Whereas oral cultures are guided by a narrative, performative style, by situated and context-dependent knowledge, our literal culture is said to have a more descriptive and abstract language and its knowledge to be more atomistic and de-contextualized. Communication in the Net combines both distinctive marks.

The general question, however, is: can this new kind of literacy really replace the domain of orality without any losses? Isn't this big fuss about micro content as a new electronic expression for situated knowledge just a big illusion? It was the firm opinion of Marc Weiser that postmodernism just multiplies the explicating program of modernism (Weiser, 1997, p. 146). An age beyond postmodernism would be needed which reestimates the body as the original and only source of situated knowledge. Following this idea, the incorporation of content and context in the digital would be an undesirable development in the sense of this kind of postmodernism which Weiser has criticized.

The influence of the Internet on our culture is not a process which takes place overnight. It is an ongoing development with an open end. Looking back at the transition from oral cultures to literacy, as it was described by Eric Havelock (1988) in regard to the introduction of the greek alphabet, we find the following situation: only the Greek alphabet (according to Havelock) was smooth enough to reflect oral speech without loss of information. Greek writing had this ability because it atomized the syllables into meaningless fragments – the alphabet.

In spite of its quality of reproducing orality, the literalization of the Greeks instigated a radical change in their cognitive structures and resulted in a repression of aspects of the former oral culture: poetry was replaced by prose, thinking became more and more abstract and the idea of a detached subject emerged.

But nothing has ever been so smooth (and atomized) as the digital code. It was, first of all, the digital code which was apt to reproduce pictures and sound. As it seems, multimedia does not repress orality, on the contrary, it seems to be able to replace it.

The general question, however, whether situated knowledge (narratives transmit situated knowledge) can be exhaustively expressed in electronic form, needs a closer look. It can be answered only after a clear analysis of situated knowledge, what it is and how it works.

Such an analysis can be found in Cognitive Science. The faults of the computational theory of mind enforced the demand for a reassessment of the (cognitive revolution) of the science of the "mind." Jerome Bruner's "Acts of Meaning," Hubert Dreyfus' critics on de-contextualized knowledge as it is applied in expert systems, Hilary Putnam's critics on methodological individualism, directed the attention from formal algorithms to content. All those critics together paved the way for a new cognitive revolution which picks up again what "algorithmic" cognitivism seems to have neglected: Content, Context and the situatedness of our knowledge.

A short historical review shows how this reassessment of knowledge emerged in Cognitive Science. Proceeding on the assumptions of Cartesian dualism, the question arises: how can something purely mental (e.g., the intention to raise one's arm) be the cause of something purely physical (e.g., raising one's arm). Put in others words, the question of such a dualistic position is: how can we achieve a psychological explanation of our intentional behaviour which is compatible with the laws of physics? According to those laws, the only causes we can count on are physical causes, there is no room for other causes which would be qualitatively different from physics.

As a first reaction to this kind of dualism, early psychologists tried to reduce mental vocabulary to observables. But, as it soon turned out, behaviourism was going too far, throwing out the baby with the bathwater. In particular, it did not correspond with the use of psychological vocabulary according to common sense. The ascription of psychological states plays an important part in explaining behaviour. This point is stressed by so-called folk psychology. For explaining behaviour, we need such ascriptions and for those ascriptions in turn, we need a model of the mind.

The question of how to retain psychological explanations without violating the laws of physics was answered by the computational model of the mind. In order to maintain common sense psychology and at the same time respect scientific standards, Cognitive Science postulated a multilevel of the mind. According to that model, psychological states and physical states are not two separate and incompatible ontological domains; instead the psychological is understood as just another level of description of the physical. Psychological states are converted into syntactic structures like computer programs and those programs in turn are realized in physical structures – the "hardware" of the programs.

But, as it turned out, this multilevel approach in its attempt to "catch" intelligent behaviour by its transformation into formal rules and models was exposed to the same problems as in rationalism.

Cognitive Science, still dependent on basic assumptions of Cartesian philosophy, took over the same mistakes as classical computational models. Instead of being treated as mere or pure explanations of mental processes, in hindsight, these models have been mistakenly used as more or less literal causal descriptions of the (working of the) mind. Rules for the explanation of knowledge, however, are something quite different then the actual production of knowledge.

In that way, we lost our grounding in the earthly world: accustomed to follow the rules of explanations, we got caught in the inherent dynamism of our computational constructions of reality. Always relying on our digitally remastered world, we run the risk of unlearning those parts of our skillful behaviour which resist a complete and adequate transformation into formal rules. Especially, two kinds of knowledge have proved to be very obstinate (resistant) against all efforts of formalization: doing something and being something – the former is prevalent in purely tacit skills like riding a bicycle; the latter in social knowledge, like to be a good teacher. Such a kind of knowledge cannot be acquired by learning explicit rules by heart, it emerges from participation and empathy, like apprenticeship learning (as in the case of learning tacit rules) or storytelling (as in the case of social knowledge a good story has a "point" which is contextually situated; it roots the general in the particular without mentioning it explicitly; cf. Brown, 2004, p. 65).

For both kinds of knowledge, there is no necessity of ever becoming aware of them; on the contrary they make up the transparent background of our everyday activity.

A very simple example might illuminate what I mean. Martin, my assistant in my e-learning classes, asked me one day where I had stored a file in my computer. But I could not explicitly tell him that location. I had to sit down in front of the computer and find the file by a mouse-click. The knowledge of the location of the file was not in my mind, yet it was in my hand, which moved the mouse on the pad.

The crucial question now is how to disclose such a kind of knowledge without destroying it in the process of its disclosure. If tacit knowledge belongs intrinsically to the transparent background of our coping activities, how can we ever pass on this knowledge in such a way that it will not be falsified by terms?

As I mentioned above, there are techniques which fulfil this demand, one of which is storytelling. By telling a story, we are able to indirectly address a moral or point without making it explicit. Stories, as I explained before, provide a context for anchoring understanding.

Stories exploit a technique which was dominant in former oral cultures and which was repressed in the course of the literalization of our western tradition, namely, to trigger participation and empathy. Stories draw people in and engage feelings. This revival of the narrative was not a feature confined to real meetings at conferences, workshops and so on; it – and this sounds paradoxical at first sight – took place in the community of the Net. In instant messaging, in chats and blogs, the new generation @ does not exchange simple information as happened at the beginning of the Internet; instead, social contacts are cultivated. The average player in the web nowadays is not an expert in programming, it is the housewife, the neighbour next door just interested in small talk.

But, we have to ask, does the Internet provide the right rails to establish and transfer transparent knowledge? Can communication in the Net preserve the implicit without distorting it by its transfer in a digitally recreated world? Can empathy and participation really be transmitted just by written symbols as happens in instant messaging, in blogs and in chatrooms?

The answer to this question is quite tricky. We have to take a closer look at both of them, at blogs and chats.

Blogs and Chats

Let us start with blogs. In a very simplified way, we can define a blog as a content management system with dated entries. A blog contains thoughts of a biographic character, as well as annotated links through the Net (Stone, 2002). Whereas a classical homepage is static, frozen at the moment of its creation, blogs are dynamic. Blogs are pathfinders through the Net. So why not read them as ways of digital storytelling? The answer to this question depends on what makes up a story. An interesting hint is given to us by John Seely Brown (Brown, 2004, p. 93): "What's so interesting about a story is it always gets re-purposed in the context in which it's told. The telling and the listening to the story, both active processes, are always very situated. And the 'situatedness' of it is what creates the power." Digital storytelling, on the contrary, is just a reduction to the explicit. It is for that reason that we don't learn anything new through video-conferencing.

The essential objection in this argument is that digital storytelling is missing the interactive element. Without this interactive element, no regulation (emotional and cognitive) is possible between the speaker and the listener, and without that regulation a story can never become re-purposed. Such a regulation can be found in chatrooms. Communication in a chatroom is interactive and almost synchronous. So why not use chats to alleviate the deficits of digitally told stories?

In chatrooms we find a strange mix of elements of oral and written language. It seems as if writing has learned to speak. When I was observing social interactions in chatrooms (Leidlmair, 2001) two things caught my attention: a high degree of involvement, and intense emotionality. Only the beginner experiences messages on the monitor as symbols created by animated cartoons. Tools such as the keyboard, monitor and chat-software are in the foreground of his attention. The advanced user, on the other hand, is practically drawn into the middle of the chatroom. A feeling of proximity to the other participants arises, even though they may be separated by thousands of miles. This feeling can be best described as a kind of flow which connects the users in a very intense and intimate way.

One possible explanation, among others, for this phenomenon is the high speed of exchange in chatrooms compared with face-to-face communication. At first glance, this fact sounds strange because speaking is normally faster than writing. But we have to take into account that in a chatroom many people are talking with each other and whereas in ordinary conversation only one person can speak, in the chatroom all participants can write their messages simultaneously. The written messages flit across the monitor at a very high speed and force the reader to formulate his own answers without any further reflection. This circumstance causes the user to fall into a situation of flow in which time passes unnoticed and all reflection about one's activity ceases, which results in a kind of unconscious "mindless" coping with the chat-community.

Another important factor is the special language used in chatrooms. Very often, shortcuts (onomatopoeia) are used such as *n8* (German) or *u* (English). This allows for fast conversation and connects the letters to their oral phonetics. Another remarkable feature is its performative style. Saying something does not describe an action, it embodies the action itself. Thus, the new language of the Internet contains many features which have been ascribed to former oral cultures.

But, to take up the previous question: does the Internet provide the right rails for anchoring context? I will break this question into two parts, a practical question proceeding on the techniques of electronic communication available nowadays and a more philosophical and speculative one.

As I explained before, a story has the ability to anchor context by recreating it together with the listener. This works only in an interactive dialogue. A direct confrontation with face-to-face communication, however, is remarkably different from electronic communication as it happens now in chatrooms. Those differences are practical problems, resting upon the current state of the art.

In direct speech, the speaker always gets some feedback from the listener in the very moment of his own speech. Such a feedback can be mimicing a nod, or even some short utterance like "Mmh." It is this feedback which regulates and repurposes the story told by the speaker to the listener. Such a feedback now is totally absent in the case of chat communication. The reader of the messages has no chance to control the story in the very moment when it is written by the remote partner.

In this connection, Dreyfus, quoting David Blair, makes a very interesting observation: It is not possible (given the current state of the art) to have direct eye contact by video cam: "To look into another person's eyes, I would have to look straight into the camera but then I would not be able to see the eyes of the other person since, to do that, I would have to turn from the camera to the student's image on the screen. You can look into the camera or look at the screen, but you can't do both." (Blair, personal communication, quoted in Dreyfus, 2001, p. 60)

The lack of physical presence has other consequences, as well: sometimes we attribute to a speaker's voice a special charisma, but we cannot explain explicitly from where this charisma stems. Is it really the timbre of the voice, or maybe something else, maybe it is the posture of the speaker?

But what does all that imply? Does communication in the Net encourage only very superficial social interactions? In his study on Carnegie Mellon University, Robert Kraut (1998) maintained that in the Internet, strong social ties are substituted by weak social ties. Critics of that study, however, claimed that the sample used was not representative and Kraut (2002) himself modified his polemic in a later statement. In another study, Parks and Floyd even argued that users of chatrooms are more socially active then others. The reason for this social behavior may be found in the fact that virtual escapism, the radical withdrawal from real friends and relatives, is not the normal behavior of chat participants. Even in chatrooms, people after a while come together in reality; meetings are organized especially for chatters.

In a more speculative way, however, we can ask: what if communication in the Net were to become a central issue in our social behavior?

Electronic Communication and Derived Intentionality

One general objection to electronic communication might be the following: in electronic communication, we use only one aspect of communication, namely that one which can be transmitted in explicit, written terms. However, not everything we experience can be completely explicated. In order to understand something which has been said explicitly, we must presuppose an implicit understanding. This understanding remains in the background. The understanding of written terms works only as long as we can rely on the fact that all the participants in the electronic communication share the same common understanding.

Remember the technique of perspective in western painting: a smaller man is a man standing at a greater distance. When we look at a painting, we don't think about the fact that our perception of the little man is an interpretation instilled in us by our western tradition. The idea that the man is further away comes to us willy-nilly, quasi automatically, as if spatiality were something built in, an intrinsic feature of the painting.

But think about the case of a child who says to his father: "look, look at the little man standing there on the top of the hill."

What the example illuminates is the simple fact that perspective foreshortening is something which has to be learned. And in order to learn it, we need experiences which are not embodied in the painting. Just think what would happen if we would try to learn perspective only by exchanging paintings. Nothing in the paintings would give us the key for understanding the spatiality of the painting. In Chinese culture, for example, the small size of a man indicates his minor social status.

So, in order to understand written symbols, we must rely on socially shared standard experiences which we have to know from the very outset. In electronic communication, therefore, nothing really new can be learned. Instead, we always remain within the limits of some standard experiences and stick in this way to what is already known.

Against such a criticism of electronic communication, the following objection may be raised: the argument is right, as long as electronic communication is reduced to the exchange of written symbols. But the Internet has long since exceeded the limits of writing. And it will not be long before the Internet will allow the transmission of all kinds of impressions which we can get with our other senses, including haptic and olfactory sensations (introducing high-resolution television, surround sound, and adding touch and smell channels).

But even if we use such supplements in electronic communication, the general question remains: are all those supplements really rich enough to be able to replace face-to-face communication without any losses and shortenings? Let me give you the following example.

There is a new variant of cybersex in which people can touch each other with a stick operated by remote control. But even in that case, we must already know something about sex in advance in order to be able to understand a touch of a stick as a touch by our remote partner. If we hadn't already had such sexual experiences, such a touching would not have meaning for us at all.

Such an argument, however, seems to leave us impossibly stuck into some kind of total skepticism. Even in face-to-face communication, the impressions we get from our partner have to be interpreted. In all our sensations, we can find this uncertainty concerning their meaning. If every signal, every message we receive has a meaning, which, even in real life, is only derived, how does it ever come about that we understand each other? How is communication ever possible?

In asking about the origin of meaning and intentionality, how can one avoid just begging the question? A clear and thorough answer can be found only by clarifying what that rumor about derived and intrinsic meaning means. Let me give you an example.

Let us suppose that a European painting is shipped to China. In China, a Chinese person points at a little man in the painting and says: look at this insignificant person. Is our Chinese person wrong? As long as he is interpreting the painting, I would say no.

Because the painting is only an artifact and its meaning is only derived, its meaning is in the eye of the beholder.

We can say: the small size of the man does not really indicate distance. There is no built-in spatiality in the painting. It indicates it only in the context of a special tradition.

It would be a quite different story if our Chinese person would interpret the intentions of the European painter from the background of his culture. If he would say, for example, that the painter intended to show, with size, a man of minor social position, he would make an error.

Now what can we learn from this short lesson about intrinsic meaning? We can learn two things: 1) Not the painting itself really means this or that by itself, only we mean by the painting this or that. We are the meaning-makers, it is up to us what the painting, what the signal, what the message really means. 2) What is meant intrinsically is not relative to a context any more. Would the latter be the case, we could never make an error.

I am saying all this now – and this I want to emphasize – without any ontological assumptions concerning intrinsic or derived intentionality. What I am doing instead is only a very modest commentary on the everyday usage of the attribution of meaning. I just want to explicate how our ordinary understanding of intrinsic meaning works and what "really meaning" implies. By really meaning spatiality, for example, we fix the meaning for all possible contexts. And we can do this by virtue of our own immediate directedness towards spatiality – an ability which no artifact has.

But after all this, I am coming back to the former question: how are we ever able to fix meaning, if the meaning of all the signals we get is derived? Do we not reach the conclusion that all meaning is derived, a view which, by the way, such different philosophers as Dennett and Derrida would share?

So what about intrinsic meaning? The answer is very simple: it is the situation as a whole which cannot be cut up into single chunks of experiences and from which something like intrinsic meaning emerges.

This statement sounds like a deus ex machina. If there is something like intrinsic meaning, it must emerge from somewhere, so why not take the situation of our being in the world as a whole? This is not the end of my analysis, however; on the contrary, it is the beginning. First of all, we have to state that that Quinian rumor about the indeterminacy of all signals we receive is a very artificial view of our everyday communication. In a normal situation, we don't first hear noises and then furnish them with a meaning, what we hear instead are verbal messages which always already have a meaning. Only in the mode of detached philosophical reflection are we able to strip those messages of their meaning.

In everyday life, on the contrary, we are involved in a meaningful world which has a social dimension from the very outset. I don't want to loose much time on this. Because everything that needs to be said about this topic has been explained in Dreyfus' reading of Heidegger, a few words will suffice for my purpose.

Heideggerian Intentionality

In everyday life, we don't stare at things in the mode of detached reflection, things don't simply occur. Instead, we encounter them as something available in the process of an involved coping activity. This concerned coping in a world is grounded in turn in a basic familiarity which penetrates all our everyday activity in such a way that all equipment we cope with is encountered as something embedded in a whole set of other equipments. But this equipment whole, although it is a constant companion of our everyday activity, remains in the background of our attention. Invisible and transparent as it is, it can be very easily overlooked. And in fact, it has been ignored in the tradition of western philosophy. A lot of the epistemological skepticism contained in the above mentioned ambiguity concerning our understanding of sounds and other signals has its origin in this ignorance of our primordial settledness in such an equipment whole. But as I said before, I don't want to belabor this point.

What I want to ask instead, is whether this Heideggerian approach does not amount to some kind of pragmatic reductionism.

The main target of this question, let me emphasize this point, is not how to find an adequate understanding of Heidegger. On the contrary, the real question I am interested in is how to explain anchoring of meaning. Only by answering this question can we understand which deficits (if any) we are exposed to by electronic communication. The argument that in electronic communication the meaning of the exchanged signals always remains derived, whereas only in a communication "in reality" original meaning can be achieved shall be explored by analyzing Heidegger's approach to original intentionality. So, can primordial settledness in an equipment whole completely explain original intentionality?

First of all, we have to see that Heidegger's analysis of equipment in *Being and Time* is in relation to his main purpose, namely to explain the phenomenon of world as transcendence, of minor importance. He even stresses this point in a footnote in "Essence of Reasons" (Heidegger, 1978, p. 153), where he explicitly says that the nexus of equipment can never be identified with his phenomenon of world.

I am coming now to a difficult point, for which I can give only some basic clues within the limits of this article. The question is how to understand disclosing in the right way. First of all, I want to come back to the above mentioned fact that we don't hear noises and give them an interpretation in hindsight, that we instead listen to meaningful messages from the very outset. Heidegger calls this phenomenon in *Being and Time* the primordial openness of the human being. He offers several different examples of how this openness can ever be experienced. I will pick out only one, namely anxiety. In this connection, two questions may be in order:

1. What is anxiety?
2. What does anxiety disclose?

1. Anxiety is a special affectedness which happens in situations of a total breakdown of our familiar coping with things.

2. In anxiety, we become aware of the tacit background of our concerned coping activity with which we are familiar from the outset. But we don't become aware of it in the sense of a deliberate cognitive process, but rather in the mode of finding ourselves already settled in it. We have called this settledness in an equipment whole something primordial. Now it turns out that something even more primordial is lurking in the background, namely finding ourselves in total unsettledness as it happens in the case of anxiety. Heidegger even emphasizes that all our familiar dwelling in a world is only a mode of this unsettledness and not the reverse.

For the very reason of the human's ability to experience the total breakdown of familiarity in the case of anxiety he can disclose a world. To put it in another way, we can also say: transcending the borders of the known in the case of breakdown, we root our understanding in the unknown. And, I must add, this is not a problem of epistemology, in the view of Heidegger, it has to do with the way our being is situated in a human world.

This kind of transcendence is not grounded in a special mental power of the human being like in the case of an *intuitus originarius*, it is a transcendence born out of a weakness which enables us first of all to respect the Other as something having a stand in itself.

What we have, I suggest, is a *weak ontological attitude*. What I mean by a weak ontological attitude may be best explained if we go back to the example of a cybersex scenario in which a stick or something similar is operated by remote control. As I explained before, we must know in advance what a sexual relationship is in order to be able to interpret a touch by a stick as a touch by our partner in the Net. Without that ontological attitude, we could not even be deceived. Heidegger is asking a similar question, which has to be understood only in a rhetorical sense: if we mistake in the darkness a tree for a man, does that mean that our intention is directed towards a mere representation of a man and not the man himself? His answer is: no, the deception is possible only because we erroneously intend the man himself. Without that ontological attitude, we could not distinguish between illusion and reality. But what is weak now about that ontological attitude?

Due to the experience of total breakdown, we leave the door always open for entering the unknown. (Please note that I am not talking about propositional knowledge.) That means that our directedness towards the ontological cannot be reduced to what we are just familiar with.

So if we take all that talking about our coping activity as being absorbed into the familiar background of an inconspicuous equipment whole, we have to see that this is only the one side of the coin. What completes the coin is just the same background in the mode of its withdrawal. We can also say: only by having a stand in the abyss of the unfamiliar do we disclose a world. If we would be totally absorbed by our tacit background coping activity, no openness whatsoever would be possible.

Electronic Communication without Roots to the Unknown

What does all that imply now for Internet communication? First of all, I have to draw our attention to the simple fact that Internet communication is a computer mediated communication. Mediated communication, in turn, is a reframed communication. In order to reframe communication, we have to know in advance all relevant facts which we use in direct communication to understand each other. If we implant that knowledge now in a computer network, all information we can get from our remote partner will be frozen to just this technical realization of the knowledge. No new experiences outside of this technical model of communication will ever come about. What we have is a communication without surprises, a communication without roots to the unknown. And what we are actually doing is a communication via representations of communication.

An example might help to illuminate what I mean. In chat communication, the only information about our partner which comes to our attention is not an immediate impression, but rather only what our partner is saying about herself. So we can say: in chat communication, the only information which is exchanged is based upon our mutual self descriptions. But such descriptions, even when we are not lying, give only a distorted impression of ourselves. The social relationship we can deal with in chatrooms is therefore always restricted to some standard roles we already have in mind when we start the communication. A new relationship, however, is only built by direct interaction with a person whose character is full of surprises and unexpected reactions. It is for that reason that only in the very moment when two people meet in reality do they have a chance to build a relationship.

And last not least, in front of a class room we draw our listeners in by developing an idea on the blackboard. The more vivid our demonstration becomes, the better will be the understanding of our students. Sometimes even an error, at least if it does not happen too often, might be helpful to attract attention.

In this connection, Nonaka (1995) says something interesting: the externalization of the implicit as the motor by which new knowledge is created needs a breakdown in our daily routines.

In blogs and chats, on the contrary, communication always remains restricted to what we already know about communication, passing over the risky experience to which we are exposed when we encounter somebody new in real life. This is not only a problem for the current state of the art. However sophisticated electronic communication will become in the future, enriched by additional communication channels, entering cyberspace and leaving behind the fragility and vulnerability of our embodied life, we will run the risk of *unlearning learning*.

In order to learn something new (a new experience, a new friend), we have to take a further step which can never be replaced by electronic tools: we have to come together in reality, a teacher in a classroom, a lover in a meeting face-to-face. Only by being exposed to the risk of a total breakdown of our expectations about our remote partner, will we be open for new experiences.

Electronic communication, therefore, can at best be an additional (and doubtlessly useful) tool, a possibility of bridging space and time. Such a tool can work fine as long as we don't forget its limitations. We should never confound the tool with the task for which it is put to use.

References

Brown, J.S. et al. (2004) *Storytelling in Organizations: why Storytelling is Transforming 21st Century Organizations and Management.* Burlington: Elsevier Butterworth-Heinemann.

Brown, J.S. (2004) Narrative as a knowledge medium in organizations. In: op. cit., pp. 53–95.

Bruner, J. (1990) *Acts of Meaning.* Cambridge MA: Harvard University Press.

Dreyfus, H.L. & Dreyfus, S.E. (1986) *Mind Over Machine.* New York: The Free Press.

Dreyfus, H.L. (1991) *Being-in-the-World. A Commentary on Heidegger's Being and Time.* Division I. Cambridge: MIT Press.

Dreyfus, H.L. (2001) *On the Internet.* London/New York: Routledge.

Havelock, E.A. (1988) *The Muse Learns to Write: Reflections on Orality and Literacy from Antiquity to the Present.* New Haven: Yale University Press.

Heidegger, M. (1978) Vom Wesen des Grundes. In: Heidegger, M. *Wegmarken.* Frankfurt a.M.: Vittorio Klostermann, pp. 123–173.

Kraut, R. et al. (1998) Internet paradox: a social technology that reduces social involvement and psychological well-being? In: *American Psychologist*, 53 (9), pp. 10171–031.

Kraut, K. et al. (2002) Internet paradox revisited. In: *Journal of Social Issues*, 58 (1), pp. 49–74.

Leidlmair, Karl (2001) Sexualität im Netz. Wenn die Schrift zur Stimme wird. In: *Sexuologie*, 8 (3/4), pp. 119–144.

Leidlmair, K. (1991) *Künstliche Intelligenz und Heidegger.* München: Wilhelm Fink.

Lyotard, J.-F. (1984) *The Postmodern Condition: A Report on Knowledge.* Minneapolis: University of Minnesota Press.

Nonaka, I. & Takeuchi, H. (1995) *The Knowledge-Creating Company.* New York: Oxford University Press.

Parks, M.R. & Floyd, C. (1996) Making friends in cyberspace. In: *Journal of Communication*, 46 (1), 80–97.

Putnam, H. (1975) The meaning of 'meaning.' In: Gunderson, K. ed. *Language, Mind and Knowledge*. Minneapolis: University of Minnesota Press, pp. 131–193.

Stone, B. (2002) *Blogging. Genius Strategies for Instant Web Content*. Berkeley: New Riders.

Weiser, M. (1997) Periphery and the FleshFactor. In: Stocker, G. & Schöpf, C. eds. *FleshFactor. Informationsmaschine Mensch*. Wien/New York: Springer, pp. 136–147.

Playing History: Reflections on Mobile and Location-Based Learning

Joost Raessens

> *Don't know much about history*
> Sam Cooke, 'Wonderful World'

In this chapter, the author analyses the ways in which mobile and location-based technologies can be used as microlearning tools. He focuses on *Frequency 1550*, a mobile city game that was developed by the Dutch Waag Society in Amsterdam in 2005. In this game, small groups of pupils, aged 12 to 14, playfully acquire specific historical knowledge about the city of Amsterdam. With the help of the Internet, smart phones and GPS technology, Amsterdam changes into a medieval playing-field. After a brief description of the activities of Waag Society, the author describes the pilot of *Frequency 1550*, the game's provisional didactic results, and research plans related to these results. The game will be played ten times in the period 2006-2007. At the end of this chapter, the author describes existing plans for a Dutch National Historical Museum and the role micro-games such as *Frequency 1550* could play in this respect.

1 Waag Society

Waag Society is a media lab located in De Waag (The Weigh House) at the Nieuwmarkt in Amsterdam. De Waag is the oldest secular building in the city. It was built in 1487 as the Saint Anthonis gate, one of Amsterdam's three late-medieval city gates. As such, it was part of the medieval defences of the city. In 1617, the Saint Anthonis gate was converted into the city's weighing house (i.e. the place where commodities were officially weighed for trade).

Waag Society started its projects in 1996, and has since developed into an acknowledged institute that is internationally active in research and development of, and experimentation with, new technologies in the domains of health care, art and culture, society and cultural education (see www.waag.org). Waag Society has been involved in cultural education from its very beginning. In 2001, the Dutch Ministry of Education, Culture and Science made Waag Society the Center of Expertise for Cultural Education and ICT. In September, 2006, its activities in the educational domain came together within the Creative Learning Lab as part of De Zwijger, Warehouse for Culture and Media, in the Amsterdam harbour.

Five basic assumptions are at the heart of Waag Society's domain of cultural education: creation, digital lifestyle, social learning, presentation and reflection. Together, these assumptions form the Waag's didactics. Cultural education is predominantly seen as a creative process which does not treat pupils as passive consumers with standard skills, but as active knowledge and media producers who focus on innovation and creativity. When producing animations, newspaper articles, stories and web magazines, for example, pupils learn how media work. Whereas the goal of traditional approaches to media literacy is to educate people in such a way that they are not "duped" by media messages (see Gee, 2006), Waag Society wants pupils to become designers and producers of media messages. Through the production of media, pupils learn that media are not presenting reality in an objective way, but are themselves actively constructing reality (creation refers to this aspect). By using digital media such as computer games, cell phones, the Internet and locative technology (GPS), cultural education comes closer to pupils' lifestyles and, thereby, becomes more engaging in the process (digital lifestyle). Digital media are also used to stimulate collaboration between pupils and their peers, thereby encouraging, instead of reducing, the social learning process (social learning). Finally, pupils find the media content they produce more meaningful if they have to present their results to a wider audience, be it friends and/or family. Pupils learn to reflect on the creative process and the impact of these media by discussing the media messages they and others have produced, the challenges they had to overcome and the choices they have made (presentation and reflection).

From 1999 onwards, Waag Society has introduced games and game elements to improve cultural and historical education. I will give three examples of games made for pupils of primary and secondary schools. Waag Society developed *Teylers Adventure*, a mixed media adventure game, for the Dutch Teylers Museum in Haarlem. In this game, the female character, Minx, asks the players to help her. They can save the museum's collection by accomplishing all kinds of assignments in the physical space of the museum. In the adventure game *Demi Dubbel's Teletimemachine* (2002), the vain professor Demi Dubbel uses a time machine to teletransport herself into the era of the Flemish painter Pieter Breughel, in the first half of the sixteenth century. Pupils take on the role of assistant inspector of police, and prevent her from portraying herself in all kinds of Western and non-Western works of art exhibited world-wide. In the online world *MonsterMedia* (2005) pupils adopt and feed little media monsters. By producing an online exploratory expedition of media history, answering questions and completing assignments, pupils can teach these media monsters to become the smartest of the web. Though research into the use of games in educational contexts is still in its early stages, these examples of game-based learning show that games can be effectively used in primary and secondary education.

2   Frequency 1550

In close collaboration with the Montessori Comprehensive School Amsterdam and telecom company KPN Mobile, and with the help of the Municipal Archives Amsterdam, Waag Society developed *Frequency 1550*, a mobile learning game pilot that took place from 7 to 9 February 2005 (see freq1550.waag.org).[1] It is a location-based city game networked in technology and collaborative in principle, that was developed for secondary-school pupils aged 12 to 14.

Back-Story. *Frequency 1550* is an interesting game and story mix. The interplay between game and story is one of the central issues of the so-called ludology-narratology debate. A standard reason in this debate for describing games as narratives is that "most games feature narrative introductions and back-stories" (Juul, 2005, p. 219). This is, indeed, the case with *Frequency 1550*. Before the pupils actually start playing the game, the designers of Waag Society place the game in the context of a larger story (back-story), and create an ideal story that the players have to realize. Theo Hug describes the purpose of such a storyline in an educational game such as *Frequency 1550* as follows. A storyline:

> constitutes a narrative framework for the structuring of learning contents, networked episodes, tasks and activities. It follows a narrative outline (setting the scene in time and place, introducing characters, creating ways of living) and a pedagogical outline with reference to key questions, learning tasks, activities, resources, media and cooperative interactions (Hug, 2005, p. 11).

According to the back-story of *Frequency 1550,* the Waag Society development team ran into some technical difficulties with the Amsterdam UMTS-network during network testing. Frequency 1550 is magically interfering with a different time period, the year 1550 of the late medieval era. Via the UMTS-network, the medieval city's bailiff is getting in contact with the present, that is 21st century Amsterdam. Through all kinds of misunderstandings, the bailiff takes the developers – and then the pupils – for pilgrims visiting Amsterdam in 1550 in order to visit the Holy Host, a special relic associated with The Miracle of Amsterdam.[2] The relic has mysteriously disappeared, and the bailiff suggests a deal: he will give them easy access to citizenship, provided they help him retrieve the holy relic. Six teams of four pupils – two of them located at

---

1   The following people collaborated on the making of this game: Aske Hopman (game design); Saar van Kouswijk (educational design); Joes Koppers (interaction design); Ronald Lenz (mobile phone software development); Just van den Broecke (game server software development); Bente van Bourgondiën (HQ software development); Marco Meijer (media design).

2   "According to tradition, on 15 March 1345, a man lay seriously ill in his house on the Kalverstraat. [the name of a street in Amsterdam]. Thinking he was about to die, he called for a priest to administer the last rites, including the Blessed Sacrament. After receiving the host, the man became sick and finally vomited. As was the custom, what he had brought up was thrown on the fire. The next morning, the host was discovered undamaged in the ashes. It was put into a box and taken by a priest to the parish church (the present-day Oude Kerk), but on two occasions it miraculously made its way back to the house on the Kalverstraat. This was the beginning of the tradition known in Amsterdam as the Miracle Procession, since people had taken it as a sign that they should spread word of what had happened." Available from: http://www.stille-omgang.nl/pagina_eng.htm [accessed 17 September 2006] According to Dutch historian Geert Mak, "the remarkable blossoming of Amsterdam after 1350 was not due simply to trade. Almost certainly it also had a religious stimulus (...) The city was an extraordinarily popular place of pilgrimage" (Mak, 1999, p. 45).

Headquarters (HQ) at De Waag, the other two walking the streets of Amsterdam – each take up their roles as competing pilgrims, and thus step into the game's world.

Technical Infrastructure. The two members of the team who wander through Amsterdam are equipped with a Nokia 6600 GPRS Gamephone linked to a Global Positioning System (GPS) receiver, and a Sony Ericsson Z1010 UMTS Videophone. Their two colleagues at HQ have a Videophone too, and a laptop with an Internet connection. All smart phones have Internet connection, and the Gamephone is constantly connected to the Game Server at Waag Society's lab.

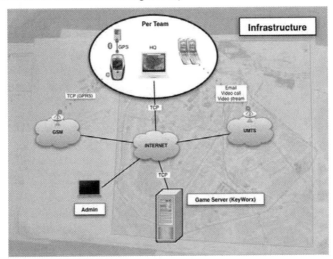

Figure 1. Infrastructure *Frequency 1550* © Waag Society

With the help of a GPS receiver, a Gamephone displays the position of its team on a medieval map of Amsterdam. Using their Videophone and Gamephone, a team can make (video) calls to their HQ, receive and watch pre-recorded video messages figuring medieval characters, and make and send assignments (video clips and pictures) to HQ located at De Waag. Using their laptops, team members at HQ have a game application with Internetaccess in order to look up information, check out historical references and send relevant information to the players out there in the city, thereby helping them to make their assignments (figure 2). Because they are able to see each player walk through the city in real time as colored dots – on a medieval map (figure 3), as well as on a current map of Amsterdam (figure 4) – they can work out the team's strategy and use their phones to guide their team toward scoring locations. At the end, HQ is responsible for the collection of all the data in an online presentation.

Figure 2. Playing at Headquarters © Waag Society

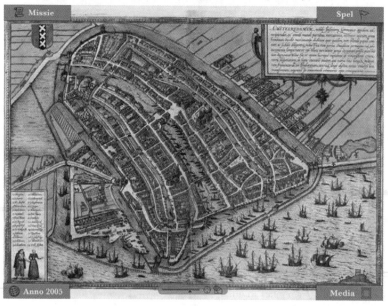

Figure 3. Map of medieval Amsterdam © Waag Society

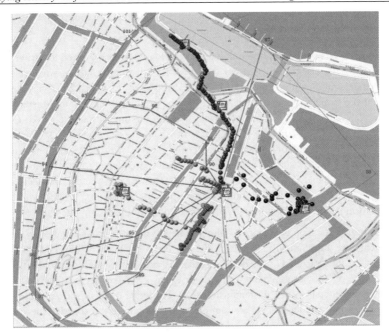

Figure 4. Contemporary map of Amsterdam © Waag Society

Goal of the Game. "You are a member of a pilgrim's order that comes to town to see the Host of the Miracle and to found its own monastery in Amsterdam. But first of all, you have to deserve the right to built a monastery by becoming a burgher (citizen)," according to the game's manual. A team can earn burghership or citizenship by collecting as many of the required 366 so-called "Days of Burghership" as possible. According to Aske Hopman: "These 366 points refer to the medieval year-and-a-day rule, which is the period you had to be living inside the city walls to earn citizenship rights." The team which manages to acquire burghership first earns the right to keep the Holy Host in its monastery and wins the game. Each team of pilgrims gets assigned a certain starting sector of the city it needs to explore, map, and master in a multimedial way. As the team moves around in the streets of (medieval) Amsterdam, it receives pre-recorded video clips with characters from the Middle Ages who provide information on historical locations and on the strange disappearance of the holy relic. Along the way, these medieval characters reveal bit by bit what happened to the relic, allowing players to piece this story together.

At the same time, the teams are competing with each other. Each team of pilgrims has to decide to stay away from other teams or call on a confrontation – their order determines who wins. The winning team takes away hard-earned medieval Days of Burghership from the team who loses. Team members can also earn a monk's habit, which makes them invisible to the other teams, and they can drop virtual bombs to kill each other's communication facilities with HQ.

According to Henry Jenkins, the ludology-narratology debate I referred to earlier over-emphasizes "the question of whether whole games tell stories and not whether narra-tive elements might enter games at a more localized level" (Jenkins, 2004, p. 121). The fact that the game's spatial experience of moving around in the city of Amsterdam is crucial to *Frequency 1550* does not mean that there is no narrative context. On the contrary, I would like to argue that the way in which the game space is structured fa-cilitates different kinds of narrative experiences. That is why Henry Jenkins refers to the design of these "spatial games" as "narrative architecture" or "environmental storytelling" (idem). The back-story of the Holy Host gives structure and meaning to the pupils' gaming experiences and provides a play area or staging ground where they can perform historical micro-narratives in order to fulfill their assignments.

Assignments. As soon as a team of pilgrims has reached a certain location, video as-signments are automatically sent from the server of De Waag to the UMTS Video-phone with the help of GPS. The team receives commands such as: "Now watch a video clip of the Schreierstoren [Schreierstower]." In order to obtain Days of Burghership, a team needs to demonstrate its knowledge of medieval Amsterdam by doing small location-based media assignments and by answering specific questions on the city's history, for example regarding the Schreierstoren.

Each team can complete all of the eighteen assignments that are related to specific lo-cations. Pupils are encouraged to fulfill at least two assignments per sector, in order to open up a new sector with a new story and assignment locations. They can win points for these assignments, helping them to win the game. To be able to do so, they have to study the historical buildings and sources. At the same time, they are experiencing the story, and reaching the game's learning goals. All the assignments are short-term learning activities that deal with relatively small learning units, two aspects of what has been called "microlearning" (Hug, 2006). These assignments enable the pupils to participate actively in the learning process without forcing them to obtain a complete overview of Amsterdam's history. Each assignment starts with an introductory video clip, and then the pupils are asked to do research and enact some kind of historical situation that they have to register and send to HQ with their smart phone.

The first example of such an assignment I will discuss here is related to the Schreiers-toren. The pilgrims have to portray the development of the legend of the name of the Schreierstoren in a video clip. HQ helps its team members by searching the Internet for the two possible explanations of the tower's name and communicating them as quickly as possible.

The Schreierstoren is a defensive tower in Amsterdam that was part of its city wall. The building of the tower was completed around 1487. It is the only remaining defen-sive tower. Its original name was the Schreyhoeckstoren, because the city wall makes a sharp (= 'schrey') angle (= 'hoeck') on this spot where the Geldersekade and the Oudezijds Kolk – two streets – meet. However, the Schreierstoren has gone down in history as the "wailing tower." At this spot, the wives of sailors bewailed the departure of their beloved husbands. In 1569 or shortly after, a tablet that depicts this scene (figure 5) was placed in the tower adding to this second interpretation. With her right hand, a female figure in a long robe points to a ship that is sailing away. She keeps her left hand in front of her face in desperation. Above this scene it says 'Scrayer-Hovck 1569.'

Although this story is frequently told and believed by many, historians agree that its authenticity is problematic. As Geert Mak writes: "it is commonly assumed that the name [Schreierstoren] means 'wailing tower,' though in fact it has nothing to do with sobbing sailors' wives waving goodbye and everything to do with the *schreye*, the sharp angle on which it is built" (Mak, 1999, p. 58).

Figure 5. Tablet Schreierstoren © Municipal Archive Amsterdam (Gemeentearchief Amsterdam)

The second assignment concerns the building at Zeedijk number 1. The pilgrims have to find the name of the building and discover its relation to a well-known saying and express the latter in a video clip. An additional question concerns a change in the construction of wooden houses. A special law of 1452 forbade owners to use wood for the sidewalls of their houses. HQ is asked to help its team members via an Internet search.

The building's name is 't Aepgen (the Little Monkey). The house is one of the oldest in Amsterdam and was built around 1550. Apparently, the following Dutch expression, which is still frequently used, finds its origin in this house: "in de aap gelogeerd zijn" (to be housed in the monkey) meaning "to be duped." According to the story, the owner of the sailors' inn kept monkeys that sailors brought back home from their voyages around 1600. These animals had fleas and other vermin and when somebody walked around the Zeedijk having a good scratch, he was said to be "housed in 't Aepgen." As is the case with the Schreierstoren, this story is disputed. According to Riemer Reinsma: "The core of the story is false. In the past centuries, there was no bar residing in that house at the Zeedijk" (Reinsma, 2006, p. 204). According to Reinsma, it is plausible that the saying is related to a notorious inn called The Ape, but that is all we know. "The sailors and the fleas are made up. Meanwhile this nonsensical story is almost ineradicable" (idem). Today, the building's ground floor is a café and the upper floors are part of the Barbizon Palace Hotel.

Zeedijk 1 is one of two remaining wooden houses in Amsterdam. It has sidewalls of stone. Initially, Amsterdam consisted of wooden houses. Stone houses were only built on a large scale from 1600 onwards. Most of the wooden houses burned down in the two big city fires of 1421 and 1452. The latter fire destroyed three quarters of the city. In the wake of this fire, the sidewalls of the houses had to be of stone.

The learning goals of both assignments are diverse. Pupils were asked to indicate the place of the Schreierstoren and Zeedijk 1 on contemporary and medieval maps. They learned about the city walls, for instance that the Schreierstoren is the only remaining part of the wall and that its name can be explained in several ways. Though a definite answer was not always at hand, they had to learn to choose the best explanation and argue for it. This example shows that the mere facts are insufficient to construct a true image of the past and that one has to select, organize and interpret these facts, a process in which stories can be helpful. Pupils learned that originally all Amsterdam houses were made of wood, that fire was one of the biggest dangers facing a medieval city, and that the city council took all kinds of measures to reduce the devastating effects of a city fire. Furthermore, they learned all kinds of skills related to historical knowledge: how to use arguments in discussions, how to be critical of all kinds of interpretations and of Internet or physical sources (such as parts of a building, e.g., the Schreierstoren tablet), how to determine differences and similarities between past and present situations.

3   Learning Results

Frequency 1550 had six different learning targets: five of them are a specification of the basic assumptions of Waag Society's domain of cultural education I discussed above. The sixth one is specific to *Frequency 1550* and concerns the acquisition of historical knowledge about Amsterdam.

Creation. One of the research findings of the *Frequency 1550*-pilot is that the use of smart phones, GPS-technology and the Internet, but also and foremost the creation and communication of images (pictures, video), sound and an online presentation had a positive impact on pupils' digital media literacy. According to Saar van Kouswijk, educational staff-member of Waag Society, the game showed that: "learning by doing (constructive learning) does, indeed, provide better results than learning by being taught (instructive learning)."

What *Frequency 1550* also shows is that the strict dichotomy between instructionist and constructionist philosophies of education is an untenable one. When we adopt the split between "playing" and "making" games in education as discussed by Yasmin Kafai (2006), *Frequency 1550* clearly reveals aspects of an instructionist philosophy of learning. For pupils are instructed how to play this well-designed game, both by exploring an unknown medieval world and by selecting possibilities that were programmed in advance. In this way, the game makes it easier and more pleasurable for pupils to learn the medieval history of Amsterdam. At the same time, however, these pupils have to construct the knowledge essential to playing and winning the game – what is generally called "constructivism." They have to construct multimedia messages to do so, elements that belong to a constructionist philosophy of learning. What we are witnessing here is what Paul Kirschner has termed "a fusion of the extremes" (Kirschner, 2006, p. 5). *Frequency 1550* shows that pupils are no longer mere consumers of culture, but that they also can be instructed in how to participate in its production, namely by exploring, selecting, and constructing all sorts of cultural and historical meanings and practices (see Raessens, 2005).

Digital Lifestyle. The second result showed that pupils felt motivated to learn about Amsterdam's history not only by using digital media such as computer games, cell phones, the Internet and locative technology (GPS), but also by using a combination of a game and a story. Although *Frequency 1550* takes place outside the classroom, it is not a form of "informal learning," but of "formal education" involving intention and commitment. What is remarkable about the game is that it appeals to the informal learning skills that pupils playfully acquire using digital technologies outside school (see Smith, 1999). It is important to notice that the success of the game depended largely on faultless, rather unobtrusive technology. On the first day, the pupils Savannah and Scarabee thought the technology difficult to handle: "It took a while before we got used to it. But on Tuesday [the second day] we already did much better" (Rippen, 2005). Both pupils agreed that, in the end, playing the game had enhanced their technological skills. And according to Saar van Kouswijk, the technology was transparent enough not to disturb the game play.

We understand better how pupils became motivated by the gaming elements of *Frequency 1550* by referring to three different relationships between entertainment and education (Ritterfeld & Weber, 2006): the motivation paradigm, the reinforcement paradigm, and the blending paradigm. Firstly, the game experience serves as a motivational facilitator for processing information about the history of Amsterdam. The educational content on the Middle Ages is enriched through entertainment (the motivation paradigm). Secondly, the scores, the achievement of the assignments, and the reward of progress by the game are reinforcement strategies to keep the pupils interested in the game's educational value (the reinforcement paradigm). According to

Ritterfeld & Weber, "both the motivation and the reinforcement paradigm are based on an additive concept of entertainment and education, in which educational information is added to an entertaining program or vice versa (...) Yet (...) entertainment-education unfolds its greatest potential strategy if the information provided becomes an essential part of the entertainment experience" (Ritterfeld & Weber, 2006, pp. 407-408). According to both authors, role-play is a game-format that perfectly blends education and entertainment: "we assume that the mimic of role-play is most sufficient in providing highly immersive experiences with entertainment and education combined. We consider the experience of nonmediation (presence) an indicator for a successful blend" (idem, p. 410) (blending paradigm). As players take on the identity of pilgrims and immerse themselves in historical practices to perform acts like the sobbing of the sailors' wives, they experience these moments of presence.

The pupils described their motivation for the game as follows: "You take much of it in. But especially the struggle with the other teams makes it really nice. Much nicer than a normal history lesson. We are very glad that our teacher was able to arrange this." (Rippen, 2005) In response to the question whether they had learned more from playing the game than from a book, they answered: "H'm, yes I think so." (idem) The pupils had no difficulties with the non-linear structure of the game; they enjoyed the freedom that it provided. The narrative scenario also turned out to be an effective way to make them enthusiastic about this historical game.

But some aspects of the story and the game were problematic. Some of the pupils identified themselves so strongly with the story that they had difficulties differentiating between the fictional story elements (such as the role of the medieval city's bailiff in the game's back-story) and the real source material (such as the story of The Miracle of Amsterdam). And though it seems to be a good idea to use a narrative framework for bringing together the micro-elements of the game, some pupils thought that the storyline was not sufficiently sustained by the game elements and vice versa. Some also thought that the scenario was too complex, which made it difficult for them to fully understand the goal and the mission of the game and limited the flow of the game. One of the aims of this pilot was to find out how long the game ideally ought to take. Many commented that the game should take no more than a few hours, instead of two days. Last, but not least, some of the pupils thought there was too much emphasis on the learning part, which spoiled the fun part of the game for them.

Social Learning. While playing the game and discussing game tactics, for example, pupils used and further developed their communication and collaboration skills. Therefore, Waag Society seems to be right in calling *Frequency 1550* a form of social learning, or, as Paul Kirschner says, a form of dependent learning. This is "the acquisition of competencies which include not only individual knowledge and cognitive skills, but also attitudes and interpersonal skills (i.e. social and affective). The learning process is a group process leading to group achievement and is assessed as such" (Kirschner, 2006, p. 8). At first sight, the game does, indeed, seem to oppose "independent learning." Within the independence paradigm, "learning, which is often seen as the acquisition of knowledge and skills, is considered an individualistic achievement of each learner herself/himself and is assessed as such. Goal achievement is autonomous and unrelated to what other students do" (idem, p. 7).

According to Paul Kirschner, however, "independence" versus "dependence" is another dichotomy we have to criticize, comparable to the "instructionism" –"constructionism" dichotomy I discussed earlier. A better way of understanding what happens in *Frequency 1550* is what Kirschner calls "interdependent learning." *Frequency 1550* has both an independent aspect (each pupil has his/her own individual responsibility) and a dependent one (as part of a team, they are all dependent on each other). An individual pupil is not 'only' or 'just' an element of a team of pilgrims, but an entity on his/her own that has to be taken into account. A team of pilgrims can profit from the recognition that each individual member already possesses specific knowledge and skills necessary for the group as a whole to win the game. And the effects of the game depend heavily on previous experiences of each individual pupil. The learning effects of *Frequency 1550* seem to be the result of a productive interplay between dependent and independent aspects.

Presentation and Reflection. On the third day, after two days of playing, all teams gathered at HQ to see what they did best, and to collectively reflect on the media produced, their answers to the questions, and the strategic decisions taken during the game. These aspects became even more meaningful to them when they had to present their results to a wider audience of classmates. By discussing the results, their choices, and the challenges they overcame with team members, but also with 'outsiders,' they learned to reflect better on the creative process in which they were involved.

In this whole process, pupils were encouraged to play with, to take on and reflect on old and new identities. As James-Paul Gee writes: "Learning (...) requires identity work. It requires taking on a new identity and forming bridges from one's old identities to the new one" (Gee, 2003, p. 51). One of the identity issues involved is related to the question of whether learning about Amsterdam's cultural legacy influenced pupils' Dutch cultural identity – a question I will return to at the end of this chapter. Another identity issue relates to the question of how playing the game influenced their identity as "problem solvers," for example. Pupils could only play *Frequency 1550* when they were willing and able to take on the identities of problem solvers (the pupils at HQ searching the Internet for solutions), and/or performers (those pupils who were performing as the sobbing wives of sailors). Although this aspect was not researched thoroughly, pupils who felt comfortable with their new identities must have profited greatly from their old identities, for example, if they already had ICT and/or theatrical competences. It is likely that the presentation and discussion of the game helped them to transform their identity and to reflectively take on these new identities, and, by doing so, internalize them.

History. Is it the case that an active experience of history through the immersing qualities of a location-based game really adds to historical awareness, knowledge and appreciation of the city and its history, and enhances competences such as the interpretation of historical sources and references? This question can be answered positively. However, it is more difficult to determine whether this playful instrument of historical education ought to be privileged over traditional means of dealing with the curriculum.

On the third day of the pilot, educational staff-member of Waag Society Saar van Kouswijk extensively evaluated the game with the participants. The pilgrims had to do a test to determine what they had learned. The test consisted of twelve questions, partly related to the game's back-story, partly related to the factual historical knowledge they had acquired. Some of these questions were: What is the story behind the Miracle of Amsterdam? How did this miracle contribute to the rich and prosperous nature of the city of Amsterdam? What is a bailiff? What is a burgher? How did one become a medieval burgher of the city of Amsterdam? Can you think of a contemporary profession that is comparable to the bailiff's job? What is the meaning of the Schreierstoren (optional question, depending on the zone in which they played the game)? According to Van Kouswijk, "It is clear that they have learned a lot, and that they are also very enthusiastic. The results of the test were better than we had expected. Such a view on the daily life in the Middle Ages has apparently stayed in their memories quite strongly." But the educational concept of the game was also problematic in some respects. Though the test results were positive, some pupils also thought that there were too many assignments, which were too complex for this target group. They also remarked that there were too many learning goals.

Frequency 1550 partly matches the goals of the official History curriculum, in particular those concerning the period: "The time of cities and states: 1000-1500." It is important to notice that the game is not meant to replace, but to complement and reinforce small units of the compulsory subject matter. *Frequency 1550* avoids the criticism of traditional histories that pass on from the past only that which seems relevant today, as formulated by the Italian philosopher Gianni Vattimo: "At school we studied the dates of battles, peace treaties and even revolutions, but they never told us of radical changes in forms of nutrition, or in sexual attitudes, or things of that kind. History speaks only of events involving those who count, the nobles, the souvereigns, or the middle- classes once they became powerful. The poor, and those aspects of life considered 'base,' do not 'make history'" (1992, p. 3). *Frequency 1550*, on the other hand, enables people to participate in a game that is a guided tour along the most significant historic buildings and sites of Amsterdam (such as the Schreierstoren) and learn about their architecture and preservation on the basis of episodes from the life stories of ordinary people (such as the innkeeper of 't Aepgen). The game offers a compelling reconstruction of micro-aspects of everyday life in the medieval city of Amsterdam.

4 Future Research *Frequency 1550*

In 2006-2007, *Frequency 1550* will be played ten times with a slightly adapted educational concept. The effects of the game will be researched more systematically and in more detail when compared to the pilot. The learning results I described earlier are based upon the evaluation of the game by the designers and players, their personal observations, and on the test, not on an extensive evaluative study. This future research will focus on four aspects: the knowledge of Amsterdam's cultural heritage acquired by pupils; the impact of gaming and storytelling on pupils' motivation for, and engagement with, the learning process; cognitive skills, such as spatial abilities, media literacy, decision making, problem solving; and the pupils' potential for further, life-long learning (so-called metacognitive learning-to-learn competences). Metacognition refers to the fact that pupils are conscious about their strategies for knowledge acquisition or problem-solving for example. We will also look at the possible restrictions of this approach in terms of costs and application in other fields such as physics, mathematics, biology, etc.

In educational terms, *Frequency 1550* is a mediated learning environment in which pupils cooperate and communicate with each other on historical locations, using today's technology, such as PCs, the Internet, cell phones, and GPS. What makes this a special case is the presence of the game and a story line which situates pupils in the historical context itself. The teams interact with the system and compete with each other, and, thus, they influence the course of the game. In order to measure the effects of *Frequency 1550*, the game will be compared with a project-based collaborative learning environment in which the game and story elements are missing.

Two hundred and fifty pupils will play the game, from ten classes at the Montessori Comprehensive School Amsterdam and the Open School Community Bijlmer (both are secondary schools). The same number of pupils from ten other classes at these schools will receive comparable assignments in a learning environment where small groups of pupils will be collaborating via PCs and the Internet. The four types of effects will be measured immediately before, immediately after, and two months after the playing of the game. The comparability of the game and non-game settings are guaranteed by taking into account four variables that can interfere with the end results, namely the differences between boys and girls, between competent and less competent students, between students with a varying degree of ICT competences, and between students with different ethnical backgrounds. Why is the latter variable important? The *Yearbook ICT and Society. The Digital Generation* (De Haan and Van 't Hof, 2006) argues that migrants' use of the Internet is decreasing when compared to native students. If the number of migrant and native students in both populations differs considerably, the researchers could end up with a study of ethnic differences instead of a study of the impact of gaming.

Qualitative and quantitative empirical research will be carried out by the Graduate School of Teaching and Learning (University of Amsterdam), and the IVLOS Institute of Education (Utrecht University). Research assistants will observe the students, and students and teachers will be interviewed. The four effects will be measured quantitatively. Research will look at the different effects of *Frequency 1550* on the groups mentioned above, taking the four variables into account. Research of the identity issues at stake is part of the research program *Playful identities. From narrative to ludic self-construction* (see www.playful-identities.nl). The impact of these kinds of spatial games and environmental storytelling on learning processes will be researched within the GATE-project: *Game research for training and entertainment* (see www.gameresearch.nl). Both projects belong to the New Media and Digital Culture department (Utrecht University).

5   Dutch National Historical Museum

In September, 2006, the Dutch government decided upon the establishment of a National Historical Museum in the Netherlands (NHM[3]). Just as is the case with *Frequency 1550*, the goal of the NHM is to reinforce the Dutch population's historical knowledge and understanding. Taking as its starting point "The Canon of the Netherlands," the things everybody should know about Dutch history and culture, the museum wants to present a complete and coherent chronological overview of Dutch history that is divided into ten periods. As we have seen above, one of those periods – "The time of cities and states (1000–1500)" – is at the center of *Frequency 1550*. The museum is aimed at a wide audience, in particular pupils of primary and secondary schools, and will be part of the teaching activities within the History curriculum. To reach this audience, the NHM wants to be a place of "living" instead of "frozen" history. The basic principle underlying the NHM is that not only Dutch historical consciousness, but also Dutch cultural and historical identity need to be strengthened, in order to improve the social cohesion of Dutch society. "Without knowledge of their history the Dutch do not know who they are" summarizes the motto of the NHM succinctly.

The idea of a National Historical Museum was disputed from its beginning in 2003, not only because the idea of a single history of a single nation is being undermined by processes of globalization and fragmentation, but also because such a history is undesirable to some critics. In their view, it would ignore the cultural diversity and multiculturality so typical of the Netherlands. This does not mean, however, that it is impossible to define cultural identity or that cultural citizenship forming would not be desirable. Citizenship can be defined as the membership of a community based on a set of common values, not only in an economical and political, but also in a social and cultural sense. It is crucial that people have the right "to belong to an identity, to contribute to its definition or to withdraw from belonging in order to create new meaning" (Alberto Melucci, 1989, as cited in Uricchio, 2003, pp. 9-10). They must be free to

---

3   See http://www.nationaalmuseum.nl

question old values and identities and search for new ones. The ability to do so, that is, to participate in the kinds of cultural practices the NHM wants to focus on (as I have discussed in this chapter), constitutes an important condition for the formation of citizenship and the diversity mentioned before. As I have discussed above, pupils who play *Frequency 1550* have to collect so-called "Days of Burghership" to acquire burghership or citizenship. Because they want to win the game, they acquire competences that are a necessary condition for becoming empowered social and cultural citizens in today's world, to echo William Uricchio (2003).

We could take Jenkins' idea of "environmental storytelling" as a metaphor for such an interplay between a unified and diversified identity. The chronological overview of Dutch history could function as a back-story that not only gives structure and meaning to the performances of a multiplicity of micro-narratives, but also functions as a play area or staging ground for these performances. In the plan that sketches the outlines of the NHM, the author Wim van der Weiden pays attention to this. According to Van der Weiden, the NHM must not only focus on "the 'highlights' of our history" (think of the Schreierstoren), but also on "the history of everyday life" (think of 't Aepgen), not only on "those things we can be proud of" (our self-image as a tolerant nation, for example), but also on "the black pages of our history (for example the slave trade and the police actions"[4] (Van der Weiden, 2006, p. 6). This is why on Prinsjesdag 2006, Queen Beatrix referred to the founding of the NHM with the words "Culture binds and enriches."[5] In conformity with these words, the NHM must have in mind the cultural enrichment of Holland as the result of migration, and the solidarity between the different cultures present in the Netherlands.

Digital media play an important role in this plan. Thanks to the media-specific characteristics of cell phones, the Internet, and serious games, the public will be able to experience the history of the Netherlands in an interactive and multi-medial way. Though *Frequency 1550* is not mentioned in the plan, Van der Weiden is enthusiastic about elements that also play a decisive role in this particular game: the use of quests inside and outside the museum, short documentary video clips received on cell phones, the use of various media that strengthen each other, and the use of a strong story that a visitor to the museum can experience him/herself. All of these elements evoke the image of a game like *Frequency 1550*. Games and stories are not only appropriate metaphors for cultural identity, as I suggested above, they are also important and powerful tools for individuals and collectives to actively and reflexively construct their identi-

---

4   "The police actions (Dutch: politionele acties) were the two military operations that the Netherlands undertook on Java and Sumatra against the Republic of Indonesia to reestablish colonial rule after World War Two. The first operation took place from July 21 until August 5, 1947, the second in December 1948 and January 1949. The operations took place during the time of the Indonesian fight for independence." Available from:
     http://en.wikipedia.org/wiki/Politionele_acties [Accessed 17 September 2006].

5   On Prinsjesdag, the Queen of Holland delivers a speech to a joint session of the Senate and House of Representatives, in which she sets out the government's plans for the year to come. Available from: http://www.koninklijkhuis.nl/english [Accessed 17 September 2006].

ties (see www.playful-identities.nl). It is likely that mobile and location-based learning games like *Frequency 1550* are going to play an important role in a future Dutch National Historical Museum. Although they are still small in number and micro-sized, the impact of these kinds of serious games on established cultural practices may turn out to be greater than we would expect at first sight.

Acknowledgments

This chapter is partly based upon descriptions of *Frequency 1550* on the game's website (see freq1550.waag.org). I would like to thank Saar van Kouswijk, Aske Hopman and Henk van Zeijts for providing me with unpublished documents on the game, for discussing the technological infrastructure and educational concept of the game with me and for helpful comments on this chapter. I would also like to thank Paul Kirschner for his useful feedback and Christien Franken for editing this chapter. This text was written in the context of the Media Research programme at Utrecht University, the Netherlands (see www.let.uu.nl/umr).

References

Gee, J.P. (2003) *What Video Games Have to Teach Us about Learning and Literacy.* New York: Palgrave Macmillan.

Gee, J.P. (2006) *Media literacy & gaming literacy.* Symposium of the Games, Learning and Society Conference 2.0, June 15-16 2006, Madison Wisconsin. Available from: <http://www.mediasite.com> [Accessed 17 September 2006].

Haan, J. de & Hof, C. van 't (2006) *Jaarboek ICT en samenleving. De digitale generatie.* [Yearbook ICT and Society. The Digital Generation]. Amsterdam: Boom.

Hug, T. (2005) *Microlearning and Narration.* Paper presented at the fourth Media in Transition conference, May 6-8, 2005, MIT, Cambridge (MA), USA, Available from: <http://web.mit.edu/comm-forum/mit4/papers/hug.pdf> [Accessed 17 September 2006].

Hug, T. (2006) Microlearning: a new pedagogical challenge (Introductory Note) In: Hug, T., Lindner, M. & Bruck, P.A. eds. *Microlearning: Emerging Concepts, Practices and Technologies after e-Learning.* Innsbruck: Innsbruck University Press, pp. 7–11.

Jenkins, H. (2004) Game design as narrative architecture. In: Wardrip-Fruin, N. & Harrigan, P. eds. *First Person. New Media as Story, Performance, and Game.* Cambridge, MA: The MIT Press, pp. 118–130.

Juul, J. (2005) Games telling stories? In: Raessens, J. & Goldstein, J. eds. *Handbook of Computer Game Studies.* Cambridge, MA: The MIT Press, pp. 219–226.

Kafai, Y. (2006) Playing and making games for learning. Instructionist and constructionist perspectives for game studies. In: *Games and Culture. A Journal of Interactive Media*, 1 (1), pp. 36–40.

Kirschner, P. (2006) *(Inter)dependent Learning. Learning Is Interaction.* Inaugural address spoken upon the acceptance of the position of Professor of Educational Psychology, Utrecht University. Available from: <http://www.uu.nl/content/OratieKirschner-Learningis Interaction-Geheel-A4-FINAL.pdf> [Accessed 17 September 2006].

Mak, G. (1999) *Amsterdam. A Brief Life of the City*. London: The Harvill Press.

Melucci, A. (1989) *Nomads of the Present: Social Movements and Individual Needs in Contemporary Society*. London: Hutchinson Radius.

Raessens, J. (2005) Computer games as participatory media culture. In: Raessens, J. & Goldstein, J. eds. *Handbook of Computer Game Studies*. Cambridge, MA: The MIT Press, pp. 373–388.

Reinsma, R. (2006). Zo oud als de weg naar Kralingen. Hebben Nederlandse spreekwoorden en uitdrukkingen toekomst? [As old as the road to Kralingen. Do Dutch proverbs and expressions have a future?]. In: *Onze Taal*. Den Haag: Genootschap Onze Taal, pp. 202–205.

Rippen, R. (2005) *UMTS pilot in middeleeuws Amsterdam* [UMTS pilot in medieval Amsterdam]. Available from: <http://www.computable.nl/artikel.jsp?archive=1&id=1415901> [Accessed 17 September 2006].

Ritterfeld, U. & Weber, R. (2006) Video games for entertainment and education. In: Vorderer, P. & Bryant, J. eds. *Playing Video Games. Motives, Responses, and Consequences*. Mahwah, NJ: Lawrence Erlbaum Associates, Publishers.

Smith, M. (1999) Informal learning. Available from: <http://www.infed.org/biblio/inf-lrn.htm> [Accessed 17 September 2006].

Uricchio, W. (2003) Cultural Citizenship in the Age of P2P Networks. Available from: <http://www.hum.ku.dk/modinet/Conference_aug/Uricchiofinal.pdf> [Accessed 17 September 2006].

Vattimo, G. (1992) *The Transparent Society*. Cambridge, UK: Polity Press.

Weiden, W. v.d. (2006) *Het Nationaal Historisch Museum. Een visie* [The National Historic Museum. A vision]. Den Haag: Ministry of Education, Culture and Science [http://www.minocw.nl].

When Remix Culture Meets Microlearning

Ravi Purushotma

Educators have often tried to shrink the gap between formal education and every-day life by trying to incorporate elements from popular culture into their formal curriculum. In the past, this was extremely challenging as popular media, such as a television broadcast, was often in a format that could not readily be manipulated or customized to suit learning goals. As a result, educators were prevented from layering educational microcontent inside popular media itself, but rather would need to hold any media at a distance and instead create separate textual materials for adding pedagogical content (i.e. creating a worksheet to be filled out after watching a video).

Today's popular media, however, is often designed specifically to be manipulated, customized and extended. Combined with the wide proliferation of home-user media production tools, the practice of editing, mixing and reshaping popular media has become a central part of popular culture. This chapter aims to identify different methods employed by participants in popular culture to interact with, manipulate and mix together popular media. Curriculum designers are then encouraged to try some of the same direct manipulation techniques in order to create natural hooks where they can connect microlearning content directly into popular media content.

A nation housing over one-third of the earth's illiterate population (NLM 2000), India has always been under immense pressure to improve its education system. Yet their challenge is formidable, for many of the cash-strapped provincial governments the extensive investment in proper classrooms and infrastructure required to support a modern educational system is simply not feasible. Furthermore, even those governments capable of stretching their budgets far enough to provide schools and literacy training to their citizens often encounter lackluster results, as they struggle to motivate students to set aside their work and everyday obligations in order to attend classes and devote time to studying materials that have little apparent connection to the rest of their life. As a result, many adults ultimately choose to live their lives without any regular exposure to literacy training.

If we look at the slums of Ahmedabad city, however, we see a very different picture. While formal schooling is still well outside the reach of much of the population, many of them do have some form of access to a television. In particular, many of them choose to watch the popular television series Chitrageet, a weekly broadcast of music videos for popular Gujarati film songs. Noticing this, rather than constructing a traditional educational infrastructure focused on dedicated study periods, literacy researchers opted to instead insert pedagogical interventions directly into Chitrageet (Kothary, Padey & Chudgar, 2004). Building upon techniques previously used for foreign lan-

guage subtitling, they are able to modify Chitrageet to deliver same-language synchro-
nized subtitles designed to facilitate literacy at a cost of US$ 0.0065 per year per per-
son. While initially there were concerns that such a simplistic layering of pedagogical
content would simply be ignored by viewers, the results from their study show a significant increase in viewer literacy rates versus a control group over a period of 16 episodes. Interestingly, rather than seeing the pedagogical interventions as detracting
from their entertainment experience, 99.5% of respondents (N=704) indicated a preference for the intervention over the unsubtitled version – as literacy became a tool that
could help them better understand the lyrics used in Chitrageet. Additionally, many
viewers pro-actively requested further educational materials related to Chitrageet.

In the developed world, we are fortunate enough to be able to devote a reasonable portion of our disposable income towards building an educational infrastructure capable
of delivering dedicated and focused educational content, rather than being forced to
build upon the infrastructure of popular culture such as was done with Chitrageet.
While this is undoubtedly a good thing in many cases, we need to question if our current means is always the best way of constructing a learning experience. Would learners in Ahmedabad city have been more successful if they had been asked to attend a
classroom so that they could formally study Chitrageet lyrics? More likely, the integration of learning into their pre-existing weekly practice of watching Chitrageet and
the utilization of the small moments waiting between song verses to skim the available
subtitles was precisely what facilitated the success with the Chitrageet study.

One concern with trying to apply pedagogical techniques like the same language subtitling used in Chitrageet to the entertainment media used in western culture is that our
media landscape is far more complex than a typical Ahmedabad villager's and that
their situation was unique because of their ability to harness pre-existing technologies
like subtitling. If we look closely at the cultural practices surrounding today's popular
media, however, we see that not only is layering, modifying and remixing content
technologically easier than ever – but that it is already widespread in contemporary
youth entertainment culture. In this chapter I outline how playing video games,
browsing and searching the web, social networking and other activities prevalent in the
lives of today's youth are built upon modular media pieces that can easily be extended
by educators. Besides creating more entertaining and engaging curriculum, this
approach opens numerous possibilities for challenging expectations for how we
engage with educational materials. Often youth will engage with popular media in a
highly asynchronous manner, continually rotating between different activities as best
suits them. With traditional educational materials, however, learners are asked to put
aside all "distractions" such as video games and social web applications in order to
complete a full assignment. By inserting pedagogical content directly into popular
media we encourage learners to adopt the same patterns of micro-engagement used

elsewhere when working with educational content. In particular, I focus on foreign language learning as a discipline particularly well suited to these kinds of experiences.

Video Games

In the early 90's, video games seemed a panacea for educators hoping to sneak small fragments of learning content inside the everyday entertainment activities of youth. Back then various "edutainment" titles abounded; however, most failed so spectacularly that today game developers routinely go out of their way to ensure that people do not consider their games as educational. This is because rather than meaningfully including learning experiences as part of a larger well-designed game experience, the original wave of edutainment titles unfortunately were built upon poorly designed games that occasionally halted, forcing players to learn educational content before allowing them return to the game. As Henry Jenkins, co-director of the MIT Education Arcade project describes it, "most edutainment products combined the entertainment value of a bad lecture with the educational value of a bad video game" (IT Conversations, 2005).

As kids would sometimes even prefer their school homework to an edutainment video game, the market soon capitulated with many designers concluding that an educational game could never compete with an entertainment game. Fortunately, education and entertainment games no longer need to compete with one another. If we look at today's entertainment video games, many bare little resemblance to the games prevalent in the early 90's when educators first attempted to insert small fragments of learning content inside games. Back then, game worlds were relatively fixed, asking the player only to play out the action of a pre-programmed story. Today, however, games are considerably more open-ended, with many of them encouraging players to take an active role in the construction of the game itself through the use of various 'mod' tools.

For example, the current number one selling video game The Sims 2 does not prescribe any explicit goal or way to win. Rather, the game presents itself as a "virtual doll house" in which users play out and optionally share stories with one another. As a result of the enormous flexibility of this game, tens of thousands of player created content pieces or game modifications are freely available on the internet. Surprisingly, so far little has been attempted by educators to use the extensive mod tools available for games such as The Sims 2 to insert learning content in a way that naturally integrates with the larger game experience.

For example, mod tools for many games provide access to all the language data used in all the different international versions of a game. This allows curriculum designers to easily manipulate popular video games to create opportunities for foreign language microlearning (see Purushotma, 2005).

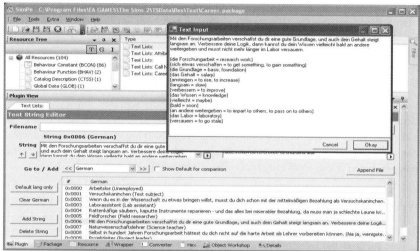

Figure 1. The mod tool SimPE is used to add English annotations to the German language data for the game The Sims 2 in order to create an annotated video game similar to the annotated readers currently used in foreign language classrooms. (available at http://www.langwidge.com/simsfiles.html)

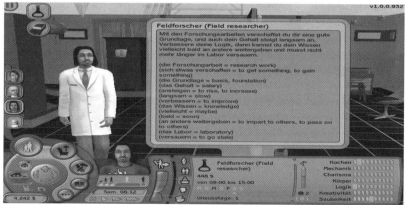

Figure 2. The resulting game screen from the modifications in figure 1 are shown, whereby the mod tool automatically integrates annotations into The Sims 2. Students learning German can then play the actual German version of the game, but learning content is always easily available to players should they have difficulties.

Educational researcher Kurt Squire used a customized map in the game Civilization III in order to provide teachable moments in world history classes (Squire, 2004). The MIT Education Arcade team modded the medieval dungeon game Neverwinter Nights to provided students a virtual recreation of the Virginia town Colonial Williamsburg as it existed in the Spring of 1775 (Education Arcade, 2006). The Sims 2 ships with a customizable literature theme in which all the characters in the game world are taken from Shakespearian plays (Wikipedia, 2006b). The Center for Advanced Research in Technology for Education used the shooting game Unreal Tournament as the basis for a game teaching Iraqi customs, culture and language (CARTE, 2006). Smilebit modified the zombie shooter The House of the Dead to rapidly produce The Typing of the Dead – perhaps the most engaging typing tutor ever created (Wikipedia, 2006a).

While there is no single system or technique for modding across all video games, most fan websites for any major game today will list examples of mods created for a given game. By studying the ways in which youth are modifying games for entertainment purposes, educators can often discover ways in which pedagogical content can seamlessly be blended into an already successful commercial game.

Walking the Virtual Dog

Another change in video games important to understand when designing microlearning interventions is the evolution of the different player feedback systems used today. Originally, many games relied simply on providing "points" as players made correct choices, similar to the way schools award high grades to students who provide correct answers. If we look at NeoPets, the number one online kids game with 115,033,662 pet owners bringing 339,343,790,000 page views to the site (Neopets, 2006), we can see how player feedback in the game world has evolved. The first thing a player entering the Neopets site does is to adopt one of many different species of virtual pets for them to raise as their own. In playing the game, kids need to take care of their pets: feeding them, playing with them and buying them items. For kids who spend their lives being told what to do by parents, games like Neopets gives them the chance to shift themselves into the role of being the caretaker (albeit of a virtual pet). If a player fails to feed their pet when they become hungry, rather than simply loosing points, they witness their pet struggling with starvation and begging the player to take better care when they next log online. As a result, kids become highly attached to their pets and motivated to constantly maintain their pet's well-being at regular intervals.

At first, many parents like Mr. Shih Chi Ning became concerned that his daughters "would spend hour upon hour at the site to earn enough NeoPoints to buy rare items for their pets" rather than working on their homework. "I wanted to put their pets up for adoption at the virtual pound but they cried and cried" he explains, "they were so attached to their pets, I thought that attachment had a potential to motivate the child to do his schoolwork first." A businessman working with as managing director of

Micromax Technologies, Mr. Shih then went to the Neopets Asia division and created a partnership whereby diligent students could receive virtual money to buy treats for their neopets in exchange for doing their homework (Soh, 2002).

In educational settings, curricular designers often try to keep feedback as simple and efficient as possible. Neopets would suggest, however, that providing rich feedback with an affective dimension could improve motivation and engagement. Rather than developing microlearning experiences in which feedback is provided through quantitative scoring or direct responses, we should also explore the possibilities for providing qualitative feedback in which learner responses have meaningful consequences on characters with emotional depth. If the success of Neopets is an indication, this might result in an increased motivation by learners to remain engaged throughout the day.

While we are still only at the very beginning of understanding the best reward and feedback structures to motivate players and learners, research in game studies can give us some clues. In one study, researchers wired participants with a series of psychophysiological measuring devices (EEC, EKG, EMC and SCL) and had them play the video game Super Monkey Ball 2 (also referred to as Monkey Bowling 2). While the underlying mechanics of Super Monkey Ball 2 resemble that of traditional bowling, the game replaces the bowling ball with an adorable animated monkey running inside a semi-transparent sphere. In the event that the sphere misses the bowling pins and instead falls outside of the bowling lane, the player is presented with an amusing animation sequence depicting the monkey falling off into the void of outer space.

From a functional perspective, this event represents nothing more than a failure condition, in which an educational designer might have simply told the user "You failed, please try again." However, when the monkey instead implicitly gives the feedback of failure in Super Monkey Ball 2 by falling off into outer space, all psychophysiological measures indicated a sense of enjoyment by the players. As the researchers describe "thus, although the event in question represents a clear failure [by the player], several physiological indices showed that it elicited positively valenced high-arousal emotion (i.e., joy), rather than disappointment. This is an important finding suggesting that event characteristics such as visual impressiveness and excitingness may be more potent determinants of the emotional response of the player compared to the meaning of the event in terms of failure or success."

The researchers next created a condition in which players explicitly received negative feedback after a poor throw. Contrary to their previous findings, they discovered that players

> appeared to elicit depressed affect characterized by a combination of negative valence and low arousal. The data of the present study suggest that the valence of the emotional response to game events may vary as a function of the active participation of the player. Recall that a putatively negative event the player

actively participated in (falling off the edge of the lane) elicited a positive emotional response. In contrast, [this event] characterized by passive reception of negative feedback elicited a negative emotional response. This finding is in line with our prior research (Ravaja, et al., 2004) showing that, when playing Super Monkey Ball 2, the valence of the emotional response was positive when the player actively participated in a putatively negative game event, but it was negative when the player passively perceived a replay of the same event. (Ravaja, et al., 2005)

These results suggest that when trying to design appropriate feedback mechanisms for microcontent embedded in a larger activity, we must be careful not to break the larger flow of a user's participation. Rather than breaking from an experience to provide learners with external meta-descriptive feedback, we need to instead devise feedback mechanisms that continue the learner's involvement with the base content – such as humorously playing out possible consequences of a wrong answer.

Figure 3. Super Monkey Ball 2

Foxes, Monkeys and Purple Bunnies

The overwhelming success of Neopets has also surprised many in the games community by its use of relatively simplistic web technologies. Whereas most popular video games today require players to launch a separate game application in order to play, Neopets is designed to be playable entirely within a web browser from neopets.com. As a result, the graphics and game features in Neopets are often considered drastically inferior to most modern video games – presumably far more of a degradation than is worth the additional step loading a separate game application. Yet, in practice, the integration of Neopets into a user's web-browser creates a far more important psychological link for players. Each time a player is browsing the web for another purpose and has a short break from their work, the thought of quickly dashing to neopets.com to feed their pet becomes naturally ingrained into their mind.

Besides video games, another popular target for amateur media modders are their own web browsers. Following the decline in popularity of the original Netscape Navigator web browser, Netscape Corporation decided to try a new strategy of making the underlying program code openly available to anyone who wanted to help improve or modify the browser. Originally re-branded as the Mozilla web browser and subsequently as Firefox, a large community of worldwide volunteers began tinkering with the underlying structure of Firefox and making it even easier for others with less technical experience to join in. Today, thousands of amateur produced browser extensions are freely available for download from the Firefox site.

As with video games, it is surprising how few extensions have been developed for educational purposes. Particularly for those interested in delivering microlearning experiences, browser extensions open a rich pool of possibilities for intelligently combining learning content with a user's everyday activities. In interviewing foreign language learners, I found that many of the more successful students didn't set aside dedicated study times as was prescribed by their teacher, but would instead use the commercial breaks while watching television as opportunities to review vocabulary words. This matches with the Kaiser Family foundation reports (2005) that two-thirds of youth in America either watch television, talk on the phone, instant message, listen to music, or surf the Web for fun some or most of the time they're doing homework. Besides only doing homework, the report showed that overall youth today spent an average of an extra hour per day multitasking between multiple different media forms as compared to 5 years ago. Particularly, as youth encounter pauses in one media form – such as a commercial break or waiting for websites to load – they are more apt to try and temporarily engage in another task until the pause completes.

To take advantage of this, I developed a small browser extension that analyzes a user's browsing patterns, then automatically updates a small portion of the screen to deliver a new foreign language vocabulary word whenever they are waiting for a website to load. Rather than creating new flashcard sets, a teacher simply enters the week's vocabulary words onto a central server and they are then automatically pushed to students at the moment when their attention is least scarce.

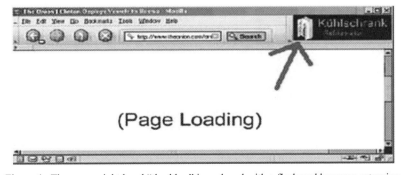

Figure 4. The upper-right hand "throbber" is replaced with a flashcard browser extension, designed to give learners new words at key moments while their attention is least scare.

With high speed connections now commonplace, capturing the time spent waiting for pages to load is no longer as effective as it once was. Still, browser extensions offer extraordinary power for creative educators to devise new mechanisms for augmenting a web browsing experience to include microlearning moments. For example, extensions like Outfoxed, Netmite and Purple Bunny allow friends and fellow website visitors to post comments directly into other viewer's website windows. Normally these programs are used for users to flag things like inaccurate content for subsequent viewers, but they provide the flexibility for anyone to easily insert customized annotations of any type into a specified website.

Perhaps the most interesting Firefox extension, Greasemonkey (Mozdev, 2006) allows users to selectively replace javascript code on specific websites. For example, one script provides Toronto users viewing Amazon.com with inline information and links notifying them if a particular book they are looking at is available in their local library. Another tells customers if the book they are looking at is available cheaper from another merchant.

Using Greasemonkey, curricular designers could intelligently augment the way any mainstream website appears to a student in order to also include in-line pedagogical content. For example, numerous scripts exist to remove advertisement images from websites. However, the resulting websites often look awkward as they try to adjust for the empty space where advertisements once were. One could easily modify these extensions to replace advertisement images with images filled with any learning content such as foreign language vocabulary relevant to the current site.

Figure 5. A book listing on amazon.com is modified to inform viewers that a particular book is also available free at the local public library, with a link provided to the library catalog description.

Chasing Bee's Across 40,000 Payphones

While video game and browser modding represent two of the earliest forms of remix culture, as more technologies and services enter the Web 2.0 age, in which all media content is designed to be remixed and interconnected into all other media, it is important to realize what we are seeing so far is actually part of a much larger cultural shift that is taking place. Going forward, we should expect entirely new media experiences to be constructed from the remixing of other media content. The key for constructing microlearning experiences, then, will be understanding how different media is mixed together and learning how to intelligently layer learning experiences at the points of connection. Already we are seeing the emergence of popular games constructed by connecting together a variety of transmedia experiences:

On July 16t[h] 2004, a number of popular website owners received mysterious packages at their doorstep (Szulborski, 2005). The package were ostensibly from a company named "Margaret's Honey" and included a sample bottle of honey from the company. Also included in the package were a series of cutout letters, including the letters "B", "I", "L", "O", "S", "V" and three of the letter "E". After playing with the letters, a number of the recipients noticed that the letters could be arranged to form the sentence "I Love Bees", which prompted them to then try looking up "ilovebees.com." Upon reaching the website, which displayed a page for Margaret's Honey, the site appeared as though it had been hacked with strange messages appearing:

HALT – MODULE CORE HEMORRHAGE
Control has been yielded to the
SYSTEM PERIL DISTRIBUTED REFLEX.
This medium is classified, and has a
STRONG INTRUSIVE INCLINATION.
In 5 days, network throttling will erode.
In 19 days this medium will metastasize.
COUNTDOWN TO WIDE AWAKE AND PHYSICAL:
32:15:38:10:831
Make your decisions accordingly.

At the end was an appeal from Dana, Margaret's niece, asking visitors to help her figure out what was wrong with the website. Many of the recipients then posted notes on their websites asking others to help them trace down the cause of the hacks to Dana's website. As their friends looked over the website, some noticed the images were scrambled in systematic ways which ultimately held encoded messages within them. Rather than answers, however, those messages contained even more perplexing messages bringing viewers even deeper into the game world of I Love Bee's and requiring them to bring in even more friends to help. Ultimately, I Love Bee's swelled to include over 600,000 players world wide, comprising one of the largest pools of collective intelligence assembled for history's most challenging scavenger hunt.

Throughout the course of the game, clues would lead players to a series of GPS coordinates and time codes. Each of the GPS coordinates would correspond to one of a series of 40,000 payphones scattered across all 50 U.S. states and 8 countries which would ring at the specified time. By intelligently networking between the 600,000 players and effectively using technologies such as SMS, players were able to identify and relay instructions to players nearby key payphones scattered across vast geographic distances, within 20 seconds of notification. At the payphones, players would receive 15 second fragments of a 6 hour radio drama they then reconstructed on the web (McGonigal, 2005).

What is interesting about I Love Bee's is that it was a game constructed entirely out of technologies more commonly used for other purposes. In fact, at no point during the game did I Love Bee's even admit that it was a game. For many of the players, the result was a confusingly immersive experience in which they began to see much of the real world in the context of the game world. As one of the players described in an online posting "here we are, every one of us excited at blurring the lines between story and reality. The game promises to become not just entertainment, but our lives." In numerous cases, sites and mysteries not connected to the game were solved by confused players thinking that they were still in the game (McGonigal, 2003).

By constructing experiences out of technologies youth already commonly engage with for non-learning content, besides greatly saving on production costs, we also encourage students to blur lines and break from traditional roles of how one should engage with learning content. So far the focus on these efforts in educational settings has been on improving how actively students engage with materials, but we could easily imagine similar systems that also improve how often students engage with educational materials. Consider the Medieval Space project undertaken at Byrd middle school in Virginia. Here history teachers mocked up a MySpace clone titled "Medieval Space" for students to create social networking profiles for historical characters.

Traditionally, students working on an assignment such as this might have been asked set aside a single study session in a distraction-free environment where they would be asked to read a biography from a textbook, then fill in blanks on a worksheet. With an assignment like Medieval space, we could more easily imagine a model where students might alternatively just keep the activity open in a separate browser tab, occasionally checking in to see what updates other students had posted throughout the day – the way they do with the popular social networking site "MySpace."

Of course, we have to question if it is really worth all the effort given how easy it is to make a fill-in-the-blank worksheet as compared to programing an entire social networking application. Then again, by using services such as www.ning.com, the latter approach may actually end up easier than the former. With Ning, educators simply select a social web application from a catalog with 1,000's of sample applications. They then click 'clone this app', and need only to customize an already existing application with pedagogical content using a pallete of user-friendly tools. In this way, students are given assignments in the exact format used for the non-academic applications they already use throughout the day – encouraging them to adopt similar usage patterns.

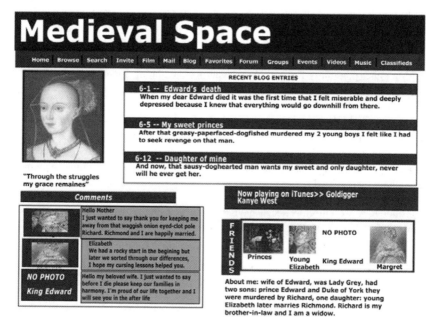

Figure 6. Medieval Space entry for Queen Elizabeth. They were started off with Richard III as an example page and I think that was key. His "currently playing iTunes song" was "Only God can Judge Me Now" by 2Pac and that started to loosen them up. His quote was "Don't hate the player, hate the game." and they did a great job finding more suitable quotes and songs for their pages. (BionicTeacher, 2006)

Finding Directions, Learning Geography and Conquering the World

In the summer of 2005, Google released Google Earth, a free tool enabling users to navigate their way through satellite or airplane imagery and extensive geographic data. Originally, users of Google Earth would use the tool to help them locate a nearby restaurant, find driving directions or simply view images of their houses from outer space. However, by the fall of 2005, remixers and modders were already co-opting Google Earth as a tool to support extensive fictional universes. In one game, Google Earth Wars, thousands of players would choose to make virtual army bases in real world locations. Their bases would then show up on all other player's copies of Google Earth, allowing them to interact with one another, all from within the Google Earth interface.

For anyone playing these games, one level of learning possibilities is instantly clear: as Google Earth was itself a geography tool, any remix experience derived from Google Earth will naturally teach geography. By placing my personal base along the Ivory Coast such that I would be in easy striking range of the densely populated city of Lagos, I rapidly acquired a far better understanding of North African geography than from my entire formal education. However, remixing applications like Google Earth holds another possibility for learning relevant for facilitating microlearning. Like with I Love Bee's, entertainment and/or educational experiences built upon real world applications like Google Earth naturally blur the lines between real life and game or learning time. While using Google Earth for looking up driving directions to the movie theater or exploring different cities for an upcoming vacation, there is always the chance that the user will stumble upon a hidden game jewel or a poorly defended city to attack. In this way, players never really leave the game, but continue playing it throughout their everyday life.

Consider how we currently teach navigation in foreign language classrooms versus how youth are engaging with the same content in their everyday lives:

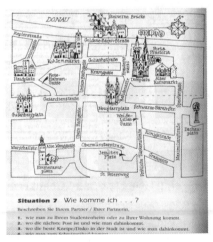

Figure 7. A page taken from one of the best selling German textbooks in California, Kontakte. This activity is designed to familiarize students with different parts of the city and understanding directions from one location to another.

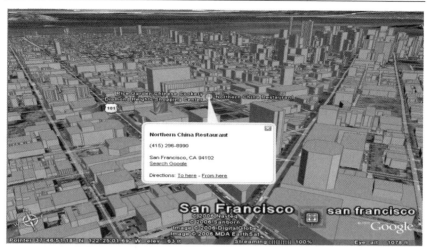

Figure 8. A sample screen of what a youth looking for Chinese restaurants in San Francisco might encounter when using Google Earth. Provides fly-through navigation of the city with street labels, landmarks and directions.

Creating learning exercises by remixing Google Earth to include educational content would have numerous benefits over the textbook page depicted in figure 7: it provides authentic materials which can be rapidly appropriated to provide highly interactive and engaging activities. Perhaps most interesting for microlearning, it places the opportunities to engage in learning activities within the same space as its corresponding everyday activities. Should a Spanish learner in San Francisco looking for directions to a Chinese restaurant become curious about how they might have performed the same task if they were in Mexico City, rather than needing to set aside time to look up a recreation of that experience in a textbook, they could simply move Google Earth to Mexico City and try the actual process – then go back to their original task.

Similarly, any discipline with content oriented around geographic spaces could benefit from innovative modifications to Google Earth. Noel Jenkins (2006), outlines his use of Google Earth to teach city planning. In his class, students synthesize numerous layers of seismographic data, then use Google Earth to sketch out their plans for a new hospital in San Francisco city. While for Jenkins, this activity was completed in a classroom session, like Medieval Space, the format of the assignment could make it easily amenable for being broken-down into micro-tasks performed throughout the day in an open Google Earth window as responses to other student's work.

Microlearning Across Space & Time

As we shift towards microlearning, many of the assumptions made historically about the nature of learning need to be re-examined. Designing an education system 200 years ago, the choice between using print or sound as the underlying media format was clear: recorded sound did not even exist. In the last 10 years, however, the technologies for both creating and consuming recorded sound have dramatically reshaped what can be achieved through aural mediums – requiring us to carefully consider where its advantages and disadvantages lie in relation to printed materials. Most apparently, print mediums give content producers control over how materials are laid out in space, but leave the speed and manner in which materials are consumed to the reader. Auditory mediums, by contrast, ask content producers to fix content in time, but are rarely laid out in space.

Much of the way we have designed educational experiences so far relies upon effective uses of spatial positioning, often juxtapositioning two items for a reader to learn through processes of comparing and contrasting. This gave print mediums a strong advantage over auditory mediums for many educational assignments. Auditory mediums, of course, have their own advantages, making them a popular choice for many popular culture activities. Most notably, as auditory mediums no not take up physical space, they allow listeners to integrate auditory materials into a variety of everyday spaces: listening to the news while driving to work, a song while jogging or a telephone conversation while cooking.

Increasingly, educators are finding ways to exploit the advantages of auditory mediums for learning purposes (Apple, 2006). However, the limitations imposed upon the spatial organization of auditory content leave it at a significant disadvantage for numerous assignments. Most auditory exercises ask students to first listen to materials and then to analyze them afterward. Given the limitations of human short-term memory (Baddeley, 1999), however, it can be difficult for students to remember the content to be analyzed until it finishes playing. This is especially true for activities like listening to songs in foreign languages, where words and sounds are often unfamiliar to the listener.

For anyone who has ever found themselves in the middle of a crowded party, listening to multiple conversations and trying to decide which to join, it is clear that it is indeed possible to simultaneously organize different audio streams spatially. Originally, audio producers tried to recreate this phenomenon by placing different sound streams in different ears – i.e. a foreign song in one ear and the pedagogical explanations in the other ear. If you have ever tried listening to different telephone conversations in each ear, however, you know that is far more difficult than listening to two conversations at a party.

If we reflect on this a little, we can see why. Nowhere in nature is there a situation in which sound enters one ear but not the other. Rather, sound becomes spatialized as the brain records the difference in time that a sound hits one ear versus the other. For example, if somebody is standing to the right of you, any sound they make will enter the right ear before it reaches the left ear. As game designers have invested considerable effort learning how to create immersive soundscapes, the calculations and tools necessary to recreate this experience are now common place in numerous audio editing programs. With the current rise in podcasting popularity, audio editing tools will undoubtedly become even easier to use, more widely available and allow for a variety of new techniques. As this happens, it is important that we consider the full range of possibilities they afford for creating microlearning experiences given their easy integration with everyday spaces and portability.

Micromixing

Historically, education has prided itself as a discipline that enables students to "stand on the shoulders of giants", scaffolding them to see and accomplish entirely new tasks. Today, however, it is the various elements of our popular culture that have learned how to effectively build upon one another to create unprecedentedly rich media experiences. Unfortunately, rather than embracing a more modular approach to media construction, many educators have pushed away popular media and sought to further distinguish between the worlds of education and our everyday entertainment lives.

In the end, we are left with an unfortunate schism between formal and informal learning. Proponents of formal learning lament how informal learning is rendered meaningless by its lack of structure or possibilities for creating meaningful interventions to guide and direct learning outcomes. Informal learning enthusiasts argue that as the informal world around us accelerates, virtually submerging us in a torrent of rich learning opportunities, the stolid educational structures we have dragged with us from past centuries are woefully ill-equipped to keep pace.

Should we choose to use it, the same modular structure that is enabling the development of popular media to accelerate at its extreme rate could be exploited to bridge the formal and in-formal schism. By modifying video games and social web applications for easier integration into the classroom, we bring the rich learning practices commonplace with these media together with the structure offered by a formal curriculum; this can be particularly useful for homework assignments. Conversely, by taking advantage of systems like greasemonkey, we can manipulate and guide the learning that takes place during everyday activities like browsing the web. Unlike non-formal learning which focuses on exploring new contexts and settings which learning activities can be orchestrated, remixing media gives us additional options for removing the respective disadvantages for either formal or informal learning without prescribing a context or setting.

As learning content shrinks to smaller and smaller units, learning contexts become increasingly important. All human memory is based on associations. In a traditional 50-minute lesson, educators often spend the first 15 minutes working to elucidate a clear context for students to associate their learning with, and then time at the end to help students make sense of their learning. A 50-second microsession may have neither of these. Rather, it becomes critical that educators devise means of forging strong connections between micro-content and the contexts provided by other activities prominent in a learner's life.

The first step will be to recognize just how different the media consumption patterns of youth today are from those even 10 years ago. In the earlier days of instructional design, broadcast technologies were the norm; media literacy education was generally separated out from mainstream curriculum and seen as a means of protecting viewers from being manipulated by media. Today, however, it is the youth who are manipulating their media to suit their goals and lifestyle patterns. Thus, for educators of all subjects, it becomes imperative that we work alongside youth to help them to manipulate their media in a productive manner. Video game modding, greasemonkey scripting, map mashing and spatialized sound layering provide simply a few examples of how microcontent can be inserted at the points of connection between remixed content. As we learn to apply these principles more broadly, however, we will undoubtedly unlock many more opportunities to insert microlearning as a seamless component of everyday life.

References

Apple (2006) *iPod in the Classroom*. Available from: <http://www.apple.com/education/ipod/> [Accessed 3 June 2006]

Baddeley, A.D. (1999) *Essentials of Human Memory*. East Sussex, United Kingdom: Psychology Press.

BionicTeacher (2006) *BionicTeacher: Medievalspace*. Available from: <http://www.incsub.org/wpmu/bionicteacher/?p=142> [Accessed 7 July 2006].

CARTE (2006) *TacticalLanguage Project at CARTE – Center for Advanced Research in Technology for Education*. Available from: <http://www.isi.edu/isd/carte/proj_tactlang/> [Accessed 2006-3-6]

Education Arcade (2006) *Revolution*. The Education Arcade. Available from: <http://educationarcade.org/revolution> [Accessed 3 June 2006].

IT Conversations (2005) *IT Conversations: Dr. Henry Jenkins*. Tech Nation. Available from: <http://www.itconversations.com/shows/detail435.html> [Accessed 29 June 2006]

Jenkins, N. (2006) *San Francisco: Visualizing a Safer City*. Juicy Geography. Available from: <http://www.juicygeography.co.uk/googleearthsanfran.htm> [Accessed 8 July 2006]

Kaiser Family Foundation (2005) *Generation M: Media in the Lives of 8-18 Year Olds*. Available from: <http://www.kff.org/entmedia/entmedia030905pkg.cfm> [Accessed 3 June 2006]

Korthari, B., Pandey, A. & Chudgar, A.R. (2004) Reading out of the "Idiot Box": Same-Language Subtitling on Television in India. In: *Information Technologies and International Development 2* (1), pp. 23–44.

McGonigal, Jane (2003) This Is Not a Game: Immersive Aesthetics & Collective Play. In: *Digital Arts & Culture 2003 Conference Proceedings*. Available from: <http://www.seanstewart.org/beast/mcgonigal/notagame/paper.pdf> [Accessed 3 June 2006]

McGonigal, Jane (2005) *Alternate Reality Learning*. *Education Arcade Panel Session on Creative Design*. Available from: <http://educationarcade.org/files /videos/conf2005/3-SessionCreative%20Design.mov> [Accessed 3 June 2006]

Mozdev (2006) *Mozdev.org – Greesemonkey: Using*. Mozdev.org. Available from: <http://greasemonkey.mozdev.org/using.html> [Accessed 7 June 2006]

National Literacy Mission (NLM). (2000) *Literacy Rates: An analysis based on NSSO survey 1998*. New Delhi: Directorate of Adult Education.

Neopets (2006) *Pet Central*. Neopets. Available from: <http://www.neopets.com/petcentral.phtml> [Accessed 3 June 2006]

Ravaja, N., Saari, T., Salminen, M., Laarni, J. & Kallinen, K. (2004) *Phasic Emotinal Reactions to Video Game Events: A Psychophysiological Investigation*. Manuscript submitted for publication.

Ravaja, Niklas et al. (2005) *The Psychophysiology of Video Gaming: Phasic Emotional Responses to Game Events*. Digital Games Research Association International Conference 2005. Available from: <http://tinyurl.com/7rsfz> [Accessed 3 June 2006]

Purushotma, R (2005) *The Sims Teach German*. The Internet Archive. Avalable from: <http://www.archive.org/details/the_sims_teach_german> [Accessed 3 June 2006]

Soh, N. (2002) Do well in studies and get a Neopets treat. In: *Straights Times*, 2002-3-18.

Squire, K. (2004) *Replaying History: Learning World History through playing Civilization III*. Dissertation submitted to the Instructional Systems and Technology Department, Indiana University, January.

Szulborski, D. (2005) *This is Not a Game: A guide to Alternate Reality Gaming*. Lulu Press.

Wikipedia (2006a) *The Typing of The Dead*. Wikipedia. Available from: <http://en.wikipedia.org/wiki/The_Typing_of_the_Dead> [Accessed 3 June 2006]

Wikipedia (2006b) *The Sims 2*. Wikipedia. Available from: <http://en.wikipedia.org/wiki/The_Sims_2#Veronaville> [Accessed 3 June 2006].

The *Doctor Who* Principle: Microlearning and the episodic nature of almost everything

Kendal Newman & Robert Grigg

This chapter explores the episodic nature of microlearning and looks at examples from game-playing, narrative and interactive learning content to find effective ways episodic structure and delivery can be used in microlearning. While the principle of episodic structure itself may seem fundamental to learning, even self-evident, implementing it is not and the discussed examples provide concrete examples of episodic content from various genres. The lessons from the discussed examples suggest two related principles for producing successful episodic content: firstly, structuring the content for episodic delivery by using cliff-hangers, story, characters, and scoring systems; and secondly, delivering episodes within appropriate intervals so that the learner neither loses continuity/interest nor is overloaded.

Introduction

The apparatus of microlearning is inherently episodic. Learning content is disassembled into discrete micro-units and reassembled into a coherent whole to be delivered with technologies and into living/learning environments which themselves impose limits on the size of the micro-units. Far from being a limitation though, episodic delivery of content can be a powerful tool for learning and engagement (Caplana and Schooler, 1999). Human perception itself is in many ways episodic (Hastie, Ostrom et al., 1980) – we are all actors/players in our own life-story and we perceive that story in terms of episodes, structured in our memories according to various categorisation schemas. The world around us makes more sense if we perceive it in terms of logical sequence; cause and effect; action and reaction, organized in memory as discrete episodes of experience that define the sum of our own life stories.

The tendency to structure perception episodically can be seen as a species-wide trait (McNeil, 1996, p. 333). The human cognitive process for sequential scripts is believed to arise from everyday occurrences that we understand by organizing them episodically into 'scripts' (Schank & Abelson, 1977; Turner, 1991; McNeil, 1996). An episodic script might be described as being similar to a concept in cognitive structure, in that it reflects generalized knowledge (Schank & Abelson, 1977, p. 41) but has the added complexity of being associated with an ordered sequence of events. There are various societal, physiological and cultural contexts within which the tendency towards episodic perception could be examined. In their work on human understanding of culpability, for example, Finkel and Groscup (1997, p. 210) describe episodic scripts as mental templates or prototypes equipping us to understand situations. Characters, locations, sequenced events, motivations, and action-response relationships are the variables of the episodic templates by which we organize our knowledge of the world. However, even though we have used the phrase in the title, it is not our intention in this chapter to present a comprehensive discussion of *the episodic nature of almost everything*, but rather to note that episodic frameworks, as we apply them to ideas about microlearning, fit within a broader discussion of episodic perception.

The title of this chapter was inspired from the long-running BBC TV series *Doctor Who*, which used a strong episodic narrative structure to great effect. A *Doctor Who* story consisted of five 30-minute episodes, and was typically broadcast each weekday at the same time, so that a new story began on Monday and finished on Friday. Without fail, every episode finished with a cliff-hanging plot twist to keep the viewer coming back each day of the week. In the last 30 seconds of every episode the Doctor was left facing certain doom, or his lovely female assistant was revealed to be in mortal danger, or some trusted friend turned out to be a nasty alien. *Doctor Who* was designed to leave the audience screaming "No!!!!" every time the end credits began to roll on an episode, and in this, certainly in this author's neighbourhood when growing up, it was very successful. It didn't matter that the audience knew the Doctor would not die, and that somehow everything would turn out ok. The suspense was intense, the wait excruciating and no one was going to miss that next episode. The key ingredients of the *Doctor Who* principle are episodic structure and the timely delivery of episodes.

It is possible today to buy DVDs of all the old *Doctor Who* series, and watch all the episodes of a story in a single sitting. It quickly becomes apparent that doing this completely destroys the sense of suspense. At the other end of the time scale interval, some broadcasters tried screening episodes a week apart instead of nightly. This was never successful either, as the wait was too long between episodes and the audience would tend to lose interest. The two key ingredients to the *Doctor Who* principle therefore are;

1. Structure the content to fit the episode (end every episode with a cliff-hanger)

2. Deliver the episodes in appropriate time intervals.

As this introduction is being written the phenomenal bestseller *The DaVinci Code* has just been released as a movie. The book uses the key ingredients of the *Doctor Who* principle to great effect. The chapters are very short, and at the end of each chapter is a sudden twist, another clue revealed, or a sudden mortal danger. No chapter end in the book feels like a good place to put the book down. When one does put it down, there is a pleasurable anticipation of the next chapter, as the experience of the book is spread over several days/sessions of reading, which echoes the *Doctor Who* experience. The movie, on the other hand, presents the story as a single unit rather than in an episodic structure, and, by its very nature, does not deliver the same extended experience of suspense and anticipation.

This chapter will first review the literature of episodic content in the interactive entertainment industry and then look at how the two key *Doctor Who* principles have been applied in a number of practical examples. The examples to be reviewed are:

- Episodic games
- The Language Market
- *Albert in the Land of the Vikings*

There are lessons to be learned from these examples that have direct relevance to the episodic delivery of microlearning.

Episodic Entertainment in Interactive Entertainment

There are a variety of views regarding the features that make an interactive entertainment product episodic in nature. Within the interactive entertainment industry, some describe episodic gaming as simply dividing up a large product into smaller products, much like splitting a book into chapters for independent release. Problematically, this definition assumes that episodes would be highly cohesive narratively. It also assumes that the structure of the game is suited to being subdivided into smaller games.

Michael's (2003, p. 301) discussions of "episodic content," in the context of Indie game development communities, identifies the creation of the "core game engine" with a series of levels or episodes. New chapters, or mini-sequels, continue the story by introducing new levels that are released as they are completed. This expands the end-user's experience and provides incentive for the player to return to future episodes.

Other definitions draw parallels to the pulp movement in literature during the 19th century, where the new-found wood pulping processes enabled the cost-effective manufacture of paper, providing the opportunity for production of smaller, yet more frequent and affordable, publications. These publications were commonly linked narratives, and gave rise to the publications we came to know as comic books, and, of course, the ultimate episodic publication genre – the newspaper. The Internet has provided an opportunity for new distribution and development approaches, and in a number of ways, has motivated experiments with episodic methods, much like pulp manufacturing processes gave rise to cheap comics, books and newspapers.

The goal of episodic content in interactive entertainment is to capture the end-user and have them return to continue to be engaged with the game content. Episodic delivery can fit gaming into shorter periods of time, making it more accessible to a wider range of users. Ultimately, the repeated exposure allows the player to explore the game content more deeply, he or she having become familiar with the interface to how the game world works.

Today, the Internet is the medium that presents the means in which episodic delivery can be a viable alternative to single product release for content providers. The Internet not only provides a cheap and fast way to distribute new content, it also provides the means by which the end-users can create and receive help from a community of other users, as well as from the content provider.

Examples of Episodic Games

Episodic games as a genre has been around for over a decade, but despite this fact, the amount of episodic gaming content is still in its infancy. The best example of the success of episodic content is still in the television industry with examples today including shows like *24* and *Lost* carrying on the episodic traditions laid down by *Doctor Who* two decades earlier. In the gaming industry today, "SiN Episodes" from Ritual are the latest and most targeted attempt at episodic gaming but are still a long way from achieving the results that the television industry obtains.

Earlier attempts to create episodic gaming were limited by the digital distribution pathways of the day. Titles such as "Wing Commander: Secret Ops" from Origin suffered from being too large to download for the majority of game players, and therefore it was decided to deliver the game in the more traditional "off the shelf – all at once" form.

"Kuma: War" is another example of an episodic game with over 60 episodes and still growing. It incorporates gaming activities that represent real world locations and conflicts for the game player to experience first hand. "Kuma Games" approached this episodic format by using world events to guide them in the content they needed to produce. Users would then experience the news interactively even if limited to one particular war incident at a time.

Everquest is an example of a very large online gaming environment with thousands of players all interacting with each other and essentially creating the story. Everquest also exhibits episodic characteristics whenever the administrators of the Everquest world introduce new items of story into the world for everyone to take on board.

Even within the console market there are interesting examples of staged release of product add-ons which have an episodic quality about them, such as Sony's Singstar franchise of games. The original singing apparatus of a microphone and Singstar game is open to many different Singstar song compilation add-ons. The overall singing theme remains the same, but new songs to expand one's repertoire are distributed frequently, and today result in a wide selection of possible Singstar add-ons. The Sony Playstation also had a series called "hack" delivered from Bandai which ended up as a game delivered in four episodes following the traditional Japanese style of storytelling called "kisho tenketsu" which consists of an introduction, rising action, a turning point, and ending.

In each case, the episodic approach is used to lengthen the time spent with the game concerned. The game interface provides a level of consistency, while the content itself may alter in ways intended to maintain user curiosity, involvement, and satisfaction.

Episodic Structure in the Language Market

Although somewhat dated now, when it was published in the late '90s, The Language Market was considered a highly innovative example of how the new interactive technologies could be used in teaching and learning. Each Language Market product (there were 12 in all) was designed to deliver a whole year course of a language other than English (LOTE) to English-speaking students in Years 6-10 without any requirement of the classroom teacher to provide content input. The intention was that the role of the teacher was to become one of a classroom manager, while the students pursued their learning under the internal (semi-intelligent) guidance of the software. The software itself was delivered into students' classrooms and homes by the first generation of *multi-media capable* desktop computers using all sorts of games, puzzles and activities to teach, drill, and monitor the student's reading, writing, and comprehension skills in the new language.

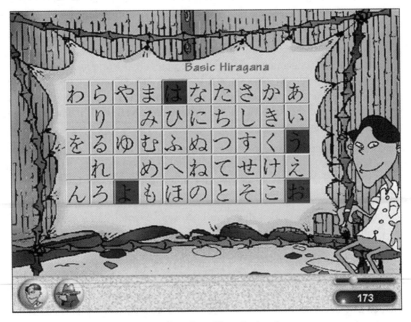

Figure 1. The calligraphy booth.

The episodic story structure was thought to have two functions in the Language Market. First, it provided a virtual space into which the user enters. Entering the space provides the trigger for the user that learning is about to take place. The user enters the space through the title screen and intro music, receiving a personalised greeting on the way. They progress into the main navigation screen of the market place where they are prompted to pick up the episode where they left off. Once inside the episode space, the user is invited to begin controlling and interacting.

The Language Market used a strong episodic structure based around a scenario of a market place with various characters within the space. Certain characters tended to be associated with certain types of learning, for example:

The Fruit Stand Lady with her fruit stand and oversized interactive cash register was always associated with activities about numbers.

Ludmilla is a shady female spy who is always gathering information on people – names, ages, country, and city.

Shaka is a free spirit who runs a new age stall in the market place, and provides the main navigation interface for the units and activities.

Bowtie is like a circus ringmaster who introduces each episode, and explains the activity.

Mr. Fuji, the calligraphy artist, introduces each script activity (see figure 1).

The second function of the episodic story structure is to provide a context, interesting locations and characters, and ways of weaving their personalities into the activities while providing a unifying structure. It was decided that a Market Place was a location that worked well in any culture and that was versatile enough in terms of the activities that could take place there. Having established this as the story, the creators then re-worked it into a space that resembled no market in the real world. A game show host and a backyard scientist appear beside the usual fruit and new-age gift stalls. Lunfeld (2000, p. 98) and others have described the idea of a virtual space as an active place containing visual pleasure and experience.

Senger (1999, p. 1227) discusses the need for designing and integrating comprehensible, interesting and engaging agents endowing the agent with human-like and narrative abilities. This resonates particularly when designing agents for children. In each episode/activity, the user is invited to manipulate elements within the space and respond to them. There are about 170 episodes in each of the languages. A typical episode with a typical level of interaction required by the student is the *Design-your-own-teddy-bear* episode. This activity was designed to teach the user about adjectives for body parts and to practice recognising the written form of body parts. Users are invited to design their own teddy bear (see figure 2).

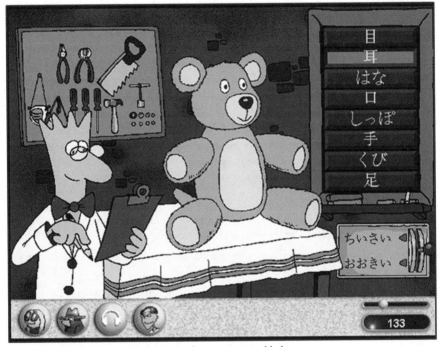

Figure 2. Design your own teddy bear.

The user clicks on a series of buttons that select a body part (eyes, nose, legs, etc.) and for each part they are given a choice of two adjectives (fat-thin, big-small, etc). The graphics respond accordingly. Once they have designed each part of their teddy bear, the *scientist* starts making statements about their bear – "This bear has a big nose." The user responds with true or false and gets points if they are correct.

The illusion here is that the user has created something (a customised teddy bear) and that the system is aware of it, and able to intelligently assess whether statements about the bear are true. The user has, of course, done nothing more than make some selections out of a given set of list variables constructed from the primary data lists for the activity. The 'engine' for this activity, then, is a series of list and index variables, run through a series of extremely specific tests and procedures. There is no complex reasoning taking place here. However, via the various algorithms which drive the activity, the illusion is created of an understanding of the user's actions, cause-and effect, time, and LOTE domain knowledge.

Each activity has a scoring value, a pass minimum, and a bonus score for a perfect result. The scoring system provided the mechanism for tracking the users' progress, directing them to continue or repeat certain sections. It also provided the basis for the users' "save" file. A point of debate arising from the scoring system was the extent to which the users' path and rate of progress through the activities should be prescribed by the program. This debate tended to divide the development team into the teachers and the programmers, with the teachers favouring a 'lock-step' approach. By this, they meant that the users would be barred from progressing to the next activity until they had achieved a pass mark in the current activity. The programmers cringed instinctively from anything that seemed like an unnecessary imposition on the user. From the teachers' point of view activities were placed in a particular order for a reason and they did not want the users to have the freedom to 'jump around'. The final compromise was to use the lock-step approach but with a game-style 'cheat' built in so that teachers could direct users to a specific episode, even if they were not actually up to that episode. For example, there were a number of episodes that related to Karneval and Easter celebrations that would be more meaningful if done during Easter week.

Feedback from users was generally enthusiastic, and it seemed like the episodic story structure was well received by the students and teachers. Some of the most interesting feedback was from a teacher using the French Language Market in a remote indigenous community in the Northern Territory. She had constant problems with students not attending classes and not engaging with learning, but when it came to the Language Market there were no problems at all. She observed students deliberately repeating episodes to get higher scores. She also observed them jealously guarding their improved solutions, and bartering and swapping solutions in the playground like valuable collector items. The students themselves came to her and asked if they could start a Language Market club so that they could have access to the computers after school. This was unheard of at this school. Best of all was the way she heard them shouting complex French phrases at each other in the playground, which convinced her that real learning was happening. In the Language Market a distinctive graphic style, interesting characters and a cohesive meta-narrative all contributed to organizing the content as an episodic structure.

Albert in the Land of the Vikings as Episodic Story-telling

In the final example, which is also the most recent, we will discuss a project which used streaming video, podcasting and blogging technologies to tell stories to an audience/community. The project, entitled *Albert in the Land of the Vikings* revolves around a teddy bear named Albert who is actually travelling around the United Kingdom and Scandinavia in search of Viking stories. These stories are presented as five-minute video documentaries, often comical in nature, but also with real embedded learning content. Each documentary includes map information about where Albert is currently, as well as an audio podcast from the supporting crew giving the "behind the scenes" on Albert's antics when off camera (see figure 3). The blogging technologies provide not only the content presentation management system, but also the communication loop between the producers and the audience. In this way, the audience becomes more like a community as they interact with Albert, discuss the stories with him as they are happening, and contribute their own suggestions to him about what the next story should be about.

The episodic time interval for this production was approximately every 3 days and it was evident from the server statistics that hits to the site tailed off very quickly if a new story took longer than this to appear. Since a lot of the audience/community also subscribed to the podcasts, they were instantly alerted when a new story had been placed on the site and this meant that visitor hits grew rapidly after each new story was uploaded. The frequent nature of the story time interval combined with the almost live nature of the production helps raise interest in the online experience. Knowing that Albert is on a trip and is leaving one destination and about to arrive at another is a style that episodically works well for maintaining interest for the next episode.

The gaming dimension appears in the form of the audience being able to converse with Albert, ask questions, and even challenge him. The results of such interactions can include:

1. Community members responding to Albert's stories
2. Albert responding to Community members through blog/emails
3. Albert's team members conversing through podcast
4. Albert obtaining commentary from a Viking expert on the topic, which is then incorporated into the creation of the next 5-minute documentary.

Although this interaction, on the surface, seems quite simplistic, the motivations in the community for people to first ask questions, and then stay tuned for the response in any one of the above methods, helped ensure their return to future episodes and hence become even more informed about the history of the Vikings and their ways. In this way the interactions between the audience, technology, and Albert were seen to heighten the audience's curiosity and therefore increase the likelihood of further learning.

The other aspect that helps maintain community interest and the engagement of the individual is the use of push technologies. In this case, the key element was the podcasting of audio content. Once a user subscribes through their own favourite media-viewing program (i.e., iTunes), they will, whenever they open the program, automatically receive any new material from Albert in the way of video or audio. Push technology was also used in the blog technology, for anyone that had an automated blog reader. Automated blog readers also automatically receive any updated correspondence from *Albert in the Land of the Vikings* when refreshed. Even without a blog reader, there is still a certain degree of "pushing" with emails being sent to members automatically about topics they were actively involved with. In both cases, the use of these two technologies did not require users to visit the Albert website through a browser. They had the option of listening to or viewing material in a mobile manner through portable technology such as iPods, PDAs and certain mobile phones.

Figure 3. Website for *Albert in the Land of the Vikings*.

The web stories were based around a road trip and related timeline of events. The stories also tended to be location based, so in England, Albert learned about the Viking history of Britain; in Denmark, he learned about the rune stones of Jelling; in Oslo, at the Viking Ship Museum, he learned about Viking ships and navigation, and so on. Each episode followed a particular aspect of Viking history. The audience/users were aware that the events of the road trip were occurring as they were viewing episodes, and this contributed to the sense of riding with Albert on the journey. The use of comedy also provided means by which to entertain users and help ensure their return. The use of a teddy bear to interview people gave the whole project a slightly comic feel and helped to relax interview subjects. Albert's enthusiasm for each story also helped to make the learning content very accessible for the audience.

Each episode would not only be at a unique location but it would also have a unique theme such as "Viking Runes" or "Norse Mythology." In this manner, the interest of the viewer would be heightened by both a new destination as well as the exploration of a new topic. The stories were linked by both the sequential nature of the destinations along the road travelled, and the overall Viking theme which linked all stories. The story also played out on another level that consisted of the occurrences of unforeseen events or politics between Albert and the team members. This played an important role in allowing the community to get to know Albert's character. It also allowed the producers to further develop Albert's character, and provided another reason for the audience/community to tune in. The light, entertaining and informal stories were quite successful in promoting engagement and communication between the community and Albert.

The types of media involved also played a role in maintaining interest. This spanned from basic text messaging through blogs, emails, and little stories on the website; audio only methods through audio podcasts; and audiovisual, with streaming movies that could be played on each topic.

Evidence of learning was demonstrated in the correspondence around each episode, and a number of members commented on the unusual way the content was being presented.

Anne Says:

June 30th, 2006 at 9:53 pm

What a great interview! I never thought to see a lecture on Vikings given to a bear – and he asked such good questions too.

Users would discuss items of interest, which often invoked further contributions of Viking information from other users, or even for some users to admit to missing that component of the material, which lead them to review the material again.

Albert in the Land of the Vikings demonstrates again the principle of timely release of episodes, and the design of episodic appropriate content. In this case, the use of humour, the sequential nature of a road trip, the exploration of stories related around a theme, and the quirky character of Albert himself, gave the stories in this project a strong episodic structure.

Summary

The examples discussed in this chapter are drawn from a diverse range of genres – TV production and broadcasting, interactive entertainment, online and console gaming, and internet-based technologies such as blogging and streaming. The examples were largely chosen because the authors were familiar with these, and in some cases actually involved in the production, but there are many other examples that could have been used in this chapter to demonstrate good use of episodic structure with potentially useful lessons for microlearning applications.

The examples discussed in this chapter represent various levels of formality in learning. The Language Market was mostly used in a formal class environment under direction of a teacher although the activities themselves crossed over into a more informal style of learning, and at the point where the children themselves asked for an after-school Language Market club and began trading solutions in the playground the learning activity had become quite informal. The learning in *Albert in the Land of the Vikings* was always highly informal in the sense that learning was not the sole or main activity of the members of the audience/community. A lot of serious Viking history was covered in the project but the audience was primarily there for their own enjoyment, and there was no assessing of learning outcomes or achievements in any conventional way (Bowyer et al., 2005, p. 43).

Delivering learning content in an appropriate time frame is a fundamental element of formal learning. In a classroom, it is, of course, usually the teacher who decides the sequence and intervals for delivery of the next lesson/unit/episode and it is one of the characteristics of the delivery of microlearning content that learning can be more self-directed and take place outside of the classroom learning times. In the discussed examples we find a range of different time intervals being used. The default delivery of Language Market episodes retains some of the formal characteristics, as it is linear delivery with a new episode being presented only when the learner has gained a satisfactory pass in the previous episode. The intervals *Albert in the Land of the Vikings* were dictated by the rate at which the production team could produce and upload episodes. Mostly this was every 3-4 days, which was sufficient to maintain the engagement of the audience/community. There was one notable period of 6 days with no new episode and during that time the daily hit rate dropped dramatically. The only conclusions about intervals to draw from these examples are that the intervals should not be so great that the learners lose the continuity, not so short that there is no chance to build suspense/looking forward to it, and consistent enough so that each episode arrives more or less when the learner is expecting it.

The intention of this chapter is not to argue that the episodic framework is inherently superior to all other ways of structuring and delivering learning content. The *Doctor Who Principle* may indeed be difficult to adopt when teaching highly abstract mathematical concepts, and learners will be very quick to spot a *contrived* structure that is not actually serving any useful purpose. The scope of our argument is that microlearning *is* inherently episodic; that there *is* a human tendency to perceive episodically that sits comfortably with microlearning; and that if an episodic structure is adopted there are some lessons to be learned from other forms of episodic content.

Having made that qualification, however, the examples shown do not actually suggest any limits to the sort of learning content for which an episodic structure is suitable. Neither is there any suggestion that episodic structure is inherently more suitable for a certain age or cultural group. The example of the Aboriginal children using the Language Market actually shows that well-structured and well-delivered content can be surprisingly cross-cultural, and perhaps with appropriate design and delivery there are no limits.

In practice, of course, there are limitations on the resources available to develop microlearning content and the competencies and funds to develop episodic structure may simply be beyond the resources of the content provider. Within the examples discussed in this chapter, there is a wide range of budget types. The Language Market had a team of 12 people working full-time on it for two years, with a budget of around $2 million Australian dollars. *Albert in the Land of the Vikings*, on the other hand, was produced with a minimal budget and minimal expertise: no professional cinematographers or film editors were used; all production was done on laptops rather than in any professional labs; and all blogging, communication and streaming functionality used existing free or inexpensive third-party applications. The total cost was around £4000 which was mostly travel and accommodation for the production team during the project.

As the technological and learning frameworks that we are here including in the microlearning polemic break out of traditional classroom and class time boundaries into the rest of our lives they become inherently episodic. The two crucial lessons we have articulated in the *Doctor Who* Principle are that learning content should, where appropriate and feasible, be designed as episodic content and delivered at appropriate time intervals, because ultimately, appropriate use of the episodic properties of microlearning will mean the experience of deeper levels of engagement and learning for the users concerned.

References

Bobrow, D. & Winograd, T. (1977) *An Overview of KRL. A Knowledge Representation Language*. Los Altos, CA: Morgan Kaufmann.
Bowyer, J. et al. (2005) *The Full Bridges Report. Promoting recognition of Youth Work across Europe*. Available from: <http://www.salto-youth.net/download/630/reportbridges.pdf> [Accessed 19 September 2006]
Caplan, L. & Schooler, C. (1999) On the Use of Analogy in Text-Based Memory and Comprehension: the Interaction Between Complexity of Within-Domain Encoding and Between-Domain Processing. In: *Journal of the Learning Sciences 8*, no., p. 43.
Finkel, N.J. & Groscup, J.L (1997) Crime prototypes, objective vs. subjective culpability, and a commonsense balance. *Law and Human Behavior* 21, pp. 209–230
Lunenfeld, P. (2000) Hardscapes and Imagescapes. In: *Snap To Grid*. Cambridge: MIT Press.
Michael, D. (2003) *The Indie Game Development Survival Guide*. Hingham: Charles River Media, p. 301.
Hastie, R., Ostrom, T.M., Ebbesen, E.B., Wyer, R.S., Hamilton, D.L. & Carlston, D. eds. (1980) *Person Memory: The Cognitive Basis of Social Perception*. Hillsdale, NJ: Lawrence Erlbaum Associates, p. 94.
McNeil, L.D. (1996). Homo Inventans: The Evolution of Narrativity. In: *Language & Communication* 16(4), pp. 331–360.
Minsky, M, (1985) *Structured Object Representations – A Framework for Representing Knowledge*. Los Altos, CA: Morgan Kaufmann.
Rittel, H. & Webber, M. (1973). Dilemmas in a General Theory of Planning. *DMG-DRS Journal 8*(1), pp. 31–39.
Schank, R. & Abelson, R. (1977) *Scripts, plans, goals, and understanding. An Inquiry into human knowledge structures*. Hillsdale, NJ: Lawrence Erlbaum Associates.

Sengers, P. (1999) Designing Comprehensible Agents. In: *IJCAI-99 Joint Conference Proceedings*, pp. 1227–1232.

Turner, M. (1991) *Reading minds. The study of English in the age of cognitive science.* Princeton: Princeton University Press.

Storytelling as a Motivational Tool in Digital Learning Games

Matthias Bopp

The following article provides a theoretical framework for the usage of storytelling in digital learning games as a motivational tool. The centre of this framework is the concept of a *virtual extrinsic motivation*. This concept is developed in reference to design structures in entertaining digital games, Rheinberg's extended cognitive model of motivation and Zillmann's affection disposition theory. Storytelling as a motivational tool in digital learning games is then illustrated by means of the *Elektra Demonstrator*, a game-based research learning software that deals with physics learning for upper intermediate pupils.

Introduction

Motivation, as a psychological term, usually refers to the initiation, intensity and persistence of behavior. The motivation of students to learn is not always as high as desired and thus there is an ongoing debate on didactic methods to support this motivation. Digital games (video and computer games, handheld games, mobile games, etc.) are a popular pastime for most of today's children, adolescents and a growing number of adults (currently, the average age of digital game players is about 29) and gaming implies learning (although usually not educational learning). Thus, it is obvious to ask if motivational design methods of digital games can be used to support educational learning.

Digital gaming is a sophisticated and fast-evolving field of social and human-computer interaction. Thus, lots of variables are to be taken into account. For example, variables concerning the player's gender, traits, experience with games, social and educational status, inner psychological processes (such as flow), and various design aspects of different game genres. Currently, there is no thorough and systematically convincing motivational theory that covers all of these variables and their interrelations. Nevertheless, it is common sense to assume that storytelling in games is one aspect that has to be considered. This article develops some theoretical perspectives on and practical suggestions for the use of storytelling as a motivational tool to support learning in digital learning games.

Motivation and Learning

A starting point for this is to look at the role of cognitions and valuations in motivational processes. A theory that includes these two elements and combines them with the distinction of intrinsic and extrinsic motivation was suggested by Rheinberg (1989, 2005). Rheinberg regards motivation as a function of:

(a) expectations concerning the result of a situation (if a person does not act), the proximate result(s) of an action (e.g., a learning action) in this situation and the consequences of this result(s),

(b) combined with the values that an actor attributes to an action itself and the consequence(s) of the results of this action (see figure 1).

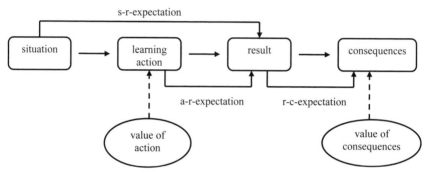

Figure 1: Extended cognitive model of motivation (Rheinberg, 2005, p. 341); translation by the author.

For example, according to this model, there are two basic processes that should motivate a student to prepare for a final exam:

(a) The student expects that doing nothing will not lead to a good score in the exam (s-r-expectation); that preparation will actually help her to achieve a high score (a-r-expectation); and that a good score will actually lead to consequences (r-c-expectation) that are of high value for her, e.g., getting a good job (value of consequences). Rheinberg calls the result of these processes a case of *extrinsic* motivation.

(b) Even if a student does not have any of these expectations and doesn't care about consequences, she will prepare for the exam if she has the feeling that learning in itself is of high value. Rheinberg calls this a case of *intrinsic* motivation.

Learning in educational contexts usually occurs due to a mix of extrinsic and intrinsic motivation. Sometimes students have a particular interest in a topic, or they are motivated by a general curiosity, achievement motivation, etc. (high value of action), which leads to intrinsic motivation. And, in addition, they often learn in order to gain social acceptance or avoid social disadvantages (high value of consequences) and thus they are motivated extrinsically.

In opposition, pupils that do not learn sufficiently can be seen as having intrinsically low motivation, and, in addition, may have unrealistic expectations concerning the unpleasant long-term consequences of not-learning in our knowledge society. As a result, they are not motivated extrinsically and do not perform in a desirable way.

Frame Stories and Virtual Extrinsic Motivation

One of several ways to deal with this problem is the usage of storytelling as a motivational didactic method or tool.[1] In a simple way, this can be done by using storytelling as a *reward* for learning tasks. For example, if a primary class performs a given task in a good way, a teacher may read out a chapter of an exiting story.

In a more sophisticated way, storytelling is used as a *frame* (see e.g., Creswell 1997) for a learning activity. Such a frame story provides a) a context for a certain learning task and b) gives the learning activity a specific form in order to link it to the context.

For example, in primary school a teacher may motivate pupils to draw by telling them the story of 'poor Pluto' who has lost his dog house in a big storm. Next, the pupil's task is to draw a new dog house for the cute pet

Digital games usually use a similar method. For example, a typical 'abstract task' in most shooter games is to quickly move a mouse pointer on a small moving part of the screen and click the left mouse button. In this perspective, shooters are a variation of psychological tests that examine the ability to coordinate hand movements and eye stimuli (see Pias, 2001). Such activities may be intrinsically motivating for people that attribute a high value to achievement in itself. But this doesn't seem to be sufficient for the motivation of a majority of players. Thus, in shooter games, usually a frame story with a hero who defends himself or his peers is introduced (see, for the use of frame theory in digital games, Bopp, 2006b). In order to link the abstract game task to this frame story, the mouse pointer morphs into cross-hairs, the small moving areas on the screen turn into ugly and mean enemies that fight the hero, and the mouse click is the pulling of a trigger.

An example of the usage of frame stories in the area of learning media is the Jasper-Project that produced a series of teaching films narrating *The Adventures of Jasper Woodbury*. Here, the hero Jasper is engaged in several practical problems the learner then has to solve by using mathematics (see Cognition and Technology Group at Vanderbilt, 1997).

Is the creation of a frame story a way to create intrinsic or extrinsic motivation? This depends on the range of the process in focus. Taking the whole story-based activity (as in the drawing of a dog house for Pluto) as one unit, a learner is motivated intrinsically if he or she attributes a high value to the action and does not care about consequences

---

1   Besides the motivational function of storytelling, in educational contexts and computer games, storytelling can also be used to give learning content *a specific form that is easy to understand and memorise*. For basic remarks on the connection between thinking and narration, see Bruner 1990.

that take place after the activity in the real world (e.g., good marks). But looking at the process of drawing (or fighting enemies etc.) in detail, this activity can be seen as a series of single actions that are performed *due to their consequences in the fictional world* in which the story takes place. In this case, not the drawing itself, but the fact that this helps the dog, Pluto, to get shelter is of high value. And not the killing of enemies itself, but the fact that, for example, a player gets a particularly 'cool sword' when he does, is rewarding.

In the long run, these activities may lead to the development of an intrinsic motivation to draw (or to have fun by shooting at enemies), but the initial motivation is not intrinsic but extrinsic in respect to the story world. To distinguish this form of motivation from the usual forms of intrinsic or external motivation, I suggest calling it *virtual extrinsic motivation*.

To sum up, processes of virtual external motivation can be described using Rheinberg's schema in the following way: The learner/player is confronted with a specific kind of situation. This situation is part of a fictional story (which basically means that it is driven by actions of and relationships between characters; see for this the next paragraph). This *story situation* provides the opportunity to perform a certain task, in learning games this is a learning activity. The actor has specific expectations concerning the result of this task/action and its consequences and attributes a high value to the results and their consequences in respect to the story-based game world (and not in respect to the real world). Thus, he or she performs the task which results in a gratification if he or she is successful.

Given this, three types of motivation can be distinguished in respect to story-based digital games:

Firstly, a player may like to do something/to learn because he or she is interested in the topic, likes learning in general, etc., and thus may be intrinsically motivated. Secondly, a player is extrinsically motivated because he or she attributes high values to the consequences of the playing/learning action in the real world, e.g., getting better marks or a high score that leads to appreciation from peers that play the game, as well. For both types of players/learners, the story of a digital (learning) game is of low importance motivationally. Thirdly, some gamers do not like the pure action/learning activity in itself and do not care about their real world consequences. They are neither motivated intrinsiccally nor extrinsically, but they feel immersed in the story, and thus care about the consequences of a learning or playing activity in the fictional world of the game, which motivates them to perform these tasks. These gamers are driven by a virtual external motivation. In reality, all three types of motivations may be more or less merged in learning (games) or they may separately dominate different episodes of a game. Learners that are not motivated by intrinsic or extrinsic processes are the main target group of story-based digital learning games.

The model of story-based motivation developed so far is rather abstract and needs re-finement, because it does not deal with the question of *how to create a frame story that leads to motivating story situations.* The following paragraphs will deal with this question in respect to the usage of (a) motivating characters and (b) didactic methods to create motivating expectations.

Storytelling and Motivation in Digital (Learning) Games

Telling a little story about Pluto, the dog that has lost its dog house can perhaps be suf-ficient to raise motivation in pet-loving children, but in respect to older students and different learning tasks, more sophisticated ways of storytelling are needed. This raises the question of whether there are any typical structures of entertaining stories that ap-peal to a broad audience of male and female students, or potential learners in general. To answer this question, it is helpful to look at the structure (or plots) of entertaining fictional stories in general, and at the psychological processes of the reception of these stories.

In a narratological perspective, the term *story* refers to a series of linked events. These events are the result of the thoughts, feelings, and actions of (usually several main) story characters in a specific setting. A *character* is a human or non-human being, with more or less individual features, that takes part in a fictional story. For the purpose of analyzing (and developing) the structure of a story, it can be helpful to label characters in respect to their function for the story (e.g., their relation to other characters). There may be the 'hero' and the 'heroine,' the 'villain,' the 'lovers,' the 'femme fatal,' the 'helper,' etc. (see in respect to digital games, Schmidt, 2004). A story is called *dra-matic* if there is a serious conflict between the goals of the main characters. The *setting* of a story describes the location(s) of the story's actions in space and time, and basic features of the story world itself: there are, for example, historical, fantastic, and real-istic settings.

Stories can be more or less elaborate in respect to all of these elements (see for differ-ent levels of narrative elaboration and their usage in microlearning, Hug, 2005 and paragraph 6 below) and there are, for example, functional simulations (see Mentz & Rattunde, 1997) that do not include a 'real story' in the sense displayed above. The following refers to rather elaborate stories.

A common theory to describe the structure and reception of entertaining stories, like soaps on TV, is the *affection disposition theory* (see Zillmann, 1996, 2004). According to this theory, recipients typically classify the characters of a story into two main cate-gories: positive characters (e.g., the heroes and heroine and their friends) and negative characters, the villains. The positive characters often incorporate a main couple in a more or less problematic romantic relationship. In more complex entertaining stories, some characters can not be easily subsumed to one of these categories, which adds suspense to the story. In a dramatic story, there is a basic conflict between the main two categories of characters. According to Zillman, the categorization of a character is the result of a moral judgment of the actions of a character. (Aesthetic judgments may be of importance as well.) These judgments lead to the emergence of emotional relations between the recipient and the characters. In respect to the protagonists, this relationship is mainly characterized by liking, caring or identification; in respect to villains, it is characterized by disliking or enmity.

Zillmann's affection disposition theory is designed in respect to traditional, non-interactive media with a recipient that has no influence on the fate of the characters and the presentation of the story. In opposition, in digital games this is more or possible: The player can control one or more characters in the virtual world. These characters are called *avatars*. In addition, there are characters that are controlled by the computer and usually interact with each other and the player's avatar. They are called Non Personal Characters (*NPCs*). Melting this distinction with the schema of positive and negative characters, there are three main types of characters in digital games: friendly and helpful NPCs, the avatar(s) that usually fulfill(s) the role of the hero/heroine, and hostile NPCs, the villains.

The ability to control an avatar and to interact with NPCs can intensify the emotional relationship between a player and the story characters, and can lead to emotions and actions *that usually do just appear in social interactions* (meaning: human-human-interaction). For example, a male player can feel attracted to a female avatar (as if it would be an actor) and start to write poems for her;[2] the player can get angry about the 'stupidity' of an NPC that is supposed to help him, but instead acts in a clumsy way, causing the player to start to shout at him; he can feel challenged by NPCs that scorn him (e.g., in *Far Cry*, Crytek, 2003), and he can feel proud if an NPC or a crowd of NPCs praises him (e.g., *Fable*, Big Blue Box, 2004). The player does this even though basically he knows that it is just a machine he is interacting with. A state of the art example of a game that is based heavily on this kind of emotional interaction between a player and an NPC (Alex, the heroine of the game) is *Half Live 2: Episode 1* (Velve, 2006).[3]

Similar feelings and actions sometimes also appear during the reception of not-interactive media (e.g., when spectators in the cinema spontaneously try to give a warning to the hero, or a TV-watching football fan shouts at a centre forward to kick the ball), but this is rather rare. In opposition, in story-based digital games these feelings and actions are rather common. To separate them from typical feelings during the recep-

---

2   See the famous character of Lara Croft, heroine of the *Tomb Raider* series, Hartmann, Klimmt & Vorderer (2001).

3   This game can be played in a 'commentary mode' that includes explanations by the game designers in respect to specific game situations, and especially of the design efforts undertaken in order to create an entertaining emotional relationship between the player and the main NPC.

tion of not-interactive media, on one hand, and from real social interactions on the other hand, they can be called *parasocial*[4] emotions, interactions, or relationships.

Why are these emotions relevant for learning? In story-based digital games, traditional as well as parasocial emotions toward characters (liking, caring, anger, to feel defiant etc.) have a motivational function. They can lead to hopes and fears concerning the future destiny of the positive characters (the avatar and friendly NPCs), hope for a bad outcome of the story in respect to the villains, and to curiosity about the final outcome of a storyline in general. In opposition to traditional media, these feelings do not just motivate the player to keep on watching, reading, etc., but they can also stimulate the motivation to perform certain actions/tasks in the game world in order to take care of the destiny of the avatar and friendly NPCs, or to frustrate the villain's plans. Depending on the outcome of these actions/tasks, entertaining feelings arise.

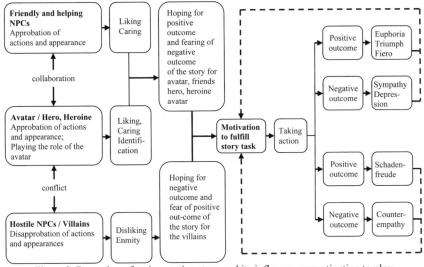

Figure 2. Reception of an interactive story and its influence on motivation to play

According to a qualitative empirical study of Lazzaro (2004), these feelings typical include euphoria, fiero (an Italian expression for the feeling of triumph after over-powering an enemy), sympathy, depressiveness, schadenfreude, or counter empathy. These emotions, in turn, can influence and foster the motivation to perform subsequent tasks (see figure 2).

---

4   The term is used slightly differently in respect to different media; see for digital games Bopp, 2005; for TV e.g., Horton & Wohl (1956) and Hoffner, 1996; for human-computer-interaction Nass & Shyam (1994). See also *affecting computing* as a theory that is focused on "computing that relates to, arises from, or deliberately influences emotions ... [it is aimed at the development of; M.B.] applications of affective computing in areas such as computer-assisted learning ... and entertainment ..." (Picard, 1995, p. 1).

This reconstruction of the basic link between the structure and reception of stories in digital games and the motivation of the player/learner to fulfill tasks can be easily merged with the concept of a virtual extrinsic motivation described above: reception and judgment of the characters, the development of (parasocial) emotions and certain expectations (hopes, fears) concerning the destiny of the characters constitute an emotionally relevant story situation.

This story situation leads to the possibility of specific actions (e.g., learning tasks) and a motivation to perform these actions on the basis of expectations concerning the results and consequences of these actions. The player's main expectations include the support of the avatar's goals and friendly NPCs and the derogation of villainous NPCs.

After the player performed the actions, their results and virtual consequences are valued in respect to these expectations (especially the character's fates), which in turn leads to entertaining feelings (euphoria, fiero, etc.).

According to the mechanisms of the storyline, a consequence of the player's actions is the emergence of a new story situation, which again provides a chance for the gamer to influence the character's destiny and the whole process repeats itself (see figure 3).

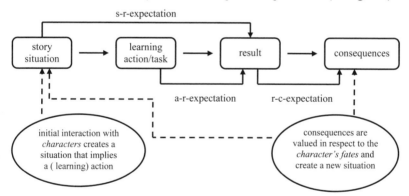

Figure 3. Storytelling and motivation as a circled process

In respect to the learner/player, this method of motivation presupposes at least two important and specific traits. Firstly, a general affection for typical entertaining storytelling, and secondly, the ability to understand and memorize the setting, the characters, their needs, motives, etc. This is especially important if storytelling is used in micro teaching contexts. Here, once a background story is introduced, it cannot be introduced again and again in every single situation. It is only possible to refer to this knowledge by using some cues in the design of the situation. Thus, the learner must be able to retrieve this background knowledge using the cues. Nevertheless, as typical soap operas on TV demonstrate, this can be easily achieved by viewers. Single TV soap episodes last about 20 to 30 minutes and contain 3 storylines, which are often shorter then 7 minutes each. Nevertheless, viewers are easily able to recall what they have to know to enjoy these 'short story pieces.'

Task-Oriented Frame Stories, Expectations in Digital Games and Micro Teaching

A story that creates a desire in a player to influence the fate of story characters is not sufficient for successful story design in digital games. In addition, the story must prompt cognition that – together with the player's wishes – motivate him to act.

– The learner/player must know what he is supposed to do in a situation,
– he must have the *expectation* that certain tasks will lead to satisfying results and consequences,
– and he must have the expectation that he is able to perform a task in an adequate way; that is, his cognitions on game play *self-efficacy* (Bandura, 1977) must be sufficiently high.

Thus, the story and every single situation in a digital learning game must be designed in a way that allows the player to acquire and create this knowledge and these expectations. How do entertaining digital games try to achieve this goal? They do so by

– defining one or a few simple main objectives or tasks,
– dividing these objectives into hundreds or thousands of single sub objectives or tasks,
– making sure that the player can link these tasks to motivating expectations concerning desired results and consequences,
– assuring that the player encounters enough little tasks he can accomplish which gives frequently experiences of success and achievement and
– praise and encouragement for the player via NPCs.

For example, take the beginning of the famous role playing game *Gothic 2* (Piranha Bytes, 2002). The setting is a fantasy world, populated by humans, orcs, mages and monsters. At the beginning, an introduction trailer imposes the task on the hero to kill several dragons that threaten the island Khorinis, where the story takes place. This is the main goal on the main story level. To fight these dragons, the hero has to get a certain amulet (1 task, first sublevel). To get this amulet, he has to talk to the governor in the town Khorinis (task 1.1., second sublevel). To be able to talk to the governor, the player has to become a member of the town's militia (task 1.1.1, third sublevel) and so on.[5]

---

5   From a psychological perspective, this narrative structure is similar to a classic cybernetic concept to describe human action plans by means of elementary action elements proposed by Miller, Galanter & Pribram (1960).

The example makes it obvious that on the micro level of tasks, a typical digital game is comprised of thousands of segments that consist of a motivational sequence of 'story situation – action – result – consequence – new story situation.' Concerning the problem of how to link motivating expectations to these single segments, it is important to notice that usually there are not just rewarding consequences in the long run ('killing all dragons at the end of the story, or getting an amulet after several hours of game play') but also a lot of rewarding *on-the-spot consequences*. Although there is no sound empirical study on this, it is possible to estimate that the time gap between rewarding consequences on the micro level of a typical game is rather small and can be measured in seconds or a few minutes, depending on the genre at hand. In addition, these small rewards are enriched by the addition of bigger rewards on different higher task levels (e.g., rewards after a successful 'big fight').

The whole concept of intermediate rewards for actions refers to the idea of programmed learning and Skinner's concepts of "on-the-spot consequences" and "reinforcement plans" (see Skinner, 1954, 1958). In simplified terms, Skinner states that behavior which always has on-the-spot-rewarding consequences will occur more frequently in the future. And "stretching the ratio" of the given rewards will lead to behavior which lasts longer, even if every single instance of that behavior is not rewarded. Although the behavioristic theory behind these assumptions is problematic, the code of practice based on it is very typical for digital games, and leads to the metaphor of digital games as modern variations of the old 'Skinner box.' Just as a pigeon in such a box gets a food pill after it has pushed a certain button, the player gets helpful tools (e.g., amour, heath packs, etc.), parasocial rewards (praise from NPCs, etc.), access to new and exiting areas of the game world, etc., after having performed a certain game task successfully (for the application of this approach to the popular online role playing game *Everquest* by Sony, see Yee, 2001, pp. 70-72).

Simultaneously, this demonstrates that storytelling is linked to the motivational design of a digital game on various levels. On the micro level, there are hundreds or thousands of short 'story situation – action – result – consequence – new story situation' sequences, glued together by a specific setting and their relation to more complex story tasks on higher levels up to one, or a "view main tasks" of the macro level of the game.

Levels of Narrativity in Entertaining and Learning Games

In addition to the problem of how to prompt motivating knowledge and expectations via storytelling, there is the question of how many development resources should be used to create good storytelling in learning games in general. Based on the answers designers gave to this question, it is possible to distinguish *levels of narrativity* in digital games.

A lot of entertaining game genres (usually shooters, simulations, and sport games) do incorporate some story elements (e.g., a main character and a "view main tasks") but, nevertheless, they have more similarity to an Ikea assembly manual ('do this, then this, then that') than to narratives to be seen on TV, or a fortiori sophisticated stories to be found in classic literature. The characters are very shallow, and NPCs are subordinated to the demands of the game play: they provide missions ('look for my child'), give the player information or tools, or they function as dumb, violent opponents and so on.

In contrast, there are genres that traditionally are on a higher level of narrativity, especially adventure games. For example, the *Gabriel Knight* series (Sierra, 1993-1999) and the *Broken Sword* series (Revolution Software, 1993-), but also role playing games like *Final Fantasy VI* (Square, 1993) and even survival horror games like *Silent Hill 2* (Kanami, 2001; see Neitzel, Bopp & Nohr, 2005) demonstrate that it is possible to combine interesting game play with a complex story that includes characters with relations to each other, with inner problems, weaknesses etc.[6]

In addition, there is currently a trend to put more stress on storytelling across all genres, even in genres like the shooter game that used very low levels of storytelling in the past. For example, the third person shooter, *Max Payne* (Remedy, 2001), which combines an innovative game play with a film noir story; or *Half Life 2* (Velve, 2004), which incorporates a rather complex political science fiction setting. The commercial reason for this trend is the attempt to attract more girls and women (who are generally more interested in storytelling with complex characters then are men) to digital gaming.

In opposition to these tendencies, *learning games* (at least on the German market) make very limited usage of storytelling and motivation via parasocial mechanisms (see Bopp, 2006a). One reason for this may be the focus on simulations like *SimCity* (Maxis, 1989) as promising examples of digital entertaining games that dominated the discourses in media didactic in the past (Dempsey, 1993).

Some Specific Demands on Storytelling in Learning Games for School

To illustrate the idea of a story-based learning game, the frame story of the *Elektra Demonstrator* is presented. This research demonstrator's purpose is to test the usage of didactic structures of entertaining digital games in digital learning environments (for

---

6   A basic design method to create such stories with complex characters in digital games (next to scripted cutscenes) is the extensive use of letters, e-mails, and phone or video calls and especially the usage of *multiple choice dialogs*. In adventure games and role playing games, the audio files for these multiple choice dialogs sometimes account for more than half of all game data, and dialogs all together can last dozens of hours.

All these games use an approach with a determined plot. In the future, maybe there will be games with more flexible stories that are determined by specific aspects of the characters of an NPC (an AI driven approach) and the actions of the player (e.g., see Hoffmann, Göbel, Schneider & Iurgel, 2005; Louchart & Aylett, 2004).

the concept of 'didactic structures in digital games,' see Bopp, 2006a). Its focus is on learning in virtual 3D environments that supports European school curricula for 13+ students in physics, mainly via homework learning.

The developers of a frame story for the *Elektra Demonstrator* had to face some problems that are typical for learning games for pupils in general.

Firstly, the less appealing the gameplay of a game, the more important good storytelling is in motivating the player. Learning games have to stress learning tasks that are probably not as appealing as purely entertaining gameplay activities (e.g., fighting, driving etc.). Thus, good storytelling for virtual extrinsic motivation is particularly important for digital learning games. But unfortunately, digital learning games for pupils cannot simply copy typical plots that are used by many successful digital games, because these stories usually incorporate violence and lots of (for example, gender) stereotypes that may foster violent tendencies in high risk groups or may be seen as offensive or discriminative.

Secondly, the story in a learning game should appeal to both boys and girls. Unfortunately, it has been clearly shown that there is a gender difference concerning preferences for entertaining stories and types of computer games in general. For example, in Germany in 2005, the favorite game for adolescent boys was the team-based shooter *Counterstrike* (a *Half-Life* modification), for girls it was The Sims series (Maxis, 2000-), a social simulation (see Medienpädagogischer Forschungsverbund Südwest, 2005).

Thirdly, a feature of curriculum related knowledge is that it is often abstract and separated from everyday situations. Typically, it aims at general knowledge ("Allgemeinwissen"), not, for example, the specific knowledge acquired in an apprenticeship. Thus, it is a challenge to create a story with learning situations that do not feel 'schoolish' but nevertheless include the learning content that is the subject of the schools curricula.

Concerning these problems, it is not surprising that a lot of digital learning games create boring frame stories that incorporate learning tasks in a rather forced way (e.g., *Physikus*, Heureka-Klett 1999).

An Example of a Frame Story for an Educational Game on "Physics"

The *Elektra Demonstrator* tries to deal with these problems by using a mystic adventure story with magic elements. The main location is Florence; the time is the present. The story is dramatic and hierarchically task-oriented. A young male (George) and female student (Mona), both of whom can be played as avatars, meet each other on holiday and get involved in the struggle between the female's grand-uncle Leo (an old professor of History of Natural Science), a crazy villain scientist (and his myrmidons) and an ancient secret society (the 'Galileans'). Leo disappears at the beginning of the plot, and George and Mona must rescue him and search for an old lost renaissance manuscript, Galileo's secret diary, which is the story's MacGuffin (as Hitchcock used to call an elusive object that propels the story). During the chase, the couple immerse themselves in the world of the Renaissance and its scientific achievements, and has to use this knowledge to reach their goals.

This plot obviously doesn't try to reinvent the wheel, but is inspired by narrative elements that are currently in vogue (e.g., the novels of Dan Brown) and the successful adventure game series *Broken Sword* (Revolution Software, 1996-). The plot, with its links to the Renaissance and Galileo Galilei, provides the opportunity to integrate content that is linked to the learning topic (physics) in a smooth way.

There are two reasons for choosing a young male and female student as the avatars of the story. Firstly, pupils in junior high school have the tendency to want to be young adults. Thus, this may foster the identification of the learners with the main characters. Secondly, it provides the opportunity to raise an issue that is of particular interest for adolescents: romantic relationships.

The main characters of the plot are surrounded by several NPCs that fulfill different functions for the story and the learning tasks. It is recommended to use a lot of NPCs as a variety of characters (and locations) provide variety in respect to storytelling. *Dreamfall. The Longest Journey*, 2006), for example, an adventure game that is highly praised for its storytelling, incorporates 156 individual characters. In addition, the NPCs serve the function of *virtual pedagogical agents* (for this term, see Gunz & Haake, 2005). They provide missions and learning tasks to the player, reward him, and give him learning hints, learning tools and so on. It is sensible to distribute this function between several characters in order to avoid any one character being interpreted as a kind of stealth 'school teacher.' This profession has negative connotations for some learners and thus this may destroy the immersion in the game world. This aspect of digital games –concealing the fact that a player actually learns something in an environment that is arranged for learning – can be called *stealth teaching* (see Bopp, 2006b).

An Example of the Integration of Frame Story, Learning and Game Play

To illustrate the implementation of a frame story on the micro level of a learning game, such a game can be seen as a sequence of three basic types of *game situations* with different functions:

- There are situations that are mainly designed to tell the story of the game. They can be called story situations (StS).
- There are situations that are mainly designed to incite learning activities and thus can be termed learning situations (LeS). LeS must be designed as 'pure learning

activities in a way that makes them compatible with the game setting and the story' (see above).

– There are gameplay situations (GpS) that include typical traditional gaming actions (driving, jump & run, fighting etc.) which are supposed to be fun and do not result in educational learning. They serve as rewards, and thus are included for motivational reasons, as are StS.

This three-part segmentation of digital learning games is cross-grained. A LeS, for example, will often be composed of several single learning activities, interrupted by short pieces of other activities (e.g., a joke from a NPC who otherwise provides learning information). The labels just indicate *the main function* of the situation.

A main challenge in respect to the creation of a story-driven digital learning game is to merge these three types of situation in a way that doesn't feel artificial. The table below illustrates a way to merge LeS on the propagation of light with a story task (free the heroine Mona who is captured behind a door) and a GpS that is typical for adventure games (solving a riddle).

Type of situation and main actions
StS 1: Mona follows a Galilean and is captured behind a strange door in her grand-uncle's laboratory. George enters the laboratory. The magical NPC Galileo Galilei (the main virtual pedagogical agent in the situation) appears and gives G. several hints that make it clear that he has to send a strong beam of light through the key hole of the strange door in order to open the door. Behind the door, the beam must shine on a specific light cell but not on anything next to this light cell.
LeS 1: If the player is familiar with the concept of a beam of light and with the 2D modelling of light as rays he can jump forward to GpS # 1 (see below).
LeS 2: If the learner has no prior knowledge, Galileo tells George to examine a lab table in the room with a little flashlight and blinds and invites him to create a narrow beam of light. Galileo gives hints, if necessary.
LeS 3: Galilei explains the concept of a ray of light in reference to the flashlight and the blinds: In order to do so, the room suddenly morphs into an abstract modelled version of itself, the camera moves into a top-down shot of the lab table and displays a schematic graphic of the lab table with its tools on it. The beam of light now is represented by several rays of light. The player can move the spotlight and the rays change their directions.
GpS 1: George has to discover that he must use a strong spotlight that stands unplugged behind a clip board in a corner of the lab (or, to make it more challenging, in a little storage room next to the lab) in order to create this strong beam of light. Galileo gives hints, if necessary.
LeS 4: The player now probably aims the spot light at the keyhole in a randomized angle. He cannot see the path of the beam in the room behind the door. Thus, nothing happens. Galileo explains why nothing happens. In order to find the correct position for the spotlight, Galileo tells George to look at his PDA. The PDA now displays a top-down 2D

graphic of the lab and the room behind the door (similar to the first abstract view of the lab table in LeS 3). It displays the position of the spotlight, the rays of light that go through the key hole and the position of the light cell in the room behind the door.
George now has to change the position of the spotlight till it shines on the appropriate light cell behind the door. In order to do so, he has to check the position of the ray of light on the PDA. If the player wants to, Galileo can give hints.

StS 2: When George succeeds, the door opens; Mona is free again and is glad to see him.

Applications and Limitations

At present, there is no sound research on fields of application and limitations concerning digital story-based learning games. But some assumptions can be made concerning the target groups of learners and possible producers.

- *Age group*: Digital story-based learning is targeted at learners who like digital games. As the current average digital gamer is 29 and gets older every year, it may be particularly suitable for children and (young at heart) adults that like playful identities.
- *Presuppositions of the learner*: Besides a general affection for digital games, there are no specific presuppositions for the learner.
- *School context*: As story-based learning is more time consuming than traditional teaching, it may be more suitable for homework instruction than for classroom teaching. As story-based learning tries to motivate learners that do not like 'pure learning activities,' a specific target group may be learners who are strongly unmotivated in specific areas.
- *Producers*: The production of story-based digital games (especially in 3D) is currently costly and requires a lot of creative personnel (similar to the movie industry). Thus, today only big educational or research institutions and commercial enterprises can produce or commission these types of games. In principle, there may be products that provide story-based learning environments that can be easily adapted by teachers to their individual needs (with exchangeable learning content, for example), but right now these are dreams for the future.

References

Bandura, A. (1977) Self-efficacy: toward a unifying theory of behavioral change. In: *Psychological Review*, 84, pp. 191–215.

Bopp, M. (2005) Didaktisches Design in Silent Hill. In: Neitzel, B., Bopp, M. & Nohr, R. F. eds.: *"See? I'm real…"* Multidisziplinäre Zugänge zum Computerspiel am Beispiel von 'Silent Hill'. Münster: Lit, pp. 74–95.

Bopp, M. (2006a) Didactic analysis of digital games and game-based learning. In: Pivec, M. ed. *Affective and Emotional Aspects of Human-Computer Interaction. Game-Based and Innovative Learning Approaches.* Amsterdam: IOS Press, pp. 8–37.

Bopp, M. (2006b) Immersive Didaktik und Framingprozesse in Computerspielen. Ein handlungstheoretischer Ansatz. In: Neitzel, B. & Nohr, R. F. eds. *Das Spiel mit dem Medium. Partizipation – Immersion – Interaction. Zur Teilnahme an den Medien von Kunst bis Computerspiel.* Schriftenreihe der Gesellschaft für Medienwissenschaft (GFM). Marburg: Schüren, pp. 170–186.

Bruner, J. (1990) *Acts of Meaning.* Cambridge, MA: Harvard University Press.

Cognition and Technology Group at Vanderbilt (1997) *The Cognition and Technology Group at Vanderbilt. The Jasper Project: lessons in curriculum, instruction, assessment, and professional development.* Mahwah, NJ: Lawrence Erlbaum Associates.

Creswell, J. (1997) *Creating worlds, constructing meaning: the Scottish storyline method.* Portsmouth, NH: Heinemann.

Dempsey, J., Lucassen, B., Gilley, W. & Rasmussen, K. (1993) Since Malone's theory of intrinsically motivating instruction: what's the score in the gaming literature? In: *Journal of Educational Technology Systems*, 22 (2), pp. 173–83.

Gulz, A. & Haake, M. (2005) *Virtual Pedagogical Agents – Design Guidelines Regarding Visual Appearance and Pedagogical Roles.* Available from: <http://www.formatex.org/micte2006/pdf/1848-1852.pdf> [Accessed 8 March 2007].

Hartmann, T., Klimmt, C. & Vorderer, P. (2001) Avatare: Parasoziale Beziehungen zu virtuellen Akteueren. In: *Medien- und Kommunikationswissenschaft 49* (3), pp. 350–368.

Hoffmann, A., Göbel, S., Schneider, O. & Iurgel, I. (2005) Storytelling-based edutainment applications. In: Tan, L. ed. *E-Learning and Virtual Science Centers.* Hershey: Information Science Publishing, pp. 190–214.

Hoffner, C. (1996) Children's wishful identification and parasocial interaction with favorite television characters. In: *Journal of Broadcasting and Electronic Media*, 40, pp. 389–402.

Horton, D. & Wohl, R.R. (1956) Mass communication and para-social interaction. Observations on intimacy at a distance. In: *Psychiatry*, 19 (3), pp. 215–229.

Hug, T. (2005) Microlearning and narration. Exploring possibilities of utilization of narrations and storytelling for the designing of "micro units" and didactical microlearning arrangements. In: *Online Proceedings of the International Conference "Media in Transition 4: The Work of Stories" at the M.I.T. in Cambridge (MA), USA, May 6-8, 2005.*Available from: <http://web.mit.edu/ comm-forum/mit4/papers/hug.pdf> [Accessed 15 August 2006]

Medienpädagogischer Forschungsverbund Südwest ed. (2005) *JIM-Studie. Jugend, Information, (Multi-)Media. Basisstudie zum Medienumgang 12-19-Jähriger in Deutschland.* Available from: <http://www.mpfs.de/fileadmin/Studien/JIM 2005.pdf> [Accessed 19 June 2006].

Mentz, O. & Rattunde, E. (1997) Simulationen in offenen Unterrichtseinheiten – Mög-lichkeiten für den Fremdsprachenunterricht. In: Burger, G. ed. *Fortgeschrittener Fremdsprachenunterricht an Volkshochschulen.* Frankfurt: Deutsches Institut für Erwachsenenbildung (DIE), pp. 75–88.

Klimmt, C. (2001) Computer-Spiel: Interaktive Unterhaltungsangebote als Synthese aus Medium und Spielzeug. In: *Zeitschrift für Medienpsychologie 1* (13), pp. 22–32. Available

from: <http://www.psyjournals.com/psyjournals/hh/zmp/   2001/01/zmp1301022.html>
[Accessed 19 June 2006].

Lazzaro, N. (2004) *Why We Play Games: Four Keys to More Emotion Without Story.*
XeonDesign. Available from <http://www.xeodesign.com> [Accessed 1 March 2005].

Louchart S. & Aylett, R. (2004) Narrative theories and emergent interactive narrative. In:
IJCEELL Journal, 14 (6), pp. 506–518.

Miller, G. A., Galanter, E. & Pribram, C. (1960) *Plans and the Structure of Behaviour.* New
York: Holt, Rinehart and Winston.

Nass, C. & Shyam, S. (1994) *Is Human-Computer Interaction Social or Parasocial?*
Available from: <http://www.stanford.edu/group/commdept/oldstuff/srct_pages /Social-
Parasocial.html> [Accessed 19 June 2005].

Neitzel, B., Bopp, M. & Nohr, R.F. eds. (2005) *"See? I'm real..."* Multidisziplinäre Zugänge
zum Computerspiel am Beispiel von 'Silent Hill'. Münster: Lit.

Pias, C. (2002) *ComputerSpielWelten.* München: sequenzia.

Picard, R. W. (1995) Affective Computing. *M.I.T. Media Laboratory Perceptual Computing
Selection Technical Report No. 321.* Available from: <http://citeseer.ist.psu.edu/cache/
papers/cs/405/ftp:zSzzSzwhitechapel.media.mit.eduzSzpubzSztech-reportszSzTR-321.pdf/
picard95affective.pdf> [Accessed 19 June 2005].

Rheinberg, F. (1989) *Zweck und Tätigkeit.* Göttingen: Hogrefe.

Rheinberg, F. (2005) Intrinsische Motivation und Flow-Erleben. In: Heckhausen, J. &
Heckhausen, H. eds.*: Motivation und Handeln.* Heidelberg: Springer, pp. 331–352.

Schmidt, C. (2004). Der Archeplot im Game. Silent Hill 2 als klassische Heldenreise. In:
Neitzel, B., Bopp, M. & Nohr, R.F. eds.: *"See? I'm real..."* Multidisziplinäre Zugänge
zum Computerspiel am Beispiel von 'Silent Hill'. Münster: Lit, pp. 20–40.

Skinner, B.F. (1954) The science of learning and the art of teaching. In: *Harvard Educational
Review*, 24 (2), pp. 86–97.

Skinner, B.F. (1958) Teaching machines. In*: Science*, 128, pp. 969–977.

Yee, N. (2001) *The Norrathian Scrolls: A Study of EverQuest (Version 2.5).* Available from:
<http://www.nickyee.com/report.pdf> [Accessed 19 June 2005].

Zillmann, D. (1996) The psychology of suspense in dramatic exposition. In: Vorderer, P.,
Wulff, H. J. & Friedrichsen, M. eds. *Suspense: Conceptualizations, Theoretical Analysis,
and Empirical Explorations.* Mahwah, NJ: Lawrence Erlbaum, pp. 199–231.

Zillmann, D. (2004) Emotionspsychologische Grundlagen. In: Mangold, R., Vorderer, P. &
Bente, G. eds. *Lehrbuch der Medienpsychologie.* Göttingen Hogrefe, pp. 101–128.

Experiences in Setting up a Virtual Learning Game Project

Pasi Mattila, Jukka Miettunen & Tony Manninen

The traditional notion of a learning environment has expanded to cover virtual spaces. Today, these virtual learning environments are often network-based and readily accessible to a certain group of students. Virtual meeting places are extremely popular among young people. Their very popularity can occasionally even present problems for everyday schoolwork. Thus, attempts to harness these new tools and environments for learning purposes are worth undertaking. These considerations have inspired the present project that has produced a 3D virtual learning environment with the aim of providing a space for microlearning activities. The space itself and its virtual inhabitants are based on historical data. The players who enter this environment learn by interacting with the game world and other players.

The games designed for this space offer challenges the players try to solve as a team. They emphasize group work skills, group interaction, and cooperation in various conflict situations that have to be negotiated inside the virtual world. Historical information plays a key role in gameplay and thus the learning experience is integrated into the events of the games, making learning fun. The environment utilizes both verbal and non-verbal communication and it does not contain violent or destructive elements, and therefore it is suitable for children of all ages and both sexes.

1   Introduction

The game concepts were produced in cooperation with the Department of Education of the City of Oulu and Ludocraft, the Game Design and Research Unit of the University of Oulu.

This article describes two projects whose aim was the creation of a virtual space designed to enhance learning. The activities embedded in this virtual space offer a game-like environment that supplies the players with bits of information which carry the plot of the games and provide an interactive learning experience. The convergence of gaming and learning environments expounded through the description of these projects challenges traditional notions of teaching and learning, changes the way these concepts are viewed, and creates an alternative perspective to the distribution of information.

2   Gaming Technology for Educational Purposes

Microlearning can be understood as a metaphor which refers to microaspects of a variety of learning models, concepts and processes. "No matter if learning refers to the process of building up and organizing knowledge, to the change of behavior, of attitudes, of values, of mental abilities, of cognitive structures, of emotional reactions, of action patterns or of societal dimensions, in all cases we have the possibility to consider micro, meso and macro aspects of the various views on more or less persisting changes and sustainable alterations of performances." (Hug 2005, p. 4).

The Snellman game and learning environment contains the following microlearning activities: information nuggets as a text, memorizing a word, selecting an answer to a question, answering questions in quizzes and playful learning with micro-games. While moving in the game- and learning environment, the students have to deal with the small information nuggets (microcontent) and have to make decisions and choices considering their own interests and job descriptions. The picture of the educational entity is build by the information gone through.

The core in developing and using the game and learning environment in teaching is Inquiry-based learning (IBL). IBL is a project-oriented learning model and pedagogic strategy based on constructivist and socio-constructivist theories of learning (Eick & Reed, 2002). This learning process by exploration of the natural or the con-structed/social world leads the learner to questions and discoveries in the seeking of new understandings. With this pedagogic strategy, children learn science by doing it (Aubé & David, 2003). The main goal is conceptual change. A microworld implements a constructivist instructional design model that lets the learner "play" within an artificial or real environment and learns by building things. The purpose is to give students the resources to build and refine their own knowledge.

Young media consumers want to be active participants in, rather than passive observers of, information. This is particularly apparent in their use of the Internet – they are at home in networks and virtual environments. Previously, the Net was con-ceived merely as a source of information, but today the social and communal nature of virtual network environments is recognized. Information is actively constructed online through the exchange of opinions and images. Furthermore, users want to be able to influence their virtual environment and not only act as consumers, but as producers of information as well. In the learning environments of the future, users will be able to manipulate content to suit their present needs. These developments, in turn, will pre-sent challenges to individual schools as well as pedagogy in general.

Young students are constantly applying new technologies creatively to suit their own purposes. According to the Scandinavian eLearning Nordic (2006) study, the use of information technology does improve learning results. The problem with new tech-nologies is that teachers often feel unqualified to apply them to teaching. Teachers and students inhabit different digital worlds and this mismatch is reflected in the learning experience. The effective use of information technology requires a departure from tra-ditional teaching methods and available pedagogical frameworks. Games and play are natural activities and part of everyday life. Before the advent of mobile and wireless technologies, games were tied to specific occasions and locations. Today, games are capable of producing a forum where people can establish and uphold relationships with others. The societal role of games is transforming gaming from a mere pleasure-seeking activity into an incremental part of modern society, especially in youth culture.

People use games as a means of expression. Gaming is a phenomenon that touches nearly everyone. Games and game environments provide a space wherein one can solve problems, interact with others, and build social networks. They also present opportunities for exploring and developing one's emotional life. Furthermore, as shown by Gee (2003, p. 205), games operate with solid principles of learning that are better than those in many of our skill-and-drill, back-to-basics, test-them-until-they-drop schools. Games are often multilayered and can contain a vast variety of activities, address any number of interests, and provide countless possibilities for human interaction. In the future, it is crucial to develop genuinely innovative educational games for large audiences in order to counterbalance the mass of violent games on the market. As such, games will have an increasingly important part to play as learning environments and methods of teaching (cf. Lim, et al., 2006).

Earlier research has suggested that games can have a positive impact on learning, since they support intrinsic motivation, and give opportunities for imitation and learning by providing feedback, fantasy, and challenges (Rieber, 1996). The purpose of play is to practice everyday skills. In order to motivate the player, a game must have a goal. This goal produces a challenge for the player and motivates him or her to develop the skills that are required to reach it. Digital games fulfill the central requirements of purposeful play (Ermi et al., 2004). Learning need not be the explicit objective of play, but any given game requires some learning to take place. The charm of play and the popularity of digital games inevitably leads to the question: can gaming be used in teaching? Through games, children are often prepared to go to great lengths in order to achieve their goals.

Playing games develops one's style of thinking towards an experimental, game-like approach to problem solving. The activities that take place within a game are circumscribed by a set of rules that have been agreed upon beforehand (Salen & Zimmerman, 2004). In addition, the game acts as a learning space in which the learner is able to take risks where real-world consequences are lowered (Gee, 2003, p. 62). Online games and various virtual game environments are steadily gaining in popularity. Gaming is as much a hobby as reading books, but often this is not recognized by parents. Children are especially attracted to action and adventure games. Furthermore, children more often than not resort to their circle of friends in their choice of games and thus gaming is at the outset a social affair. Young students view games as meaningful and motivating environments that enable them to exercise their faculties, actively explore various subjects, meet with friends, and create and uphold relationships with others. In contrast, most parents and educators view games as entertainment.

This framework is the basis on which the present research on virtual learning environments in the City of Oulu has been built. The Department of Education of the City of Oulu and the university's game research unit has produced two projects in which it has been possible to observe the benefits of educational gaming in practice. The following two cases provide information and discussion about the value of gaming in education. The cases consist of two games that bring history to life.

Figure 1. Bird's eye view of the area surrounding the Castle of Oulu

3   Two Experimental Applications of Educational Games

3.1   Case I: An Adventure in the Castle of Oulu (1641)

Research on the application of virtual environment technologies to education has been pioneered at the University of Oulu by the Research Unit for Educational Technology at the Department of Educational Sciences and Teacher Education. In this work, game design and development have been the responsibility of the university's game research unit, LudoCraft. These efforts have focused mainly on higher education and they have been documented in various publications (see, for instance, Hämäläinen et al., 2006, Manninen & Korva, 2005). Drawing from this research, the present project aimed at developing students' communal skills in a virtual environment as well as exploring further advancements in the field.

The team in charge of the realization of the project consisted of a game development group of eight people who supplied all the essential skills required for designing and constructing a game. The team was lead by a producer and a lead designer. Among the areas of expertise of the participants were programming, level design, 3D modeling, animation, audio design, script writing, graphical design, and concept art, to name a few. With this approach, it was possible to acquire the required level of quality for the outcome of the project. The game development team was supported by a group of pedagogical experts who planned the functional and educational features of the game and made sure it met the needs of players aged 9 to 16 years. The seamless collaboration between game developers and pedagogical experts enabled the project to harness two very different knowledge bases.

The platform chosen for the project was the Unreal game engine by Epic. An end user license agreement of €50 per workstation secured the use of the platform for non-profit, research, and educational purposes. A client version of the Unreal environment was installed in a number of workstations which were then connected to a server that controlled the flow of the game. Most modern PCs with adequate memory and a competent 3D graphics card can perform these tasks.

The virtual game environment emphasizes group interaction and cooperative skills, testing these skills in various challenging conflict situations that have to be resolved through teamwork. The game itself is a multiplayer game designed for up to 30 simultaneous players. It should be noted that the objective of the designers was to avoid the inclusion of any violent or destructive elements, in order to ensure the applicability of the game for educational aims and younger players. The environment is a faithful representation of the area surrounding the Castle of Oulu in 1651. The model is based on historical documents and drawings from that period. Some fictional elements were added to enhance gameplay.

The moderator sets up the game on the server according to the age and number of participants, assigns a preferred duration for the game, and adjusts the difficulty level. Each player is assigned a name, a character, and a specific mission. The assigned characters are based on typical professions and social classes of the period, such as peasant, clergyman, merchant, or soldier. A typical mission statement reads: "You are a shopkeeper and your job is to buy and trade as much merchandise as you can. In addition, you have to contribute to the mayoral campaign of the merchant Anders Mattson by acquiring votes." The other players receive similar tasks associated with various professions. Some of the players act as henchmen, creating discord and thus adding suspense to the game. The players score points according to their performance on a given mission. The teacher, acting as moderator, can assume the likeness of a bird or a dog in order to move freely in the environment as an observer.

Figure 2. Players exchanging microknowledge via headsets (voice data), characters sporting speech bubbles

The user interface of the game is simple and straightforward. Movement in the game environment is controlled by the arrow keys on the keyboard and the computer mouse. Exchanging items and other related actions take place using the function keys. Communication within the game is conducted with the aid of headsets. Contact in the virtual game world is established by approaching a character, at which time a speech bubble appears and signifies the possibility for communication. Communication via natural speech instead of the usual written chat-form was found to be a major strength of the game. However, this required some special arrangements in the game room, as it produced the need to create sound proof areas for the players. The practical solution to this problem was to erect cubicles – like in many language-learning studios – for individual workstations. A typical session consisted of playing the game for around an hour.

The objective of the project was to investigate the educational use of a 3D gaming environment targeted for students 9 to 16 years old. Given the relatively short amount of time that was available for design and production, the game itself can be considered a success. Despite the fact that before the final field experiments the game had not been tested on large groups involving more than 10 players, the game environment was found to be stable and reliable. Over 300 students took part in the ten separate game sessions during the week of the Festival. In addition to oral and written feedback, gameplay was videotaped and recorded on the computers' hard drives. This material is currently under analysis by the research group.

Preliminary findings based on the oral and written feedback suggest that a game-like approach to historical materials is motivating for the students. As with the use of print or following learning material in multimedia form, assuming a character in a virtual world can act as a valuable supplement for the learning process. New teaching programs often emphasize community, the importance of communication, and media skills. The game showed potential for the realization of precisely such objectives. This pilot project did not contain the elements required for an in-depth study (such as the use of a control group) and therefore its conclusions must remain tentative. However, the project did produce a wealth of data that can be used to benefit future research. At present, the environment is freely available for student groups through the Department of Education of the City of Oulu.

3.2   Case II: Virtual Snellman (1822)

The positive feedback from *Adventure in the Castle of Oulu* inspired the team to conceive of a second educational game. Unlike in *Adventure in the Castle of Oulu*, in which gameplay took place in a closed environment coordinated through client programs, the game's follower was designed to function on the Internet and contain the possibility of interfacing with other learning environments and technologies, such as mobile devices. The 3D game engine software created for the project was designed with future projects in mind.

Figure 3. The teacher in the past and the future

The year 2006 marks the 200th birthday of J. V. Snellman, a legendary Finnish statesman and philosopher who acted in several political roles during his lifetime. The theme of the jubilee is to celebrate the national identity of Finland, and this theme is illustrated through the colorful personal history of Snellman himself. All citizens, and especially the younger population, are encouraged to participate in various events that take place throughout the year. Virtual Snellman, a virtual learning environment situated in the year 1822, is part of these pursuits. The central idea behind Virtual Snellman is to create a virtual learning environment that contains a wealth of information about Snellman and his contemporaries, and to transport the player into their historical surroundings. The learning environment will also contain exciting game-elements, such as various objectives and goals, role-playing and colorful characters, and an exciting plot. Students will be able to develop strategic thinking, as well as problem solving and decision making skills. Furthermore, the learning environment will enable the student to be a part of a group and interact with his or her social network.

This Snellman-themed learning environment will be realized as a game in order to attract students. The purpose of the game will be to introduce the students to fascinating historical materials in an exciting way, and thus make the learning experience a captivating one. A game-like environment will offer the player the opportunity to shape the learning experience to suit his or her interests. A game that emphasizes action will make the relationship between the individual player and the information imparted by the game an active process in which interaction and communal goals are raised above the gathering of factual knowledge.

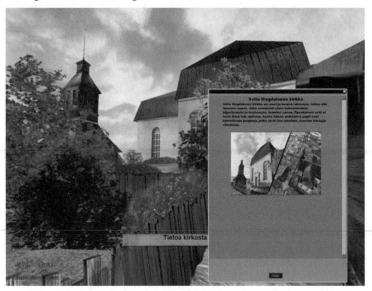

Figure 4. A learning environment containing plenty of microcontent

The objective of the Snellman project is to construct a virtual learning environment that is inspiring and rich in opportunities. The learning environment contains a wealth of information which is contextualized in the form of a virtual world. Learning in this environment occurs by exploring the virtual space, problem solving, and interacting with others.

In the design stages of the Snellman game, the following central questions have to be addressed before and during production. Firstly, what does a game have to be like in order to attract and maintain the interest of the target audience? Secondly, how to utilize the enormous amount of historical data in a manner that does not transform the game into a mere reading experience? One of the important goals of realizing the Snellman game is to make sure the application can be transported to other networks and is able to utilize different learning environments through, for instance, mobile devices. The meaning of the mobile devices is growing while the WLAN-devices are available in everyday use.

During pre-production, the requirements and demands of the target audience have been carefully mapped. In addition, the design group has compiled a list containing technical requirements for production, content, game design, audiovisual style, and the storyboard. The environment and technology used is designed to be as simple and easy to use as possible, so that every teacher and student can adapt to it. The teacher, however, has to be unprejudiced in order to benefit this new type of learning environment, which is familiar to most kids nowadays. The teacher must also be oriented in IBL. In our pilot cases, the use of the environment is free of charge. In the future, creating those kinds of environments will require planning and human resources, even though the environment and the tools are free.

The Snellman game was assigned the following properties: a virtual environment where the action takes place, three dimensional visually impressive user interface, and content respectful of the theme. The learning technology available empowers the benefit and using the tools in teaching.

Requirement	Arguments and Examples
Replayability	• Must not lack in content even if played through a number of times
Expandability	• Possibility to expand the environment in the future • Sequels, further levels and scenarios
Rich in relevant information	• Full of interesting details about Snellman's life • Not merely an encyclopedia
Visual appeal and ambiance	• Competent audiovisuals attract young gamers • Able to convey factual knowledge to the target audience
Educational	• Exploration, observation, analysis • Not only performance but atmospheric as well

Appealing to young gamers	• A genuine game, not a mere application • Goals, challenges, and rewards must be clearly visible
Easy to learn	• Everyone should be able to play the game • Low threshold but challenging enough

Table 1. Requirements relating to gameplay – activities in the environment

The learning environment consists of virtual spaces where the activities take place and information is imparted. A virtual space might be a room, the scene of an historical event, or some other space that contains the necessary selection of tools, characters, and activities. Inside the virtual world, the user can explore freely and access the knowledge. The educational objectives of the Snellman game set demands that the historical information be present in the game environment. Despite its game-like qualities, information conveyed by the environment takes center stage. However, the objective of the project is not to produce a Snellman databank. The information presented in the game can be viewed as both raw material for gameplay and educational material for students.

1. Information must be based on historical facts: (a) A critical approach to sources (b) Ensuring the authenticity of the material.

2. There must be a sufficient amount of information: (a) Collecting, recording, and transforming the material into a presentable form (b) Arranging the material into suitable blocks.

3. Information must be accessible: (a) The material must be placed into the game environment (b) Interactivity.

4. Information must be presented in an interesting manner: (a) Game-like qualities (b) Choosing perspectives and the manner of presentation.

The objective of designing the learning environment is to create a virtual space that contains all the relevant information. This information is based on historical fact, arranged in a suitable manner to cover relevant topics, easy to approach, and presented in an exciting way. The game is intended mostly for younger gamers, and therefore the information need not be only in textbook or encyclopedic form. The user must be able to experiment, explore, and engage the subject matter in a way that is exciting for them. Creating these effects through various activities and experiences can be achieved by faithfully modeling Snellman's era and being true to its historical features. Content created by the users themselves is a current topic that has generated lots of interest in gaming and virtual communities. The reason for the popularity of this feature of gaming can be explained by the individual user's desire to be a star in their own storyline and leave a mark on the given environment.

Content created by users can also present significant risks. If the content is not controlled in the proper manner, there is a danger that the environment will be filled with inappropriate materials.

4 Utilizing Games for Educational Purposes

The two case projects described in this paper approach the problematic area of educational games with a hands-on mentality. Since an educational game cannot deliver if either the educational content or the game itself fails, there is a need to combine the two domains into a seamless multidisciplinary effort. The two-year collaboration between pedagogical experts and game design researchers has provided us with a wealth of information – and critical questions – that can be used in future work. How to present information to young students in a meaningful and exciting way? How to bring books to life? J.V. Snellman, for instance, has been the subject of a biography exceeding a thousand pages and a twenty-four volume series of books, consisting of twelve thousand pages. Young students do not favor written materials of this sort. Is it possible to deliver the same information using games?

The learning process involved in gaming often proceeds in concordance with gameplay. Games require and develop various problem solving faculties and learning strategies. Children associate learning with the classroom situation, and thus games offer, as it were, a covert way of delivering information. The idea behind microcontent is to offer the players information that one could acquire from a textbook and present it in small bits, embedded in the virtual environment. One can teach various useful skills and demonstrate societal values through games. Games involving strategy and simulation have the strength of creating opportunities for experimentation and cultivating a hands-on approach to learning. Games involve learning everyday skills through direct experience, free exploration, and repetition. Furthermore, games evolve language, computer, and media skills and can instruct students in historical facts and values. Modern games can also provide learners an experience in social interaction and alternative methods of learning. The virtual learning environment supports the compounding of knowledge from information collected from the environment and the exchange of relevant facts between fellow players.

Central to the experience is the player's immersion into the world of the game. In digital games, the act of moving through space is of great importance, perhaps as important as the plot of the game and social interaction with others during gameplay. Because of this, these games emphasize exploration and discovery, finding and utilizing various objects and bits of information. It is important that the player feels at home in this virtual space, as the experience as a whole is composed to a large extent of the interaction between the player and his or her environment. The game environment acts as a micromedium that amplifies interaction, motivates the player to solve problems presented by the environment, and encourages the player to learn and continue learning. There is usually an idea of a fictional world behind games, a world where the player can act free from the restrictions of the actual world. Gaming is a multidimensional activity and it is largely dictated by the prerequisites of both game and player. The world that is opened up through games enables the player to perform feats that are simply impossible to execute in the real world. Succeeding in these virtual tasks strengthens the player's ego and self-esteem. Games are played for the pleasure they produce and the experiences they offer. As the objectives posed by the game are achieved, the goal of educational gaming, microlearning, takes place.

The virtual game and learning environment gives the concept of microlearning a new form and supplies it with fitting content. This tool enables the simulation of real-life situations which can then be tackled inside the safety of virtual reality. The environment integrates familiar Internet applications and working methods, and it enables players to browse through microcontent and accumulate useful information, microknowledge. Traveling through the environment can itself be considered a learning experience. Furthermore, the flexibility of the digital information supplied by the environment enables it to be exported into other applications and platforms, such as mobile devices, in the future. Virtual learning environments demand a fresh conception of information and teaching, but they also supply new possibilities for uniting learning in the real world and learning that occurs with the aid of computer networks.

Teachers and schools can no longer view themselves simply as distributors of information. The focus of education is shifting towards the task of understanding a computerized digital world that contains great amounts of noisy information. The functions of games and learning environments are converging, and more often than not learning in this setting occurs in a less self-conscious manner, using modern digital instruments to explore and test the large quantities of information that is available to young students. Active learning such as this produces a learning experience that the student will remember for a very long time. Learning, in this sense, consists to a large extent of adapting and processing information to suit a great variety of different contexts. Experience has shown that young students are drawn to game-like learning environments and find in them the necessary motivation to undertake the study of a given subject. Retrieving strategically placed bits of information produces a clear picture of the subject as a whole, provides an enjoyable gaming experience, and, most importantly, inspires learning.

References

Aubé, M. & David, R. (2003) Le programme d'adoption du "Monde de Darwin": une exploitation concrète des TIC selon une approche socio-constructiviste. In: Taurisson, A. and Senteni, A. eds.: *Pédagogies.net. L'essor des communautés virtuelles d'apprentissage.* Montréal: PUQ, Collection Éducation/Recherche, pp. 49–72.

Eick, C.J. & Reed, C.J. (2002) What makes an inquiry oriented science teacher? The influence of learning histories on student teacher role identity and practice. *Science Teacher Education,* 86, pp. 401–416.

Ermi, L., Heliö, S. & Mäyrä, F. (2004) Pelien voima ja pelaamisen hallinta. *Hypermedialaboratory net series* 6. University of Tampere.

E-Learning Nordic 2006. Impact of ICT on Education. (2006) Available from: <http://www.edu.fi/julkaisut/eLearning_Nordic_English.pdf> [Accessed 11 April 2007]

Gee, J.P. (2003) *What Video Games Have to Teach Us About Learning and Literacy.* New York: Palgrave Macmillan.

Hämäläinen, R. et al. (2006) Learning to collaborate scripting collaboration in a 3-D game environment. *International Journal of Internet and Higher Education* (INTHIG), 9 (1), pp. 47–61.

Hug, T. (2005) Microlearning and narration. Exploring possibilities of utilization of narrations and storytelling for the designing of "microunits" and didactical microlearning arrangements. Paper presented at the fourth Media in Transition conference, May 6-8, 2005, MIT, Cambridge (MA), USA.

Lim, C.P., Nonis, D. & Hedberg, J. (2006) Gaming in a 3D multi-user virtual environment (MUVE): engaging students in science lessons. *British Journal of Educational Technology,* 37 (2), pp. 211–231.

Manninen T. & Korva T. (2005) Designing puzzles for collaborative gaming experience – CASE: eScape. In: de Castell S. & Jenson J. eds. *Selected Papers Proceedings of Digital Games Research Association's Second International Conference, June 16-20 Vancouver, Canada,* pp. 233–247.

Rieber, L. (1996) Seriously considering play: designing interactive learning environments based on blending of microworlds, simulations and games. *Educational Technology Research and Development,* 44 (2), pp. 43–58.

Salen, K. & Zimmerman, E. (2004) *Rules of Play: Game Design Fundamentals.* Cambridge: MIT Press.

IV Connecting Micro Steps

Providing Macrostructure for Microlearning

Bernhard Ertl & Heinz Mandl

One major problem of traditional learning scenarios is that learners often acquire knowledge in a way which enables them to recall it in tests quite well, but which creates an obstacle for the application of their knowledge in later situations (see Renkl, Mandl & Gruber, 1996). This means that learners acquire isolated fragments of knowledge without any links to a potential use – the knowledge remains inert (Renkl, Mandl & Gruber, 1996). Approaches such as situated learning (see Lave & Wenger, 1991) describe learning environments with high degrees of authenticity and social interaction that aim particularly at the acquisition of applicable knowledge. Because of this authenticity and the social context, learning is embedded in the macrostructure of application. Recent approaches use the framework of situated learning in the context of computers to provide powerful learning environments (see DeCorte et al., 2003). Thereby, the computer often provides a macrostructure of learning by introducing methods that require learners to perform several microlearning activities (see e.g., Hug, Lindner & Bruck, 2006) either in a sequence or concurrently.

The most obvious way to provide a macrostructure is to sequence different microlearning activities. Such a sequence can *facilitate learners' collaborative work on the task.* In literature, such sequences are often called scripts (see King, 1999). The aim of this sequence is to introduce beneficial activities to collaboration. A second approach provides different microlearning activities concurrently. The learning environment thereby offers collaborating partners a set of resources. The contents or affordances presented by the learning environment can focus the collaborative learning discourse on particular microlearning activities, e.g. on epistemic clarifications and on argumentation moves (see Suthers & Hundhausen, 2003; Ertl, Fischer & Mandl, 2006). This approach *facilitates learners' content-specific work.* In the following, we will describe both approaches.

Facilitating Collaborative Work on the Task

Methods targeting the improvement of the collaborative work on the task often refer to approaches such as *scripted cooperation* (see O'Donnell & King, 1999). These scripts sequence learners' work on the task by the introduction of several microlearning activities; they may provide roles for the learners and different phases that encourage them to engage in several micro-activities, such as summarizing, clarifying or predicting contents of a text section. From this perspective, scripts have two main purposes: they structure the *collaborative negotiation* as well as the *proceeding in the work on the task.* Applying scripts in face-to-face scenarios mainly aims at evoking beneficial cognitive and meta-cognitive strategies of the learners. An example is the method of scripted cooperation by O'Donnell & Dansereau (1992). This script sequenced the collaboration process of the learners in four phases for individual text reading, recall from memory, peer-feedback and elaboration. However, even if this script structures the work on the task, the main motor for the comprehension processes lies in the strategies applied in the different phases (see also Rosenshine & Meister 1994). Furthermore, learners take different roles, which correspond to the application of particular strategies within each phase: e.g., one learner has the role of a recaller, while the other functions as questioner. This example also shows that scripts are independent of the content of the text: the method of scripted cooperation can be applied independent of a learning content. However, it is specific to the learning task.

Recently, scripts have gained in importance in the field of computer supported collaborative learning (see Fischer et al., 2007). In contrast to scripts in face-to-face scenarios, such scripts do not necessarily structure both the collaboration process *and* the proceeding in the work on the task. Baker & Lund (1997), for example, report a script that only directed the collaboration process. Using speech act buttons implemented on their computer screen, the collaborating learners had to agree to a modification, which one learner made in the computer screen before they were able to continue. Weinberger et al. (2005) reported a different script that guided learners proceeding through different discussion boards without specifying how to collaborate. However, most scripts use a mixture of both aspects and sequence particular strategies for the work on the task.

Ertl, Reiserer & Mandl (2005) showed one example for scripting in videoconferencing. The aim of this script was to improve learners during the task of collaborative teaching. This script structured the collaborative proceeding on the task, the roles of the learners and the application of beneficial strategies regarding the collaborative negotiation. Therefore, the script assigned the role of a teacher and the role of a learner to the learners and four micro-phases to the collaboration process. In the first phase, the learner in the teacher role explained the text material and the partner in the learner role asked comprehension questions. In the second phase, the learner in the learner role rehearsed the concepts learned and recorded important aspects on a shared computer screen. The learner in the teacher role supported the partner and clarified misinterpretations. In the third phase, both partners reflected individually and in the fourth phase, they discussed the learning material. Finally, the learner in the learner role recorded important aspects in the shared application. After these four phases, learners switched their roles and continued with another text.

Results of the study show that the script was able to facilitate learners' negotiation with theoretical concepts during the collaboration process. Regarding individual learning outcomes, the script particularly facilitated the acquisition of theoretical knowledge for the learners in the learner role (see Ertl, Reiserer & Mandl, 2005). Other studies also report beneficial effects of scripts on learning processes (see Baker

& Lund, 1997; Weinberger et al. 2005) and on individual outcomes in computer supported learning environments (see Rummel & Spada, 2005). Baker & Lund (1997)
were able to show that the script applied could foster processes of learners' collaboration. Weinberger (2003) reports a more homogeneous work on the task as well as a
higher individual learning outcome, measured by a higher score in an individual post-
test case, when scripts facilitated learning. Furthermore, Rummel & Spada (2005) report that the script was able to facilitate learners' acquisition of beneficial collaboration strategies.

Facilitating Content Specific Work

In contrast to the script approach, which mainly aims at task-specific strategies, content specific facilitation is directed at the conceptual level. This divides a content domain into different aspects at the micro-level. Attribution Theory, for example, could
be split into the aspects of causes, information about circumstances and attribution
patterns (see Ertl, Kopp & Mandl, 2005). Such facilitation aims at facilitating learners'
understanding of a particular problem. For this purpose, content specific facilitation
highlights central characteristics of the learning material by the representation of important content structures. According to Zhang & Norman (1994), this representation
of content has an influence on learners' ability to deal with the content. When provided with a beneficial representation, learners may perceive the problem in a different
manner, which enables them to deal with its content more swiftly (see Zhang &
Norman, 1994). In computer supported collaborative learning environments, the
shared screen provides a great opportunity to realise content specific support (see Ertl,
Fischer & Mandl, 2006). The term, "shared screen", in this context, means that
learners can see the same contents that are provided by the learning environment on
their screen – even if they sit at separate places. A pre-structure of the shared screen
can make important micro-characteristics of a task *salient* and can thereby function as
a representational guide for content-specific negotiations (see the concept of *representational guidance*, e.g. in Suthers & Hundhausen, 2003). The broad variety of structures for conceptual representation (see Löhner & van Joulingen, 2001) led to a wide
variety of facilitation methods, differing in the degrees of freedom that learners have,
and in the degree of support they receive when working with them. Regarding conceptual support, one can distinguish different classes of support, e.g., *templates*, and
conceptualization tools. Templates pre-structure the content domain (see Brooks &
Dansereau, 1983; Suthers & Hundhausen, 2003; Ertl, Fischer & Mandl, 2006). They
provide categories, mainly in the form of tables, which are particularly important for
content-specific negotiation. Learners fill in the empty spaces in the template and
thereby focus on important categories. However, learners cannot change the structure
of the template and model new relations. Therefore, templates aim at providing an understanding of important aspects of a content area. Finally, conceptualization tools allow the modelling of relations by the learners. In this case, the tool provides objects of

different styles and different relations important for the content area and the learners can create their own representation of the structure of a particular content (see Fischer et al., 2002; Suthers & Hundhausen, 2003). Thus, conceptualization tools aim to provide a deeper understanding of structures within the particular content area.

Ertl, Reiserer & Mandl (2005) present an example for content specific improvement of the learning environment in the form of a template (see figure 1). The template is aimed at facilitating learners' learning of text material. The template is focused – similar to the template of Brooks & Dansereau (1983) – on important micro-aspects of theories, particularly on theory concepts, evidence and personal elaborations with respect to consequences and learners' individual opinion. These rather broad categories were anchored by several prompts for micro-activities.

Theoretical concepts	Evidence
What are the core concepts of the theory?	How was the theory examined?
What are the most important statements of the theory?	Which findings support the theory?
Consequences	**Individual opinion**
Which pedagogical interventions can be derived from the theory?	What do we like about the theory? What do we not like?
Which limitations of pedagogical interventions are set by the theory?	Which of our own experiences confirm the theory? Which of your own experiences contradict the theory?

Figure 1. Content specific facilitation in a template style
(taken from Ertl, Reiserer & Mandl, 2005)

Results of the study show that the template was able to focus learners on the important aspects of the theory. Compared to a control group, they reached a higher score in evidence and spent more effort in theory elaborations (see Ertl, Reiserer & Mandl, 2005). This indicates that the template was able to direct the learning process towards the negotiation with evidence and elaborations. But many other studies have also shown beneficial effects of content specific facilitation in computer supported learning environments (see Roschelle & Teasley, 1995; Fischer et al., 2002; Suthers & Hundhausen, 2003; Ertl, Fischer & Mandl, 2006). Roschelle & Teasley (1995) report beneficial effects of simulations for transactive discourse and knowledge co-construction. Kopp, Ertl & Mandl (2004) present a template, which had beneficial effects for learners' collaborative knowledge construction as well as for their individual learning outcomes. Suthers & Hundhausen (2003) reported that a template had facilitated the learners to draw relations between theoretical concepts and evidence. Furthermore, Fischer et al. (2000) found that learners using conceptualization tools also converged regarding the knowledge acquired. This means that the post-test scores of learners with support were much more similar than the scores of the other learners.

Facilitation and Learners' Prerequisites

It has been demonstrated in several studies that combining a number of activities of microlearning for collaboration specific and content specific support has proven to be beneficial for learning. However, they should be applied in a reasonable manner, because not all of the opportunities such facilitation offers may have the desired effects (see Weinberger et al., 2005). The key for this issue often lies in the learners' individual prerequisites, e.g. prior knowledge (Shapiro, 2004; Ertl, Kopp & Mandl, 2005; O'Donnell & Dansereau, 2000), cognitive abilities (Sweller, van Merrienboer & Paas, 1998) or motivational aspects (Deci & Ryan, 1992). These prerequisites may have a different impact with respect to scripts and content-specific support.

When composing scripts with several activities of microlearning, there is the risk that they may get too rigid; thereby having a negative impact on learners' motivation (see Deci & Ryan, 1992). This could also lead to a detrimental impact on learning processes and outcomes (see Weinberger, 2003). Dillenbourg (2002) introduced the term of "over-scripting" a learning environment, which means that too many small micro-activities in the learning process may hinder the exchange of information and reduce the beneficial effects on the learning processes (see also Cohen, 1994).

Regarding content specific facilitation, one should consider the skills and the prior knowledge of the learners (see Reiserer, 2003; Shapiro, 2004; Ertl, Kopp & Mandl, 2005). Applying activities of microlearning that offer many freedoms to the learners may be too complex for beneficial activities (see Dobson, 1999). When applying complex conceptual facilitation, they may exceed learners' cognitive abilities, leading to cognitive overload (see Sweller, van Merrienboer & Paas, 1998), which may negate the facilitation effect. This means that complex methods having a high degree of freedom may be best suited for highly experienced learners, while rather restricted, highly structured methods that introduce many small micro-activities can provide the most benefits for inexperienced beginners.

However, if the facilitation is simplifying the task too much, this could lead to decreased mental activity in the learners and therefore to lower learning outcomes (see also Salomon, 1984). In this case, the combination of too many micro-activities may become a substitute for learners' cognitive activities. Therefore, whilst a certain degree of facilitation is required for beneficial learning, the focus must be placed on maintaining a high level of cognitive activity (Reiser, 2002). In general, solid theoretical considerations and aspects of usability, rather than technical feasibility should be the driving force for the design of facilitation.

Summary

In this contribution, we focused on the application of several activities of microlearning in the context of a macro structural framework. The main issue was that of how far microlearning activities can provide different kinds of facilitation for learners. Furthermore, we illustrated that learners' needs for microlearning activities depend on their prerequisites. Next, we will focus on the long-term application of microlearning. In learning environments, which extend over a longer space of time, learners work several times within the same learning scenario, which usually includes a particular set of microlearning activities. One could expect that learners would have internalized these activities with growing experience. Therefore, we should remember that the need for microlearning might be reduced by growing experience. Consequently, learning environments applying microlearning should provide a fading mechanism according to the cognitive apprenticeship approach (see Collins, Brown & Newman, 1989; Puntambekar & Hübscher, 2005). This fading mechanism should reduce the number of micro activities in the course of time and increase instead the complexity of each microlearning activity. This could increase learners' perception of self-regulation and counteract motivational losses and dropouts, when working with microlearning for longer periods (see Deci & Ryan, 1992). Moreover, such a mechanism could increase learners' mastery (according to Collins, Brown & Newman, 1989) and therefore enable them to see more and more the macro-context of the things they learn. Thereby, learners could learn to work with their knowledge, they could learn to apply it, and they could avoid the acquisition of inert knowledge.

Acknowledgements

This work was funded by Deutsche Forschungsgemeinschaft (German science foundation, DFG), Grant Nos. MA 978/13-1, MA 978/13-3 and MA 978/13-4.

References

Baker, M. & Lund, K. (1997) Promoting reflective interactions in a CSCL environment. In: *Journal of Computer Assisted Learning,* 13, pp. 175–193.

Brooks, L.W. & Dansereau, D.F. (1983) Effects of structural schema training and text organization on expository prose processing. In: *Journal of Educational Psychology,* 75, pp. 811–820.

Cohen, E.G. (1994) Restructuring the classroom: Conditions for productive small groups. *Review of Educational Research,* 64, pp. 1–35.

Collins, A., Brown, J. S. & Newman, S. E. (1989) Cognitive apprenticeship: Teaching the crafts of reading, writing, and mathematics. In Resnick, L. B. ed.: *Knowing, learning, and instruction: Essays in honor of Robert Glaser.* Hillsdale, NJ: Erlbaum.

De Corte, E., Verschaffel, L., Entwistle, N. & van Merrienboer, J.J.G. (Eds.) (2003) *Powerful learning environments: Unravelling basic components and dimensions.* Amsterdam: Pergamon.

Deci, E.L. & Ryan, R. M. (1992) The initiation and regulation of intrinsically motivated learning and achievement. In Boggiano, A.K. & Pittman, T.S. eds.: *Achievement and motivation: A social-developmental perspective.* Cambridge: Cambridge University Press.

Dillenbourg, P. (2002) Over-scripting CSCL: The risks of blending collaborative learning with instructional design. In Kirschner, P.A. ed.: *Three worlds of CSCL. Can we support CSCL.* Heerlen: Open Universiteit Nederland.

Dobson, M. (1999) Information enforcement and learning with interactive graphical systems. In: *Learning and Instruction,* 9, pp. 365–390.

Ertl, B., Fischer, F. & Mandl, H. (2006) Conceptual and socio-cognitive support for collaborative learning in videoconferencing environments. In: *Computers & Education,* 47, pp. 298–315.

Ertl, B., Kopp, B. & Mandl, H. (2005) Effects of individual's prior knowledge on collaborative knowledge construction and individual learning outcomes in Videoconferencing. In Koschmann, T., Suthers, D.D. & Chan, T. eds.: *Computer Supported Collaborative Learning 2005.* Mahwah: Lawrence Erlbaum Associates.

Ertl, B., Reiserer, M. & Mandl, H. (2005) Fostering collaborative learning in Videoconferencing: the influence of content schemes and collaboration scripts on collaboration outcomes and individual learning outcomes. In: *Education, Communication & Information,* 5, pp. 147–166.

Fischer, F., Bruhn, J., Gräsel, C. & Mandl, H. (2000) Kooperatives Lernen mit Videokonferenzen: Gemeinsame Wissenskonstruktion und individueller Lernerfolg. In: *Kognitionswissenschaft,* 9, pp. 5–16.

Fischer, F. et al. (2002) Fostering collaborative knowledge construction with visualization tools. *Learning and Instruction,* 12, pp. 213–232.

Fischer, F., Kollar, I., Mandl, H. & Haake, J.M. eds. *Scripting computer-supported communication of knowledge – Cognitive, computational, and educational perspectives.* Berlin: Springer (forthcoming).

Hug, T., Lindner, M. & Bruck, P. eds. (2006) Microlearning: Emerging Concepts, Practices and Technologies after e-Learning. In: *Proceedings of Microlearning 2005.* Innsbruck: Innsbruck University Press.

King, A. (1999) Discourse patterns for mediating peer learning. In: O'Donnell, A.M. & King, A. eds.: *Cognitive perspectives on peer learning.* Mahwah: Lawrence Erlbaum Associates.

Kopp, B., Ertl, B. & Mandl, H. (2004) Fostering cooperative case-based learning in videoconferencing: Effects of content schemes and cooperation scripts. In Gerjets, P., Kirschner, P., Elen, J. & Joiner, R. eds.: *Instructional design for effective and enjoyable computer-supported learning. Proceedings of the first joint meeting of the EARLI SIGs Instructional Design and Learning and Instruction with Computers.* Tuebingen: Knowledge Media Research Center.

Lave, J. & Wenger, E. (1991) *Situated learning: Legitimate peripheral participation.* New York: Cambridge University Press.

Löhner, S. & van Joolingen, W. (2001) Representations for model construction in collaborative inquiry environments. In Dillenbourg, P., Eurelings, A. & Hakkarainen, K. eds.: *Proceedings of the First European Conference on Computer-Supported Collaborative Learning (euroCSCL).* Maastricht: McLuhan Institute.

O'Donnell, A.M. & Dansereau, D.F. (1992) Scripted cooperation in student dyads: A method for analyzing and enhancing academic learning and performance. In Hertz-Lazarowitz, R. & Miller, N. eds.: *Interactions in cooperative groups. The theoretical anatomy of group learning.* New York: Cambridge UP.

O'Donnell, A.M. & Dansereau, D.F. (2000) Interactive effects of prior knowledge and material format on cooperative teaching. In: *Journal of Experimental Education,* 68, pp. 101–118.

O'Donnell, A.M. & King, A. eds. (1999) *Cognitive perspectives on peer learning.* Mahwah: Erlbaum.

Puntambekar, S. & Hübscher, R. (2005) Tools for scaffolding students in a complex learning environment: What have we gained and what have we missed. In: *Educational Psychologist,* 40, pp. 1–12.

Reiser, B.J. (2002) Why scaffolding should sometimes make tasks more difficult for learners. In Stahl, G. ed.: *Computer Support for Collaborative Learning: Foundations for a CSCL Community.* Boulder: Erlbaum.

Reiserer, M. (2003) *Peer-Teaching in Videokonferenzen. Effekte niedrig- und hochstrukturierter Kooperationsskripte auf Lernprozess und Lernerfolg.* Berlin: Logos.

Renkl, A., Mandl, H. & Gruber, H. (1996). Inert knowledge: Analyses and remedies. In: *Educational Psychologist,* 31, pp. 115–121.

Roschelle, J. & Teasley, S.D. (1995) The construction of shared knowledge in collaborative problem solving. In O'Malley, C. ed.: *Computer Supported Collaborative Learning.* Berlin: Springer.

Rosenshine, B. & Meister, C. (1994) Reciprocal teaching: A review of the research. In: *Review of Educational Research,* 64, pp. 479–530.

Rummel, N. & Spada, H. (2005) Learning to collaborate: An instructional approach to promoting collaborative problem-solving in computer-mediated settings. In: *Journal of the Learning Sciences,* 14, pp. 201–241.

Salomon, G. (1984) Television Is "Easy" and Print Is "Tough": The Differential Investment of Mental Effort in Learning as a Function of Perceptions and Attributions. In: *Journal of Educational Psychology,* 76, pp. 647–658.

Scardamalia, M. & Bereiter, C. (1994) Computer support for knowledge-building communities. In: *Journal of the Learning Sciences,* 3, pp. 265–283.

Shapiro, A. M. (2004) How including prior knowledge as a subject variable may change outcomes of learning research. In: *American Educational Research Journal,* 41, pp. 159–189.

Suthers, D.D. & Hundhausen, C.D. (2003) An experimental study of the effects of representational guidance on collaborative learning processes. In: *The Journal of the Learning Sciences,* 12, pp. 183–218.

Sweller, J., van Merrienboër, J.J.G. & Paas, F.G.W.C. (1998) Cognitive architecture and instructional design. In: *Educational Psychology Review,* 10, pp. 251–296.

Weinberger, A. (2003) Scripts for computer-supported collaborative learning. Available from: <http://edoc.ub.uni-muenchen.de/archive/00001120/01/Weinberger_Armin.pdf> [Accessed 20 June 2006]

Weinberger, A. et al. (2005) Epistemic and social scripts in computer-supported collaborative learning. In: *Instructional Science,* 33, pp. 1–30.

Zhang, J. & Norman, D.A. (1994) Representations in distributed cognitive tasks. In: *Cognitive Science,* 18, pp. 87–122.

From Double-Loop Learning to Triple-Loop Learning
Profound Change, Individual Cultivation, and the Role of Wisdom in the Context of the Microlearning Approach

Markus F. Peschl

What is profound change? How can it be brought about? How can profound change be realized in the context of personality development and individual cultivation? What are possible contributions of microlearning technology for these processes? In the course of this paper, it will be shown that apart from the classical concept of knowledge transfer, or (collaborative) knowledge construction, microlearning technology turns out to be an interesting candidate in a field which has not yet been covered (and discovered) by information and e-learning technology: namely, the domain of personality development and *individual cultivation*. Individual cultivation encompasses knowledge types which are neither well explored, nor considered or implemented in the context of technologically supported educational/learning processes.

That is why a typology of knowledge will be developed in this paper; it takes into account the *existential* dimension and the realm of wisdom, because they are essential for profound change and individual cultivation. The *triple-loop learning strategy* and the *U-theory* will be developed as an epistemological framework; they act as a basis for integrating these rather unorthodox types of (existential) knowledge and epistemological processes (e.g., suspending, redirecting, presencing, etc.) with the technological potentials of the microlearning approach.

In the triple-loop learning strategy, the goal is not so much to "learn something," but the *formation* of the learner on a more profound level (of the person). It will be shown that the microlearning approach offers functionalities that fit the requirements of profound change in the domain of attitudes, values, personality, etc., very well: i.e., the features of (a) ubiquitous availability, (b) continuous support, and, as an implication, (c) "continuous micro pulses," for a continuous change in (epistemological) *attitudes* turn out to be the most important ingredients for the context of individual cultivation.

1   Introduction

Commonly, learning has been seen in the context of improving intellectual capacities, acquiring new knowledge in a specific domain, training of skills, etc. In most instances, learning is concerned with drill-and-practice methods and with training "recipe knowledge." In rare cases, the goal is to *collaboratively construct* and *create* (new) *knowledge*. In even more rare cases, *reflection* on these processes of knowledge production, learning, etc., are considered to be necessary and explicit parts of the learning process (see Peschl, 2005, 2006).

The web has dramatically changed the way we look at knowledge and at how we will learn in the near future. The challenge of today's so-called knowledge society is no longer to excessively know facts by heart, or to be highly trained and highly skilled in applying certain recipes – in fact, on many occasions, these learning outcomes prove to be a hindrance rather than an advantage in the technology-based and high-speed learning and knowledge culture we are living in today. Today's *intellectual challenges* rather concern the domains of (individual and collective) knowledge creation, of (meta-) knowledge literacy and reflection, of judgment and exploration, of multimedia-, web-, and digital literacy, of social skills in knowledge collaboration contexts, etc. (see also Peschl, 2006, 2006a). Apart from these challenges, one can observe a shift towards the concrete, towards action, synthesis, "bricolage," etc. Learning becomes more situated, more constructive, more personality(-development) oriented, more social, as well as more generative and explorative. What are the implications of these developments for our understanding of learning, technologically supported learning/teaching processes (such as the microlearning approach), etc?

1.1 Personality and Individual Cultivation in the Knowledge Society

Looking more closely at what is at the heart of modern knowledge society (e.g., UNESCO 2005, European Commission (2004), etc.), one can discover that the focus on knowledge and knowledge processes has an interesting and significant implication: Whereas during the first and second industrial revolutions the individual more or less vanished and was "dissolved" by automation, the role of the individual (and in particular of *his/her knowledge* and *personality*) becomes more important in a knowledge based society/economy (compare Levy, 1997, 2001; Rifkin, 2004, Friedman, 2006, and many others). Knowledge, and especially (creative) development of knowledge, are domains, which can*not* be automated – on the contrary, these parts which can be automated are of minor interest (e.g., management and storage of explicit knowledge, etc.). The opposite applies even more to the domain of *personality*: the more the focus is on highly sophisticated knowledge, deep understanding, complex contexts, creative minds, etc., the less it is possible to simply replace the person or automate his/her particular cognitive and personal faculties.

Taking seriously the developments and goals of the knowledge society brings about crucial implications and challenges: the more the focus is on knowledge and knowledge creation, the more important will be the role of the *individual*, of his/her intellectual *as well as* personal, ethical, etc., cultivation. Ideally, this would mean a return of the value of the *person* and his/her *"individual cultivation."* Individual cultivation concerns the formation of personality, values, habitus, the "core," etc., of a person (compare, for instance, Senge et al., 2004). In many cases these issues are closely related to the domain of *wisdom*. However, in most cases, only rather simple and "intellectually simple" level forms of knowledge and knowledge transfer (e.g., classical (explicit/fact) knowledge (transfer), know-how, theoretical and recipe knowledge, (...)

and in some rare cases reflective capabilities) are offered at today's schools, colleges, universities, and educational institutions (compare also Peschl, 2003, 2006, 2006b for a more detailed classification of knowledge types and processes). In the domain of individual cultivation the situation is even worse than in the intellectual realm.

That is the point where the concept of microlearing comes in. As will be shown in the sections to come, this technology could be used to support not only the learning processes in the intellectual and cognitive domain, but it seems that this technology is *particularly well suited* for enhancing *learning processes of individual cultivation*.

2 From Double-Loop to Triple-Loop Learning and Individual Cultivation

Before focusing on the microlearning aspect, let's take a look at the theoretical background of individual cultivation. More advanced forms of learning try to go beyond the classical transfer model, i.e., the understanding of learning as a process of transferring more or less stable chunks of knowledge from one brain to another is replaced by a more dynamic perspective: learning is a continuous and active *process* of adaptation and construction in which knowledge is developed in permanent *interaction* between the cognitive system and its environment. Knowledge is not passively mapped into the brain, but actively constructed by perceiving, acting, and interacting with the environmental structures – there is a feedback loop between the realm of knowledge and of the environment. Hence, knowledge is a *process* which functionally fits into the environmental structures. This understanding of knowledge has its roots in constructivist concepts (e.g., Foerster, 1973; Glasersfeld, 1984, 1991, 1995; Maturana, 1980, and many others) and in a *situated* perspective of cognition (e.g., Clark, 1997, 2001; Hutchins, 1995). This kind of learning and knowledge acquisition is referred to as *single-loop learning* or Kolb-learning (compare also Kolb, 1984; Argyris & Schön, 1996; Scharmer, 2000; Senge et al., 1990, 2004, Peschl, 2006, etc.).

In Peschl (2006), several limitations of single-loop learning have been elaborated. The most crucial problem has turned out to be the limitation that this strategy of learning does not allow for the construction of paradigmatically new knowledge and radical innovation (see Peschl, 2006 for details). In order to overcome some of the limitations of single loop learning, a second feedback loop is introduced. It realizes a kind of meta-learning strategy. This second feedback loop takes into consideration that any kind of knowledge is always based on and embedded in a set of assumptions, premises, or a paradigm (Kuhn, 1970).

In general, knowledge always has to be seen as being embedded in and pre-structured by a particular *framework of reference*. Knowledge receives its meaning and structures from this framework of reference. Normally, this framework of reference is not explicitly present in our processes of cognition, learning, or knowledge construction. This implies that we do not have a conscious experience of these premises, assumptions, etc., on which our thinking and constructing is implicitly based. It has to be made explicit by active exploration of one's own assumptions, premises, ideological attitudes, etc. This can be achieved by introducing a process of *reflection* and "stepping out" of one's normal way of thinking.

Due to its implicit and relatively inaccessible character, it appears as if this framework of reference is stable; due to this seeming constancy it is a kind of *"blind spot"* in our thinking, perception, and understanding. A closer look reveals, however, that this framework of reference is not as stable as it seems. The double-loop learning strategy takes these changes in the framework of reference into consideration by introducing a second feedback loop. This implies that a completely new dynamics becomes possible in the whole process of learning and knowledge creation: one starts to change the framework of reference. Each modification in the set of premises or in the framework of reference causes a radical change in the structure, dimensions, dynamics, semantics, etc., of the resulting space of knowledge. By that process, a completely new space of knowledge opens up and entirely new and different theories, knowledge, patterns of perception, interpretation patterns, etc., about reality become possible. The method being applied in this process is basically the technique of *reflection*. It is a process of *radically questioning* and consistently and systematically changing the premises and studying their implications on the body and on the dynamics of knowledge. Double-loop learning has its roots in several fields, such as cybernetics, learning theory, cognitive science (e.g., Peschl, 2001), or in the domain of organizational learning (e.g., Senge, 1990; Argyris et al., 1996).

Besides the effect that double-loop learning enables processes of deep understanding and the reflection of one's foundations of thinking, it is also a kind of meta-learning strategy: one is forced to take a look at one's learning processes and, by that, it is possible to improve them. However, despite these advantages in the learning processes a fundamental level of the human person domain remains excluded and untouched in this double-loop learning strategy.

1.2 The Role of Wisdom in the Existential Dimension of Knowledge and Learning: the Triple-Loop Learning Strategy

Double-loop learning is focused mainly on the intellectual and cognitive domain and its dynamics. However, if one is interested in profound change, a *new level* has to be introduced; profound change does not only happen in the cognitive domains, but touches a more fundamental level – an *existential* level including the person and his/her attitudes, values, habitus, etc. Whereas it is possible to "play games" on the cognitive/intellectual level (in the sense of trying out or simulating intellectual positions without being touched existentially by them), one can experience that there exists a level where "intellectual games" are not possible any more, i.e., we are confronted with a level going beyond the domain of cognitive or intellectual questions touching the self in its very center.

Similarly, as in the case of double-loop learning, we discover that the whole intellectual framework, the whole domain of knowledge and representation, our sets of premises, assumptions, etc., are *embedded* in a more fundamental domain: the domain which could be described as "myself" – that is the level where I am myself in an *existential* sense. Philosophically, one can refer to this domain as the "person." It goes beyond the level of personal skills, competencies, personality, etc., because it transcends the domain of personality traits, behavioral and cognitive patterns, solely quantifiable data, etc. It touches the person on his/her fundamental level of being, and, in many cases, concerns the domain of *wisdom* – in most cases, it is rather difficult to talk about it in classical scientific terms. It goes even beyond what Polanyi (1966) and the more recent discussions in the field of knowledge management (e.g., Easterby-Smith et al., 2003; Krogh et al., 2000; Nonaka et al., 1995, 2003, and many others) refer to as *tacit knowledge*. The introduction of this existential domain implies that a third loop has to be introduced in our model of learning processes: *triple-loop learning*.

2.2   Learning as Change on Various Levels: an Overview

Hence, the goal of learning processes on that existential level is *profound change*. What does that mean and how can it be realized? While classical learning strategies focus on changes in the domain of knowledge, the intellect, or skills, the triple-loop approach also includes changes on the existential level and in the domain of the "will/heart."[1] Looking more closely at the processes of change and learning various levels of "intensity" of change can be identified (compare also Scharmer, (2000) and Senge et al., (2004)):

(i)   *Reacting and Downloading*: The simplest way of responding to change (e.g., if one is confronted with a problem, change, task, or challenge) is to simply react. In other words, already existing and well established behavioral, perceptual, or cognitive patterns are applied to solve the problem or the learning/adaptation task. This is the most convenient and most economic way of reacting to change, because it requires only downloading of already prefabricated solutions, knowledge, etc. The price of this simple response is quite high: (i) the reactions are highly rigid and (ii) the resulting solutions or changes do not go very deep and in most cases do not even scratch the underlying issues of the problem.

(ii)   *Redesign and Adaptation:* Alternatively, it is possible to not only apply already existing patterns, but to use these patterns as a blueprint which is adapted slightly to the current situation. From a cognitive perspective, this is a highly efficient learning strategy, because it is not as rigid as level (i) learning

---

1   Classical philosophy shows that there is a close relationship between the "heart" and the will. Both are concerned with the orientation, the finality, etc., of the human person.

processes, but it can be done with minimal cognitive effort; namely, to make use of already existing patterns, change them slightly (e.g., changing values of variables) and apply them to the new situation, task, etc. From the field of cognitive (neuro-)science, these processes are well understood – these are the classical learning and adaptation processes well known from the domains of connectionism or computational neuroscience (Bechtel et al., 2002; Hebb, 1949; Peschl, 2001; Rumelhart et al., 1986; Varela, 1991a, and many others). From this perspective it becomes clear that these processes are mathematically equivalent with processes of *optimization, i.e.,* we are searching for an optimum in an already pre-structured space (of solutions). What we are doing in single-loop learning is structurally equivalent with these level-(ii) processes of redesigning and adaptation.

(iii)   *Reframing:* In most cases, downloading, adaptation, and optimization (i.e., level-(i) and level-(ii) learning/change processes) are sufficient for mastering everyday problems and challenges. In a way, these solutions are not very interesting, because they do not bring forth fundamentally new knowledge, insights, or understanding. As has been discussed in the context of double-loop learning, fundamental cognitive change is always connected with reflection and stepping out of the – more or less consciously – chosen framework of reference, i.e., going beyond the boundaries of the pre-structured space of knowledge and "reframe" it in the sense of constructing and establishing new dimensions and new semantic categories. This process concerns the level mental models, premises, and assumptions and their change.

Profound Existential Change and "Presencing": On a more fundamental level, change goes beyond reframing and does not only concern intellectual or cognitive matters any more. On that level, questions of *finality, purpose, heart, will,* etc., come to the fore. As has been shown above, that is the domain of the triple-loop learning strategy. "Why do change initiatives based on culture and learning sometimes also fail? One explanation is that the rhetoric of change was in disconnection to what really matters most ... Thus, a fifth approach to coping with change is to focus on deep intention, purpose, and will. Now the responses of [previous] levels (...) become part of an even more subtle set of contextual variables, which are referred to as purpose, (shared) vision, or common will." (Scharmer, 2000, p. 9) In this mode, change is not solely based on cognitive reflection any more, but more importantly, on *existential* reflection and learning. In a way, the goal is to bring the existential level, the person, his/her will, his/her acting, as well as his/her cognitive domain, into a status of inner unity. What might sound esoteric is in fact a very old theme and philosophical issue going back at least to Aristotle's (1985) Nikomachian Ethics and to most Western and Eastern philosophical and religious traditions. Very often, these questions concern the domain of wisdom. Due to its existential character, Scharmer (2000) and Senge et al., (2004) refer to this mode of change/learning as *"presencing."*

These modes of change/learning cannot be seen as being separated from each other. It is only in the mode of analysis that these domains have to be distinguished. In the mode of action, these domains and loops are closely intertwined and depend on each other. I refer to this perspective of learning which takes into account all of the above levels of change (and especially the existential level) as *"individual cultivation,"* if it is conducted on an individual level.

3   Individual Cultivation, Presencing and U-theory

3.1   An Epistemo-Existential Strategy for Profound Change

How can these processes of profound existential change or learning be realized? Which steps are necessary to implement this process of individual cultivation being suggested by the triple-loop learning strategy? There are many ways of supporting this process of individual cultivation ranging from classical upbringing in families and (not only school and university) education, to the very old classical concept of the relationship between a master and his/her student(s) (e.g., in the ancient Greek philosophical schools, in Western and Eastern religious traditions of monasteries, etc.,). However, taking a closer look at most modern educational institutions reveals that they are not capable of offering such an educational setting any more.

On a more general level, a relatively new (and at the same time very classical) theoretical framework capturing this process of individual cultivation and profound change has been developed by C.O. Scharmer (2000, 2001, forthcoming) and Senge et al. (2004, 2004a); it is referred to as "U-Theory" or "presencing." In the following section I am going to present a condensed overview of a further development and adaptation of this approach, in order to get an idea which processes are necessary for profound learning and change in the context of individual cultivation (as well as in the collective/organizational context).

One can describe that process as a U-shaped curve, which is realized in a series of states: the left branch going down the "U" focuses on issues of *observation*, perception, *sensing*, discovery of patterns of thought and cognition, and on how to leave these patterns behind oneself in order to be cognitively and emotionally "prepared" and open for profound change. At the bottom, one finds him-/herself in the state of presencing: it can be characterized as a condition of high receptivity and openness and as a state where radically new knowledge/change can emerge. The upward branch deals with issues concerning the *realization*, prototyping, and embodying of these changes in the (external or internal) environment.

3.2   Observing, Sensing and Seeing Radically Different:
From Downloading to Letting Go and Presencing

– *Suspending*: A conditio sine qua non for any form of profound change, learning, or innovation is an attitude of suspension, i.e., in order to achieve the goal of profound change it is necessary to free oneself from well established patterns of perception and thought. That means that – in the first place – it is necessary to suspend one's instant recipes, judgments, solutions, etc., Being confronted with a new situation or a complex problem, we are always tempted to simply download already well-proven and well-established solutions (compare the downloading process of the level-(i) form of change; section 2.2). From an epistemological perspective, this means that we are projecting our knowledge, judgments, patterns, and mental models onto the world. By doing so, we are missing the point of what learning and change are really about: namely, being receptive and open to what happens in the world and – despite all constructivist claims – trying to lower the level of construction and projection activities. This will open up the view for new perspectives and for new perceptual and cognitive categories (compare also Varela, Thompson & Rosch, 1991, 2000; Depraz, Varela & Vermersch 2003). In a social/collective context, this process of suspending is a precondition for a successful process of dialogue (cf. Bohm, 1996; Isaacs, 1999; Schein, 1993).

– *Redirecting*: In this step, one redirects his/her attention towards the interior; "… you change the *direction* of attention, which tunes out the spectacle of the world, so you can return to the interior world. In other words, you substitute an *apperceptive* act for perception." (Depraz, Varela & Vermersch, 2003, p. 31) Metaphorically speaking, one turns his/her gaze back towards the source of this perceptual act and tries to look at it consciously and reflectedly through his/her perceptual patterns. "It is the idea that normally the habitual thing is that one should redirect attention outward. Redirect it to what is emerging as an object, as a content, which has its own intentionality. The point about redirection is that you reverse that. You keep it within, but toward the source, toward the source of the mental process rather than the object. (Varela, 2000, p. 6) (…) Suspension will lead to very early emerging events, contents, patterns, gestures, whatever. Then you can actually redirect your attention to them. That's where the new is. So the suspension creates a space, the new comes up, and then you can redirect. Redirection is a specific gesture." (Varela, 2000, p. 5) This process of redirecting goes beyond reflection; it does not only aim at uncovering and questioning premises and cognitive patterns, but at exploring the source of these patterns and, by that, opening up a new space, a space that enables the emergence of new constructions, new profound insights, fundamental change, etc.,

– *Letting-go*: In order to reach this state of emergence it is – at first – necessary to *let go* of what one has discovered in this process of redirection and exploration of one's own premises, assumptions, etc., "… you have to change from voluntarily turning your attention from the exterior to the interior, to simply accepting and listening. In other words,... you go from 'looking for something' to 'letting something come to you,' to 'letting something be revealed.' What is difficult here is that you have to get through an *empty time,* a time of silence, and not grab onto whatever data is immediately available, for that's already been rendered conscious, and what you're after is what is still unconscious at the start." (Depraz, Varela & Vermersch, 2003, p. 31) Of course, this process can cause existential fear in some cases, because one loses "(epistemological) control" and the (epistemological) ground on which one is standing and which normally provides a rather stable cognitive framework. This is a well-known state in the constructivist framework (if it is adopted in a reflected manner). Being in a state of receptivity always means to be in a relatively passive role, which brings about a higher chance of being (epistemologically and existentially) hurt. However, surrendering into this rather receptive and open state does not imply that one is completely passive; rather the contrary is the case: in a way, one finds him-/herself in an active state of extremely high attention towards what is coming up without trying to project one's own expectations, plans, knowledge, etc. It is a bit of a paradoxical situation: on the one hand, one is waiting seemingly passively for what is going to happen and on the other hand, this is a highly active state concerning one's attention and receptiveness. These processes of trying to get empty and at the same time to be attentive towards what is going on "out there" are well known from art or religious traditions as well as from Husserl's phenomenological approach (e.g., the concept of epoche).

– *Presencing*: In this state, one enters into an *"intimate epistemological dance"* with reality. In other words, due to the high level of receptiveness and attention, it is possible to "catch the wave" of the environmental dynamics and "surf" it in a process of smooth and intimate interaction between the cognitive and environmental dynamics. Ideally, this is E.v.Glasersfeld's (1984, 1991, 1995) concept of functional fitness in its perfect realization; or Maturana's (1970, 1980) notion of (structural) coupling in its most sophisticated form. Epistemologically, this leads to a process of what Rosch (1999) and others refer to as *"deep* or *primary knowing."* In that moment constructivist and realist attitudes come very close and almost collapse, which sometimes makes it difficult to talk about. What is important in our context of the question of profound change and learning are the following points:

– This is a way of constructing highly sophisticated and profound knowledge about an environmental aspect with trying to keep the influence of projection on a minimum level. By that it is possible to achieve a profound understanding of the phenomenon under investigation. This understanding goes beyond a purely cognitive and intellectual penetration in most cases; it also includes the existential dimension in the sense that not only the intellect, but more importantly the person, is related to the phenomenon under investigation.

– This is a prerequisite for enabling profound change or learning. Having a deep understanding about a phenomenon implies that one also comes to know or "see" its potential(-ity) ["potentia"];

– In other words, one comes to see what could or what wants to emerge in the participating systems and, more importantly, out of the interaction between one's cognitive activities and the environmental dynamics, i.e., it is not only about exploring the potentials of one of the participating systems, but about potentials, radically new structures/knowledge or innovations emerging out of the *interaction* between the participating systems.

– One does not only enter into a "contemplative" dance of understanding with reality, but also into an organic process of co-construction, co-formation, co-design, co-influencing, co-changing, i.e., the potentials/-ities of both the cognitive system and the environment/phenomenon it is interacting with begin to organically connect into a joint dynamics in which radically new structures, processes, dynamics, knowledge, etc., may come into being in an emergent process.

– For these processes to happen, both the involved systems and their close interaction are necessary; the systems involved are mutually respected in and respecting their dynamics, possibilities, determinations, and limitations, i.e., the goal is not to project one's own prefabricated knowledge and mental models on the phenomenon and try to change it according to these ideas. Rather, the goal is to organically co-evolve and co-develop a dynamics which brings both partners into a state where it is possible to enter into a process of mutual blossoming and realizing more of one's finalities and perhaps completely new structures, processes, potentials, etc.

– Metaphorically speaking, one can compare this process to the interaction between a good artist and the material she/he is working with: both systems unfold and blossom in the process of this interaction by respecting as well as cultivating the potentials/-ities of the other. In a way, the stone already has the form of the statue (in potentia) in itself and the artist brings forth this form by both being inspired by that stone and by his own cognitive activities, mental models, plans, talents, etc.

– If one takes this approach seriously, this would have an enormous impact on our understanding, and, foremost, on our way of doing science. Bortoft (1996) sketches a scenario of what such a kind of science could look like.

In this downward branch of the U-theory, much of what we are used to do in science and our everyday thinking is turned upside down. Depraz, Varela, and Vermersch have summarized this as follows: "Thus what we're talking about here is reversing two of your usual thought processes, the first of which is the condition of the second: (i) You have to re-direct your attention from the exterior to the interior. (ii) You have to change the quality of your attention, moving from an active search to an accepting let-ting-arrive. This means that while the first reversal actively moves between the dueling poles of the exterior and the interior, the second reversal moves from activity to a passive and receptive waiting, thereby doing away with any duality remaining from the first reversal." (Depraz, Varela, and Vermersch, 2003, p. 31)

It is important to note that these processes are not only intellectually challenging, but also have a deep impact on the domain of intent/finality, and on the emotional and existential level, because they touch the innermost domains of the person (or organization) who/which is going through this process. From what has been said above, it is clear that these processes and their results are highly fragile, and it is very difficult to make them explicit in natural language. However, they are a conditio sine qua non that profound change in the sense of triple-loop learning can happen. It is only this kind of change process that makes a real difference (compared to classical adaptive or optimization approaches) and may bring about radically new knowledge, radical innovation, completely new social, political, or organizational structures, etc.

3.3   Acting Profoundly Different: from Presencing to Prototyping, Embodying and Institutionalizing

– *Letting-Come and Crystallizing*: As a consequence of this phase of presencing, it is possible that profoundly new interaction patterns, knowledge, perspectives, etc., can emerge. This is not only a form of radical innovation, but also a kind of *emergent innovation*, i.e., it does not so much arise from an external source which projects his/her ideas on the phenomenon. Rather, it has its source both inside the cognitive system and in the object/phenomenon to be changed (and in their interaction). In a way this new structure *crystallizes* in an emergent process of letting-come. Of course, this is not the result of just passively sitting there and waiting (see above), but it has something to do with an attitude of both being patient, receptive and epistemologically humble and at the same time being active and precise in attention; i.e., to wait with a high level of attention, intellectual accuracy, and to get into a very close and almost intimate relationship with the phenomenon which one wants to study and/or change. This process of letting-come is the other side of the process of letting-go. In other words, one shifts the focus from surrendering to looking at what wants to emerge and what is new. This is an epistemologically fragile process in which new ideas and changes emerge and converge ("crystallize") towards a specific vision, concept, idea, etc.

– *Enacting and Prototyping*: At some point it is necessary that what has emerged in this process of presencing and crystallizing starts to manifest in some kind of external form – be it in material form, or in a concrete plan, in a concrete action, model, product, service, etc. Of course, this very first externalization can only be a kind of *prototype* which gets "tested" in the environment. The goal of this phase of prototyping is, however, that what has emerged in the interior gets externalized so that it can be verified, seen by the others, discussed by the others, slightly adapted, etc.

– *Embodying and Institutionalizing*: The final step consists in implementing the adapted prototype in the daily routines, in established practices, in everyday action, in the repertoire of reaction patterns, etc. In other words, switching back from the mode of radical innovation and presencing to the modes of downloading and adaptation (compare also sections 2.2).

These steps must not be seen as a recipe which can be blindly executed and one ends up with fundamental change. Rather, it is framework helping us to orient ourselves in this considerably complex domain. These steps do not have to be executed mechanically in the above order; this would be a contradiction to the very character of this process! This proposed structure sketches a framework which captures the most important phases and functionalities. In many cases, it will be necessary to adapt this process to the specific situation, question, domain, etc., and to introduce loops and jumps in this order. The concrete instruments being used in order to implement this framework will differ by the specific domain in which it is applied. Finally, it has to be mentioned that this way of looking at profound change and learning processes can not only be applied on an individual level ("individual cultivation"), but also in the *collective* domain of organizations, social systems, etc.

What are modern means of realizing this U-process of individual cultivation? What can modern technologies in general and microlearning technologies in particular contribute to that process?

4   Triple-Loop Learning and Microlearning

4.1   Epistemological Implications from the Triple-Loop Learning Strategy for Knowledge Oriented (Micro-)Didactical Approaches

Taking seriously the triple-loop learning approach, and its realization in the U-theory, has crucial implications on the epistemological level, as well. Apart from the classical typology of knowledge the triple-loop learning strategy forces us to take into consideration the domain of individual cultivation, the existential domain, and its epistemological consequences. From a (micro-)knowledge-didactical perspective this means that both an extended knowledge typology and a corresponding typology of (micro-)didactical interventions has to be developed.

Highly sophisticated and well-established knowledge typologies exist for the classical approaches to learning (e.g., single- and double-loop learning; Meder, 2000; Swertz, 2004; Peschl, 2003, 2006, etc.). These cover the cognitive and "intellectual domain" and sometimes include the level of skills and reflection. Apart from these fields of knowledge, the U-theory/presencing approach forces us to expand and broaden these typologies in a couple of dimensions:

(a) *Cognitive/Intellectual Domain:* these types of knowledge are covered by the classical typologies. This domain includes all the classical (didactical) knowledge types (such as explanatory knowledge, factual knowledge, orienting knowledge, etc.; e.g., Meder, 2000).

(b) *Skills and Competencies:* these types of knowledge cover the more practical domain of acting. In the context of individual cultivation/U-theory these skills are particularly important with respect to *epistemological skills* of reflection, suspension, redirecting, etc.

(c) *"Augmenting Knowledge":* knowledge which is necessary for supporting the process of observation or profound understanding, i.e., additional knowledge is offered in a process of profound change in order to enable the achievement of a deeper understanding of the current situation, observation, etc.

(d) *Cognitive/Epistemological Attitudes:* this domain does not fit into the classical knowledge typologies, because it is a kind of meta-domain concerning the question of how one is dealing with epistemological issues, such as receptivity, projection of one's own patterns of thought, how to deal with biases, prejudices, etc. This covers both a highly reflective capability and the domain of attitudes concerning the personal (epistemological) relationship to reality.

(e) *Values:* whereas epistemological attitudes have a focus on epistemological issues, values cover the more general domain of ethical attitudes, general attitudes towards life and the other, etc.

(f) *Existential Issues and Wisdom:* as has been discussed in the context of the U-theory and of the triple-loop learning strategy, changes in these processses concern the existential level – both internally (i.e., concerning my own person) and externally (i.e., concerning "substantial issues" of an external entity). The notion of wisdom is of particular interest in this context.

Table 1 integrates this expanded knowledge typology with the phases of the U-theory; each step in the U-process requires different kinds of knowledge and, consequently, a specific strategy for how the creation of this knowledge or change can be supported by (micro-)didactical measures and interventions.

	cognitive & intellectual	skills & competencies	augmenting knowledge	epistemological attitudes	values	existential issues & wisdom
observing & suspending	●	●	●	●		
redirecting		●		●		
letting-go		●		●	●	

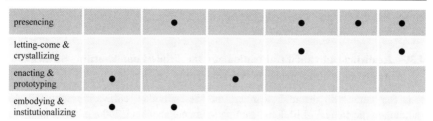

presencing		•		•	•	•
letting-come & crystallizing				•		•
enacting & prototyping	•		•			
embodying & institutionalizing	•	•				

Table 1.   Extended knowledge types and the phases of the U-theory. The dots ("•") mark which types of knowledge are involved in the respective phase of the presencing process.

4.2   Specific Features of the Microlearning Approach

Before taking a closer look at this integration of microlearning and presencing processes, we have to clarify what are the specific features making the microlearning technology different from classical learning approaches. Apart from classical forms of learning/teaching as well as from classical media-supported forms of learning/teaching (e.g., eLearning, communication tools, knowledge management tools, etc.), the microlearning approach offers features and possibilities going beyond these forms. These "microlearning-features" provide solutions and procedures which are very interesting for the triple-loop learning approach presented above. Here is a short list of selected features which are of high relevance for our question of individual cultivation (see also Hug et al., 2006): (i) Learning takes place in *micro steps*. (ii) These micro steps have proven to be the basis for a learning success with a high level of *sustainability* (e.g., Hug et al., 2006). (iii) Furthermore, these microlearning steps facilitate the process of *deep understanding* and creation of *profound* knowledge and understanding, if the microlearning process is embedded in an appropriate learning design/setting (e.g., Peschl, 2005, 2006). (iv) Microlearning offers the possibility of *ubiquitous* learning and, by that, (v) supports a *continuous* process of learning over a longer period of time. (vi) *Ubiquitous* learning and *mobile technologies* provide the basis that microlearning can be realized as situated learning (*situatedness*) implying, for instance, learning from direct interaction with reality.

Most of these features turn out to be highly relevant for the process of individual cultivation. Due to its continuous and ubiquitous character microlearning technologies are especially well suited for a more or less permanent accompanying process in the field of the personality (development) and existential issues. It is not a particular feature that is responsible for a successful process of learning, knowledge creation, or individual cultivation. Rather, it is the combination of these functionalities bringing about the high impact of the microlearning paradigm. If these features are combined and the concept of triple-loop learning is integrated into that approach, the microlearning paradigm becomes even more powerful in a wide field of applications; a field which goes far beyond the classical knowledge domain and the realm of skills and competencies, a field which is still open for exploration.

4.3   Realizing Individual Cultivation and the Triple-Loop Learning Strategy by Applying Features from the Microlearning Technology

It is clear that both the microlearning and the individual cultivation approach are standing in the context of lifelong learning (compare also Hug, 2006, p. 8). Contrary to classical learning, triple-loop learning is not so much concerned with intellectual and cognitive issues, but rather with existential, personal, philosophical, ethical, as well as wisdom issues. This is a relatively new field for a technological approach to learning, education, and personality development. That is why we will not talk so much about concrete content, but rather take a closer look at the areas in which such an integration between microlearning technology and U-theory seems promising.

What are possible contributions of microlearning in the particular stages being laid out by the U-theory (see above; Scharmer, 2000, forthcoming, Senge et al., 2004)? Which types of knowledge are involved (compare section 4.1) and how can they be supported by the microlearning approach?

Observing and Suspending

Before a process of profound change becomes possible, one has to achieve a profound understanding of his/her internal and external situation. The first step to get there is by *observation*. This concerns all kinds of processes of collecting data, gauging, going "out in the (external or internal) field," creating descriptions (or any other kinds of recordings) of observations, etc. From an epistemological perspective this is a "hot spot" for the process of profound change, as these observational data are the basis for almost all the other forms of knowledge and its change. That is why it is particularly important to take a closer look at these processes and at how these processes could be improved by applying microlearning techniques.

Every observation is a micro-step in the process of learning and individual cultivation – the microlearning approach can support these processes in the following ways: Due to its ubiquitous features and in combination with mobile technologies, the microlearning paradigm can not only support the process of observation and recording data, but can be used for providing *context information* for the observation process. This process can be interpreted as an *"augmented observation process."* In many cases – especially if the learner is not experienced – this leads to more precise and more comprehensive observational data. Furthermore, in combination with (theoretical) background knowledge, the learner gains deeper insights, as he/she can *make more sense* out of what he/she has observed. This is a particularly important feature in the context of profound change. In general, microlearning technologies support the process of observation by providing a ubiquitous and comprehensive strategy of *documentation* which is not limited by storage issues or other problems of this kind.

On the other hand, the process of *suspension* pursues an opposite strategy: the goal does not consist in providing additional information for the observation process, but in getting rid of one's patterns of thought and reactions during that process. As this is a task happening primarily inside our cognition and on the level of (epistemological) attitudes, the support by an external microlearning strategy can be only minimal: as the goal is to establish an *attitude of suspension* this microlearning process has to be realized in the form of continuous "microlearning-pulses" (e.g., by reminding the learner of the importance of suspending, by giving specific hints of how to suspend one's opinions, thoughts, etc.; for more specific suggestions see Bohm, 1996). Due to its ubiquitous character, the microlearning technology may support that cognitive activity of suspension in almost every situation or context. It is important to design this process in such a way that a good balance between providing augmented information and getting rid of well-known patterns is established. The results of this process of suspension can be documented in the microlearning environment, although it has to be clear that these results will be situated more in the internal domain (of epistemological attitudes and skills; see 4.1) of the learner – microlearning technology plays only the role of documenting these processes (e.g., in the form of a learning journal or [e-]portfolio).

Redirecting, Letting Go, and Presencing –
Cultivating Epistemological Attitudes

As has been shown in section 3.2, the stages of redirecting and letting-go are highly sophisticated epistemological processes in terms of cognitive and emotional activities. From a microlearning perspective, they do not primarily concern "knowledge or intellectual issues," but rather the domain of epistemological attitudes and epistemological skills. In this field, the microlearning approach is not so much concerned with providing information or knowledge, but rather with accompanying these epistemological processes in offering a continuous "epistemological cultivation and coaching program." This is a relatively new challenge in that field which still has to be developed in detail – a lot could be learned from the domains of reflection, observation techniques, dialogue, coaching, philosophical methods, or even perhaps meditation techniques. The goal is *not* to produce a standardized result/change, but to provide a (microlearning-technologically enriched) *enabling space* providing the necessary means that these processes of redirecting, letting-go, and profound change can surface! The microlearning approach is particularly well suited for these processes, because this technology makes available epistemological and personal services for which, normally, personal coaches, etc., would be necessary. This does not imply, however, that these human coaches, guides, etc., are not necessary any more when these technologies are applied! The "mechanical parts" of these processes can be enriched and partly replaced by the microlearning technology.

Due to its highly internal and existential character, the process of presencing itself is relatively hard to support by (microlearning) technological means. The only possible support is in the field of awareness formation and documentation.

Letting-Come and Crystallizing

The (cognitive) operations being involved in the stage of letting-come and crystallizing are epistemologically fragile, because they are emergent processes with an open outcome. In most cases, a bunch of new ideas, knowledge, and changes surface, and it is necessary to converge on one of them. This process can be supported by microlearning technologies in the following ways: (i) support by providing visualization or any other form of representation of the field of ideas, visions, etc., in order to achieve some kind of overview; (ii) providing decision criteria and tools for finding the "right" decision, and (iii) documentation functionalities for future purposes (perhaps one wants to come back to one of his/her ideas and wants use them for inspiration).

Prototyping, Embodying and Institutionalizing

In these phases, the classical tools supporting the processes of innovation management, idea management, prototyping, etc., can be applied. The knowledge being necessary in that domain is on the explicit and intellectual level, which is well handled by the arsenal of classical e-learning, innovation/project management tools, and knowledge management techniques.

5   Conclusions and Open Questions

An essential question is hidden behind our considerations: how can these epistemologically fragile processes of triple-loop learning/presencing be supported and handled with microlearning technology in an efficient, and, most importantly, *non-destructive* manner? And, more importantly, do we really want that?

Pushing our concepts into a more extreme position this implies that we are confronted not only with "lifelong learning," but that we could be led by "lifelong learning *devices*" continuously feeding us with content: not only on the abstract/knowledge level (which is partly reality today), but on the more profound existential level concerning our very person. It is obvious that there opens up a wide spectrum of possibilities of abuse.

Apart from the classical concept of knowledge transfer, or (collaborative) knowledge construction, microlearning technology has turned out to be an interesting candidate in a field which has not yet been covered (and discovered) by information and e-learning technology; namely the domain of personality development and, even more profoundly, of *individual cultivation*. The reasons are obvious: as has been shown in sections 2.2, 3.1, and 4.1, processes of individual cultivation encompass knowledge types which are neither well explored, nor considered or implemented in the context of technologically supported educational processes. That is why a typology of knowledge has been developed in this paper; it takes into account the *existential* dimension of profound change and individual cultivation. The approaches of the triple-loop learning strategy and the U-theory have been developed as an epistemological framework; they act as a basis for integrating these rather unorthodox types of (existential) knowledge and the epistemological processes necessary for their forming and dynamics (e.g., suspending, redirecting, presencing, etc.) with the technological potentials of the microlearning approach.

Among the most important features of the microlearning approach, the following functions have turned out to be central in the context of the process of individual cultivation: (a) ubiquitous availability, (b) continuous support, and, as an implication, (c) "continuous micro pulses" for a continuous change in (epistemological) *attitudes* and virtues. The process of intellectual learning and the focus on knowledge is complemented by a *formation* of attitudes and values in the triple-loop approach. In the triple-loop learning strategy, the goal is not so much to "learn something," but the *formation* on a more profound level (of the person). The microlearning approach offers functionalities fitting the requirements of this profound change in the domain of attitudes, values, personality, etc. This is the foundation for any process of individual cultivation.

The clue to these processes of profound change are the concepts of *deep knowing* and *profound understanding*; according to the triple-loop/U-theory approach they are a conditio sine qua non for every process of profound change or individual cultivation. This implies that the triple-loop learning strategy requires the development of alternative learning cultures and learning environments. They go far beyond classical classrooms, learning labs, or environments for real or virtual knowledge construction. In a way, these learning environments are rather simple, because they are realized by our everyday contexts in most cases – everyday situations become "living labs" and "training camps" for awareness formation (of, for instance, epistemological attitudes). Beyond that, we will need distinct spaces (as well as periods of time; see, for instance, Peschl, 2006c) for going through these processes of profound change, as has been suggested by the presencing approach. As has been shown, both contexts can be supported very well by microlearning technologies. One thing has to be clear, however: in order to trigger radical change or radical innovation, a radical change in our understanding and concept of learning has to occur – a perspective of learning which does not exclude existential matters and the notion of wisdom.

References

Argyris, C. & Schön, D.A. (1996) *Organizational Learning II. Theory, Method, and Practice.* Redwood City: Addison-Wesley.

Aristoteles (1985) *Nikomachische Ethik.* Hamburg: Felix Meiner Verlag.

Bechtel, W. & Abrahamsen, A. (2002) *Connectionism and the Mind. Parallel Processing, Dynamics, and Evolution in Networks.* Malden: Blackwell Publishers.

Bohm, D. (1996) *On Dialogue.* New York: Routledge.

Bortoft, H. (1996) *The Wholeness of Nature. Goethe's Way of Science.* Edinburgh: Floris Books.

Clark, A. (1997) *Being There. Putting Brain, Body, and World Together Again.* Cambridge: MIT Press.

Clark, A. (2001) *Mindware. An Introduction to the Philosophy of Cognitive Science.* New York: Oxford University Press.

Depraz, N., Varela, F.J. & Vermersch, P. (2003) *On Becoming Aware. A Pragmatics of Experiencing. Amsterdam.* Philadelphia: John Benjamins Publishing Company.

Easterby-Smith, M. & Lyles, M.A. eds. (2003) *The Blackwell Handbook of Organizational Learning and Knowledge Management.* Oxford: Blackwell Publishing.

European Commission (2004) *Innovation Management and the Knowledge-Driven Economy.* Brussels: European Commission, Directorate-general for Enterprise.

Foerster, H.v. (1973) On constructing a reality. In: Preiser, W.F.E. ed. *Environmental Design Research.* Stroudsburg: Hutchinson & Ross.

Friedman, T.L. (2006) *The World is Flat. A Brief History of the Twenty-First Century.* New York: Ferrar, Straus and Giroux.

Glasersfeld, E.v. (1984) An introduction to radical constructivism. In: Watzlawick, P. ed. *The Invented Reality.* New York: Norton.

Glasersfeld, E.v. (1991) Knowing without metaphysics. Aspects of the radical constructivist position. In: Steier, F. ed. *Research and Reflexivity.* London: Sage Publishers.

Glasersfeld, E.v. (1995) *Radical Constructivism: A Way of Knowing and Learning.* London: Falmer Press.

Hebb, D.O. (1949) *The Organization of Behavior: A Neuropsychological Theory.* New York: Wiley.

Hug, T., Lindner, M. & Bruck, P.A. eds. (2006) *Microlearning: Emerging Concepts, Practices and Technologies after e-Learning.* Innsbruck: Innsbruck University Press.

Hutchins, E. (1995) *Cognition in the Wild.* Cambridge: MIT Press.

Isaacs, W. (1999) *Dialogue and the Art of Thinking Together: A Pioneering Approach to Communicating in Business and Life.* New York: Doubleday Currency.

Kolb, D.A. (1984) *Experiential Learning: Experience as the Source of Learning and Development.* Englewood Cliffs: Prentice Hall.

Krogh, G.v., Ichijo, K. & Nonaka, I. (2000) *Enabling Knowledge Creation. How to Unlock the Mystery of Tacit Knowledge and Release the Power of Innovation.* New York: Oxford University Press.

Levy, P. (1997) *Collective Intelligence: Mankind's Emerging World in Cyberspace.* Cambridge: Perseus Books.

Levy, P. (2001) *Cyberculture.* Minneapolis: University of Minneapolis Press.

Maturana, H.R. (1970) Biology of cognition. In: Maturana, H.R. & Varela, F.J. eds. *Autopoiesis and Cognition: The Realization of the Living.* Dordrecht, Boston: Reidel.

Maturana, H.R. & Varela, F.J. eds. (1980) Autopoiesis and Cognition: The Realization of the Living. Dordrecht, Boston: Reidel.

Meder, N. (2000) Didaktische Ontologien. In: Ohly, H.P., Rahmstorf, G. & Sigl, A. eds. *Globalisierung und Wissensorganisation. Neue Aspekte für Wissen, Wissenschaft und Informationssysteme.* Würzburg: Ergon.

Nonaka, I. & Takeuchi, H. (1995) *The Knowledge Creating Company. How Japanese Companies Manage the Dynamics of Innovation.* Oxford: Oxford University Press.

Nonaka, I. & Toyama, R. (2003) The knowledge-creating theory revisited: knowledge creation as a synthesizing process. In: *Knowledge Management Research and Practice*, 1, pp. 2–10.

Peschl, M.F. (2001) Constructivism, cognition, and science. An investigation of its links and possible shortcomings. In: *Foundations of Science*, 6(1), pp. 125–161.

Peschl, M.F. (2003) Structures and diversity in everyday knowledge. From reality to cognition and back. In: Gadner, J., Buber, R. & Richards, L. eds. *Organising Knowledge. Methods and Case Studies.* Hampshire: Palgrave Macmillan.

Peschl, M.F. (2005) Acquiring basic cognitive and intellectual skills for informatics. Facilitating understanding and abstraction in a virtual cooperative learning environment. In: Micheuz, P., Antonitsch, P. & Mittermeir, R. eds. *Innovative Concepts for Teaching Informatics.* Wien: Ueberreuter.

Peschl, M.F. (2006) Modes of knowing and modes of coming to know. Knowledge creation and knowledge co-construction as socio-epistemological engineering in educational processes. In: *Constructivist Foundations*, 1(3), pp. 111–123.

Peschl, M.F. (2006a) The challenge of triggering profound processes of understanding in microlearning environments. Theoretical foundations and a case study for a "Microlearning Laboratory." In: Hug, T., Lindner, M. & Bruck, P.A. eds. *Microlearning: Emerging Concepts, Practices and Technologies after e-Learning.* Innsbruck: Innsbruck University Press.

Peschl, M.F. (2006b) Knowledge-oriented educational processes. From knowledge transfer to collective knowledge creation and innovation. In: Budin, G., Swertz, C., & Mitgutsch, K. eds. *Knowledge Organization for a Global Learning Society.* Würzburg: Ergon.

Peschl, M.F. (2006c) Raum für Innovation und Knowledge Creation. In: *Lernende Organisation*, 29(2), pp. 56–64.

Polanyi, M. (1966) *The Tacit Dimension.* Garden City: Doubleday.

Rifkin, J. (2004) *The End of Work.* New York: Putnam.

Rosch, E. (1999) Primary Knowing: When Perception Happens from the Whole Field. (Conversation with E. Rosch; Berkeley, Oct 15, 1999). Available from <http://www.-dialogonleadership.org/Rosch-1999.pdf> [Accessed 6 May 2005].

Rumelhart, D.E., Hinton, G.E. & Williams, R.J. (1986) Learning internal representations by error propagation. In: Rumelhart, D.E. & McClelland, J.L. eds. *Parallel Distributed Processing: Explorations in the Microstructure of Cognition Foundations.* Cambridge: MIT Press.

Scharmer, C.O. (2000) Presencing: learning from the future as it emerges. On the tacit dimension of leading revolutionary change. Helsinki School of Economics, Finnland and the MIT Sloan School of Management. Conference On Knowledge and Innovation, May 25-26, 2000. Available from <http://www.dialogonleadership.org/ PresencingTOC.html> [Accessed 2 February 2005].

Scharmer, C.O. (2001) Self-transcending knowledge. Sensing and organizing around emerging opportunities. In: *Journal of Knowledge Management*, 5(2), pp. 137–150.

Scharmer, C.O. (forthcoming) Theory U: A Social Technology for Leading Profound Change.

Schein, E.H. (1993) On dialogue, culture and organizational learning. In: *Organization Dynamics,* 22(2), pp. 44–51.

Senge, P.M. (1990) *The Fifth Discipline. The Art and Practice of the Learning Organization.* New York: Doubleday.

Senge, P. et al. (2004) *Presence. Human Purpose and the Field of the Future.* Cambridge: Society for Organizational Learning.

Senge, P. et al. (2004a) Awakening Faith in an Alternative Future. Reflections. In: *The SoL Journal on Knowledge, Learning, and Change,* 5(7), pp. 1–16.

Swertz, C. (2004) *Didaktisches Design. Ein Leitfaden für den Aufbau hypermedialer Lernsysteme mit der Web-Didaktik.* Bielefeld: Wilhelm Bertelsmann Verlag.

UNESCO (2005) *Towards Knowledge Societies.* Paris: United Nations Educational, Scientific and Cultural Organization (UNESCO World Report).

Varela, F.J., Thompson, E. & Rosch, E. (1991) *The Embodied Mind: Cognitive Science and Human Experience.* Cambridge: MIT Press.

Varela, F.J. (1991a) Allgemeine Prinzipien des Lernens im Rahmen der Theorien biologischer Netzwerke. In: Schmidt, S.J. ed. *Gedächtnis. Probleme und Perspektiven der interdisziplinären Gedächtnisforschung,* pp. 159–169. Frankfurt/M.: Suhrkamp.

Varela, F. (2000) Three gestures of becoming aware. (Interview with F.Varela; Paris, 12 January 2000). Available from <http://www.dialogonleadership.org/Varela-2000.pdf> [Accessed 27 April 2005].

Small Steps Towards a Culture of Deliberative Learning: Media Supported Pyramid Discussions

Christiane Schmidt

The basic idea of deliberative didactic is to improve decision competency in discussion and research. Based on the philosophy of deliberation (known from the program of the journal *Deliberation-Knowledge-Ethics*) well-considered alternative positions and their comprehensible representation are seen as essential for well-founded decisions. The following article refers to the didactical approach developed by Bettina Blanck. The article focuses on a specific deliberation method: the pyramid discussion. In these discussions, deliberations, valuations and solutions are developed by the team members and represented as the steps of a pyramid. Experiences in using media supported pyramid discussions in university seminars are described and considered as small steps towards the deliberative managing of knowledge diversity in virtual teams.

Introduction

At first glance, the didactic approach of deliberative learning and current approaches of microlearning – especially those emphasizing prepared microcontent with push character for media supported learning in short time – seem to be based on incommensurable ideas. In both contexts – deliberative learning and microlearning – information overload is considered to be an important pedagogical challenge at present, but contrasting strategies are offered. Microlearning focuses on the handling of small units in learning-processes. In a broader sense, microlearning is defined as learning with microcontent, which is characterized by small units of content and short learning times. A variety of new microlearning approaches and the integration of microlearning in various didactic concepts has been developed in recent years – mainly in the context of e-learning and knowledge management (cf. Mosel, Hug & Gstrein in prep.; Wikipedia, 2006; for details see also the contributions in this book). In view of information overload, some of these approaches recommend knowledge fragmentation and aim at small learning steps and short effort with prepared microcontent. "Unlike 'traditional' elearning approaches, microlearning often tends towards push technology through push media, which reduces the cognitive load on the learners" (Wikipedia, 2006). Deliberative learning focuses on knowledge diversity and reflexive learning. The basic idea of deliberative didactic is to improve decision competency in discussion and research. With respect to information overload, the deliberative approach recommends knowledge justification by considering and representing alternative positions. Deliberative learning tends to be time-consuming and labour-intensive. From a sceptic's point of view, the differences may be briefly characterized as lean-learning against long-winded learning.

Looking more closely and open-mindedly on microlearning and deliberative learning, we also find some points of contact. In this article, an attempt is made to describe the basic idea of deliberative didactic, to give an example of a deliberation method and to discuss its connection with basic ideas of microlearning. As will be seen, achieving decision competency starts with small steps of deliberation. The presented method, the "deliberation oriented pyramid discussion," is reflected as a special type of micro-collaboration. The given example of pyramid discussions in two collaborating university seminars describes first experiences with deliberations in virtual teams. A comprehensible representation of the deliberation process in pyramid discussions – of traditional as well as of virtual teams – supports the students in finding and building knowledge structures. In the described teams, digital media supported the collaborative structuring of knowledge. The given example therefore touches upon pyramid discussions as a specific view of a virtual knowledge space. Finally, differences to microlearning – especially to prepared micro content with push character – are discussed and open questions are pointed out.

The Deliberative Didactic Approach

The deliberative approach has been developed in the research group "culture of deliberation" at the University of Paderborn. The group started in the middle 1980s discussing deliberation as a requirement of knowledge justification with respect to the responsibility of scientific research. The group members Frank Benseler, Bettina Blanck, Rainer Greshoff and Werner Loh made the upcoming philosophy of deliberation to the conceptual fundament of a scientific discussion journal. This journal, first named *Ethik und Sozialwissenschaften* and later changed into *Erwägung – Wissen – Ethik (EWE) Deliberation – Knowledge – Ethics*, has been published since 1990. In the 90s an interdisciplinary circle started discussing and refining the deliberation approach (cf. Benseler, Blanck, Greshoff & Loh, 1994; for the program of the journal, see *EWE* 13, 2002, p. 174). First deliberation seminars have been designed and explored.

The deliberative didactic approach is based on the main ideas about a culture of deliberation. It is seen as important:

- to distinguish between solution oriented and deliberation-oriented handling of alternative positions.
- to consider alternative positions not only in the context of discovery, but also in the context of justification.

- to be conscious about the connection between solution and deliberation: the deliberated alternatives help to qualify the justification of a founded (tentative) solution.
- to document and preserve the deliberated alternatives which allows for examining the state of deliberation and supports a (self-) critical view on solutions.
- to reflect the limits of deliberating.

The aim of deliberative didactic is to improve decision competency in discussion and research. Based on the philosophy of deliberation (in the sense of the program of the aforementioned journal), well-considered alternative positions and their comprehensible representation are seen as essential for well-founded decisions. Bettina Blanck, who developed the didactic concept, defines a decision as a combination of deliberation and valuation: the deliberation of one or more possibilities and the positive or negative valuation of the deliberated possibilities (cf. Blanck, 2002, p. 236). Decisions aim at solutions. Blanck points out that it is not possible to gain all solutions by decisions. Decisions are only one way to get solutions. For instance, traditions or routines may determine a solution. Solutions may also be determined by preceding personal decisions or preceding decisions of others (cf. Blanck, 2002, p. 237). Decision competency, therefore, is not only a competence to handle deliberations and valuations but also a competence to reflect the feasibility of deciding. A decision may also be the decision not to decide. Decision competency includes, furthermore, the ability to reflect the adequacy of previous decisions.

To provide a culture of deliberation in university seminars cannot be done simply by adding controversial scientific positions to the topic of a traditional seminar. The ways of handling alternative positions have to be reflected. Methods supporting the students' getting used to a deliberation oriented handling of alternatives are necessary. On the level of deliberation, it is essential to make use of knowledge diversity, to open a range of alternatives, to be creative, to share knowledge, to develop one's own positions, to debate the positions of others, and to accept corrections. On the level of deliberation, there are no false or forbidden positions, nobody is to blame for his/her contributions. An essential element is to develop scientific curiosity (cf. Blanck, 2004, p. 5).

In deliberation seminars, therefore, methods like brainstorming, gathering examples and writing diaries of research are used. Moreover, special deliberation methods have been explicated and explored, for instance, forms of written discussion, like the position-commentary-response method and the deliberation oriented pyramid discussion (cf. Blanck, 2005). Let us now look more closely at the latter.

Deliberation Oriented Pyramid Discussions

Pyramid discussions are designed to support the finding, explication, structuring and representation of a variety of alternatives. Deliberation oriented pyramid discussions are mostly written discussions in teams. The produced texts are represented in the form of a pyramid. An important aim of this form of representation is to make it easier to handle knowledge diversity and explore differences and similarities of positions (cf. Blanck, 2005, p. 546). A good size for such a team is eight members. In principle, the pyramid discussion is a special type of debating and arguing: each student of the team of eight members reflects and describes his/her personal ideas, interpretation or expertise to a given problem, or question, or text, or other starting material, so that there are eight positions on level one. In a form of micro-collaboration, the members of four subteams (with two members each) – by discussing their level one positions – find four more-or-less new positions on level two. These new positions can be repetitions, transformations or deliberative integrations of the original positions. Now each of these subteams builds together with another subteam a new subteam (two subteams with four members each) – and by deliberating their level two positions – find two more-or-less new positions on level three. Next, all the eight members of the team work together, deliberating their level three positions until they find the one position on level four. Each collaboration step ends by writing down not only the developed position, but also the remaining points of disagreement.

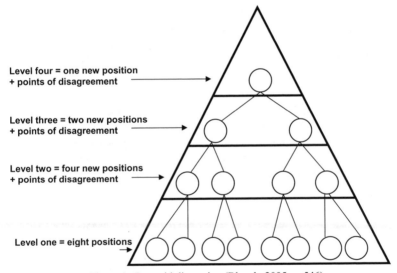

Figure 1. Pyramid discussion (Blanck, 2005, p. 546)

There may be more or less than eight students in a pyramid team. If there were, for example, nine students, they would have to build one subteam of three and three subteams of two students on the second pyramid step. If there were less than eight, the pyramid would have only three steps.

For a well-done deliberation, it is important that the participants of the pyramid discussion neither only try to maintain their own position, nor only try to enforce the team to agree on one unified position. They, rather, should explore as thoroughly as possible the differences of diverse positions. In the view of the deliberation philosophy, not to achieve a joint position is also seen as a good result of a pyramid discussion: to adhere to different positions may be appropriate, if there are, for instance, not enough arguments in favor of one position (cf. Blanck, 2002; Blanck & Schmidt, 2005)

Pyramid Discussions in the Virtual Knowledge Space opensTeam

Writing positions and arguments implies the production of a big number of documents. Therefore, one reason to look for possibilities of media supported pyramid discussions was to get the documentation clearly structured. Other requirements for media support were to enable

- the availability of the documents
- a simple handling of all contributions
- personal areas and shared group areas
- possibilities to comment or annotate the documents of others
- links between the documents
- a comprehensible representation of the history of the discussion.

In several research projects of Reinhard Keil-Slawik and his team at the University of Paderborn, these requirements of pyramid discussions and other deliberation methods have been explored in connection with the development of collaborative virtual knowledge spaces. In interdisciplinary discussions and projects, the ideas of deliberative didactic have been connected with ideas of cooperative knowledge organization:

"Our research in Paderborn focuses on finding new and innovative methods for the collaborative structuring of knowledge (...). For a number of years now the open source platform opensTeam has been used for the technical implementation of our concepts (...). The key conceptual element of our work is the virtual knowledge space. It brings together and focuses a variety of digital services. People (users/learners) meet in virtual knowledge spaces, structure knowledge collaboratively and use different digital means of communication (...). The various media involved are stored in the knowledge space and mapped via a specific view of the space." (Hampel & Heckmann, 2005, pp. 1942–3; cf. Hampel, Keil-Slawik & Selke, 2005).

In a pilot project, pyramid discussions were developed as such a specific view of the virtual knowledge space opensTeam. The technical realization was developed by Patricia Heckmann, the didactic approach by Bettina Blanck who tried out the method together with Christiane Schmidt in two collaborating university seminars (Heckmann, 2004, Blanck & Schmidt, 2005). The pyramid discussions in these seminars are described in the next section. Then connections and differences between pyramid discussions and microlearning will be discussed.

Media Supported Pyramid Discussions in Two Collaborating University Seminars

The now considered example of pyramid discussions took place in 2004 at two German universities: Paderborn and Hildesheim. The involved seminars differed in topic and timetable. The topic of the seminar in Paderborn – managed by Bettina Blanck and addressed to advanced students – was "How to handle diversity at school." The seminar in Hildesheim – managed by Christiane Schmidt and addressed to beginners – was an introduction to scientific work for students in educational science. These seminars cooperated only during certain weeks, as can be seen in figure 2.

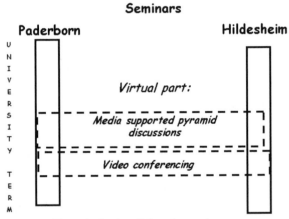

Figure 2. Partly collaborating seminars

In a shared group area of the virtual knowledge space ^{open}sTeam, the students worked on two pyramid discussions. The students in Paderborn deliberated, in their pyramid, the question "What is a well-done diversity reflecting teaching?" (Was ist ein guter heterogenitätsbewusster Unterricht?). The students in Hildesheim chose one of several given proposals of statements as a starting point of their pyramid discussion. The statement they picked out was "Teachers who attempt to have all children learn the same things will only support 'low performers' and neglect the 'high performers.' (Lehrerinnen und Lehrer, die sich bemühen, dass alle Kinder das Gleiche lernen, fördern nur die 'Schwachen' und vernachlässigen es, auch 'starke' SchülerInnen zu fördern). Each local pyramid team had eight members. In Hildesheim, thirty students took part in the seminar. They could choose between conventional working groups – preparing and presenting papers – and media supported pyramid discussions. Most of them chose the first option. In the shared area of ^{open}sTeam, the students could store their positions and discuss and develop them collaboratively in asynchronous, as well as in synchronous, communication. Reaching the third step, the students in Hildesheim referred to literature to justify their arguments (according to the regulations of seminar examination).

To encourage the communication between the teams of the two collaborating seminars, each student had to write a comment to one of the level-one-positions of the pyramid of the other team and to trace and comment on the history of this position. So it was possible for the students to accompany a member of the other team from step one to step four by writing comments. The collaboration of the teams was intensified and reflected by videoconferencing between both seminars (cf. Blanck & Schmidt, 2005).

Let's now have a look at the following summary of a selected aspect of the deliberations of the pyramid discussion in Hildesheim. The selected aspect "support of 'low performers' by special courses" is mentioned in several step one positions and is partly picked up in step two and three. There are also some comments from the other team on this aspect. It is not the central aspect of the deliberation, but explicitly mentioned and easy to trace. Therefore, it is selected here to illustrate a small section of the deliberation process.

On the first step of the pyramid, we find different opinions about the support of "low performers" by special additional courses. Arguments for special courses, for instance, are the advantages of working in small groups and the advantages of individualized learning time. Personal experiences of the students regarding how their teachers tried to manage diversity in the classroom are partly reported to support and partly mentioned to contest the idea of special groups. An argument against special courses on this pyramid step is that heterogeneity in the classroom may encourage the pupils to learn from each other.

On the second step, most of the students reflected the differences and similarities between their positions and tried to construct together a new "mixed" position. For instance, one subgroup with different opinions about special courses for "low performers" discussed that ideally there shouldn't be special courses, but that in present praxis such courses are still necessary. The members of one of the subteams on level two – they were good friends – did not touch upon the differences between their positions. They mainly adapted one of both positions, screening off the contrary points.

In the third step, the four students of one of the subteams picked up the aspect of special courses for "low performers." They pointed out the importance of giving all pupils equal access to education. They voted for individualized support and discussed special courses as a possibility to realise this support. The idea of different learning areas, in which the pupils could help each other, was discussed and valued as a better realisation of individualized support.

The students in Paderborn wrote several comments to the first- and second-step-positions of the students in Hildesheim. One of those comments – referring to the aspect of the special courses – may now continue our example. One of the students in Hildesheim had written that – in her opinion – the best way to support "low performers" would be to offer special courses in addition to regular courses. The commentator did not agree. She thought this separation would lead to an exceptional position of the supported children. She also rejected the separation for the "high performers." If "low performers" and "high performers" were supported in the classroom the children would learn that diversity is normal and that "low performers" are not stupid and "high performers" are not better than the others.

Pyramid Discussions and Microlearning

In a broader sense, the steps of a deliberation oriented pyramid discussion may be interpreted as micro-steps of deliberation and of collaborative knowledge structuring.

Each student was involved in writing from the very beginning – working alone on step one of the pyramid, answering to the question (Pyramid of Paderborn) or taking position to the statement (Pyramid of Hildesheim). Problems like uncertainty in how to start the discussion or difficulties because of unequal participation in the beginning of the discussions – well known in discussions of virtual teams – did not occur. To write down one's own position was the presupposition for the following teamwork. Our impression was that the stepwise enlargement of the collaborating subteams supported the development of the deliberation process. Every student could be sure about the inclusion of his/her more-or-less small contribution. The first steps in this stepwise enlargement of the collaboration may be seen as micro-collaboration, which supports in small steps the development of the team (see for the term "micro-collaboration" Neuhold & Lindner, 2006, p. 21).

The documentation of the contributions, in the shape of a pyramid, supported the structuring of positions in the teams. The shared group area of the virtual knowledge space opensTeam facilitated the structured documentation of the deliberation process of the positions. These small steps of deliberation are one way to inspire the students to find and build knowledge structures and to handle knowledge diversity in teams. Here we may find some points of contact of deliberative learning with the background of microlearning, where the microlearning discourse refers to "the process of medialization, mediation, transformation and order of knowledge" (Hug, 2006, p. 2).

The comments on the positions of the other team in our example may be interpreted as very first steps to learn how to handle knowledge diversity in virtual teams. ICT (Information and Communication Technologies) – supported virtual teams have become an important form of co-operation in education and at work. Like a traditional team, a virtual team is a group of people, built to realize a task. While the members of a traditional team use to meet at the same place, communicating mostly face to face, the members of a virtual team are at different places, often even in different countries, communicating mainly via media, partly synchronously, partly asynchronously (Hauenschild, Schmidt & Wagner, 2005, p. 14; Schmidt, 2005). The building of partnerships with members at two different campus universities in two collaborating seminars may be seen as a pre-exercise to such virtual teamwork.

To comment critically on a statement of another student in writing is no simple task. To handle different positions/opinions in team discussions and especially to handle criticism – to criticize others, as well as to be criticised – is a special challenge of handling knowledge diversity and social relations in teams. In our example, each student had to comment and trace a position of another student. In the beginning, there were several misunderstandings of the younger students in Hildesheim when getting comments from the advanced students in Paderborn. The first commentary, written by a student in Paderborn, was long and detailed. The commented-upon subteam in Hildesheim was shocked about the length and felt attacked. This commentary extended the uneasiness of the beginners in Hildesheim about writing comments on the texts of the advanced students in Paderborn. To learn to value criticism and to learn to handle it in a deliberative way is part of a long process of changing the discussion culture in university and society. The initiation of a new way of handling criticism in a deliberation oriented pyramid discussion has to go along with reflections on the experiences made learning by doing. Pyramid teams that are not experienced in deliberative discussions need external support for these reflections.

If members of a virtual team communicate mainly asynchronously and in writing, problems of handling criticism may be augmented. Based on our observations of the commentary-partnerships, we suspected that the reflection of these problems needs synchronous communication. In the seminar, the problems of the virtual partners to handle criticism came up for discussion and could be reflected during the synchronous communication in the videoconference.

Small steps in media supported micro-collaboration in the deliberative didactic approach are embedded in reflexive learning and knowledge structuring. As the problems of handling criticism show, to improve decision competency in discussion and research cannot be learned micro-step by micro-step. There are roundabout ways, leaps and bounds, feedback looping, deepening thoughts and changing processes over time. The small steps in a deliberation-oriented pyramid are not knowledge nuggets to be collected by the students. They have to write and justify their own positions. Dimensions of microlearning like "relatively short effort," "rather simple issues," "narrow topics," and "micro content with push character" (Hug, 2006, p. 9; cf. also EAMIL, 2006), like, for example, language training on a screen saver (cf. Hug, 2005, p. 7) are in sharp contrast to these dimensions of deliberative learning.

Up to this point, we have been looking at microlearning elements of deliberation oriented pyramid discussions. To look at microlearning from a deliberative perspective raises many open questions beyond the scope of this article. Some of these questions are: Do different allied learning topics and different types of knowledge resolve the contrasts between microlearning and deliberative learning? What about elements of deliberative learning like reflection, feedback, and criticism in microlearning contexts? Microlearning is derived from microteaching, which is mainly characterized by feedback of peers to experienced interaction (cf. Hug, 2006, p. 8; see for the tradition of microteaching, for example, Fricke & Thiele, 1982). Is micro content with push character – offered for learning by short effort – compatible to ideas of reflexive learning by doing and collaborative knowledge structuring?

References

Benseler, F., Blanck, B., Greshoff, R. & Loh, W. (1994) *Alternativer Umgang mit Alternativen. Aufsätze zu Philosophie und Sozialwissenschaften.* Opladen: Westdeutscher Verlag.

Blanck, B. (2002) *Erwägungsorientierung, Entscheidung und Didaktik.* Stuttgart: Lucius & Lucius.

Blanck, B. (2004) "Man sollte meinen, die hätten völlig verschiedene Artikel gelesen ...." Seminarbericht zur Suche nach einem Erwägungsforschungsstand – Eine Auseinandersetzung mit einer EuS-Diskussionseinheit zur Koedukation In: *Erwägen – Wissen – Ethik*, 15(1), pp. 3–32.

Blanck, B. (2005) Erwägungsmethoden. Umgang mit Vielfalt und Alternativen als Herausforderung für Forschung, Lehre und Praxis. In: *Erwägen – Wissen – Ethik,* 16 (4), pp. 537–551.

Blanck, B. & Schmidt, C. (2005) "Erwägungsorientierte Pyramidendiskussionen" im virtuellen Wissensraum open sTeam. In: Tavangarian, D. & Nölting, K. ed. *Auf zu neuen Ufern! E-Learning heute und morgen.* Münster New York, München, Berlin: Waxmann, pp. 67–76.

European Academy for Microlearning (EAMIL) (2006) *Mission. "Mikrolernen" im engeren Sinn.* Available from: <http://www.eamil.org/mediawiki/index.php/Mission> [Accessed 11 August 2006].

Fricke, R. & Thiele, H. (1982) Trainingskurse zur Veränderung des Lehrverhaltens. In: Kury, H. ed. *Interdisziplinäre Beiträge zur kriminologischen Forschung.* Vol. 2. Köln: Carl Heymanns Verlag.

Hampel, T. & Heckmann, P. (2005) Deliberative handling of knowledge diversity – the pyramid discussion and position-commentary-response methods as specific views of collaborative virtual knowledge spaces. In: *SITE 2005 Proceedings,* pp. 1942–1974.

Hampel, T., Keil-Slawik, R. & Selke, H. (2005) Verteilte Wissensorganisation mit semantischen Räumen. In: *i-com 1/2005,* pp. 34–40.

Hauenschild, C., Schmidt, C. & Wagner, D. (2005) Managing Diversity in virtuellen Teams – didaktische Strategien zur Unterstützung eines wertschätzenden Umgangs mit kultureller Vielfalt. In: Beneke, J. & Jarman, F. ed. *Interkulturalität in Wissenschaft und Praxis.* Hildesheim: Schriftenreihe der Universitätsbibliothek, pp. 211-224. Available from: <http://web1.bib.uni-hildesheim.de/edocs/ 2004/390120634/meta/> [Accessed 11 August 2006].

Heckmann, P. (2004) *Medienbrüche in kooperativen Lernsystemen – Individuelle Sichten auf Räume*. Diplomarbeit vorgelegt am Lehrstuhl Informatik, Fachgruppe Informatik und Gesellschaft. Universität Paderborn. Available from: <http://www.open-steam.org/ Dokumente/docs/patricia_heckmann_diplomarbeit.pdf> [Accessed 11 August 2006].

Hug, T. (2005) Microlearning and narration. Exploring possibilities of utilization of narrations and storytelling for the designing of "micro units" and didactical microlearning arrangements. Paper presented at the fourth Media in Transition conference, May 6-8, 2005, MIT, Cambridge (MA), USA. Available from: <http://web.mit.edu/comm-forum/mit4/papers/hug.pdf> [Accessed 11 August 2006].

Hug, T. (2006) Microlearning: a new pedagogical challenge. In: Hug, T., Lindner, M. & Bruck, P.A. eds. *Microlearning: Emerging Concepts, Practices and Technologies after e-Learning. Proceedings of Microlearning 2005. Learning & Working in New Media.* Innsbruck: Innsbruck University Press, pp. 7-11. Available from: <http:// microlearning.org/micropapers/microlearning2005_proceedings_digitalversion.pdf> [Accessed 11 August 2006].

Mosel, S., Hug, T. & Gstrein, S. (forthcoming) *Perspektiven des Mikrolernens – dargestellt am Beispiel des integrierten Mikrolernens® mit dem Knowledge Pulse®*.

Neuhold, E. & Lindner, M. (2006) Quo Vadis, eLearning? (Introductory Note). In: Hug, T., Lindner, M. & Bruck, P.A.. eds. *Microlearning: Emerging Concepts, Practices and Technologies after e-Learning. Proceedings of Microlearning 2005. Learning & Working in New Media.* Innsbruck: Innsbruck University Press, pp. 19 – 22. Available from: <http://microlearning.org/micropapers/microlearning2005_proceedings_digitalversion .pdf> [Accessed 11 August 2006].

Schmidt, C. (2005) *Challenges of asynchronous communication in ICT-supported learning groups – a case study.* Paper presented at Education and Knowledge Economies, European Conference on Educational Research (ECER), September 7 – 10 2005, Dublin, Ireland. Available from: <http://www.leeds.ac.uk/educol/ documents/143880.htm> [Accessed 11 August 2006].

Wikipedia (2006) Microlearning. In: *Wikipedia. The Free Encyclopedia.* Available from: <http://wikipedia.org/wiki/Microlearning> [Accessed 12 October 2006].

RTFM! Teach Yourself Culture in Open Source Software Projects

Mirko Tobias Schäfer & Patrick Kranzlmüller

RTFM (Read The Fucking Manual) and *FAQ* (Frequently Asked Questions) are acronyms for the "teach yourself" attitude that has become a crucial aspect of Internet culture.[1] Often communities and software projects are peeved by simple questions from new users and therefore refer them to the documentation in the *ReadMe* files and the Frequently Asked Questions. In commercial software projects, the end user – often considered as *PEBKAC* (Problem Exists Between Keyboard And Chair) – led to the development of tutorials and simple interfaces. *Clippie*, the animated paperclip in Windows Word explains to the user how to write letters, format texts, etc. The latest Adobe Photoshop came with sophisticated video tutorials explaining how to use the program. However, in open source projects, the financial and human resources for providing documentation and information for less skilled users are limited. The usage of this software often requires a higher competence in teaching yourself, or connecting to a community that is willing to help beginners without a rude RTFM reference. *Microlearning* could offer a methodology for integrating the user and stimulate the teach yourself process.

1   Knowledge Communities

With the introduction of the first home computers in the early 1980s, with the Atari 800 XL and the Commodore 64, the computer acquired the status of a teach-yourself technology. Contrary to driving a car, using a machine, or working with tools, using the computer was not taught by experienced professionals. Users had to work themselves through handbooks, manuals and detailed descriptions. Often, they joined computer clubs, where people met regularly to train and help each other. Knowledge of computer technology and how to use and to write software was developed in these early user communities. A teach-yourself attitude has been established over the years, requiring users to get started by themselves by reading manuals, FAQs and documentations, as well as learning by trial and error.

An asymmetric knowledge of computer usage developed, caused by the gap between connected, knowledge sharing core users and beginners, as well as casual users. Graphical user interfaces were supposed to lower the barrier for using the technology. The computer was to become a medium, a medium that would be interactive, in the sense that the machine would reply to the user and support the process of learning (Kay, 1990, p. 193). The design and use of interfaces constructed – as Lev Manovich

---

1   For detailed information on these terms, consult the Jargon File, a glossary of hacker slang: http://www.catb.org/~esr/jargon/html/lexicon.html.

has pointed out – a cultural code, the language of new media (Manovich, 2001). Computer literacy is accomplished not only by interacting with the computer, but also by the possibility of communicating with other users. The computer and its user are not only connected to the Internet, but also to a plurality of other users, who can find help and support in user communities, or receive tips from friends and colleagues. Although the netiquette stimulates support for so-called *newbies*, one often struggles with the materials provided to get a basic grip on the software. Asking questions that are answered in the FAQ is an accepted *"don't."* Codes of communication and social skills must be considered when interacting with user communities. The culture of the information society is a culture of participating and interacting in computer mediated communication and adapting to the different habits in various user communities.

Microlearning could help to diminish the gap of asymmetric knowledge, because it suits the very aspects of computer technology and would be easily adaptable for both experienced users and beginners. The methods of Microlearning can be used for developing a practice of knowledge production and distribution that is easy to acquire and can be shared by the heterogeneous communities that are globally connected in the age of the Internet. The asymmetric knowledge is not a mere problem of understanding technology, but a social challenge, as well. Microlearning could be a way to build information systems that correlate with heterogeneous user groups, different habits and different cultures.

2   The Notion of Microlearning

The term microlearning describes a phenomenon of knowledge acquisition in the context of information and communication technology. It describes how people acquire knowledge by learning in small steps and consuming information in small pieces that form a broader and deeper connected knowledge in the long term. This practice often differs from the established learning curricula in schools and universities. The way users learn to work and play with computers is much more related to the practice of microlearning than to the learning processes in educational institutions, because they mostly learn without handbooks and don't follow a formalised methodology or curriculum. In view of these practices, microlearning is perceived as a process of taking up small pieces of information, of portioning knowledge into modules that can be learned separately at any time when access to a learning environment is granted (Gabrielli et al., 2005).

The concept of microlearning theorises how learning in small steps and pieces constitutes a new understanding of education and knowledge, and observes how the process of learning unfolds outside established institutions of education (Hug, 2005). Langreiter and Bolka identify microlearning as "ever-increasing fragmentation of both information sources and information units used for learning" (Langreiter & Bolka, 2005).

The aspects of computer technology, the modularity and versatility, stimulate the process of so-called microlearning. Instead of reading an entire handbook, the information is consumed as micro-content. Micro-content describes a piece of information that is necessary in a certain situation, and therefore has to be retrievable in the right moment. The micro-content, e.g., a posting in a weblog, is self-contained. In order to fit into the overall knowledge structure, it has to be connectable with related information and its context.[2] This comes close to the way in which knowledge is acquired and distributed in user communities. Therefore, the term microlearning describes processes that are already part of the knowledge space and the collective intelligence (P. Lévy, 1999).

Fragmentation of complex knowledge into small portions is part of teach-yourself-processes in user communities. A formalised practice could probably be used for improving the development and documentation of open source software projects, which will stimulate and foster the use of the software. Most notably, microlearning has to be realised as a social practice. Rather than a mere way of learning in an e-learning environment, microlearning describes the production and distribution of knowledge in user communities. In these communities, participants are constantly expanding the knowledge by creating micro-content. This practice is based on the current premises of a specific developer's community. The way a community is deciding to write and access the documentation of software has influences on the work process and the communication of the group. It determines how new users are integrated and how the software product is communicated to them.

3   Cooperative Structures

Especially in the field of software development and software acquirement, new methods of knowledge production and distribution have emerged. Here, the aspects of software and computer technology are intertwined with users and producers. The communication concerning open source software takes place in communities whose members are connected via the Internet. Open source software originates in interdependency with a collective of users and developers (Raymond, 1998). A software proposal is posted online and people who are interested in developing or using it can hook up and collaborate in the development. Eric Raymond differentiates the loose connections, the flat hierarchies, and the dynamic of collaborations and alliances as the *bazaar*, while the metaphor of the *cathedral* represents the top down organised method of engineering (Raymond, 1998). The open source software developers form the bazaar where anybody can collaborate in the production of software and anybody can use

---

2   A good example would be the so-called tagging of content online. Users add a tag, a piece of meta information to a picture, a sound file or to text, in order to provide information on the stored information. Tagging promises a more efficient and semantically correct information retrieval, because a plurality of users is providing the taxonomy of content stored online. For an introduction, see Mathes, 2004.

and modify the outcome. Within these communities, both new ways of dealing with code (programming), and new ways of making that process visible (documentation), have evolved, that are significantly different from established ways of engineering. They reveal a different approach to the production and distribution of knowledge. Examples would be *eXtreme Programming*, a method for software development, which tries to help developers and users collaborate. A prototype of the application – or a part of it – is developed very fast and then tested and modified in the process (Wake, 2000). For developing web applications, the software company 37signals published guidelines on how to develop and release software using so-called *Rapid Web Development* (37 Signals, 2006).

Software engineering is different from other forms of building artefacts. With regard to its structure, software is similar to language. People who are interested in learning how to write code and willing to invest the necessary time, can learn to write software by themselves and with the help of online connected communities. For software engineering, the classic institutionalised education is not necessary. Everybody who writes software contributes to the resource of already written software and is able to make extensive use of it. Developing a software application does not require the building of a model first; it is possible to contrive immediately in the software development kit or the Integrated Development Environment (IDE). In these aspects, programming software is totally different from classic engineering (Reeves, 1992). The labour of software development often takes place in a more playful mindset, which is not necessarily driven by a monetary motivation. And as heterogeneous as the reasons are for writing software, so are the persons doing it (Rieder, Schäfer, 2005). Collaborative software development in online communities can be attractive even to unskilled users, because they are able to make suggestions for the functions an application should include, or they can report what problems the use of software causes. The open source project Mozilla, which develops and maintains the Internet browser Firefox, has built a program called Bugzilla as an interface between developers and users. It facilitates the feedback of users and reports problems and errors, as well as users needs in functionality and usability.

4 The Programmer's Dilemma

For the last ten years, open source software was generally considered as a hobby of computer freaks. With the popularity of the Internet browser *Firefox* and the political debates for open source software in public administrations, the general opinion is now more balanced. The open source web server *Apache* dominates over its proprietary competitors and held a market share of 69% in 2005.[3] Almost every project associated with Web 2.0 is based on open-source software such as development frameworks (like

---

3   Netcraft ServerWatch, October 2005, http://www.serverwatch.com/stats/article.php/3554746

RubyOnRails or *Django*) or *AJAX* (Asynchronous Java and XML) libraries (like *Dojo*, *MochiKit* or *JQuery*).

However, the development of graphical interfaces, providing comprehensible documentation, manuals or a knowledge base for teach yourself processes, which respond to the user's knowledge and experience, is difficult even for well-financed enterprises. For small software development communities such as *Helma* or *Django*, this seems unachievable. A lot of software projects confront the user with bad documentation, a non-existing support system, and updates that are difficult to find and implement. Technically and socially inexperienced users are easily discouraged by the technical challenge of installation and the rude replies when asking questions that are considered – by the community – as inappropriate. Small software projects without bigger funding often have no documentation manager, no individual who is responsible for keeping track of all the changes and updates and who is able to communicate with the different groups who are involved, such as programmers, early adopters, designers, project managers, and end-users. The lack of information design, the often sloppy documentation and the communication in open source software development is rooted more in the aspects of software and the methods of software development than in a lack of social or economic skills. Firstly, the documentation is often neglected as less important in the early stages of production. Secondly, documentation is difficult to handle if a software project is portioned in countless modules that are programmed individually by a large number of programmers, and only assembled in the end. Thirdly, programmers of open source software are quite often their own users and fit the programs to suit their own needs. They develop the software in collaboration with a peer group that shares the same social codes and technical understanding. Finally, the documentation is often written by developers who know their product/application very well and who are unable (or unwilling) to reconstruct the users' course of action. Furthermore, they are often better at writing code than in describing their application.

The developer's culture has a significant impact upon the code. For someone who has to review the code of others, this causes a lot of understanding problems. There does not exist any standardised or formalised way of programming. As language allows the speaker to say something in very different ways, a programmer has countless possibilities to use a programming language. Code is, therefore, very personal and the outcome of the programmer's individual style of using a programming language.[4]

The problems at hand are initially caused by the very aspects of software. Software is modular and therefore the program code consists of various modules and different parts that together build the application. In order to improve the software, new mod-

---

4   While this is mostly true, object oriented programming (OOP) and programming-languages like
     Python and *Ruby* tend to restrict the personal choices. *PHP* is a good example of a programming
     language that allows many choices in how to achieve something that offers less structure and
     regulation.

ules and patches are added. Software is not a coherent and completed artefact, and it is of high complexity.

Secondly, the communication of complex software to users is often neglected. Documentation is necessary as a meta-level connecting all parts in a transparent and comprehensible way. This meta-level also has the task of translating the programmer's very personal way of writing code. The translation of the code from developer to user often fails, because of inappropriate information design, undisciplined communication, neglecting of user needs, etc.

Thirdly, the social issue of different groups interacting is multiplying these problems.

5   A Survey of Documentation and Information Systems

Manuals and answers to frequently asked questions (FAQs) are common tools for explaining software to end-users. User forums are used as an interface between developers and users and support the communication of both developers among each other and between users who seek support from experienced users and developers. A review of the tools of different open source software solutions will provide a deeper insight into problems of documentation and information design in open source software. In the end, the general acceptance and usage within different settings, based on the given documentation material, is a key factor for the success and the further development of the application. A choice of different open source software products were reviewed to analyse the quality of documentation, update system, information design and user support.

Beginning with the installation, the available material and sources (documentation, manuals, tutorials, FAQs, mailinglists, forum, etc.) were used and reviewed, in order to set up an application and to successfully use it. The selection included software that is used by experienced users and developers such as web development frameworks, which are used for building web applications; software that is used by skilled users, such as weblog software; and software that is widely used among common users, such as an Internet browser. With special regard to Web 2.0, documentation and user support material from the following open source software projects were reviewed:

Kind of application	Name	Consulted material
Web Development Framework	RubyOnRails	Screencast, Wiki, Books, Tutorials, Mailing-lists, Weblog
Web Development Framework	Django	Wiki, Tutorial, Documentation, Mailinglists, Weblog, Trac, IRC
Web Development Framework	Helma	Wiki, Documentation, Mailinglist
AJAX Library	Dojo	Wiki, Manual, Mailing-list, FAQ, IRC

Rich Text Editor	FCKEditor	Wiki, SourceFourge Knowledgebase
Rich Text Editor	TinyMCE	Online Documentation, Forum
Weblog	Expression Engine	Documentation, FAQ, Forum
Weblog	Symphony21	Documentation, FAQ, Mailinglist
Weblog	Squarespace	FAQ, Examples
Wiki	StikiPad	Wiki, FAQ

Table 1. Selection of open source software

This selection consists of applications that might seem irrelevant for most users. The Internet browser Firefox could be described as the only exception of open source software that is widely used by common users. But there is an increasing use of software products that facilitate the construction of HTML websites, such as weblog software and wikis. These are very popular among skilled users and do not necessarily require programming skills. Both systems are widely used on the Internet, distributing information and exchanging knowledge. The most popular wiki is probably the free encyclopaedia *Wikipedia*, which is built from the *mediawiki* software. Weblogs and wikis are expected to aid learning processes, both in e-learning and in software usage and software development. Moreover, the selection of open source software products describes means of production of an emerging software-industry that is using open source tools for building individual solutions for their customers. The usability of open source software has an economic impact, too. The more easily software designers can apply certain software, the faster they can produce websites, web applications and software solutions.

Currently, documentation is usually split up to one or more of the following tools:

- FAQ, a list answering the most frequently asked questions.
- Screencast, a short movie showing the screen of somebody, while this person explains what she is doing right now. Aimed at beginners, screencasts usually explain common problems (e.g., how to install the software).
- Manual/Documentation, an online-handbook explaining the software application. Probably the most essential part of the documentation, the manual usually describes the different modules of the software.
- Tutorials, step by step guide on how to use the application, often include screenshots or videos.
- QuickStart, a short explanation of how to get started with the application
- Mailinglist, often separated lists for users and developers for exchanging information and asking questions.
- Examples, a list of short tutorials, usually aimed at advanced users.

- Wiki, a website with an integrated html editor that allows every user to post and modify information. The wiki can be used as a substitute for manuals, or to give an overview of the stored information and documentation.
- Weblog, a website that allows commenting on posts; the weblog is an easy to use interface for user-developer communication and allows everybody (as the wiki does) to participate.
- Books, the most continuous form of documentation and the most coherent manuals, often written by professionals for successful open source projects. Usually not up-to-date, but well written and proof-read.
- Chat, IRC, chat software, or often channels on the Internet Relay Chats for real-time communication.
- Discussion Forum, a website where questions can be posted.
- Open repositories (e.g., SVN), file-storage-systems where different users can simultaneously work with files. Usually coupled with some kind of project-management system and an integrated wiki (see TRAC-Software), which makes it possible to submit code-patches and coordinate the project with milestones and tickets.
- Project Management Systems, such as TRAC, which are coupled to open repositories (e.g., SVN). These systems coordinate the project with milestones and task management. They offer an overview on the recent source-code changes and the development of the project.[5]

The main weakness of online tutorials, manuals, FAQs, wikis and weblogs is that they are usually not the result of an organised learning-environment including developers, designers and test-groups. The information provided is incoherent, unorganised and incomplete. There is often no formalisation or categorisation of information. One may find information on a certain topic in several places, usually without any additional explanation and connection to related material.

The issue is not adding information; the problem is to find and retrieve appropriate answers and information in a labyrinth of available, yet disconnected fragments. The information is provided in small pieces, to use the terminology of microlearning, the information is available as micro-content or as a knowledge nugget. Retrieving the necessary piece of information is the matter at hand. Storing information of complex contiguity requires a meta-level that can connect the small pieces of information and allows recognising the context. It is necessary to connect the small pieces of information to a meta-level, which organises them into the appropriate context.

Writing the documentation is as tentative and modular as its developing process. Besides, documenting software is often neglected by the developers and compensated for later. A coherent and continuous documentation is often not achievable. This is why the micro-content that is produced during the process of development, or added

---

5   TRAC: http://trac.edgewall.org

later, needs to be linked to a macro-level. Providing the micro-content with meta-information could facilitate the connection to the context. It must be possible to connect the small pieces of information and provide a method of information retrieval that can replace the old-fashioned way of documentation that is still similar to the linearity of handbooks. It is essential to gain knowledge of the macro-context while dealing with its micro aspects.

The problem can't be solved on a technological level only. It requires a rethinking of methods of storing information and adapting technology to cultural practice, and a rethinking of formulating and organizing language to describe action processes. Additionally, social aspects have to be taken into account. The questions that have to be taken into consideration are:

- how to find relevant information
- how to ask questions (the smart way) and where to do that
- how to add information
- how to label information (metadata)
- how to design documentation systems (style, context, reusability, connectivity, self-contained and able to implement)
- how to describe the changes (metadata)
- how to keep track of the changes (e.g., using feed-aggregators)

Information systems online are used by a vast number of users. It is impossible to expect a user to read a handbook first for participating in an online project. Although netiquette was a favoured concept in the '90s and is still visible in the various posting guidelines of countless mailing lists, a guideline would not improve users' input to software projects. The tools used for storing and extending the information must meet the cultural practice and should not be a hassle to those who add value to the system by contributing information. Contrary to the coherent group of employees of a company, students of a faculty, or members of a team, the plurality of users is dynamic, heterogeneous, continuously changing and unknown to the maintainers of the system. As Ciborra correctly points out, an information system is only useful if it is able to integrate its users and allow them to implement the system in their context (Ciborra, 2002, p. 32). A guideline for how to fill in information won't be sufficient as well as the formulation of standards, which are not adopted by users. In software development, technical and social processes are complex and dynamically intertwined.

6   From Complex Information to Comprehensible Knowledge

The common documentation-material as listed above can be replaced by less confusing and time-consuming tools. It seems appropriate to take advantage of cooperative structures (based on a given information design) that build a knowledge data-base, which is easy to access and easy to extend. There are hundreds of different wiki tools, almost all with special features and individual handling of data and content. Choosing the right tool for specific needs may solve a lot of potential problems beforehand. When using several tools, it is indispensable to explain the different objectives and possibilities.

Microlearning offers a terminology and methodology that seems to be useful for open source software development. Following some basic guidelines, developers could support and improve the documentation process. If a certain function requires more information, the developers could build a link to a help library explaining this particular function. This could be perceived as a microlearning step. The information provided would be a micro-content. A collection of such micro-contents could be developed during the first stage of building the software. Meta-tags added to each micro-content would ensure that the various pieces of information are connected retrievably.

If users are looking for help, for information on a certain function, or want to solve a problem, a good information system avoids having the user work herself through hundreds of postings, FAQs and manuals. Connecting all those pieces of information with a meta-level – which could be realised by tagging information – a search function could direct the user to the necessary piece of information. Adding new information to the system must require the connection to that meta-level. That way, a knowledge base will be created that could easily be extended and maintained by users themselves.

The database becomes the central place for storing information; the process of storing and retrieving this information is the key to efficient usage. Since micro-content tends to get lost without the necessary connections, it is crucial to not only store these knowledge-nuggets, but also to relate it to other information as much as possible, making it visible within different contexts. This leads to well-designed micro-content, readable within different paths or levels of information retrieval. Maintaining the database would entail correcting and improving the stored information by adding or changing tags. Instead of constantly expanding the given documentation material in countless directions, this approach forces the reader/writer to thoroughly re-think the context of the material, shaping it according to its possible connections. Besides, the user stumbles across already familiar bits of knowledge now and then, without getting lost in varying descriptions of the same phenomenon.

Software design is more than the mere development of an application. Creating tools for learning how to use the application is to be recognised as a task of software engineering. Information design essentially deals with basic concepts of data formats, the accessibility of content, the preparation of useful navigation paths and finally with an overall aesthetic idea of what is to be presented. It is definitely a task within the realm of information design to integrate ways for users to interact with a program on the technological level (through RSS feeds or API), as well as the overall question of integrating the user from the earliest possible stage of development. Documentation turns the complexity of code into comprehensible knowledge.

7   Overcoming Basic Obstacles

Documentation should become an ongoing process, where participants add micro-content, which enables different paths and combinations of the given material. This makes it easier to find necessary information and turns the time-consuming quest for information into an efficient learning process. Analyzing the learning processes involved with using the aforementioned open-source applications, the whole process turns out to start all over with every single application. Instead, one should be able to adapt from software one already knows. This is primarily a consequence of the lack of standardisation and also caused by the individual communication and programming style of each single developers' community. In the case of the software *FCKEditor*, the wiki is found under the button "Support" and is basically the documentation. In the case of *RubyOnRails*, the wiki is found under the button "Community" and is a place for user contributions to the documentation. In the case of the project *Django*, the Wiki is found under "Code" and refers to the integrated TRAC-Wiki, which in this case is used as a place for almost everything (from browsing the source-code to linking to tutorials on the web). Obviously, a terminological standardisation across thousands of very different applications serving different communities is impossible to achieve. As illustrated above, it is often hard to adopt learned knowledge and procedures if there is a fundamental difference between various documentations on a basic level. The creation and consumption of micro-content is not time-consuming and can take place between different activities, in breaks or gaps within the daily work. The possibility to get a picture of the material on offer, as well as recent changes or recent news, is essential. Highlighting such changes is easy by integrating RSS feeds that keep users posted. Because the documentation of open source software is largely based on contributions by users, they are themselves responsible for making available the documentation in the most comprehensible manner. Almost every community establishes an individual way of making information accessible. This is especially problematic, because these communities have to rely on users to shape, arrange and revise the material. The preconditions to shift the responsibility on to the users are:

A transparent and comprehensive explanation of how and where to find answers, why not every question is answered immediately and how every single user is able to participate;

Easy to access and easy to understand guidelines on how to produce sharable micro-content (or link to already existent guidelines);

An information design, in order to facilitate communication among users and between developers and users, as well as to provide efficient information retrieval;

An interface design which supports using the information system and the application.

Users can develop an enormous capacity for action, and support each other in questions and answers related to the usage of an application. They share their knowledge and help new users to gain experience and solve problems.

Recommendations

New ways of software engineering, participation and adoption require overcoming established views on software documentation. These products are constantly in flux and providing documentation must follow this progression. The cultural practice of writing and distributing software needs an appropriate way of documentation.

Bringing together the collective intelligence of developers, user communities and individual users in order to provide relevant teaching- and documentation-material should be achieved by revisiting tools for documentation and interfaces for user-developer communication. This can be accomplished by the implementation of tools that facilitate both using technology and interacting on a social level. Predefined guidelines may ease the growth of documentation material that has to be reusable, modifiable and readable by machines. Furthermore, the resulting micro-content should be assembled in order to provide microlearning-steps. Users and developers would add meta-data to each micro-content and weave a web of knowledge that can be consulted and expanded. Since the single user (the one who is actually "learning") adopts the given material, she is aware of the strengths and weaknesses of this material (with regard to her very individual learning situation). The plurality of users is then able to shape and modify the material.

Dynamic Documentation

Allowing the user to extend the documentation by setting links (hyper-textual content), by making notes, that are visible to other users, by changing content and mutually correct or adjust others' contributions, and by adding new content which is self-contained, still reusable and modular.

Feasibility

Making it easy for the user to extend the documentation, by giving her appropriate guidelines (helping the user to produce micro-content explaining the notion of micro-content as is), by exactly bringing across the different tools and their meaning, making it clear where to ask what kind of questions and where (and how) to extend the given material by restricting the possibilities (e.g., avoid duplicate entries on the same issue) by standardization (if gathering and extending information is standardized across several applications, the user may adapt faster). Limiting the ways in which the given material is presented (it is more efficient to have one Wiki with elaborated information than to have tons of different tutorials and/or manuals with out-dated and isolated information), explain that decision and choose additional tools, if required. This will make it easier to find appropriate answers and to maintain the documentation.

Data Storage

Even if the information design does not allow for these possibilities, micro-content should be stored in the most hyper-textual and reusable manner (e.g., using tags). The document structure (semantics) has to be well-defined according to given standards

(W3C, microformats) and the content should be machine-readable (through metadata and/or XML-formats like RSS, for example). Moreover, it should be possible to export the documents and read them offline.

Social Connectivity

Feasible information systems will provide a functioning interface between developers and users. If early adopters are enlisted as soon as possible and assigned responsibilities with regards to documentation material, interested persons and potential end-users can participate in the process and improve the documentation according to their needs. Therefore, guidelines for documentation and participation should be published in an early stage of production.

Transparency

Providing a list of what is not working, where problems are and whether they are going to be solved or not will avoid frustrated users. If developers make clear what the problems in a given application are, they avoid answering complaints and questions concerning these problems. It may also stimulate users to participate in problem solving. Receiving help from the plurality of users requires a functioning flow of information within a well maintained information system.

8   Conclusion

Taking the open source movement to the next level would require getting rid of the *PEBKAC*, and instead getting the user on board of software development. The gap between less skilled users and the advanced ones could probably be diminished by better co-operation between developers and end-users, facilitated by suitable integration of microlearning-steps and a dynamic information system. It has become clear that software development is a highly social process that requires a different way of thinking about engineering methodology. Accessible knowledge, that is open for modification and adaptation in an environment that allows users to communicate with each other, as well as with the developers, will become inseparable from the programming process. The previously underestimated *newbie* becomes part of the community and gains knowledge through basic communication techniques. Advanced design and documentation has to meet the challenge of including diverse user-groups at different stages of knowledge and practice. Perceiving software development as a social, rather than a technical process, leads to different methods of development. Microlearning could stimulate the integration of tools into communication processes in user and developer communities and stimulate the development of dynamic information systems.

References

37 Signals (2006) *Getting Real: The smarter, faster, easier way to build a successful web application.* Available from: <http://37signals.com> [Accessed 4 June 2006].

Ciborra, C. (2002) *The Labyrinths of Information. Challenging the Wisdom of Systems.* Oxford: Oxford University Press.

Gabrielli, S., Kimani, S. & Catarci, T. (2005) *The design of microlearning experiences: a research agenda.* Available from: <www.microlearning.org/micropapers/MLproc_2005_gabrielli.pdf> [Accessed 14 June 2006].

Hug, T. (2005) *Microlearning: A new pedagogical challenge.* Available from: <http://www.microlearning.org/micropapers/MLproc_2005_hug.pdf> [Accessed 14 June 2006].

Kay, A. (1990) User interface: a personal view. In: Laurel, B. ed. *The Art of Human-Computer Interface Design.* Reading, Mass.: Addison-Wesley, pp. 191–207.

Langreiter, C. & Bolka, A. (2005) *Snips & spaces: managing microlearning.* Available from: <http://www.bolka.at/pubs/2005/snips.pdf> [Accessed 14 June 2006].

Lévy, P. (1999) *Collective Intelligence. Mankind's Emerging World in Cyberspace.* Cambridge, Massachusetts: Perseus Books.

Manovich, L. (2001) *The Language of New Media.* Cambridge, Massachussetts: MIT Press.

Mathes, A. (2004) *Folksonomies – cooperative classification and communication through shared metadata.* Available from: <http://www.adammathes.com/academic/computer-mediated-communication/folksonomies.html> [Accessed 14 June 2006].

Raymond, E. S. (1998) The Cathedral and the Bazaar. *First Monday*, 3(3). Available from: <http://www.firstmonday.org/issues/issue3_3/raymond/> [Accessed 14 June 2006].

Reeves, J. W. (1992) What is software design? In: *C++ Journal*, 1992. Available from: <http://www.bleading-edge.com/Publications/C++Journal/Cpjour2.htm> [Accessed 14 June 2006].

Rieder, B. & Schäfer, M. T. (2005) *Beyond engineering.* Available from: <http://procspace.net/berno/files/design.pdf> [Accessed 14 June 2006].

Ressources

RubyOnRails: http://www.rubyonrails.org
Django: http://www.djangoproject.com
Helma: http://www.helma.org
Dojo: http://www.dojotoolkit.org
Firefox: http://www.mozilla.com/firefox/
Expression Engine: http://www.pmachine.com
Symphony21: http://www.symphony21.com
Squarespace: http://www.squarespace.com
FCKEditor: http://www.fckeditor.net
TinyMCE: http://tinymce.moxiecode.com/
StikiPad: http://www.stikipad.com/

[All URLs accessed 1 August 2006]

V Microlearning & Higher Education

Web-based Video Conferencing in Transnational Higher Education: Pedagogies and Good Practice

Stylianos Hatzipanagos, Raphael Commins & Anthony 'Skip' Basiel

This chapter will argue for the importance of using synchronous web-based videoconferencing (WVC) as an innovative model of delivery for tutorial support and communication in a higher education context. Models of implementation will be discussed in conjunction with the underpinning e-learning theories. Two illustrative case studies in an instructional setting and the implications for the role and responsibilities of educators involved will be discussed. The notion of WVC as a microlearning environment will be explored, and finally, good-practice guidelines will be presented to emphasize the relationship between the pedagogical focus and technological developments in WVC in higher education.

1   Introduction

Videoconferencing technology allows two or more people at different locations to see and hear each other at the same time and (in some cases) to share computer applications such as internet pages, documents or software (Greenberg, 2004). A synchronous web-based videoconferencing set-up consists of computers fitted with a camera and appropriate software.

The predominant assumption about the use of web-based videoconferencing (WVC) in an educational context is that it reacts as a medium with the associated technology to allow flexibility and ease of access, and to also create 'second best' learning instances in the absence of face-to-face contact. Frequently, the primary objective has been to simulate a learning environment as good as the 'real,' face-to-face one rather than to explore the 'added value' that the inclusion of WVC could trigger. In such cases, WVC has been used with reference to a physical learning set-up, and the prime consideration was how to use the context and content of the session without alienating the users, and to engage them in a learning experience which is a valid replacement for the one they would have if they were present. Context has been important in most of these cases and determined the learning approach.

Video conventionally has been perceived to be a linear, presentational (non-interactive) medium which is unvarying and cannot adapt itself to meet a variety of student needs (Laurillard, 2002). There is also another interesting prior conception about WVC as a medium of monologue, rather than dialogue, as it is frequently associated with presentations from lecturers/'talking heads' who are not involved in a dialogical process with the learners.

However, research (Smyth, 2005) has also highlighted the potential of WVC for changing emphasis in higher education from a teacher centred to student centred focus. Changes of attitudes towards its value (Amirian, 2002; Twigg, 2001) highlight the importance of interactivity as critical for the success of any WVC-based learning set-up by helping participants to engage in social aspects of learning, negotiate meaning through interaction with peers over distance, and form communities. Engagement is an advantage, as the medium can be used to engender group formation and enhance interaction between participants either on the level of local discourse or between the two parties interacting through the WVC interface. WVC can be used on its own, or embedded within/in combination with a Virtual Learning Environment (VLE).

2   VLEs and Videoconferencing

Currently, many VLEs, such as WebCT/Blackboard and FirstClass are readily used throughout education globally. Most of these VLE systems deployed at intuitions have a complex structure of bulletin boards, chat rooms, scheduled events, thematic interest areas – and millions of 'members.' However, Brown (1999) makes the point that the vast majority of these members are not involved in much interaction with each other in their virtual community, as notions of 'temporality,' 'serendipity,' and 'connected-ness,' are ill catered for in the traditional VLE. VLEs are focused more on an Intranet model in the sense of containing activities and information, with frequently little two way traffic with external resources or participants. This can make creating an online community cumbersome, and if not moderated with skill and dedication, can lead to low student progression and retention. In addition, VLEs are generally text based, asynchronous in nature, and consequently heavily biased toward visual learners. Other learning styles (auditory or tactile/kinesthetic, see Rayner & Riding, 1997) are poorly catered for. As Alessi & Trollip (2001) point out, using a Web environment for only presenting materials to users limits the instructional potential of the Web.

For the purposes of this research, we thought it was essential to use new systems as our experience of WebCT/Blackboard was that VLEs on their own can be inadequate technologically and insular in their ethos regarding approaches to open internet and networked communications.

WVC can make a departure from the traditional functional model of the VLE and focus more on the real-time context, rather than just content. As Figueiredo & Afonso (2004) point out, the future of learning and education is not only to be found in just the production of content, but in context, that is, on making learning happen within activity-rich, interaction-rich, and culturally rich social environments.

The next section will consider a set of WVC attributes, identified in research (Greenberg, 2004) that can contribute to the effectiveness of videoconferencing as a learning technology: interactivity, technology, student centred learning, new skills, role changes and cost.

3   Attributes of the WVC Learning Experience

Interaction and Communication

It is worth noting that although WVC claims to simulate face-to-face discussion, there are a number of factors which make it differ significantly, and in some cases pale in comparison. There are issues of time and space, as well as restrictions in the media form. Whilst many forms of communication seem to transfer over successfully to electronic media, it is often a simple case of what McLuhan & Fiore (1967, pp. 73-74) call "a naïve rear view mirrorism. They claim (ibid.) that "when faced with a totally new situation, we tend always to attach ourselves to the objects, to the flavor of the most recent past...we look at the present through a rear-view mirror. We march backwards into the future." In the context of new technologies, this also means that they are approached with expectations gained by experience of the preceding medium (in this case, face-to-face contact).

An important attribute of a WVC learning event is interactivity. Interactivity transforms a medium which can otherwise be by nature static and didactic. The use of WVC can enrich and enhance the social experience of participants online, by allowing a new form of real time 'truth-forming' aligned to more traditional forms of communication, that is often absent from VLE systems. Facial expressions, as well as phatic phrases, pauses, smiles, eye contact and head movement, help authenticate communication. This form of communication is one that the users are generally more comfortable with, as it is similar to interactions they encounter daily in the 'real world.' Feenberg (1989) states that (while communicating) "the interlocutor searches for tacit signs of truthfulness or falsehood, where context and tone permit a subtler interpretation." This is certainly true for WVC. Wilson (1976) lists, in Table 1, modes of natural communication, many of which have been overlooked in the building of a typical VLE. WVC strives, albeit crudely, to overcome this void.

I	Verbal Communication: the utterance of words and sentences

II	Non-verbal Communication
	  A. Prosody: tone, tempo, rhythm, loudness, pacing, and other qualities of voice that modify the meaning of verbal utterances.
	  B. Paralanguage: signals separate from words used to supplement or modify language.
	  1. Vocal paralanguage: grunts, giggles, laughs, sobs, cries and other nonverbal sounds.
	  2. Nonverbal Paralanguage: body posture. Motion, and touch (kinesic communication); possibly also chemical communication.

Table 1. The modes of human communication (Wilson, 1976).

Technology as a Significant Pre-requisite

A common prior conception of WVC tools, as a result of the innovation in the breadth of new technologies, has been that an innovative tool with a comprehensive set of functions will take care of the pedagogy that is required. The perceived linear relationship of advanced technology and effective pedagogy has been criticised by researchers such as Amirian (2002) and Tufte (2003). A typical critique of this type highlights that it is the learning outcomes that will determine the technology used, and not vice versa. Hayden (1999) suggests that technology needs to be paired with constructivist instructional strategies (see also Kinchin, 2006). A convergence of multimedia technologies in the future will provide WVC designers with a wider variety of tools to support the learning process.

Student Centred Learning
Videoconferencing has the potential to reduce the isolation of remote learners by providing opportunities to interact with peers/experts, and engage students intellectually and emotionally by combining videoconferencing with information and communication technologies (Smyth, 2005).

New Skills
WVC can accommodate multiple learning styles: Irele (1999) has pointed out that the inclusion of WVC and associated technologies can increase the range of learning styles that can be accommodated. The use of WVC can enrich experiences for both auditory and visual or tactile/kinesthetic learners.

Role Changes
The change of medium dictates different approaches and roles for the teaching practitioners. The instructional set-ups when WVC technology is introduced are substantially different from a face-to-face setting, as are the roles of the educators involved in the learning process.

Cost
Cost effectiveness is not a straightforward attribute when applied to WVC systems. A perceived advantage of WVC tools is that they can provide relatively cost-effective solutions in comparison to custom made online learning tools. WVC is not restrictive as far as the content or structure of learning sequences that educators want to employ, and learning incidents can be tailored according to the learning needs and preferences without major cost implications for research and development. There are many systems that are free to use; however, commercial products range in price, due to the licence agreement, or offer commercial flexible options, e.g., a 'pay-as-you-go' option which allows you to 'rent' a virtual WVC meeting space for a short period of time. Other options include a distributed server service that provides access to the software but is maintained on the service providers' machines while other setups allow installation of WVC software on local servers so that control and use can be maintained locally. Table 2 summarises some of the WVC options currently (as of September, 2006) available.

WVC system	Type of service	Costs
NetMeeting	*Point-to-point*	Free with Microsoft Operating System
MSN	*Distributed server*	Free with upgrade options
Yahoo	*Distributed server*	Free with upgrade options
CUseeme	*Distributed server*	Free with upgrade options
SightSpeed	*Distributed server*	Free with upgrade options
Skype	*Distributed server*	Free with upgrade options
LearnLinc	*Distributed server*	Price linked to licence
Webex	*Distributed server*	Price linked to licence
Adobe Breeze	*Distributed server or Flash server*	Price linked to licence & pay-as-you-go option

Table 2. WVC cost comparisons

Obvious cost savings can be made with respect to expenses (travel, lost production time, etc.). But, perhaps more importantly, the savings are on a human resources level, e.g., the lack of unnecessary disruption to work schedule.

4   WVC: A Pedagogical Approach

The following two sections will offer evidence of two case studies chosen to illustrate how WVC technologies have been integrated in a learning and teaching context. According to Alexander & Boud (2001), a productive approach towards online learning is to regard it as an example of learning from experience using a new medium and access to new resources rather than simply substituting the teacher and textbook as conveyors of information. The pedagogical theory underpinning the use of WVC in both case studies was influenced by Learner Managed Learning (Stephenson, 2001), and its attributes of a student-centred approach, individually negotiated learning objectives (participants were able to negotiate their own individual sets of learning outcomes) and real-world problem-solving situations. Equally influential for the second case study was the concept of work-based learning – as adapted from the National Centre for Work Based Learning Partnerships model in the UK (Armsby, 2000), using which, student learning profiles were established by recognition and accreditation of prior experiential learning.

An action research approach was adopted: Lewin (1948, pp. 202-203) defined action research as "a comparative research on the conditions and effects of various forms of social action, and research leading to social action…a spiral of steps, each of which is composed of a circle of planning, action, and fact-finding about the result of the action." By adopting this approach, we hoped that we could directly address the practical concerns of the participants in a mutually collaborative and timely manner and both parties (students and tutors) would learn by doing and benefit from the experience both in the short and long term.

5   Case Study 1: Global Campus Project

The Global Campus project in a UK University used computer-based and online learning materials to offer interactive open and distance learning MSc programmes in Hong Kong, Shanghai, Singapore and Cairo (Hatzipanagos et al., 2002). This was a programme using a blended learning approach. UK tutors were based in London with local tutor support available in the cohort's regional office in Asia. Module learning materials were predominantly CD-ROMs and books and online mostly text-based materials.

WVC in combination with a VLE was used to implement the pedagogical model, to support student learning and to enhance learner interaction by the use of its interactive facilities. (Hatzipanagos et al. 2003). Discussion forums and VLE email were the primary means of communication between the instructors and the students.

Since the tutors only travelled to the remote locations on an occasional basis, a project investigating web videoconferencing was piloted to explore its use for aiding students' understanding of the assessment with an emphasis on coursework and exam criteria. The aim was to facilitate learning support, through interaction and communication, rather than deliver online lectures.

The tutor in London sat in front of a laptop with a web cam using WVC software. The Hong Kong cohort had their local tutors at the computer with a data projector showing the monitor's image to the entire class. Sound came from the personal computer (PC)'s internal speakers.

The tutor in London introduced and discussed assessment requirements with students and cohort tutors. Each review session lasted, on average, 45 minutes. Students would take turns in front of the connected PC to ask questions and discuss issues of concern with tutors and colleagues. This format of interaction created opportunities for 'one to one communication,' but also 'one to many.'

One issue that arose concerned the poor quality of sound over the web. In response to that, tutors adjusted their speaking style to a slower and more enunciated tone. An additional factor that made communication difficult was the level of mastery for English as a second language. Further case studies collected data from the students to determine their perspectives on the review sessions. It was felt by the tutors in London that their facilitation of the student learning experience may have been more effective if they enhanced the communication by text chat rather than just verbal exchanges. Another problem was the large variation in time zones. In this case study there was an eight-hour gap between Hong Kong and London. This lack of synchronicity between the participants (tutors and students in cohorts and London) increased the complexity of organising such sessions.

In conclusion, the adapted use of video and text chat compensated for audio-over-PC communication difficulties and created learning opportunities. In addition, the educators treated the text chat as a data source which was saved and reviewed. These data were also used for research purposes as an accurate transcription of the interaction. Text was also used as a learning and teaching aid, for example, by way of providing a Frequently Asked Questions (FAQ) supplement to the students.

6   Case Study 2: An E-learning Workshop in Gaza

An international collaboration e-learning project between an Islamic University in Palestine and a UK University contributed towards e-learning research, design and development (Cook et al., 2005). A framework for using WVC was developed. The intent was two-fold. First, students would be provided with an online learning experience and a framework would be developed for using WVC in an educational context. A secondary aim was to form, through this virtual learning experience, a local face-to-face support network of peers-learners.

The interaction via WVC took place over a period of 6 weeks and was aimed at providing students/participants (who were academic staff at the university in Palestine) with continuing and professional development in e-learning, as it was not possible to meet face-to-face. The objective was to develop participants' ability to design and use e-learning content. Participants should be able to:

– apply methods and techniques in designing and testing a simple e-learning resource
– establish evaluation criteria for self- and peer-review of the e-learning system they developed

The deliverables were for each participant to produce a VLE template that was to be used by other group members, but assessed individually. Active participation through the WVC system was built into the design of the online conferencing experience.

The Pedagogical Approach

The course designers took an online activity-based approach. Each of the tasks was linked to a core element of the design of a VLE: e-content, online communication and support, and an online assessment opportunity. Each topic was based around a two-hour videoconferencing session. Feedback was given by email and through VLE discussion board postings.

As part of the work-based learning/learner-managed learning approach, learners directed the tasks, with feedback given by the tutors in the UK. Communication, collaboration and problem-solving activities formed the basis of the pedagogical approach used.

Technology Set-up

In general, the online pedagogical models went beyond the 'transmission' mode to include higher levels of interaction and communication. The tools used included:

- a web-based videoconferencing system (figure 1),
- a VLE for asynchronous communication and access to online resources,
- ISDN videoconferencing for the final project presentations for peer review,
- a conference telephone for audio link as back-up if the videoconferencing link failed.

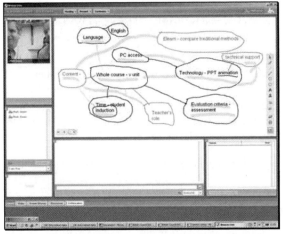

Figure 1. Video conference & whiteboard

To establish effective integration of the VLE in the learning activities, there were two levels of use. First, a central repository was established that all participants could access at a 'student' level, where copies of all digital learning materials were centrally archived for ease of access. Additionally, there were text-based threaded discussion boards to promote online discourse through problem-solving activities associated to each of the week's topics. Second, each participant was given their own personal VLE account to develop an online learning system. Other than the initial face-to-face induction, the entire course was conducted online.

Key Features for Effective Practice

As the participants had a mixed level of ICT and e-learning experience, the work-based learning/learner-managed learning approach was adopted, in addition to a set of activities, to allow each individual to progress at their own level. This approach to learning might initially have proved a challenge for participants who were used to a more traditional 'transmission' mode and content driven approach.

Each week, a new topic was introduced during a short video conference session. The discussion was initiated around a PowerPoint slide presentation. Small groups in each cohort had a representative, while the cohort as a whole had a local facilitator that sat at the web cam in the front of the lab. The image of the session was enlarged on the wall via a data projector. Individuals had access to the VLE via their PCs.

The pedagogical design was to introduce or contextualise the session's topic. Next, a discussion point would be raised. Small groups would break off for local discourse, with the web cam 'looking over the shoulder' of the lead facilitator's group. Small-group representatives would summarise their colleague's contributions, while the UK tutors would annotate the remarks using the whiteboard facility. Since English was a second language for the participants, the ability to revisit and reflect on the session could be of value. This was also helpful for those who were not able to attend the 'live' session.

Flexibility was an essential key word of the project. This could be seen at two levels. First, the logistics of the project, and second, at the curriculum design level. Contingency plans were built into every phase of the learning event.

Participants wanted to be able to download learning materials from a modem connection. The project files were made small enough for quick transmission. Also, this approach, beyond ensuring accessibility, promoted more reflection and collaboration between the stakeholders. For example, follow-up meetings were scheduled immediately after the video conference sessions, as well as events to support local group interaction. This was not in the original specifications of the project, but was suggested and implemented by the participant team in Palestine.

The cross-cultural nature of the project is another element of the experience. A sense of 'family' or bonding evolved over the weeks of online interaction. The participants used terms like 'my brothers' to communicate over the discussion boards. They were keen to learn and share with other cultures.

The tutors found the videoconferencing sessions to be quite taxing, even with the inclusion of breaks added at the request of the students. The focus and concentration needed to 'orchestrate' the learning event was more intense than in a similar face-to-face session.

Participants welcomed the opportunity of having video to add authenticity and legitimacy to the information presented in the VLE. They appreciated the opportunity to communicate verbally and visually about the subject presented. Indeed, at times, when video failed, conference calls were used as a backup. This made the 'feel' of the event seem different and in some cases even made understanding 'thorny,' as the group had subconsciously become familiar with the visual, and dependent on cues which were now absent.

Overall, the applications of use for WVC in this case study have received positive feedback from the educators and participants. The majority (72%) of stakeholders surveyed found that their learning expectations had been met in the project. 78% had rated their personal progress (knowledge and skills) as good-to-excellent. Most of the participants (83%) felt the communication and support of the online workshop was good-to-excellent.

7   WVC and Microlearning

Technological discoveries transform the fabric of human life. This applies to educational technology tools, as the choice of medium determines the learning set-ups that can transform the learners' experience. The interface, the 'surface of the medium,' determines the success of the learning experience, if it is designed to have attributes that will allow use with appropriate learning activities to support learners in their individual needs.

The nature of WVC (a flexible and modular learning platform) also dictates that learning is taken in small steps, by introducing activities that enhance the interaction between participants. Short learning videoconferencing sequences, where participants engage in computer-mediated communication, allow the technology to be used in the context of microlearning. The video supported activities subdivided the learning process into small activities. Within the WVC microlearning environment (Hug et al. 2006) these activities have the potential to reduce the overflow and complexity of information by structuring it into small linked units.

The unfolding of the microdimensions time, content, form and mediality (Hug 2005) of these activities was done in ways that enhanced the student learning experience:

- The short length of learning sequences (learning materials and WVC sessions) prompted reflection and also encouraged open ended self-reflective learning after the video-conferencing session via group interaction and on an individual basis.
- The authenticity of the WVC learning experience enhanced the legitimacy of the learning materials and the VLE-initiated communication
- Traditional learning cultures of transmissive teaching were replaced by negotiated and changed tutor/student roles.

Another advantage of WVC is that it engages participants and seems to be motivational as it provides enhancements to the concept of face-to-face learning and deals with the problem of limited use of e-learning systems. However, the synchronicity of the WVC interaction can impose difficulties in establishing time, place, and pace of learning for the synchronous events.

8   Guidelines of Good Practice

Amirian (2002) summarises significant considerations in learning and teaching via videoconferencing as:

1. Learning goals are primary,
2. Teaching via videoconferencing is different,
3. Interaction is critical,
4. Pre-planning is essential,
5. Faculty staff need development,
6. Students need scaffolding,
7. Success is measured, the process is reiterative.

While all but the second of these recommendations would also be applicable to a face-to-face session, it is the adaptation and application of these themes to a WVC context that can help design meaningful learning events.

With a theoretical foundation in place, what sort of practical recommendations can be made to the application of WVC for e-learning? Initially, a profile of participants should be done through a framework needs analysis, establishing information and communication technologies (ICT) experience and skills levels. Similarly, hardware and software limitations should be established (Basiel 1996) through a variety of research techniques such as on/off-line surveys and interviews.

Context and technical constraints determine the choice and use of the online tools. Technology should not drive pedagogy, according to Thorpe (1998), however, technical constraints can have a negative impact on pedagogy. WVC software's attributes of compatibility and interoperability, i.e. the ability of the two systems to exchange information and to use the information that has been exchanged (IEEE 1990) vary, so it is wise to test links before the actual online conference takes place. This will also establish hardware requirements. Firewalls may also interfere with connections, so a pre-test will help identify problems. Lack of a controlled videoconference suite can impose technical constraints and cause inconvenience in a public office as video conferences may interfere with people's work and vice versa. External factors, such as ambient background noise can also affect the quality of interaction. In some settings, it may be best to use a sound enhancement, such as a separate phone line, for voice in combination with the computer for the video link. However, the increasing sophistication of hardware and software videoconferencing components can make such a set-up unnecessary.

The video image can be captured to make a permanent record of the WVC interaction. This may be useful for validating the stakeholders' identity for quality assurance purposes. Audio discussion can also be digitally recorded. Lastly, as with any new technology introduced into a 'human organisation,' the adoption of WVC must be planned and staff training must be considered. A learning technology such as WVC can be a powerful tool, but only if a culture of use has been introduced and grown.

Table 3 offers a 'tick-box style' starting point, based upon the above points, to steer towards good practice in the use of WVC in an educational context:

1. Establish needs of the 'stakeholders.'
2. Determine learning outcomes and choose appropriate online tools accordingly.
3. Establish minimum technical specifications.
4. Establish a 'common' and mutually compatible software platform.'
5. Pre-test room conditions.
6. Pre-test network connections.
7. Adjust video specifications (size, frame rate, lighting, etc.).
8. 'Screen grab' or record the interaction for your records.
9. Promote a culture of use for adoption of WVC systems.

Table 3. Guidelines of effective WVC practice

9   Conclusion

The chapter explored and analysed the ways WVC can be used in creating and supporting learning environments, based on a combination of theoretical, practical and empirical grounds. There is a need in higher education for highly interactive learning programmes that use extensive branching to tailor the material to the evolving needs of the learner, however, as Rushby (2005) points out, these highly interactive learning programmes are very complex and require significant resources to design and develop. WVC as an educational medium can provide effective learning experiences in response to the needs of the learners without the shortcomings of complexity and high cost.

In the featured case studies, the distance learning environment determined the use of WVC to compensate for the lack of face-to-face contact, and create learning opportunities that are similar, if not identical to, the face-to-face ones. The physical peculiarities of a medium play a prominent role in determining the learning experience. It is only by examining the potentialities and limitations of a medium that we can enhance student learning, and in doing so, question and contrast the value of the new with traditional modes of learning and teaching. The importance of WVC lies in that though it was initially introduced to address specific learner needs, there were compensating rewards for the participants of each session through their use of the medium. As mere replication of the face-to-face experiences was not possible, the medium (videoconferencing) and the learning set-up created a different enriched code of communication between learners and tutors. The WVC microlearning environment enriched the participants' learning experience by changing the way participants interacted with each other through the medium, and by transforming traditional learning cultures within the context of trans-national higher education.

References

Alessi S.M. & Trollip S.R. (2001) *Multimedia forLlearning: Methods and Development.* 3ʳᵈ edition. Boston: Allyn & Bacon.

Alexander, S. & Boud, D. (2001), "Learners still learn from experience when online." In: Stephenson, J. ed. *Teaching and Learning Online: Pedagogies for New Technologies.* London: Kogan Page.

Amirian S. (2002) Pedagogy and Videoconferencing Conference presentation. Montclair State University, USA.

Armsby, P. (2000) Methodologies of work based learning. In: Costley, C. & Portwood D. eds. *Work Based Learning and the University: New Perspectives and Practices.* SEDA publications, Paper 109.

Basiel A. (1996) Video communication for distance learning. *MUCORT'96 Conference,* London UK.

Cook J. et al. (2005) Finding and maintaining common ground between Gaza and the UK: a framework for dialogue led e-learning. *Computer Assisted Learning Conference 2005,* Bristol UK.

de Figueiredo, A.D. & Afonso, A.P (2005) *Managing Learning in Virtual Settings: The Role of Context.* Hershey, PA: Idea Group, Inc.

Feenberg, A. (1989) The written world: on the theory and practice of computer conferencing. In: Mason R. & Kaye A. eds. *Mindweave: Communication, computers and Distance Education.* Oxford: Pergamon Press, pp. 22–39.

Greenberg, A. (2004) *Navigating the sea of research on video conferencing-based distance education: a platform for understanding research into the technology's effectiveness and value.* Available from <http://wainhouse.com/files/papers/wr-navseadistedu.pdf> [Accessed 12 September 2006].

Hatzipanagos, S. et al. (2002) Distance learning comes home: resource-based learning for campus-based students. In: *Proceedings of World Conference on Educational Multimedia, Hypermedia and Telecommunications 2002.* Norfolk, VA: AACE, pp. 719–724.

Hatzipanagos, S. et al. (2003) Blended learning for computer ccience education: a conceptual framework and a case study. In: *Proceedings of World Conference on Educational Multimedia, Hypermedia and Telecommunications 2003.* Norfolk, VA: AACE, pp. 2397–2404.

Hayden, K.L. (1999) Videoconferencing in K-12 education: a Delphi study of the characteristics and critical strategies to support constructivist learning experiences. In: *Proceedings of Conference on Distance Teaching & Learning.* University of Wisconsin, USA.

Hug, T. (2005). *Microlearning and narration. exploring possibilities of utilization of narrations and storytelling for the designing of "micro units" and didactical microlearning arrangements.* Paper presented at the fourth Media in Transition conference, May 6-8, 2005, MIT, Cambridge (MA), USA. Available from: <http://web.mit.edu/comm-forum/mit4/papers/hug.pdf> [Accessed 10 October 2006].

Hug, T., Lindner, M. & Bruck, P. A. eds. (2006) Microlearning: emerging concepts, practices and technologies after e-learning. In: *Proceedings of Microlearning 2005.* Innsbruck: Innsbruck University Press.

Institute of Electrical and Electronics Engineers (1990) *IEEE Standard Computer Dictionary: A Compilation of IEEE Standard Computer Glossaries.* New York.

Kinchin, I.M. (2006) Concept mapping, PowerPoint, and a pedagogy of access. *Journal of Biological Education,* 40 (2), pp. 79–83.

Laurillard, D. (2002) *Rethinking University Teaching: A Conversational Framework for the Effective Use of LearningTtechnologies.* London: Routledge Falmer.

Lewin, K. (1948) *Resolving Social Conflicts; Selected Papers on Group Dynamics.* New York: Harper & Row.

McLuhan, M & Quentin Fiore (1967) *The Medium is the Message.* New York: Bantam Books.

Rayner, SG. & Riding, RJ. (1997) Towards a categorization of cognitive styles and learning styles. In: *Educational Psychology,* 17, pp 5–28.

Rushby, N. (2005) Where are the new paradigms? In: *British Journal of Educational Technology* 36 (3).

Smyth, R. (2005) Broadband videoconferencing as a tool for learner-centred distance learning in higher education. In: *British Journal of Educational Technology,* 36 (5), pp. 805–820.

Stephenson, J. (2001) Learner Managed Learning: a holistic approach to work-based learning. In: Boud, D. and Solomon, N. *Work-Based Learning: A New Higher Education?* Milton Keynes: OU Press.

Thorpe, M. (1998) Keynote presentation for the Open Learning Forum, University of Sussex, England / Institute of Educational Technology, Open University, UK.

Tufte, E.R. (2003) *The CognitiveSstyle of PowerPoint.* Cheshire, CT: Graphics Press.

Twigg, C. (2001) *Innovations in online learning: moving beyond no significant difference.* The Pew Learning and Technology Program. Available from <http://www.thencat.org/Monographs/Innovations.html> [Accessed 12 September 2006].

Wilson E. O. (1976) *Sociobiology: The New Synthesis.* Cambridge: Belknap Press.

On the Relationship of Didactical Characteristics and the Use of ICT

Sigrid Blömeke & Christiane Müller

In this paper, we present core findings of an exploratory video study on teaching with information and communication technologies in Mathematics, Computer Science and German. Twenty-five lessons are videotaped and analyzed with respect to didactic dimensions, e.g., direct teaching vs. student- and problem-centered teaching, as well as to verbal interaction, e.g., questions provoking factual knowledge vs. evaluative or meta-cognitive questions, and to the kind of ICT used, e.g., microlearning tools vs. comprehensive tools. Our data show that it is possible to identify three teaching patterns: an "innovative ICT teaching script," a "traditional ICT teaching script," and a "modern traditional ICT teaching script." The types can be classified on the dimension "linear-directive teaching," with a use of comprehensive ICT tools, versus "student- and problem-centered teaching" with a more flexible use of microlearning tools.

1   Introduction

The teaching and learning process in classrooms has been investigated empirically in different traditions during the past several decades: on the one hand, research has focused on didactical dimensions, i.e. broader characteristics that structure a lesson sequence like teaching methods. In Germany, this is a well-known perspective taken by authors like Klafki, Heimann or Meyer. On the other hand research has focused on the verbal interaction between teachers and students. This is a perspective especially well known in English-speaking countries, taken by authors like Flanders, Amidon or Hough. Since these two perspectives are a matter of deeply rooted cultural research traditions, they are only rarely brought together. Our exploratory video study tries to overcome this gap. Teachers' behavior is analyzed with respect to didactic dimensions, e.g., direct teaching vs. student- and problem-centered teaching as well as to verbal interaction, e.g., questions provoking factual knowledge, versus evaluative or meta-cognitive questions.

With the information and communication technologies (ICT) coming up a third research tradition emerged that focuses on the use of media from a more technological point of view. Its research on teaching and learning with ICT is mostly carried out in laboratories and focuses on effects of single characteristics, like the kind of coding. So, we know only very little about the teachers' use of ICT: how do they make use of ICT in classrooms? And how does their ICT use relate to didactical and interaction categories? Is it possible to identify certain patterns? These are the leading research questions of the present paper. ICT is defined as computer-based digital Information- and Communication systems, -media, -techniques, -tools, and -products (Reusser, 2003).

2   Theoretical Framework

Often, ICT is seen as a "change agent" that nearly automatically changes routines and habits on different levels (OECD, 2001; Kozma, 2003). On the instructional level, it is assumed that ICT changes teaching methods since the presentation and examination of subject matter can be realized in a new and more effective manner. On the curriculum level, ICT is expected to influence the curriculum development. Finally, on system level, it is expected that the use of ICT promotes a change of the education system. The present study focuses on the instructional level.

Identification of teaching patterns has recently received a lot of attention in instructional research since the first TIMS-Video Study showed distinctive cultural differences in what happens in German, Japanese and US-American classrooms (Stigler et al., 1996). Based on Schank & Abelson (1977) these patterns are called teaching "scripts." The two authors define scripts as mental representations of systematic action sequences which are comparable to routines. A well-known example is the restaurant script: regardless of the type of restaurant, the sequence of actions is widely the same, and everybody with our cultural background knows how it works. Nevertheless, the script is slightly flexible, since subscripts can cover differences (like the difference between an average restaurant and an elite restaurant, in which you are seated, or McDonalds, where you have to pay before you can eat).

Focusing on teaching scripts can be understood as an adequate balance between laboratory studies and the complexity in the concrete teaching and learning environment. Scripts can be used as a coherent model to describe the complex teaching situations. We have only a little empirical research on how teaching scripts occur (Blömeke, 2004). During schooling students repeatedly experience the same teaching patterns. It is expected that these experiences result in "teaching scripts" over time. Due to this long-lasting process, scripts are only altered insignificantly during teacher education and they stabilize furthermore during a teacher's professional practice (Blömeke, Eichler & Müller, 2003; Richardson & Placier, 2001; Wideen, Mayer-Smith & Moon, 1998).

Now, what happens if a new feature comes in? In our case, this question concerns the implementation of ICT. Pedagogical studies concerning their implementation in classrooms are primarily evaluation studies of major pilot projects, e.g., Apple Classroom of Tomorrow (Dwyer, 1994), ImpaCT (Hammond, 1994) and SITES (Pelgrum, 2001). In general, these studies emphasize the notable potential of ICT to realize constructivist learning principles, to promote co-operative learning and a pedagogy of understanding. The assumption that ICT can support constructivist learning has been prevalent since the beginning of the 1990s (Hooper & Rieber, 1995; Papert, 1998; Kerres,

2000). It is expected that the use of ICT supports independent student work on complex assignments, which provoke a high level of cognitive activity (Scott, Cole & Engel, 1992; Pelgrum, 2001; Blömeke et al., in press) and advances social interaction between students (Kamke-Martasek, 2001). In addition, ICT can increase the level of authenticity of subject matters and student interaction (Kerres, 2000; Jonassen, 1996). Furthermore, Pelgrum (2001) postulates a changing role and activity of teachers and students in computer-based lessons.

In the beginning, ICT meant mostly expensive, and due to its size and weight, hardly manageable hardware. The use of software needed a lot of expertise and could rarely have been described as interactive. In contrast, more recently ICT is decreasing in costs, size and weights, as well as in the required prior knowledge. This development gives a lot more flexibility in the use of ICT at any time and anywhere, according to the needs of teachers and learners. "Microlearning" is the term that covers most of the movements that are based on a use of these advantages.

Against this background, one important didactical decision to be taken by a teacher is what kind of ICT he or she wants to use in instruction. We know that 98% of German schools have bought computers for instructional purposes; 86% have realized a server-based network (BMBF, 2004). Nevertheless, the concepts in which these technologies are integrated differ widely. Often computer laboratories are realized. The whole class has to move to these special rooms to be able to make use of the computers for one or two hours. This is still a relatively inflexible idea of ICT use with temporal as well as with spatial limits. The same problems apply to a very common solution schools have chosen over time: to buy common computers and data projectors that can be borrowed by teachers for single lessons. A more flexible solution is the implementation of single computers in all classrooms. The teacher, as well as students, can use them like the blackboard or an overhead projector. Still, this means being restricted to the classroom space and lesson times. Only some schools work with notebooks or computer-based calculators for all students and wireless LANs. In these cases, microlearning processes can be realized easily, since every teacher and every student has access to digital information without temporal or spatial limits. They can use ICT during the lessons, but they can also use them during the breaks, in the afternoons, on their ride to school, etc. (Schaumburg, 2003, 2006).

Since the implementation of ICT is a complex process that requires changes and adaptation on the instructional, curriculum and system level of schools (Prasse et al., in press), it is plausible to expect a close relation between the choice of ICT and other didactical and interaction categories. Student-centered learning processes can be supported more easily by a use of flexible technologies, whereas static solutions hold the risk of pure teacher-centered instruction. Even if most studies give clear evidence for the potential of ICT in teaching and learning processes, it remains an open question how teachers make use of this potential. Critics of computer integration into instruction, such as Cuban (1993), suggest that all too often teachers merely integrate ICT into traditional teaching patterns. Empirical research supports this criticism by failing to establish clear links between quantitative indicators of ICT use and student achievement (see as an overview, Blömeke, 2003). Thus, the following research questions were investigated in this study:

- How do teachers use ICT in instruction?
- Is it possible to identify teaching scripts?
- How do lessons in which microlearning tools are applied differ from lessons in which a comprehensive tool is used?

3   Methods and Data Source

The majority of existing results on the use of ICT in classrooms is based on survey studies with students and teachers about their perceptions of ICT implementation in instruction. However, survey studies are always influenced by the subjective point of view. There exist only few analyses of teaching patterns with regard to ICT by independent observers (e.g., Schaumburg, 2003). Therefore, this videotape study analyzes in detail the behaviour of eighteen teachers (in one lesson each) according to core categories of instructional quality. A teacher-centered camera is used in their lessons of Mathematics (n=12), Computer Science (n=4) and German (n=2). These teachers instruct high school classes (grades 11 to 13) in 16 different schools in 6 federal states of Germany. All teachers participated voluntarily.

With reference to other video studies (Stigler et al., 1996; Pelgrum, 2001; Clausen, Reusser & Klieme, 2003) a detailed low-inference coding scheme was developed for this analysis. It includes the observation of the interaction between teacher and class (e.g., complexity of questions, teacher and student roles) and didactic dimensions (e.g., cognitive complexity of tasks, type of ICT use) in time sampling. Except for the verbal interaction categories, a one-minute-time code is used. The verbal interaction is analyzed using a five-second time code to capture the complexity of the verbal interaction between teacher and class. Based on the coding of three independent observers the exact inter-rater agreement is computed (Cohen's kappa). The agreement ranges between good and very good ($.68 \leq \kappa \geq .92$).

4   Results

The video codings are analyzed using a cluster centroid analysis to identify different teaching scripts. On the basis of empirical findings and theoretical considerations regarding learning environments, a three cluster solution is favoured. The solution is replicated by a discriminant analysis. All teachers are classified correctly on the basis of the relevant characteristics (variables) to one out of three groups. There is a 100% concordance between the results of the cluster centroid analysis and the discriminant analysis. Furthermore, the three cluster solution is replicated by a factor analysis. Basis for the factor analysis was a transposed data matrix, in which the cases (teachers) serve as variables and the variables serve as cases. The solution with three factors explains 74% of variance. The identified factors replicate exactly the three different clusters.

The three teaching scripts can be described as follows:

- a "traditional ICT-teaching script" (n=5) with ICT used in a cram-like kind of instruction,
- an "innovative ICT-teaching script" (n=8) to promote student- and problem-centered learning, and
- a "modern traditional ICT-teaching script" (n=5) with ICT used in a mixed kind of instruction.

Teachers with a "traditional ICT teaching script" use the computer mostly to present content to the students. Power-point presentations lasting for 30 to 45 minutes and completely prepared before the lesson in German or mathematics are a perfect example for this kind of instruction. When ICT is used, it is controlled by the teacher. In approximately 76% of the lesson time, the teacher plays the active part, dominating the communication with directive statements (60% of a lesson). They use whole-class work as the dominant instructional pattern. A high proportion of class work is teacher-directed class discourse (80%). Furthermore, the proportion of complex assignments is low. These teachers rarely apply tasks of a high didactic quality, such as evaluation tasks, or complex problems which are expected to provoke a high level of complexity. Regarding the use of non-ICT media, this group uses most often the blackboard.

Teachers with an "innovative ICT teaching script" realize the highest proportion of student activities in the classroom. Whole-class discourse is used in only 19% of the lesson time. The teacher is not the main actor (39% of a lesson) but students play an active role during the lesson (approximately 50% of a lesson). In this group, teachers do not dominate the communication (only 27%). They show the highest task quality by employing a high number of complex tasks. The time in which the teacher controls the computer is minimal (7% of lesson time). ICT is mostly used as a flexible tool for working on tasks by students. Computer-based calculators for an experimental approach to functions are an example for this kind of instruction. With regard to the use of non-ICT media, ICT is mostly accompanied by work sheets.

Finally, with regard to their activity teachers of the "modern traditional ICT teaching script" rank in between the other two groups. They dominate the communication (32%) a bit more than the innovative type and less than the traditional type. This group is also mid-range regarding the activity of students (30% of lesson time). Tasks with high cognitive demands are less often used compared to the innovative type (34% of the lesson time). For nearly half of a lesson, all students of the class work together. Almost the same time is spent in class discourse guided by the teacher. Like the innovative type, teachers of this group use ICT intensively as a tool and much less for presentation purposes.

Figure 1 summarizes the results.

This convincing 5-8-5 solution emerges if the interaction and didactic variables go into the cluster analysis in its full complexity. The more the variables are aggregated to factors, the smaller the two groups of teachers with innovative or traditional ICT teaching scripts are. The majority of teachers seem to be a kind of "mixture" then.

To determine if there are differences between the subjects taught, the data is analyzed using a cross-classified table. The result confirms a relation between the subject matter taught and the use of ICT (χ^2(4, 18)=14.87; p_{exact}=.003). The "traditional ICT teaching script" is only observed in the group of mathematics teachers (n=4). In contrast, the innovative type mostly occurs in the group of Computer Science teachers (n=4) and only one mathematics teacher shows an "innovative ICT teaching script" (n=1). All examined German teachers (n=2) and seven mathematics teachers use ICT in a modern traditional way.

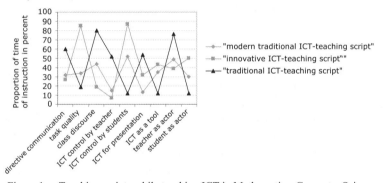

Figure 1.   Teaching scripts while teaching ICT in Mathematics, Computer Science and German classes.

5   Discussion

The presented study yields interesting insights into the kind of ICT integration in instruction, even though the number of lessons analyzed is rather small. Nevertheless, three distinguishable ICT teaching patterns can be identified: the "innovative ICT teaching script," which is student- and problem-centered, the "traditional ICT teaching script," with great resemblence to a cram-like kind of teaching, and the "modern traditional ICT teaching script," which can be located between these two different teaching scripts. The identified types of ICT use can be classified on the dimension "linear directive teaching" (step-by-step classroom discourse is the dominant teaching pattern) and "student- and problem-centered teaching" with a flexible use of technologies in the second case. The teaching patterns are well established in instructional research, while the presented study extends these findings to ICT usage. In this context, it is remarkable that the use of non-ICT media fits perfectly into the patterns described with teachers showing a traditional teaching script using the blackboard, which means an additional loss of flexibility and innovative teachers using work sheets.

Empirical research shows that teachers with characteristics like those described in the "traditional ICT teaching script" have a relatively low instructional quality (Mariage, 1995; Brophy, 2000; Klieme, Schümer & Knoll, 2001). Teachers with characteristics like those described in the "innovative ICT teaching script" use complex tasks and support self directed- and problem-centered learning. These dimensions correspond to indicators of high instruction quality and effective teaching (Gutiérrez & Slavin, 1992; Cohen, 1994; Anderson, Reder & Simon, 1997; Brophy, 2000).

Studies which expect a nearly automatic change through ICT integration to achieve constructivist teaching could not be confirmed by this study. It seems that teachers do not use the full potential of ICT. Most of the teachers show teacher-directed use of ICT ("traditional and modern traditional type"). Only a small group of teachers use ICT in a more student-centered environment ("innovative ICT teaching script"). But even these teachers do not use ICT to its full extent. They rarely apply ICT for communication and documentation purposes, or as a quick source of information. So, the whole range of microlearning processes could not be observed. The various possibilities neither occur in the subgroup "innovative ICT users" nor in the whole sample. In contrast, the common scheme of ICT corresponds with a concept that has been called "Lehrmittelsystem" by media didactics for decades (Tulodziecki, 1997). For a long time, they had hoped that more technical flexibility would go along with a more flexible didactical concept (like that represented in a "Lernumgebungskonzept" based on constructivist learning theories) but obviously this has not happened.

To sum up, it can be said that teachers do not use ICT automatically in the sense of constructivist teaching. Furthermore, they do not achieve a high level of quality of instruction while using ICT. This is even more surprising, since this sample is a positively selected sample of teachers who volunteered to participate.

From the perspective of the three examined subjects, the results of our study suggest that mathematics teachers integrate ICT in their traditional linear concept of instruction. The results of this sample indicate that mathematics teachers may have a higher affinity to the "traditional ICT teaching script" than their colleagues in Computer Science and German. Only a few use the possibilities of ICT for a high instructional quality. In fact, it seems that this group simply substitutes e.g., Power Point presentations for black board lessons. Additionally, the results point to further evidence for different teaching cultures (Feiman-Nemser & Floden, 1986) and confirm the influence of subjects on the use of ICT (Jones, 1999).

From a methodological point of view three remarks are to be made:

Firstly, the number of lessons analyzed is rather small. This has to be seen as a limitation with regard to more general conclusions. In addition, the study was restricted to one episode per instructor.

Secondly, the question has to be raised whether the three teaching scripts identified really build a scale. We have interpreted our data in this way. But is it possible that a complex construct like teaching is one dimensional, that it is a latent trait? We doubt it. We even doubt that the scripts are latent classes. Unfortunately, it is not possible to answer this question on the basis of our data. To be able to apply mixed-rasch models or latent class analyses we would need a much bigger sample.

Thirdly, and this was one of the most surprising results of our study from a methodological point of view: it is interesting that the convincing cluster solution which we could replicate with all kind of statistical procedures, that this solution changes if the interaction and didactical variables do not go into the cluster analysis in its full complexity anymore. The more the variables are aggregated to factors, the smaller the two groups of teachers are which show an innovative or a traditional ICT script. The majority of teachers belongs to the mixed ICT script, then. Even if this is plausible from a statistical point of view, this result does also point to the broad complexity of teaching, with important differences hidden in the details. It may be that we have to be very, very careful in aggregating classroom characteristics.

6   Conclusions

We will continue with our research in this field and build on the results presented in this paper. We plan to replicate our data with a much bigger sample of teachers and subjects. We have already videotaped a second and a third lesson of the teachers in our sample in which they either use ICT for other purposes, or they do not use ICT at all. First results indicate that there is not much difference in their behaviour.

A bigger sample size will give us the possibility to do further research on the level of aggregation, as well. Do we really need a coding scheme with hundreds of categories, or is it sufficient to do the analyses on an aggregated level? In addition, with a bigger sample size, we will be able to clarify whether teaching scripts is a latent trait or are latent classes.

In the long run, we plan to use our videos to create a teacher-training program. Since we need data on student achievement first in order to be able to judge the quality of the teaching scripts, this will take a while – but our idea is to show the different teaching scripts to teacher candidates and practicing teachers and to have them analyze the videos. We have some evidence from other research groups in Germany that this is a very effective way of teacher education.

References

Anderson, J.R., Reder, L.M. & Simon, H.A. (1997) Situative versus cognitive perspectives. Form versus substance. In: *Educational Researcher*, 26 (1), pp. 18–21.

Blömeke, S. (2003) Lehren und Lernen mit neuen Medien. Forschungsstand und Forschungsperspektiven. In: *Unterrichtswissenschaft*, 31 (1), pp. 57–82.

Blömeke, S. (2004) Empirische Befunde zur Wirksamkeit der Lehrerbildung. In: Blömeke, S. et al., eds. *Handbuch Lehrerbildung*. Bad Heilbrunn/ Braunschweig: Klinkhardt/ Westermann, pp. 59–91.

Blömeke, S., Eichler, D. & Müller, C. (2003) Rekonstruktion kognitiver Prozesse von Lehrpersonen als Herausforderung für die empirische Unterrichtsforschung. Theoretische und methodische Überlegungen zu Chancen und Grenzen von Videostudien. In: *Unterrichtswissenschaft*, 31 (2), pp. 103–121.

Blömeke, S. et al. (forthcoming) Aufgabenqualität im Unterrichtsfach Mathematik. Analyse von Aufgaben aus didaktischer und fachlicher Sicht. In: *Unterrichtswissenschaft*, 34.

BMBF (2004) *IT-Ausstattung der allgemein bildenden und berufsbildenden Schulen in Deutschland*. Bonn: BMBF.

Brophy, J.E. (2000) *Teaching*. Brussels: IBE (Educational Practices Series, 1).

Clausen, M., Reusser, K. & Klieme, E. (2003) Unterrichtsqualität auf der Basis von hochinferenten Unterrichtsbeurteilungen. In: *Unterrichtswissenschaft*, 31 (2), pp. 122–141.

Cohen, E.G. (1994) Restructuring the classroom. Conditions for productive small groups. In: *Review of Educational Research*, 64 (1), pp. 1–35.

Cuban, L. (1993) Computers meet classroom: classroom wins. In: *Teachers College Record*, 95 (2), pp. 185–210.

Dwyer, D. C. (1994) Apple Classrooms of Tomorrow: what we have learned. In: *Educational Leadership*, 51, pp. 4–10.

Feiman-Nemser, S. & Floden, R.E. (1986) The culture of teaching. In: Wittrock, M. C. ed. *Handbook of Rresearch on Teaching. A Project of American Educational Research Association*. New York: MacMillan, pp. 505–526.

Gutiérrez, R. & Slavin, R.E. (1992) Achievement effects of the nongraded elementary school. A best evidence synthesis. In: *Review of Educational Research*, 62, pp. 333–376.

Hammond, M. (1994) Measuring the impact of IT on learning. In: *Journal of Computer Assisted Learning*, 10, pp. 251–260.

Hooper, S., & Rieber, L.P. (1995) Teaching with technology. In: Ornstein, A.C. ed. *Teaching: Theory intoPractice*. Needham Heights, MA: Allyn and Bacon, pp. 154–170.

Jonassen, D. H. (1996) *Computers in the Classroom. Mindtools for Critical Thinking*. Englewood Cliffs, NJ: Prentice Hall.

Jones, A. (1999) Teachers' subject subcultures and curriculum innovation. The example of technology education: In: Loughran ed. *Researching Teaching. Methodologies and Practices for Understanding Pedagogy*. London: Falmer, pp. 155–171.

Kamke-Martasek, I. (2001) *Allgemeine Didaktik des Computer integrierenden Unterrichts*. Frankfurt: Peter Lang.

Kerres, M. (2000) Internet und Schule. In: *Zeitschrift für Pädagogik*, 46 (1), pp. 113–130.

Klieme, E., Schümer, G. & Knoll, S. (2001) Mathematikunterricht in der Sekundarstufe I. "Aufgabenkultur" und Unterrichtsgestaltung. In: Bundesministerium für Bildung und Forschung ed. *TIMSS – Impulse für Schule und Unterricht*. Bonn: BMBF, pp. 43–57.

Kozma, R.B. ed. (2003) *Technology, Innovation, and Educational Change: A Global Perspective*. Oregon: International Society for Technology in Education.

Mariage, T.V. (1995) Why students learn. The nature of teacher talk during reading. In: *Learning Disability Quarterly*, 18, pp. 214–234.

OECD (2001) *Learning to Change: ICT in Schools*. Paris: OECD.

Papert, S. (1998) Agents of change. In: Moura Castro, C. de ed. *Education in the Information Aage*. New York: Inter-American Development Bank, pp. 93–97.

Pelgrum, W.J. (2001) Obstacles to the integration of ICT in education: results from a worldwide educational assessment. In: *Computers & Education*, 37, pp. 163–178.

Prasse, D. et al. (forthcoming) Medienintegration in Unterricht und Schule. Bedingungen und Prozesse. In: van Buer, J. & Wagner, C. eds. *Qualität von Schule. Entwicklungen zwischen erweiterter Selbstständigkeit, definierten Bildungsstandards und strikter Ergebniskontrolle. Ein kritisches Handbuch*. Frankfurt/M.: Lang.

Reusser, K. (2003) "E-Learning" als Katalysator und Werkzeug didaktischer Innovation. In: *Beiträge zur Lehrerbildung*, 21 (2), pp. 176–191.

Richardson, V. & Placier, P. (2001) Teacher change. In: Richardson, V. ed. *Handbook of Research on Teaching*. Washington, DC: American Educational Research Association.

Ritter, M. (1994) *Computer und handlungsorientierter Unterricht*. Donauwörth: Verlag Ludwig Auer.

Schank, R.C. & Abelson, R.P. (1977) *Scripts, Plans, Goals and Understanding. An Inquiry into Human Knowledge Structures*. Hillsdale, N.J.: Lawrence Erlbaum.

Schaumburg, H. (2003) *Konstruktivistischer Unterricht mit Laptops? Eine Fallstudie zum Einfluss mobiler Computer auf die Methodik des Unterrichts*. Dissertation. Berlin: Freie Universität Berlin. Available from: <http://darwin.inf.fu-berlin.de/2003/63/> [Accessed 7 August 2006].

Schaumburg, H. (2006) Elektronische Textverarbeitung und Aufsatzleistung. Empirische Ergebnisse zur Nutzung mobiler Computer als Schreibwerkzeug in der Schule. In: *Unterrichtswissenschaft*, 34 (1), pp. 22–45.

Scott, T., Cole, M. & Engel, M. (1992) Computers and education: a cultural constructivist perspective. In: *Review of Research in Education*, 18, pp. 191–251.

Stigler, J. et al., (1999) *The TIMSS Videotape Classroom Study: Methods and Findings From an Exploratory Research Project on Eighth-Grade Mathematics Instruction in Germany, Japan and the United States*. Washington DC: U.S. Department of Education, National Center for Education Statistics.

Tulodziecki, G. (1997) *Medien in Erziehung und Bildung. Grundlagen und Beispiele einer handlungs- und entwicklungsorientierten Medienpädagogik*. Bad Heilbrunn: Klinkhardt.

Wideen, M., Mayer-Smith, J. & Moon, B. (1998) A critical analysis of the research on learning to teach: making the case for an ecological perspective inquiry. In: *Review of Educational Research*, 68 (2), pp. 130–78.

What is Quality University Learning and How Might Microlearning Help to Achieve it?

Beverley Oliver

This chapter argues that the key generic graduate outcomes of a university education at all levels, but particularly at the undergraduate level, are incorporated in the achievement of advanced information literacy, which includes critical thinking, information management and processing, and communication. These skills are best acquired at university by deep approaches to learning in engaging learning experiences. Early attempts to use web-based and web-enhanced instruction, which often consisted of linear texts adapted for the Web, were rarely more successful than traditional methods in effecting student learning in this area. Microlearning, however, enables more text-free and interactive digital environments in which to engage the mobile and connected Net Generation undergraduate. Today's university students are likely to carry their own micro devices and expect to be able to use them to engage in immediate, complex and challenging information tasks. The chapter concludes with a provocative scenario showing how a typical university lecturer might use microlearning artifacts to engage typical undergraduate students in learning experiences which ensure quality educational outcomes.

1 Introduction: What are the Appropriate Goals of a University Education?

There is much discussion about the appropriate aims of university education, and what differentiates it from other forms of higher education. Many agree that its goal is to go beyond memorisation and skill acquisition (Biggs and Collis, 1982, Chalmers and Fuller, 1996, Laurillard, 1993, Ramsden, 1992, Ramsden, 2003). Laurillard describes academic learning as the acquisition of articulated knowledge which "is located in *our experience of our experience* of the world – it is known through exposition, argument, interpretation, and reflection on experience of the world [emphasis added]" (Laurillard, 1993, p. 25). Biggs argues that university learning must go beyond declarative knowledge to changing the way the student sees the world: "Once you really understand a sector of knowledge, it changes that part of the world; you don't behave towards that domain in the same way again" (Biggs, 1999b). Few would quibble with his claim that an appropriate aim of university education is to learn to think (Biggs, 2003).

Many agree that university education is most effective when students adopt a deep approach to learning (Biggs & Collis, 1982; Chalmers & Fuller, 1996; Laurillard, 2002; Ramsden, 2003). Students with a deep approach to learning can "apprehend and discern phenomena related to the subject, rather than what they know about them or how they can manipulate them" (Ramsden, 2003). It is evidenced by students whose intention is to understand the broader subject and what it means in relation to other subjects (for example, the underlying concepts involved in solving a problem), relate previous knowledge to new knowledge across courses; relate theoretical ideas to everyday experiences; distinguish evidence and argument; and organise and structure content into a coherent whole. A deep approach to learning is encouraged by learning experiences and assessment methods that foster active and long-term engagement with learning tasks; stimulating teaching which demonstrates the lecturer's personal commitment to the subject matter and stresses its meaning and relevance to students; clearly stated academic expectations; and choice in the method and content of study (Ramsden, 2003).

Common university learning experiences and assessment practices encourage surface approaches to learning (Ramsden, 2003). Students who adopt a surface approach to learning are driven to complete assessment tasks (which are seen as external impositions), and focus on particular and unrelated details of the task (such as the formula needed to solve a problem). These students memorise information for assessments, associate facts and concepts unreflectively and fail to distinguish principles from examples (Ramsden, 2003, Biggs, 1999a). Surface approaches to learning are encouraged by university teachers, particularly at the undergraduate level, who demand mostly memorisation, rote learning and a focus on marks through assessment (creating anxiety). They also overload the curriculum with excessive material (and focus on 'covering content'), give little or no feedback on progress, and little choice in methods of learning (Ramsden, 2003; Laurillard, 2002; Margetson, 1996; Chalmers & Fuller, 1996).

Surface and deep approaches to learning are not unrelated to what university students are expected to learn: since the 1980s, universities in the western world, including Australia, have experienced reduced government funding, increased competition from local and international universities, the introduction of new information technologies, and intense market competition for students (Markwell, 2003). At the same time, employers of their graduates have indicated that now, more than ever, graduate employees need broader skill sets than just discipline content knowledge: employers look for creativity and enthusiasm, the capacity for independent and critical thinking, flexibility, problem solving and communication skills, logical and orderly thinking, and time management skills (Markwell, 2003; Curtin University of Technology, 2000; McInnis, 2003; ACER, 2001; Department of Employment Education Training and Youth Affairs, 1998). Such employer demands, as well as market forces, have in part led universities to formulate lists of their graduates' attributes, also known as generic skills or generic graduate attributes (Barrie, 2004). While there is some institutional variation in these published lists of attributes, all include key generic skills such as critical thinking. Many universities continue to recommend schemata of higher order thinking skills, such as Bloom's taxonomy or its derivatives, as a guide to creating assessment tasks appropriate to university level education (Bloom, 1956; Ennis, 1987; Andrich, 2002; Association of College and Research Libraries, 2000, Biggs & Collis, 1982; Biggs & Moore, 1993). The key aspects of Bloom's taxonomy are that higher order thinking skills go beyond memorisation and comprehension to those associated with making meaning: specifically, application, analysis, synthesis and evaluation (Bloom, 1956).

2 Advanced Information Literacy Captures the Core Goals of a Quality University Education

Key generic graduate attributes associated with making meaning have a familiar ring to those in the field of information literacy education, even though the boundaries of that field are contested (Spitzer et al., 1998). Once synonymous with library skills and bibliographic instruction, a more contemporary view of information literacy includes the process of information management (Snavely & Cooper, 1997), the mastery of information processes (Burnhein, 1992, p. 193), literacy with a range of contemporary tools (Shapiro & Hughes, 1996), media literacy and visual literacy (Tyner, 1998, p. 93); in fact, "a literacy that combines information collection and analysis and management skills and systems thinking and meta-cognition skills with the ability to use information technology to express and enhance those skills" (Tinkler et al., 1996). This concurs with the claim that the key characteristics of the undergraduate are an inquiring mind, helicopter vision, a sense of personal agency, a repertoire of learning skills, and information literacy (Candy et al., 1994). There is a view that information literacy is a process rather than an endpoint (Candy, 2000, p. 146), and that the process is about meaning creation which requires critical skills in negotiating meanings (Mutch, 2000, p. 155). Students' epistemological beliefs associated with making meaning are central to Perry's (1970) view that undergraduates often begin higher education with a simplistic (absolutist) belief that information is either right or wrong, and that their task is to find "right" answers and regurgitate them on demand. As they progress, students' faith in this absolutistic world is severely shaken and that the goal is not to find the "answers" but to be able to make judgements about information from apparently equally convincing sources. Eventually, students who develop to the highest levels on Perry's nine-point continuum come to see all knowledge as provisional (Perry, 1970, p. 5). Limberg's more contemporary analysis outlines three ways students deal with information in higher education: trying to find the "right answer", choosing the "right answer" based on relative quantity and availability of information, and creating an answer based on analysis of a variety of information sources (Limberg, 2000). In this context, information literacy is clearly in the realm of deep rather than surface learning approaches because "in its fullest sense, [information literacy] is a complex, recursive, context-dependent idea best understood as the relationship between an individual and his or her construction (or understanding) of the information task at hand" (Candy,

2000, p. 149). Because information literacy augments students' competency with evaluating, managing, and using information, it is considered a key outcome for university students (Association of College and Research Libraries, 2000; American Association for Higher Education, 2000; Australian and New Zealand Institute for Information Literacy (ANZIIL) and Council of Australian University Librarians (CAUL), 2004). This suggests that a core element of a quality university education is the acquisition of advanced information literacy.

3   How do we Ensure Graduates Achieve Advanced Information Literacy?

It is widely accepted that the aim of university teaching is to make student learning possible (Ramsden, 2003), and that the key to quality learning is engagement (Coates, 2005; Kuh, 2001; McInnis et al., 2000; McInnis, 2001; Mentkowski, 2000; Zhao & Kuh, 2004; Scott, 2005; Sweany et al., 1996). In particular, engagement with undergraduate co-learners in ill-defined and problem-solving activities encourages students to see knowledge and meaning as negotiated rather than fixed, challenging undergraduates to move from absolutist to relativist thinking (Perry, 1970). Many universities attempt to engage the beginning undergraduate in information literacy education in the initial semesters of the undergraduate curriculum through stand-alone credit-bearing courses, learning experiences embedded in required courses, optional online tutorials and workbooks (Spitzer et al., 1998, p. 182). Each of these methods appears to have varying degrees of effectiveness. While no study has been able to show one method as superior, it is clear that students profit from information literacy education (Oliver, 2001), particularly when those skills are taught in context and across the curriculum (Spitzer et al., 1998, p. 182). However, if we refocus on the aim of encouraging deep approaches to learning, the literature suggests that open learning and alternative delivery methods are useful (Candy et al., 1994, p. xii) as are a choice of methods of study (Ramsden, 2003).

4   Information Literacy Education and Early Attempts at Web-based Education

These ideas meant that the introduction of the Web offered exciting new opportunities in information literacy education; partly because the medium was the message (McLuhan & Fiore, 1967), the Web had the potential to enhance the substance of what was taught (Appleton & Orr, 2000, p. 11), and also because it enabled students to use flexible delivery of other courses more effectively (George & Luke, 1996). It was rightly claimed at that time that computer-assisted instruction allowed students to work at their own pace, and to access resources at the point of need rather than simply when a class in information literacy was scheduled (Fjallbrant, 2000; Fjällbrant & Levy, 1999; Appleton & Orr, 2000). Early claims of success were widespread but often unsubstantiated (Ramsden, 1992, p. 159; Snyder, 1997, p. xxii; Tyner, 1998 p. 72); while they were launched in a flurry of excitement, early evaluation studies failed to reveal the much anticipated improvement in learning outcomes (Alexander & McKenzie, 1998; Alexander, 1999). Sceptics predicted that no medium, however useful, could solve fundamental educational problems or alter the ways teachers understood teaching (Ramsden, 2003), that no single medium was likely to have properties that made it best for all purposes, and that most instructional functions could be performed by most media (Tyner, 1998, p. 73). Students' scepticism about early attempts at web-based learning (when it was new and usually unsophisticated) was confirmed in research on the learning preferences of a sample of beginning undergraduates in Australian higher education. The students were wary of the benefits of new educational technologies. The research found:

- A strong and consistent preference for face-to-face instruction, coupled with a suspicion and dislike of unsophisticated, overly frequent or careless use of teaching technologies which did not permit easy interaction with teachers or peers, or opportunities for questioning or collective discussion, or seemed to be simply replacing face-to-face teaching rather than complementing it;
- It is important to provide students with a diversity of teaching styles and learning opportunities: some students welcomed the "virtual university" and significant online learning methods, but most clearly preferred to work with other students and a teacher (or teachers) and welcomed the use of these technologies only as an enhancement for classroom activities;
- An appreciation of those computer-aided learning opportunities perceived as contributing to classroom, tutorial and laboratory instruction; and
- A concern about difficulties of access to and use of facilities, especially in libraries and computer laboratories (Pargetter et al., 1998, Ch. 8).

Also at that time, Laurillard explored the use of various media in effecting quality university learning. She claimed that "a mix of teaching and learning methods will always be the most efficient way to support student learning, because only then is it possible to embrace all the activities of discussion, interaction, adaptation, and reflection, which . . . are essential for academic learning." She noted that while traditional teaching methods focus on having students "attending" through listening and reading, computer-based learning (as it was at that time) could provide opportunities for "practising" and "articulating." Her conclusion was that no one medium could do it all, but all of them could do something, and that judicious combinations of media could do quite a lot (Laurillard, 1996).

One of the contributing factors to moderate success with the Web for learning is possibly the use of hypertext with learners for whom it was a completely new phenomenon. On one hand, its newness was likely to increase hypertext's attractiveness, particularly when it allowed more student-centeredness and interactivity than had previous learning environments (McKenna, 1995; Reed, 1996). However, hypertext was known to have confounding characteristics for learning such as disorientation, navigation inefficiency, cognitive overload, flagging commitment, unmotivated rambling and time constraints (Heller, 1990; Rouet, 1996; Sweany et al., 1996). For example, in a study with undergraduate students, comparisons were made between groups receiving class lecture alone and those receiving class lecture in combination with either hypertext-based instructional programs or linear drill-and-practice programs. Not only was there no significant difference in academic achievement or problem-solving ability, but the students preferred the linear-style program to the hypertext approach (Reed et al., 1996). Similarly, a study in the learning effectiveness of using web-based materials in first year undergraduate education found that students welcomed the convenience of having materials available electronically but that their use effected little real difference in the quality of their learning (Oliver, 2001). This was largely due to the use of primitive and much less interactive rather than robust hypertext (Ayersman, 1996). Students enjoyed the electronic delivery of information, but it required little engagement. This use of the Web for course materials is still often implicitly encouraged by the architecture of some learning management systems: university e-learning initiatives faltered because they failed to capitalise on interactivity, which is the distinguishing feature of hypertext, as well as central to student engagement.

5   Information Literacy Education of the Digital Natives

It is sobering to recall that what we now term "early attempts" at web-based learning took place only about a decade ago. In that time, web technologies have clearly become much more sophisticated, less text-based, and as in Web 2.0, more interactive and more easily edited through blogs and wikis (O'Reilly, 2005). Contemporary university students are no longer naive users of hypertext and they are likely to be familiar with the common artefacts of microlearning environments. Our younger students have been termed "digital natives" (Prensky, 2001) because they grew up using the Internet. They belong to the Net Generation who are multi-taskers, like to be connected and "always on" (Oblinger & Oblinger, 2005), and carry with them sophisticated portable and convergent devices which allow constant access to information, entertainment and socialising opportunities (Millea et al., 2005). The younger generation's electronic habitat has rapidly become far more sophisticated and portable, and the lines between formal learning tools and socialising tools have blurred. Oblinger and Oblinger claim that today's U.S. "Net Genners" began using computers between the ages of five and eight, and in their teenage years, they used the Web extensively for school research (Oblinger & Oblinger, 2005). They "are more comfortable working on a keyboard than writing in a spiral notebook, and are happier reading from a computer screen than from paper in hand" (Frand, 2000) and they stay connected through messaging applications (Crittenden, 2002). They are typically intuitive visual communicators, can integrate virtual and physical environments, learn better through discovery than by absorption, respond quickly to visual stimulus, and shift attention rapidly (Oblinger & Oblinger, 2005). Convenience, connection and control are the three factors which drive their steadily increasing take-up of information and communication technologies (Caruso, 2004; Caruso & Kvavik, 2005). Results from a recent Australian study suggest that Australian undergraduates' device ownership and adoption of emerging applications is comparable to the their North American peers (Oliver, submitted), and this is likely to be similar among European students.

6   How Universities Might Engender Deep Approaches to Learning Advanced Information Skills by Engaging them with Microlearning Artifacts

In spite of changing technologies, the fundamental principles for quality university learning are likely to continue to apply: quality will be achieved when graduates are high-level thinkers who can find, analyse, evaluate and synthesise information from a range of sources, and communicate it effectively in context and to various audiences. In pre-Web times, this level of thinking, requiring the encompassing skills of advanced information literacy as described here, would have been achieved by having students create extended written arguments investigating a particular topic – this is known as the academic essay. The merits of this type of assessment task are not to be underestimated, and it is still favoured as an excellent way to have students transition to university and to adopt academic discourse (Krause, 2001). It also likely to continue to be used by academic teaching staff who are typically an aging population (Hugo, 2004) who were late-comers to hypertext and in general tend to prefer oral and print texts. This is probably one reason why traditional face-to-face learning experiences are still the norm in many western countries, with e-learning adopted as supplementary and complementary to in-class interaction (Bell et al., 2002). Given the aging workforce and digital habits of the academic teaching staff in typical western universities, this seems unlikely to change. Add to this the slowness of most large universities to respond quickly to change – such as the adoption, maintenance and adjustments to learning management systems – and there seems little incentive for the typical university lecturer to use new and emerging technologies to attempt to engage their students.

Nevertheless, microlearning, even as an ill-defined concept (Hug, 2005) possibly taking its roots from an amalgam of mobile learning and Web 2.0 discourses, has much to offer as an additional and more sophisticated supplementary tool for complex university learning. The term is currently used as follows:

– a learner's short interaction with a learning matter broken down to very small bits of content ... Learning processes that have been called "microlearning" can cover a span from some seconds (e.g., in mobile learning) to 15 minutes (learning objects sent as e-mails)

- the way more and more people are actually doing informal learning and gaining knowledge in Microcontent and Micromedia/Multitasking environments ... especially those that become increasingly based on Web 2.0 and Wireless Web technologies (2005)

While the academic essay remains an excellent way to have students acquire higher order thinking skills and advanced information literacy, microlearning experiences have the added advantage that they are brief and mobile – they can provoke engagement with chunks of learning while the student is in transit, alone or in groups, and particularly in between formal learning experiences.

7   Conclusion: A Scenario for Using Microtools and Events to Engage Students in Quality University Learning in Advanced Information Literacy Tasks

Given that the focus of this chapter is undergraduate education, this concluding scenario addresses the challenge of engaging the beginning undergraduate student in complex critical thinking and advanced information literacy tasks. The context is a generic undergraduate course, but the examples presented here could be applied in very discipline-specific courses. The purpose of the scenario is to show how microlearning experiences, applications and devices can be used to engage even the somewhat resistant surface learner in higher order thinking tasks.

Our hypothetical student is Joe, a 19-year-old male engineering student whose prime interests centre around sport and socialising. Joe travels by train to an urban university campus four days a week. He carries some books and papers, a mobile phone, an iPod and a USB memory stick. His lecturer in Engineering Communication 101 is attempting to engage him in writing his first full length academic research paper on the benefits and challenges of nanotechnology. The task is proving a challenge. As per her instructions, Joe is using the Web and the university's library database to access research publications related to the topic, but he is having difficulty deciding which papers are well-argued, and which are spurious. He has also found an article from the national newspaper which presents a highly emotional and poorly reasoned argument related to his topic. He cannot see why he is being discouraged from using it in his essay – if a resource is in print it must be acceptable. His lecturer knows that although the research papers her students have found consist of arguments which are complex and lengthy, they are based on microchunks of rationality called logic. She decides that her students need a course in logical thinking, but being young and energetic Net Genners, Joe and his peers are unlikely to want to read anything too advanced or lengthy, particularly when most of them just want to get their essays finished and submitted.

The lecturer plans a microlearning approach. She begins by emailing the class a weblink to a short story called *Love is a fallacy* (Shulman, 1953). She tells them it is a story about a young man of their age trying to impress his girlfriend by teaching her how to think. In fact, the story uses tiny episodes and examples to teach the reader logical fallacies such as Hypothesis Contrary to Fact, Slippery Slop and Dicto Simpliciter. Joe's interest is sparked when he uses Google to discover that this story was in fact an episode of *The Many Loves of Dobie Gillis*, an American sit-com from the '60s. He makes a note to get hold of the DVD. His lecturer knows that he and his peers are not keen readers, so she searches the Web for a podcast. There isn't one, so she makes one and uploads it for the students. Joes downloads it on his iPod, and is really amused by the story, and shares his enthusiasm on the class wiki – a place where the students can share anything that helps their learning. The students enjoy it and listen to it repeatedly. In the meantime, his lecturer is keen to get them to practice their understanding of the logical fallacies so they can make better judgements about their nanotechnology research papers. Before she gets to that, she decides she will send the students some short argument scenarios on SMS, and get them to reply with their analysis of the validity of each. The arguments are based on topics that are sure to get their interest, such as the legal drinking age. At the next lecture, she shares a selection of the responses with the whole group and gets them to select and justify the best ones. She gets the whole class to form blog groups of five students – each group creates and evaluates micro argument scenarios, and posts their judgements on the validity of the arguments to the other blog groups. They can use the well-known *Stephen Downes Guide to the Logical Fallacies* (Downes, 2000) to broaden their understanding as well as short excerpts from *Smart thinking: Skills for critical understanding and writing* (Allen, 1997). If they prefer, they can conference or work in pairs on IM or Skype. At first, the arguments are trivial and amusing, but they soon start to get more complex and serious. They even start to relate to the nanotechology research topic under discussion.

The semester progresses and the students have drawn on their knowledge of logic and reasoning to evaluate the research papers they have found. Now they begin to compose their essays. The lecturer notes that several students have difficulty writing well and concisely. She does not have time to run extra writing classes for them, and she knows they are unlikely to attend anyway. She decides she will once again adopt a microlearning approach. She invites students to contact her at the point of need in their essay writing – when they are unsure of their writing, they can send her one sentence by SMS and ask her to check that it is correct. She often sends them a sentence as well, asking them to judge its correctness. She uses her PDA phone to receive and send the SMSs – because she can handwrite her answers using the stylus, this is not too onerous, and she can do it when she has a few spare moments. It is a lot more manageable than her previous practice of allowing the students to email their entire essays so she can read their first drafts. In that case, her comments and suggestions for improvement were so overwhelming that the students tended to become despondent. After some time using the SMS assistance, she notices sentences are improving – Joe tends to send them when he is on the train, all the while listening to his iPod – but now paragraphs need some attention. She switches to email, and invites her students to send her a paragraph at a time so she can comment and assist. After a few attempts at this level, they seem to have the concept. They sometimes use the discussion board to chat about this.

The end of the semester is approaching and the students' essays are coming in. She looks at them with relief – they are far from perfect, but they are much better than the work of cohorts from several years back when she felt overwhelmed with the marking load at the end of the semester. Even her previous attempts to put course materials in the university's learning management system (LMS) had met with limited success – her students found the web materials rather unengaging, and they were just too mobile to engage in tasks associated with spending lots of time seated at the desktop computer. As a consequence, she still uses the LMS as a web presence where course materials can be accessed as needed. Without her current panoply of microtools, she had little chance to meet with and help individual students. Now she can assist them at the point of need, and students like Joe can use his in-between travel time to get nuggets of learning. She also knows that these students are on the way to becoming more sophisticated thinkers, and that they have a solid foundation in the level of information literacy required at university and in the professional world. She also knows that her students have been engaged in the process of making meaning (Mutch, 2000) and have been challenged to move beyond the absolutist thinking typical of beginning undergraduates (Perry, 1970), and they have created new arguments based on analysis and synthesis of a variety of information sources (Limberg, 2000). Like all good teachers, she has used a "judicious combination" (Laurillard, 1996) of teaching and learning contexts and tools – some technological, others not – to engage her students. Her student evaluation feedback shows that many of the students changed their view of learning and reading because of her methods. She plans to share her teaching and learning techniques with her colleagues at the next staff forum: she knows that some of them believe she is wasting her time, and believe that students really just have to know the subject thoroughly. She understands their views, and probably where they are coming from, but she remains unshaken in her belief that regardless of the degree in which the students are enrolled, their greatest need is to learn to think.

References

ACER (2001) *Graduate skills assessment: summary report GSA Entry 2001.* Available from: <http://www.acer.edu.au/unitest/gsa/pdf/UNIENTRY> [Accessed 11 September 2001].

Alexander, S. (1999) An evaluation of innovative projects involving communication and information technology in higher education. In: *Higher Education Research and Development,* 18, pp. 173–184.

Alexander, S. & McKenzie, J. (1998) *An evaluation of information technology projects for university learning.* Committee for University Teaching and Staff Development, Canberra.

Allen, M. (1997) *Smart thinking: skills for critical understanding and writing, Melbourne:* Oxford University Press.

American Association for Higher Education (2000) Nine principles of good practice for assessing student learning. Available from: <http://www.aahe.org/assessment/principl.htm> [Accessed 15 June 2001]

Andrich, D. (2002) A framework relating outcomes based education and the taxonomy of educational objectives. *Studies in Educational Evaluation*, 28, pp. 35–59.

Appleton, M. & Orr, D. (2000) In Bruce, C. & Candy, P. eds.: *Information literacy around the world: advances in programs and research*. Wagga Wagga NSW: Centre for Information Studies Charles Sturt University, pp. 11–24.

Association of College and Research Libraries (2000) *Information literacy competency standards for higher education*. Available from: <http://www.ala.org/acrl/ilintro.html> [Accessed15 October 2000]

Australian and New Zealand Institute for Information Literacy and Council of Australian University Librarians (2004) *Australian and New Zealand Information Literacy Framework: principles, standards and practice*. Available from: <http://www.caul.edu.au/info-literacy/InfoLiteracyFramework.pdf> [Accessed 1 September 2006].

Ayersman, D. J. (1996) Reviewing the research on hypermedia-based learning. In: *Journal of Research on Computing and Education*, 28, pp. 500–526.

Bell, M., Bush, D., Nicholson, P., O'Brien, D. & Tran, T. (2002) *Universities online: a survey of online education and services in Australia*, Department of Education, Science and Training. Available from: <http://www.dest.gov.au/highered/occpaper/02a/default.htm> [Accessed 1 September 2006]

Biggs, J. (1999a) What the student does: teaching for enhanced learning. In: *Higher Education Research & Development*, 18, pp. 57–75.

Biggs, J.B. (1999b) *Teaching for quality learning at university: what the student does*. Society for Research into Higher Education. Buckingham: Open University Press.

Biggs, J. (2003) *Teaching for quality learning at university: what the student does*. Society for Research into Higher Education. Buckingham: Open University Press.

Biggs, J.B. & Collis, K.F. (1982) *Evaluating the quality of learning: the SOLO Taxonomy*. Sydney: Academic Press.

Biggs, J.B. & Moore, P.J. (1993) *The process of learning*. London: Prentice Hall.

Bloom, B.S. ed. (1956) *Taxonomy of educational objectives: the classification of educational goals. Book 1: Cognitive domain*. London: Longman.

Burnhein, R. (1992) Information literacy – A core competency. In: *Australian and Academic Research Libraries*, 23, pp. 188–196.

Candy, P. (2000) In Bruce, C. & Candy, P eds.: *Information literacy around the world: advances in programs and research*. Centre for Information Studies Charles Sturt University, Wagga Wagga NSW, pp. 139–152.

Candy, P., Crebert, G. & O'Leary, J. (1994) *Developing lifelong learners through undergraduate education*. Higher Education Council, Australian Vice Chancellors Committee, AGPS, Canberra.

Caruso, J. B. (2004) *ECAR study of students and information technology, 2004: convenience, connection, and control*, EDUCAUSE. Available from: <http://www.educause.edu/KeyFindings/1165> [Accessed 1 September 2006].

Caruso, J.B. & Kvavik, R.B. (2005) *ECAR study of students and information technology, 2005: convenience, connection, control, and learning key findings*, EDUCAUSE.

Available from: <http://www.educause.edu/ir/library/pdf/ers0506/rs/ers05061.pdf> [Accessed 1 September 2006].

Chalmers, D. & Fuller, R. (1996) *Teaching for learning at university: theory and practice*. London: Kogan Page.

Coates, H. (2005) The value of student engagement for higher education quality assurance. In: *Quality in Higher Education*, 11, pp. 25–36.

Crittenden, S. (2002) Silicon daydreams: digital pastimes of the wired generation. In: *virginia.edu*, VI.

Curtin University of Technology (2000) *Graduate attributes survey report*, Available from: <http://www.aair.org.au/jir/1999Papers/pickett1.pdf> [Accessed 26 December 2006].

Department of Employment Education Training and Youth Affairs (1998) *Research on employer satisfaction with graduate skills*, Evaluations and Investigations Programme, DEETYA. Available from: <http://www.dest.gov.au/archive/highered/eippubs/eip99-7/eip99_7pdf.pdf> [Accessed 26 December 2006].

Downes, S. (2000) Stephen Downes guide to the logical fallacies. Available from: <http://web.uvic.ca/psyc/skelton/Teaching/General%20Readings/Logical%20Falllacies.htm> [Accessed 1 September 2006].

Ennis, R.H. (1987) A taxonomy of critical thinking dispositions and abilities. In Baron, J. & Sternberg, R.: *Teaching thinking skills: theory and practice*. New York: W. H. Freeman, pp. 9–26.

Fjallbrant, N. (2000) In: Bruce, C. & Candy, P. eds.: *Information literacy around the world: advances in programs and research*. Centre for Information Studies Charles Sturt University, Wagga Wagga NSW, pp. 25–36.

Frand, J.L. (2000) The information-age mindset: changes in students and implications for higher education. In: *EDUCAUSE*, September/October, pp. 15–24.

George, R. & Luke, R. (1996) The critical place of information literacy in the trend towards flexible delivery in higher education contexts. In: *Australian Academic & Research Libraries*, 27, pp. 204–212.

Heller, R. (1990) The role of hypermedia in education: a look at the research issues. In: *Journal of Research on Computing and Education*, 22, pp. 431–442.

Hug, T., (2005) Microlearning: A new pedagogical challenge. In: *Microlearning 2005: Learning & Working in New Media Environments*. Available from: <http://www.microlearning.org/micropapers/MLproc_2005_hug.pdf> [Accessed 27 December 2006].

Hugo, G., (2004), The Demography Of Australia's Academic Workforce: Patterns, Problems And Policy Implications In: *Monash Seminars on Higher Education*. Monash University. Available from: <http://www.atn.edu.au/docs/Demography_Australias_Academic_Workforce.pdf> [Accessed 27 December 2006].

Krause, K.-L. (2001) The university essay writing experience: a pathway for academic integration during transition. In: *Higher Education Research and Development*, 20, pp. 147–168.

Kuh, G. D. (2001) *The national survey of student engagement: conceptual framework and overview of psychometric properties*. Bloomington, In: Indiana University Center for Postsecondary Research.

Laurillard, D. (1993) *Rethinking university teaching: a framework for the effective use of educational technology*. London: Routledge.

Laurillard, D. (1996) *The changing university.* Available from: <http://itech1.coe.uga.edu/ itforum/paper13/paper13.html> [Accessed 27 November 1997].

Laurillard, D. (2002) *Rethinking university teaching: a framework for the effective use of educational technology.* London: Routledge Palmer.

Limberg, L. (2000) Is there a relationship between information seeking and learning outcomes? In: Bruce, C. & Candy, P. eds.: *Information literacy around the world: advances in programs and research.* Wagga Wagga: Centre for Information Studies Charles Sturt University, pp. 197–208.

Margetson, D. (1996) *Current educational reform and the significance of problem-based learning.* Available from: <http://www.gu.edu.au/gihe/gihe_op/op1_margetson.html> [Accessed 24 November 1996].

Markwell, D. ed. (2003) *Improving teaching and learning in universities: B-HERT NEWS,* Business/Higher Education Round Table, Fitzroy, Victoria.

McInnis, C. (2001) *Signs of disengagement? The changing undergraduate experience in Australian universities,* Centre for the Study of Higher Education. Available from: <http://www.cshe.unimelb.edu.au/downloads/InaugLec23_8_01.pdf> [Accessed 27 December 2006].

McInnis, C., James, R. & Hartley, R. (2000) *Trends in the first year experience in Australian universities.* Centre for the Study of Higher Education, University of Melbourne. Available from: <http://www.detya.gov.au/highered/eippubs/eip00_6/execsum.htm> [Accessed 27 December 2006]

McKenna, S. (1995) *Evaluating interactive multimedia: issues for researchers.* Available from: <http://www.csu.edu.au/division/oli/oli-rd/occpap17/eval.htm> [Accessed 1 September 2006]

McLuhan, M. & Fiore, Q. (1967) *The medium is the massage.* New York: Bantam Books.

Mentkowski, M. (2000) *Learning that lasts: integrating learning, development, and performance in college and beyond.* San Francisco: Jossey-Bass.

Millea, J., Green, I. & Putland, G. (2005) *Emerging technologies: a framework for thinking.* education.au limited. Available from: <http://www.det.act.gov.au/publicat/pdf/emerging technologies.pdf> [Accessed 1 September 2006].

Mutch, A. (2000) Information literacy: a critical realist perspective. In: Bruce, C. & Candy, P eds.: *Information literacy around the world: advances in programs and research.* Wagga Wagga: Centre for Information Studies Charles Sturt University, pp. 153–162.

Oblinger, D.G. & Oblinger, J.L. eds. (2005) Educating the net generation. An Educause e-book, available from: <http://www.educause.edu/ir/library/pdf/pub7101.pdf> [Accessed 27 August 2007].

Oliver, B. (2001) *The effect of web-enhanced and traditional instruction on the information literacy, self-efficacy and transition to university of beginning undergraduates.* Unpublished doctoral thesis, University of Western Australia, Perth.

Oliver, B. (forthcoming) Australian undergraduates' use and ownership of emerging technologies: implications and opportunities for creating engaging learning experiences for the Net Generation. In: *Australian Journal of Educational Technology.*

O'Reilly, T. (2005) *What Is Web 2.0: Design Patterns and Business Models for the Next Generation of Software.* Available from: <http://intervention.ch/rebell.tv/presse/ O'Reilly%20Network_%20What%20Is%20Web%202.pdf> [Accessed 1 September 2006].

Pargetter, R. et al. (1998) *Transition from secondary to tertiary: a performance study.* Department of Education, Training and Youth Affairs. Available from: <http://www.detya. gov.au/archive/highered/eippubs/eip98-20/contents.htm> [Accessed 1 September 2006].

Perry, W.G. (1970) *Forms of ethical and intellectual development in the college years: a scheme.* San Francisco: Jossey-Bass Publishers.

Prensky, M. (2001) Digital Natives, Digital Immigrants. In: *On the Horizon,* 9. NCB University Press, Vol. 9 No. 5, October 2001, pp. 1-6, available from: <http://www. marcprensky.com/writing/Prensky%20-%20Digital%20Natives,%20Digital%20 Immigrants%20-%20Part1.pdf> [Accessed 27 August 2007].

Ramsden, P. (1992) *Learning to teach in higher education.* London: Routledge.

Reed, W.M. (1996) Assessing the impact of computer-based writing instruction. In: *Journal of Research on Computing in Education,* 28, pp. 418–438.

Reed, W.M. et al. (1996) Summary of special issue on assessing the impact of computer-based learning since 1987. In: *Journal of Research on Computing and Education,* 28, pp. 554–556.

Rouet, J.-F. ed. (1996) *Hypertext and cognition.* New Jersey: Laurence Erlbaum Associates.

Scott, G. (2005) *Accessing the student voice: using CEQuery to identify what retains students and promotes engagement in productive learning in Australian higher education,* HEIP. Available from: <http://www.dest.gov.au/sectors/higher_education/publications_resources/ profiles/access_student_voice.htm> [Accessed 1 September 2006].

Shapiro, J.J. & Hughes, S. (1996) *Information literacy as a liberal art: enlightenment proposals for a new curriculum.* Available from: <http://www.educause.edu/pub/er/review/ reviewarticles/31231.html> [Accessed 1 September 2006].

Shulman, M. (1953) Love is a Fallacy. In: *The Many Loves of Dobie Gillis.* Garden City: Garden City Press, available from: <http://www1.asknlearn.com/ri_Ilearning/English/631/ elang-ilearning/page3a.htm> [Accessed 27 August 2007].

Snavely, L. & Cooper, N. (1997) The information literacy debate. In: *Journal of Academic Librarianship,* 23, pp. 9–13.

Snyder, I. ed. (1997) *Page to screen: taking literacy into the electronic era,* St. Leonards: Allen & Unwin.

Spitzer, K.L. et al. (1998) *Information literacy: essential skills for the information age.* Syracuse, NY: ERIC Clearinghouse on Information and Technology.

Studio eLearning Environments (2005) *MicroWiki: a wikiweb of definitions and thoughts on microlearning, microknowledge and related subjects.* Available from: <http://www. microlearning.org/MicroWiki.html> [Accessed 1 September 2006].

Sweany, N.D. et al. (1996) The use of cognitive and metacognitive strategies in a hypermedia environment In: *EdMedia Conference, Boston.* Available from: <http://ccwf.cc.utexas.edu/ ~mcmanus/physics/poster/poster.html> [Accessed 1 September 2006].

Tinkler, D., Lepani, B. and Mitchell, J. (1996) *Education and technology convergence: a survey of technological infrastructure in education and the professional development and support of educators and trainers in information and communication technologies.* Canberra: Australian Government Publishing Service.

Tyner, K. (1998) *Literacy in a digital world: teaching and learning in the age of information.* New Jersey: Lawrence Erlbaum Associates.

Zhao, C.-M. & Kuh, G. D. (2004) Adding value: learning communities and student engagement. In: *Research in Higher Education,* 45, pp. 115–138.

VI Evaluation, Implementation & Quality Management

A Generative Model for the Evaluation of Micro-Learning Processes

Wolfgang Hagleitner & Theo Hug

1 Introduction

Over the past few years, digital educational media and their evaluation have taken on increasing importance in various fields. Before the first e-learning hype, there was a general feeling of techno-euphoria, whereas, meanwhile, many of those responsible for selecting adequate e-learning solutions have come to admit that positive learning results can only be achieved by choosing didactical solutions meeting the individual learner's needs in the particular context. According to Geser (2005, p. 10), "tailor-made solutions – based on the appropriate learning model, without excessive use of technology – will sweep the board", and now we have come to acknowledge that constructivist orientations have helped most to create adaptable learning conditions.

Alongside options favouring multi-perspective, self-determined, situation-oriented, practical and social learning, micro-perspectives of teaching and learning processes have attracted growing attention. On the one hand, new areas of multi-media, multimodal and multi-codal communication are being analysed and implemented (cf. Weidenmann, 2002; Kress, 2003). On the other hand, a wide variety of pocket-sized learning options termed m-learning or microlearning are being developed.[1]

Evaluation of m-learning options is not limited to issues of quality development. It combines aspects of acceptance, market and effect research on a technical, creative and didactical level, depending on the situation and the goal.

The present article introduces a generative model for the evaluation of a microlearning process which, taking into account individual media usage habits, integrates small learning units into the daily working routine and workflow. Even though this model can be put to use in a great variety of areas, we will take a closer look at one special technology, Knowledge Pulse® (referred to as KP in the following), and one practical example of KP evaluation (cf. Hagleitner, Drexler & Hug, 2006).

---

[1] "Micro-teaching" has been an established term in teacher education since the 1960s (cf. Dwight & Ryan, 1969), whereas "microlearning" is a fairly recent creation (cf. Gassler, 2004; Hug, 2005; Gstrein & Hug, 2006; Wikipedia, 2006). Even though the concept of microlearning had already existed long before the appearance of digital media, new phenomena, which have hardly been discussed so far, have emerged. Innsbruck University, among others, has started to undertake research into these areas in a media-pedagogical and cognitive theoretical context, promoting several applications, such as Knowledge Pulse® (KP), which was developed at eLearning Environments (eLe), a studio based in Innsbruck, Austria, of Research Studios Austria at the Austrian Research Centers GmbH, from 2004–2006. The eLE project was supported by the Federal Ministry of Economy and Employment and the Tyrolean Future Foundation. For recent microlearning developments originating from Innsbruck see http://www.hug-web.at.

First of all, we will provide an overview of the basic concept of the generative evaluation model (GEM), linking different perspectives in a methodically controlled way (multi-method triangulation). Subsequently, we will present each of the three central dimensions of GEM, discussing them on the basis of a Venn diagram (cf. chapter 3). Finally, we will look at future chances and evolutionary perspectives of GEM.

2 Towards a Generative Evaluation Model (GEM)

2.1 The Basic Concept of GEM

Micro-learning is a concept that, to date, has hardly been empirically examined. It is due to the steady increase in the use of digital, mostly web-based learning systems – which characteristically consist of the smallest learning units and elements of knowledge – that we are offered the perfect chance to make this concept more tangible and concrete, thus meanwhile establishing the basis to improve current learning models. KP, one of these learning systems that has been put into practice, is a web-based client system which unobtrusively delivers small learning stimuli directly to the learner's mobile phone or PC. In adaptation to the individual usage of the respective medium, the next learning step is made available at the appropriate moment. Presently, KP is largely used in combination with, addition to and preparation for various continuing education courses, mostly in the certification market and continuing medical education.

Comprehensive evaluation of digital learning systems must fulfil the requirements of both market-related research and methodically correct and proper work. To this purpose, a generative evaluation model, which is designed as a mainly formative concept and combines facets of product, market and accompanying empirical research, as well as monitoring and quality management aspects, is being developed, tested and established in the current context. In this case, generative stands for a broad portfolio of data collection instruments that are available at any time, quickly adaptable, but, at the same time, standardised to a certain extent, and divided into modules. In market-related research, they must meet both pragmatic requirements and evaluation standards (Sanders, 2006). The aim is to improve the quality of digital learning systems, including technical, creative and didactical aspects. Figure 1 gives you an idea of which quality aspects can be of significance for quality management and evaluation during the lifetime of a digital learning system. However, as shown in the graph, we also need to integrate group and person-specific perspectives (of experts, users and administrators) as well as evaluation approaches based on criteria, theory and legal perspectives. Administrators, for instance, are interested in simple content administration, whereas experts attach greater importance to technical quality, simple dialogue design, attractive layout, drop-out rates, internal differentiation and gender-neutral content. For users, user-friendly handling, accessibility and a harmonious colour design are of primary importance. Naturally, group-specific interests overlap in various fields. Accessibility, for instance, must be viewed from the user, criteria and legal perspectives, while the user and theory perspectives are more important for the integration of constructivist elements. Of course, GEM cannot and is not meant to fulfil all these expectations. Measuring and ensuring return on investment (ROI summarized under "cost-benefit analysis"), in particular, has grown into a proper science, which has developed its own situation-specific concepts, some of which are highly complex. Nevertheless, GEM is meant to remain adaptable to specific needs through its generative design. At the moment, GEM still represents a form of self-evaluation, yet in the middle term it will also form the basis for external evaluation. Besides, it primarily aims to serve the purposes of process evaluation, rather than product or summative evaluation, which will only gain significance towards the end of the development stage during effect analyses. After all, GEM optimises not only quality management, but also the study and description of microlearning.

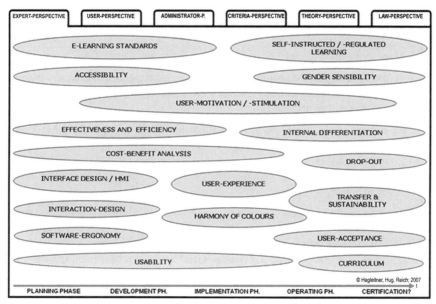

Figure 1. Quality aspects that can be of significance for evaluation during the lifetime of a digital learning system.

2.2 Method Triangulation Based on the Convergence and/or the Complementary Model

Dealing with empirical phenomena which, so far, remain relatively unexplored, we need to establish adequate means of operationalization and methodical approaches. In the present case, this task is even more difficult, as both microlearning and the evaluation of online-based teaching and learning systems rest on weak empirical foundations. Consequently, it is even more important to adopt a cautious approach, which, on the one hand, takes into account the novelty of the subject and does not limit a priori the theoretical length, width and depth of a concept but, on the contrary, acknowledges its diversity and multidimensionality. On the other hand, it must allow the construction of hypotheses, as well as the combination of established methods employed in the social and education sciences in a convergent and complementary way.

In the late '50s, Campbell and Fiske (1959) recommended combining different measuring instruments in order to determine the degree of measurement consistency (discriminant analysis) with various methods and concept validity of psychological test results (multitrait multimethod). Webb (1996) was the first to adopt the term triangulation, which was originally used in land surveys and navigation, for social sciences. Denzin (1989) established and specified the term in the context of qualitative research. He (1970) distinguishes between

a) data triangulation, demonstrating the diversity of social phenomena and social reality,

b) observer triangulation, reducing inaccuracies caused by one-sided observations,

c) theory triangulation, helping to investigate social phenomena on the basis of different theories so as to construct hypotheses, falsify and, if necessary, create theoretical networks, and

d) method triangulation, which is further divided into the within-method, i.e. triangulation within the method by combining different evaluation procedures for one set of data, for example, and the across-method, i.e. triangulation between methods by combining different methods employed for the exploration of an empirical object.

This method aims to "combine different methodologies in the study of one phenomenon" (Denzin, 1978, p. 291; quoted after Flick, 1995, p. 432). It is, above all, capable of "linking different perspectives and looking at all aspects of the subject at hand" (Flick, 1991, p. 433). In this context, GEM is a means of method triangulation, thus helping to provide the theoretical foundation of microlearning as a concept. In other words, different methods are adopted to show different aspects of one (supposed) reality – microlearning, in this case – to be part 'not of a holistic, but a kaleidoscopic picture' (Köckeis-Stangl, 1980, p. 363).

The introduction of this apparently simple method brings about far-reaching consequences. Different methods generate data that can be congruent/convergent, complementary or contradictory to each other. For lack of a theoretical framework, it is becoming increasingly difficult to make definitive statements or, even less, predictions (cf. Prein; Kelle & Kluge, 1993, p. 24, p. 57). Therefore, our model must be defined and adapted in accordance with the circumstances surrounding each situation, and the problems and questions raised in the particular case. It has also been made clear that this method does not necessarily help to increase validity (cf. Fielding & Fielding, 1986). To this purpose, 'the various data pools must specifically be combined and connected with each other' (Jakob, 2001). Basically, we can distinguish between three models trying to integrate quantitative and qualitative approaches (source: Prein, Kelle & Kluge, 1993, p. 9):

— "The *stage model of method integration*, according to which the validity of qualitative results is generally much more questionable than of quantitative results. Qualitative procedures should, therefore, be adopted to formulate hypotheses, whereas quantitative procedures should help to verify hypotheses. These two methods should follow each other in a chronological order: the qualitative preliminary study is carried out before the quantitative investigation.

— the *convergence model* of triangulation, which was developed by qualitative methodologies, also tries to reinforce qualitative and quantitative results by using them for mutual validation. However, unlike the stage model, the convergence model assumes that results for both methods are virtually equal in terms of validity and reliability.

— the *complementary model*, which is based on the presumption that qualitative and quantitative methods apply to different fields of investigation. As a consequence, the results of qualitative and quantitative investigations cannot be used for mutual validation, but may complement each other in a specific way."

A convergence model, such as the multitrait-method (MTMM), can assess both convergent and discriminant validity, since it measures the subject in question with the help of different methods. The complementary model, in contrast, enables us to link different perspectives and look at all perspectives of the subject at hand, which will 'present' itself in the way it is constituted by each method (Flick, 1991, p. 433).

We could continue the methodological discussion about the relation between qualitative and quantitative research (cf. Heinze, 2001; Sale et al., 2002) to further include aspects of epistemology (cf. Goodman, 1978) and model theory (cf. Stachowiak, 1973). In evaluation research, it is common practice to combine elements that are linked with different perspectives and observing modalities (cf. Datta, 1997; Stone et al., 2005, pp. 540ff). GEM employs these models, according to the subject at hand, in an eclectic way. The stage model of method integration, for instance, is used for an in-depth investigation of the microlearning concept. When comparing the learner's subjective perception of his/her quantitative learning performance as opposed to an objective assessment, however, GEM applies the complementary model.

3 Dimensions of GEM

3.1 Qualitative Enquiry

In this context, the qualitative enquiry may be[2] described as an inductive, holistic, explorative, comprehending and describing form of investigation assessing subjective and inter-subjective connections and individual experiences (cf. Lamnek, 1993, p. 244; cf. Spöhring, 1989, pp. 98ff). Even though all three approaches are of equal status, we will look at the qualitative method first, not by coincidence but because it can produce results where the other two approaches fail and which they rely upon, after all. This is the case, for example, when the goal is

a) to show subjective attitudes, impressions, manners of behaviour, perspectives, individual life stages and person-specific backgrounds,

b) to formulate hypotheses that can be verified with the help of resource-saving means, or

c) to back up quantitative results that have provided contradictory data or unsubstantial or uninterpretable results.

The qualitative approach is a time-consuming but indispensable method when trying to understand user perceptions and behaviour patterns as far as individual learning biographies and habits, the usage and perception of (educational) media and personal reasons for participating in further education courses are concerned. The key factors affecting the acceptance of a learning system are most learners' increasing dislike of highly technological solutions (cf. Geser, 2005, p. 10) as well as person-specific tendencies, such as learning types and styles. This raises a number of relevant questions: What are learners' experiences with regard to continuing education? What is the role of digital educational media? How can people's perception of (highly technological) digital learning applications be described? Which learning types do learners ascribe to themselves, and which learning style do learners prefer under which learning conditions?

As indicated above, another focus is on the exploration of microlearning and integrated microlearning. To what extent have the integration of these methods and their incorporation into every-day life proven themselves of value? Do learners – in the case of KP – feel supported, encouraged and motivated by push technologies, or rather obstructed, impeded and annoyed? Do they feel that their ability to memorize facts is enhanced by the mathematical algorithm of the card sequences based on Sebastian Leitner's flash card system? Would different card sequences – if presentation frequency would be in-/decreased, for example (figure 2, model 1 or 3), or occur at regular intervals (figure 2, model 2) – be more efficient? Do learners get the subjective impression that they have learned more in a shorter period of time? What comparison

---

2 "Rather" because the characterisation of the contrasts between quantitative and qualitative methods is "bipolar," not "dichotomous" (cf. Bortz & Döring, 2003 p. 298).

can be drawn to learning methods that are similar at the didactical, technical and integrative level, systems that are created differently and typical e-learning solutions?

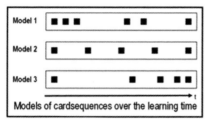

Figure 2. Models of cardsequences

The study entitled "Evaluation of a prototypic version of Knowledge Pulse in the context of a management course" (Hagleitner, Drexler & Hug, 2006) was based on a largely qualitative approach. On the basis of its results, hypotheses were formed and tested with the help of an online-questionnaire employing the qualitative method. The purpose of the questions being of an explorative nature, participants were asked, for example, in which way they used KP and to what extent their learning success was enhanced by using the mobile version of KP. Verbal comments were divided into different categories, according to learners' potential reasons for using KP (1. for learning; 2. for self-evaluation; 3. to practise the handling; 4. gaming aspects; 5. other reasons). These were then quantified in the framework of the questionnaire. The result showed that all participants used KP for learning and self-evaluation, some also for other reasons (figure 3).

Category	Frequences*	%-Rate / Persons*
Learning	8	57,1%
Self-Evaluation	6	42,9%
Other Reasons	3	21,4%
Gaming Aspect	2	14,3%
Practise Handling	1	7,1%
Total	**20**	**142,9%**

*Multiple Response / N = 14

Figure 3. Reasons for using KP

3.2   Quantitative Enquiry

In contrast to the qualitative approach, the quantitative method rather corresponds to the deductive, particular and explanatory approach, which helps to quantify, measure, explain, and make predictions as to the possible degree of learning success, transfer, sustainability and retentivity. This approach is primarily used for:

a) analyses, prognoses and statistical evaluations,

b) hypotheses testings,

c) the formulation of first models of integrated microlearning,

d) effective and efficient diagnoses and analyses of negative aspects in design, and identification of positive aspects and potential capacities that can be used for advertising purposes (accessibility), and

e) the creation of a database for long-term meta-analyses and comparative studies.

Here, a newly adapted method of investigation, which has already been adopted for a master's thesis, is employed (Hagleitner, 2005). Each aspect, referred to as "scales" in GEM (e.g. "font," Figure 4), is first evaluated with the help of a global item (e.g., "I like the font and characters …). If evaluation results are bad, a more differentiated set of questions (additive items) (e.g., Additive item 01: "Line spacing enhances legibility"; Item 02: "Font tracking reduces legibility"; Item 03: "…") and/or one or more container items (Container item 01: "Font: size, type, thickness, width and height of font enhances legibility") are formulated for the next questionnaire. In this manner, the problem can be approached, identified and solved. This method also makes use of the qualitative approach, since every scale also provides the possibility to write down other ideas and additional comments, which otherwise would not be taken into account.

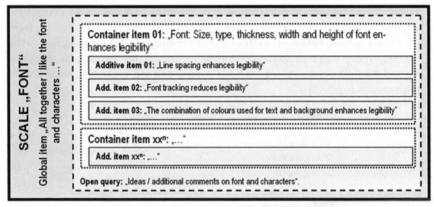

Figure 4. Basic model for the quantitative approach of GEM

At the same time, this approach offers several possible ways of implementing quality factors. The additive items may generally be treated like scales, including the use of all adequate statistical options (reliability, test power, etc.). With the aid of variance and regression analyses, the additive and container items, as independent variables (predictors), and the global item, as a dependent variable (criterion), serve as an indicator for concept validity and highly reliable predictors for user satisfaction. If you add the additive and/or container items to get a common average value[3] or a second global item, the two global items correlate, supplying additional information about further aspects of reliability and validity. The core items are used more frequently, creating a

---

3   Possible, for example, in SPSS using the syntax command "mean.^{n}(x^1, x^1, x^n, ...)"

database which provides the basis for firm statements and comparative studies. Marginal items bear little relevance and are only used in certain cases. There are several points of interest, such as screen design, user interface, usability, accessibility, software ergonomics, colour harmony and overall satisfaction with applications. Various studies on aspects of accessibility and colour harmony, for example, have been carried out lately. They showed that many users strongly criticized the combination of font and background colour (rating scale 1-7 [1=best rate], Average rating = 6.0). A contrast analysis proved that brightness and contrast were far below the recommenddations given by W3C. Besides, legibility was strongly limited for colour-blind people (Hagleitner, 2006).

3.3 Login Statistics

As opposed to interviews and written questionnaires, log file analyses are a "nonreactive, technology-based form of online-monitoring", which enable the evaluation of the learning activity at the indicator level. In this way, formative and design-oriented ways of evaluation can be carried out, helping to identify dropout problems, for instance (Wienold, p. 91), which in turn can be analysed more closely with the help of further interviews. Apart from that, log file analyses help to identify and quantify false estimations and memories at the end of a continuing education course (cf. Berker, 2003). In the current context, log file analyses will be carried out in order to:

a) reduce the duration of the other two procedures for users,

b) validate the data obtained from the quantitative and qualitative procedures,

c) enable users to access the statistics about their own learning progress,

d) establish user profiles,

e) compare subjective evaluations of users to the factual data, and

f) receive information on the technical and/or didactical quality of the flash card system.

To this purpose, clearly defined user activities must be recorded and saved, which requires a certain amount of extra programming. Log files, like the other two approaches, have certain limits. They serve as indicators that allow one to draw conclusions that are valid to a certain extent, providing information about invisible procedures, but not about usage quality, alertness, learning quality, learning behaviour or retentivity (cf. Wienold, p. 90).

KP's most distinct feature is that it delivers small learning stimuli directly to the learner's mobile phone or PC in accordance with personal learning habits and settings. Every now and then – depending on each user's individual learning achievements – clients can change their cards via the Internet, thus creating a base of their own interconnected and anonymized data on the server, which will remain available for download and further processing in the form of statistical reports. Furthermore, every user will be able to access a selection of statistics from their personal account. This is some of the information that can be obtained about each user in this manner:

- the date and time of the user's last request[4],
- the total number of client logins, with or without request,
- the average number of client logins per second, day, week, etc.,
- the average duration of a learning unit measured in seconds,
- the average number of learning units completed per hour, day, week, etc.,
- the total number of all positive/negative learning units, etc.

At present, only the simplified version of this statistical model is available. Its significance already became clear in the course of a login analysis and can be illustrated as follows: The model and the weekly report presently register the number of logins that have occurred in the past seven days/since the beginning of the course, and each user's learning progress in percentage terms. Figure 5 shows the number of logins of each user over five weeks. The bold, dashed line and the corresponding numbers stand for the average value, which shows a continuous increase in logins over five weeks, thus indicating learning activity and learning progress. Figure 6 shows each user's learning progress, which is calculated with the aid of a mathematical algorithm, in percentage terms. As opposed to figure 5, a steady decline in learning progress can be seen over the same period of time. In practice, this means that users made active use of the learning programme, but experienced negative learning results as soon as they stopped using the programme for a couple of days. The problem was caused by an incorrect SQL statement.

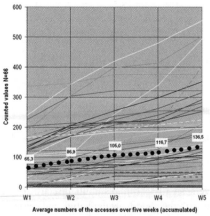

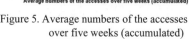

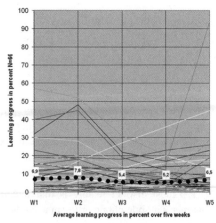

Figure 5. Average numbers of the accesses over five weeks (accumulated)

Figure 6. Average learning progress over five weeks

---

4   "Request" in this case stands for the client's automatic connection with the server and the exchange of data or the request of new learning cards.

Log files will also be used to quantify requests, learning units and learning durations per learning day and hour of all users participating in a certain course. Figure 7 employs an imaginary scenario to show how the data could be displayed. Let us take a look at the "marketing basics" course, for instance, where 43 participants are preparing to pass the final exam with the help of KP. The table contains three dimensions (D1, D2, D3): Dimension 1 shows the number of requests, dimension 2 the number of learning steps and dimension 3 the "time on task." The y-axis measures these three dimensions within the 24 hours of the day, whereas the x-axis does the same for each course day. The z-axis quantifies the data of all three dimensions, achieving visu-alisation through colour coding: the darker the colour, the higher the corresponding value. Of course, this form of visualisation may equally be substituted by real data, which would make more sense for smaller amounts of data or user-specific feedback. These data help to establish how microlearning is integrated into the daily routine, in other words at what times of the day, how often and how long learning activities occur. They also show whether users learn more at the end of a course than at the beginning, which, among other things, is indicative of the way in which this learning system is used. Finally, the data can be compared to test and exam results, current living circumstances and demographic and socio-graphic background information of learners. This information helps us to understand how learning card sequences can be optimised in didactical terms so as to improve the transfer to long-term memory. The data obtained from log files cannot be interpreted unequivocally, either. If necessary, they must, therefore, be further analysed in a multi-dimensional approach with the help of other methods of data evaluation. Of course, all procedures must comply with the current data protection legislation.

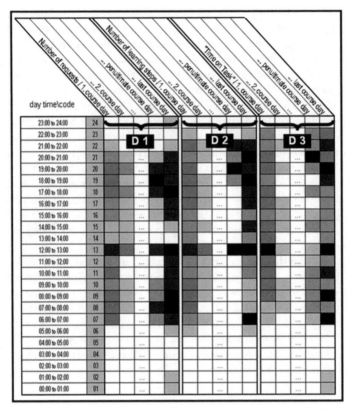

Figure 7. Quantification of requests, learning steps and "time on task"

3.4   Interfaces

Positioning the evaluation model described above including the methods of data evaluation involved, we are fully aware of the fact that there are certain grey areas and interfaces. The interfaces consist of clearly defined subjects that have to be evaluated with the help of two or three methods. The qualitative and the quantitative approach, in particular, cannot be clearly separated. Quantifications, for example, can also be given by participants of interviews and online questionnaires when asked about their sub-jective impression of their personal learning progress, for instance. In this context, participants are asked about the relation between the time spent learning and the amount and quality of what they learnt (cost-profit-estimation). Furthermore, they are asked how many times, on average, they had to learn each card, according to their subjective feeling, until the information was committed to long-term memory, and how many learning units they had gone through per day. Comparing user estimations and login data allows us to draw certain conclusions about how microlearning works and how learning units can be integrated into every-day life. If, for example, the number of daily learning units estimated by learners lies below the number of units recorded through the login data, this could indicate that the hypothetical concept of "casual learning" actually works and can easily be integrated into the daily routine, learning does not feel like a burden, and, according to learners' subjective impression, they spend less time learning than they actually do. Users may, as well, not perceive any advantage compared with other learning systems. The comparison between learners' estimations and the actual login data could be the basis for further hypotheses, which might result in the modification of card sequences, for example, as shown in figure 2.

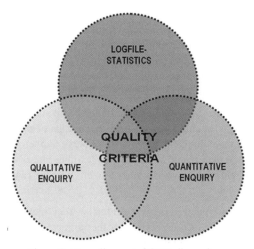

Figure 8: Venn diagram of GEM dimensions

Triangulation is mainly used in method research, where discrepancies in measuring results lead to further attempts at improving investigation methods. This strategy "may serve as a heuristic in the formulation of hypotheses: the method specifically aims to find discrepancies, which will then be accredited, by way of interpretation, with certain features of the subject of the investigation (not the method)" (Bortz & Döring, 2003, p. 370). Discrepancies between results are also likely to occur with GEM, or even desired, within the interfaces between the three methodical approaches. They are the source and origin of new hypotheses and findings, which will eventually lead to a multi-dimensional picture of the microlearning concept. Last, but not least, these interfaces also promote mutual validation of investigation results, as explained under 2.2.

4   Outlook

There are numerous novel systems of learning and information management, some of them even mobile, that are currently being developed or have already been launched on the market. KP, which we have introduced to you as just one example of new learning applications, distinguishes itself through the unobtrusive push and the delay in access. In addition, KP features a modified version of Sebastian Leitner's flashcard system and integrates a number of small learning units into the daily routine and workflow. In this context, microlearning, in particular, offers enormous potential, which, with regard to possible practical user applications, we will try to exploit to a maximum extent by adopting a multi-perspective approach. In order to confirm this well-founded and sophisticated theory, we are now facing the challenge to empirically prove the practicability of the pedagogical/didactical scenarios presented. Evaluation models, such as GEM, are of considerable use in this context.

Over time, it will be our task to differentiate the three methodical approaches provided by GEM and optimise quality performance. Programming log files, as shown in figure 7, will also have to be further developed. However, GEM can already be put to efficient use with other approaches of digital learning, like mobile or game-based learning. Thanks to the generative nature of GEM and the range of instruments used, the necessary adaptations do not require much effort.

The risk of records related to certain user activities being abused is particularly high. On the one hand, log files could be exploited as a means of technicistic control and surveillance, but, on the other hand, they may also serve to overcome rationalistic orientations of ordinance with regard to democratic learning processes. What Chelimsky & Shadish (1997) said about evaluation in the 21st century can also be applied to GEM:

"Finally, evaluators, in whatever field of evaluation they may be, are likely to find themselves, at least sometimes, at odds with the political actors, systems, and processes in their countries that militate against the free flow of information required by evaluation. This means that as the world becomes more politically diverse and complex in the 21st century, evaluators will be called upon to exhibit considerable courage in the normal pursuit of their work." (Chelimsky & Shadish 1997, p. xiii)

Computer aided evaluation methods tend to sharpen distinctions: They either obscure facts and contexts, and they hinder the free flow of information, or they promote enlightenment, refinement and transparency.

It is, therefore, each evaluator's responsibility to maintain flexibility, a certain degree of method diversity, diligence, as well as the capacity of ethnic reflection, and demonstrate the ability to find the right balance between contradictory demands (cf. Gastager & Patry, 2006). In addition, the evaluator must meet high standards of character. It is often hard to predict the outcome and "undesired side-effects" of evaluation as well as the way in which results may be ab-/used in certain cases, which makes it even more important to remain aware of these dangers. To this purpose, evaluators should seek to reach the standards set by the Joint Committee on Standards for Educational Evaluation (Sanders, 2006), for instance. If they succeed, evaluation research is as demanding a field of research as any other science.

References

Berker, T. (2003) *In Protokolldaten geronnenes Nutzerverhalten.* Available from: <http://infosoc.uni-koeln.de/girlws/abstracts/sa_08.html> [Accessed 8 July 2007].

Bortz, J. & Döring, N. (2003) *Forschungsmethoden und Evaluation für Human und Sozialwissenschaftler.* 3. überarbeitete Auflage.Berlin, Heidelberg, New York: Springer-Verlag.

Campbell, D.T. & Fiske, D.W. (1959) Convergent and discriminant validation by the multitrait-multimethod matrix. *Psychological Bulletin*, 56, (2), March, pp. 81–105.

Chelimsky, E. & Shadish, W. R. eds. (1997) Preface. In: *Evaluation for the 21st Century: A Handbook.* London et al.: Sage Publications, pp. xi-xiii.

Datte, L.-E. (1997) Multimethod Evaluations. Using Case Studies Together with Methods. In: Chelimsky, E. & Shadish, W. R. eds. *Evaluation for the 21st Century: A Handbook.* London et al.: Sage Publications, pp. 344–359.

Denzin, N. K. (1970) *The Research Act in Sociology. A Theoretical Introduction to Sociological Methods.* Chicago: Aldine.

Denzin, N.K. (1989) *The Research Act; A Theoretical Introduction to Sociological Methods.* New Jersey : Prentice-Hall, Inc. (3. Ed.), pp. 234–247.

Dwight, A. & Ryan, K. (1969) *Microteaching.* Reading, Mass.: Addison-Wesley.

Ehlers, U.-D., Schenkel, P. (2005) Bildungskontrolling im E-Learning – Eine Einführung. In: Ehlers, U.-D. & Schenkel, P. (Hrsg): *Bildungskontrolling im E-Learning: Erfolgreiche Strategien und Erfahrungen jenseits des ROI.* Berlin Heidelberg New York: Springer, pp. 1–13.

Fielding, N.G. & Fielding, J.L. (1986) *Linking Data. Qualitative Research Methods*, Vol. 4. London: Sage.

Flick, U. (1991) Triangulation. In: Flick, U., Kardoff, E. v., Keupp, H., Rosenstiel, L. v. & Stephan Wolff, S. (Hrsg.). *Handbuch qualitative Sozialforschung.* Munich: Psychologie Verlags Union, pp. 432–434.

Gassler, G. (2004) *Integriertes Mikrolernen.* MPhil. thesis, University of Innsbruck (Austria).

Gassler, G., Hug, T. & Glahn, C. (2004) Integrated Micro Learning – an outline of the basic method and first results. In: Auer, M. E. & Auer, U. eds.: *International Conference on Interactive Computer Aided Learning*, ICL 2004, Sept. 29 – Oct. 1, 2004, Villach, Austria (CD-ROM).

Gastager, A. & Patry, J-L. (2006) 'Allen Leuten recht getan ...'. Widersprüchliche Anforderungen an Evaluatorinnen und Evaluatoren. In: Böttcher, W., Holtappels, H.G., Brohm, M. (Hrsg.) *Evaluation im Bildungswesen. Eine Einführung in Grundlagen und Praxisbeispiele.* Weinheim and Munich: Juventa, pp. 109–121.

Geser, G. (2005) *Zentrumsprojekt Digital Content Engineering, F&E- und Marktoptionen, Studienergebnisse Teil IV, Trendradar: E-Learning.* Salzburg: NewMediaLab, Kompetenzzentrum für Neue Medien. Available from: <pp.newmedialab.at/fsDownload/ dce-studie_iv_trendradar_elearning_050226.pdf?forumid=275&v=1&id=310684>_[Accessed 8 July 2007].

Goodman, N. (1978) *Ways of Worldmaking.* Indianapolis: Hackett Publishing Company.

Gstrein, S. & Hug, T. (2006) Integrated micro learning during access delays: a new approach to second-language learning. In: Zaphiris, Panayiotis ed. *User-Centered Computer Aided Language Learning.* Hershey/PA: Idea Group Publishing, pp. 152–175.

Hagleitner, W. (2005) *Evaluation des Semoki-Klubs, ein außerschulisches Enrichment-Programm für begabte Kinder und Jugendliche.* (Unpublished thesis, University of Salzburg).

Hagleitner, W. (2006) Qualitätsbeurteilung des Screen Designs der PV-Version des Knowledge Pulse®, Teil 1. Research Studios Austria, eLearning Environments. (Unpublished work, Innsbruck, Austria).

Hagleitner, W., Drexler, A. & Hug, T. (2006) *Evaluation of a prototypic version of Knowledge Pulse in the context of a management course.* Paper presented at the MapEC (Multimedia Applications in Education Conference) 2006, September 4-6, FH Joanneum, Graz, Austria.

Heinze, T. (2001) *Qualitative Sozialforschung. Einführung, Methodologie und Forschungspraxis.* Verlag Munich Vienna: R. Oldenbourg, pp. 28–36.

Hug, T. (2005) *Micro learning and narration – exploring possibilities of utilization of narrations and storytelling for the designing of "micro units" and didactical micro-learning arrangements.* Paper presented at the fourth Media in Transition conference, May 6-8, 2005, MIT, Cambridge (MA), USA, p. 5.

Jakob, A. (2001, February) *Möglichkeiten und Grenzen der Triangulation quantitativer und qualitativer Daten am Beispiel der (Re-) Konstruktion einer Typologie erwerbsbiographischer Sicherheitskonzepte* [69 Absätze]. *Forum: Qualitative Social Research* [Online Journal], 2(1). Available from: <http://www.qualitative-research.net/fqs-texte/1-01/1-01jakob-d.htm> [Accessed 8 July 2007]

Kerres, M. & de Witt, C. (2004) Pragmatismus als theoretische Grundlagen für die Konzeption von eLearning. In: Meyer, H. O. & Treichel, D. (Hrsg.), *Handlungsorientiertes Lernen und eLearning. Grundlagen und Beispiele.* Munich: Oldenbourg, pp. 68–87.

Köckeis-Stangl, E. (1980) Methoden der Sozialisationsforschung. In: Hurrelmann, K. & Ulich, D. (Hg.). *Handbuch der Sozialisationsforschung.* Weinheim, Basel: Beltz, p. 363.

Kress, Gunther (2003) *Literacy in the New Media Age.* New York: Routledge

Lamnek, S. (1993) *Qualitative Sozialforschung. Band 1: Methodologie.* Weinheim: Psychologie Verlags Union, p. 244.

LERNET-Begleitforschung (MMB Institut für Medien- und Kompetenzforschung und Adolf Grimme Institut) (2003): *Zehn aktuelle Trends des E-Learning in der beruflichen Weiterbildung.* Available from: <http://www.uni-oldenburg.de/multimedia/aktuelles/10eLearningTrends.pdf> [Accessed 8 July 2007].

Prein, G., Kelle, U. & Kluge, S. (1993) *Strategien zur Integration quantitativer und qualitativer Auswertungsverfahren.* Arbeitspapier 19 des SFB 186, Universität Bremen. Available from: <http://www.sfb186.uni-bremen.de/download/paper19.pdf> [Accessed 8 July 2007].

Sale, J.E.M., Lohfeld. L.H. & Brazil, K. (2002) Revisiting the quantitative-qualitative debate:implications for mixed-methods research. In: *Quality & Quantity*, 36, pp. 43–53.

Sanders, J.-R. (2006) *Handbuch der Evaluationsstandards –Die Standards des "Joint Committee on Standards for Educational Evaluation"* (3. Auflage). Wiesbaden :VS Verlag für Sozialwissenschaften/GWV Fachverlag GmbH.

Schenkel, P., Tergan, S.-O. & Lottmann, A. (2000) *Qualitätsbeurteilung multimedialer Lern- und Informationssysteme: Evaluationsmethoden auf dem Prüfstand.* Nürnberg: BW Bildung und Wissen Verlag und Software GmbH, p. 5.

Schneeberger, A. & Mayr, T. (2004) *Berufliche Weiterbildung in Österreich und im europäischen Vergleich: Forschungsbericht im Auftrag des Bundesministeriums für Wirtschaft und Arbeit.* Vienna: IBW – Institut für Bildungsforschung der Wirtschaft (foreword).

Spöhring, W. (1989) *Qualitative Sozialforschung.* Stuttgart: Teubner, pp. 98ff.

Stachowiak, H. (1973) *Allgemeine Modelltheorie.* Wien/New York: Springer.

Stangl, W. (2006) [werner.stangl]s arbeitsblätter: *Hyperlearning, Hypermedia, Hypertext.* Available from: <http://www.stangl-taller.at/ARBEITSBLAETTER/LERNEN/Hypertext lernen.shtml> [Accessed 8 July 2007].

Stone, D., Jarrett, C., Woodroffe, M. & Minocha, S. (2005). *User Interface Design and Evaluation.* San Francisco: Morgan Kaufmann.

Webb, E.J. et al. (1966) *Nonreactive Measures in the Social Sciences.* Chicago: Rand McNally.

Weidenmann, B. (2002) Multicodierung und Multimodalität im Lernprozess. In: Issing, L.J. & Klimsa, P. (Hrsg.): *Information und Lernen mit Multimedia und Internet: Lehrbuch für Studium und Praxis.* 3. Auflage. Weinheim: Psychologie Verlags Union, Verlagsgruppe Beltz, pp. 45–62.

Wikipedia – The Free Encyclopedia (2007) *Microlearning.* Available from: <http://en.-wikipedia.org/wiki/Microlearning> [Accessed 8 July 2007].

Quality Management for the Implementation of E-Learning

Susanne Kinnebrock, Berit Baeßler & Patrick Rössler

Abstract

This article focuses on the organizational dimensions of e-learning by merging the concept of quality management and the process of implementation. We suggest a circular model of eight phases to structure the whole process of developing, producing and implementing e-learning systems in public institutions.

Our circular model connects processes on different levels: during the initial phase of analyzing resources, priority is set to macro level objectives. Phases of course development and implementation are mainly to be placed on a meso level. While developing and implementing web-based instruction, however, knowledge about microlearning processes and their didactic support has to be taken into account. Moreover, evaluations that complete every phase of implementation refer to microlearning processes, because data is mostly collected on a micro level. This micro level data is mainly used to modify the process of further development and implementation, which means that it is applied to meso- or even macro-level problems.

1   Introduction

In spite of the continuous growth in the virtualization of teaching in the past decade, the e-learning euphoria of the first years has vanished. The initial phase in which diverse support programs boosted the exponential growth of e-learning offerings at universities appears to be completed worldwide and replaced by the so-called "Trumble-Back"-phase. Failed projects, and the insight that the implementation of e-learning does not automatically lead to improvements in the learning and teaching process, have slowed down the initial enthusiasm. Thereby, the view shifted onto e-learning being successfully and sustainable implemented only if projects are not based on isolated, single initiatives. Rather, it requires an active and coordinated support by educational institutions with all their organizational units, which have to perform an *"organizational cultural change"* (Ehlers, 2006, p. 37). It seems, however, that this change has not yet taken place. At least the OECD report on e-learning stated that internationally we are still deeply located in the "Trumble-Back"-phase (Garrett, 2005). In the third and last phase, the so-called "Re-Birth"-phase, gained experiences are reflected on, e-learning projects are redesigned according to guidelines of a strict quality management, and, above all, they are incorporated into the respective educational institution. Yet, only a few single educational institutions appear to have entered this phase so far (Ehlers, 2006, p. 37).

This article addresses precisely the transition between the "Trumble Back"- and "Re-Birth"-phase and shows how effective quality management can assist the sustainable implementation of Internet-based e-learning or web-learning. Both theoretically-conceptual considerations and first experiences that were made at the University of Erfurt during the implementation and evaluation of a web-based learning environment are made accessible.[1] In detail – starting from the characteristics and potentials of web-learning – a model of the process of implementation is developed, whose basis is composed of both pedagogical research results and quality management strategies. This process of implementation will also be discussed against the background of a new perspective on web-based e-learning, i.e. microlearning.

2 Basic Concepts

E-Learning, Web-Learning, Microlearning

Basically, web-learning means the acquisition of knowledge and behaviours within the framework of web-based instruction. Web-based instruction, in turn, is defined as a hypermedia-based teaching program, which uses the characteristics and offerings of the world wide web to create a meaningful learning environment, in which learning is encouraged and facilitated (Astleitner, 2002, in reference to Abbey, 2000 and Horton, 2000). The terms web-learning and e-learning are often used interchangeably, although the generic term 'e-learning' subsumes the exposure to both offline computer-based and web-based learning programs.

Web-learning requires the existence of networked workstations. Thus, web-based learning environments are not only – like traditional courseware – highly *modularized*, *multimedia-based*, and *machine-interactive*, but also *human-interactive*[2] (i.e. learners can interact with each other, or with a human tutor, and thereby use the synchronous and asynchronous communication opportunities of the WWW, e.g., chats, video conferences, e-mails, discussion forums, etc.), *human- and computer-controlled* (i.e. learning is not only guided by the courseware, but also by human tutors), and *open*

---

1   More precisely we are talking about the Internet-based learning system CLIC (Computer-based Learning in Communications), that has been developed at the University of Erfurt. So far, it consists of an authoring system (for course development and administration), a communication platform (for the interaction between students and instructors via Internet), and of a learning interface for students, that can be used both online and from CD-ROM. Up to now, two courses have been developed in Erfurt, a comprehensive "Introduction to Communication Science" and an "Introduction to Scientific Research," which is more strongly based on the principles of blended learning. Both courses are incorporated into the communication science curriculum at the University of Erfurt as central required first semester courses. More information is available at www.clic-online.de.
     For the sustainable implementation of the learning system CLIC, an Eight-Phase-Model has been developed simultaneously. It has already been introduced – although with a focus on the specifics of communications teaching (Kinnebrock & Baeßler, 2004).

2   The differentiation between machine-interactive and human-interactive is borrowed from Gerpott & Schlegel (2000, pp. 349-50).

(i.e. students have the possibility to move outside of their immediate learning environment and use other sources of information from the WWW). In contrast to a merely computer-based learning system, web-based learning environments are furthermore characterized by a greater *content-related flexibility*. Learning contents can be centrally (by a tutor) modified, updated or adjusted to the learning capacities of the students. However, it is common again to both web- and computer based learning environments that they can be used *independent of time and place*. Learning can take place in a self-regulated way, i.e. at a self-chosen place, at any time and at the respective adequate learning pace (Astleitner, 2000, p. 17).

A perspective on e-learning under networking conditions that has lately received substantial attention can be described with the term 'microlearning.' Even though this term has not yet been clearly outlined, it is becoming apparent that it represents comparatively short-lasting, in daily routines (subtly) embedded learning processes, which are initiated by highly modularized contents (also called micro content) (Hug, 2005, pp. 2-8). Unlike web-learning, whose learning processes and learning materials can be located equally on a macro level (e.g., as curricula or an entire course), on a meso level (e.g., as lessons or topics), and on a micro level (as a singular learning matter), microlearning focuses on the interaction between learner and highly modularized contents, whose technical distribution can not only be carried out by Internet-capable PCs, but also – and that differentiates microlearning from traditional web-learning – by mobile end devices like cell phones.

Should the potentials of web-learning, and its subform, microlearning, be used for teaching in universities; should thus high quality learning environments emerge, that initiate efficient learning processes – then the question emerges of what quality with regard to learning environments means, and how it can be ensured.

Quality

In everyday speech, the term "quality" describes the "property," the "excellence," or the "value" of an object (cp. Bruhn, 2003, p. 27). It would, however, be too narrow to define quality as being merely product-oriented within the realms of web-learning – namely as the property of a courseware – and in the process to apply established product standards, that are most often defined by producers or instructors.[3] Since learning environments are developed for students, it is useful to complement the product-related definition of quality with a consumer-related one. This perception, rooted in business marketing studies (e.g., Bruhn 2003, p. 29-30), has, in the meantime, expanded to pedagogical research, which deals with the various forms of e-learning (e.g., Astleitner, 2002; Carstensen, 2006; Astleitner, 2006; Ehlers, 2006). Carstensen even talks about a *"paradigm shift from teaching towards learning"* (2006, p. 13). Expec-

---

3   A summary of the central quality criteria for web-based learning can be found in Astleitner & Sindler (1999, pp. 121-38), a summary of principles of good teaching in Astleitner (2005).

tations that students have of teaching or web-based learning environments, their perception of the provided learning offerings, and finally, their evaluation of the initiated learning process should equally be considered. *"Quality in the context of e-learning is a co production between the learner and the learning arrangement"* (Ehlers, 2006, p. 34). Quality can therefore be defined as the property of a learning product or a learning process with the ability to fulfill the attributes, that have been agreed on between web-learning-providers and web-learning-customers (Astleitner, 2002).[4]

Quality Management

To meet the manifold expectations of both providers and users of web-learning as best as possible, measures to ensure quality have to be implemented. However, they do not only start with the final product, the learning environment. The 'philosophy' of quality management, especially of Total Quality Management[5], rather assumes that the entirety of all objectives and activities of an organization should be related to quality (Bruhn, 2003, p. 54; Zollondz, 2002, pp. 192-3). All planning, controlling and organizational activities, that arise with the implementation of various quality assuring measures, are consequently referred to as 'quality management.' So quality management constitutes an extremely complex process, in which a series of different quality assuring methods – e.g., situation analyses, employee trainings and product evaluations – are employed, combined with each other and coordinated.

Especially in business studies, there is a vibrant debate about different forms of quality management (Zollondz, 2002). This microeconomic discussion will not be reproduced here. It should be mentioned, however, that with the implementation of learning environments particularly three approaches of quality management become increasingly relevant: Total Quality Management, Knowledge Management[6], and Benchmarking[7] (Astleitner, 2002).

---

4   Astleitner (2002) derives, as does currently Ehlers (2006, p. 39), this definition from the quality and quality management concept that is defined in the concept standard DIN EN ISO 9000:2000-12. This standard defines quality as the property configuration of units regarding quality requirements (Zollondz, 2002, p. 192).

5   Total Quality Management is conceived of as all structures, procedures, directions, regulations, instructions, and measures, that serve to ensure and continuously improve the quality of products and services of an organization in all functions and at all levels through the participation of all employees in due time and at low costs, in order to allow an optimal satisfaction of needs of the consumers and the society (Oess, 1993, p. 89). The holistic approach of Total Quality Management thus aims at the check and reformation of organizational structures with the objective of achieving customer- and with it competition-oriented quality improvements. The three constituent factors are customer, process, and employee orientation (Astleitner, 2002).

6   Knowledge Management can here be understood as a frame that encompasses all plans and activities, to permit individuals and organizations to act intelligently. It is to be seen as a cyclical, on single learning processes based process, that concerns the finding, organization, distribution, application and evaluation of knowledge (Astleitner, 2002).

3   Quality Management Approaches Regarding Web-Learning

In the following, the process of quality management has to be structured and related to the implementation of web-based learning environments. Although, from a pedagogical perspective, there is still a lot of research necessary concerning the production, implementation, and evaluation of Internet-based learning systems in universities (cp. summarizing Astleitner, 2000), a few quality management strategies, especially for web-learning-projects, have already been developed (cp. e.g., Koring, 2001, specified by Baeßler et al., 2003; Niegemann, 2001, pp. 157-72; Astleitner, 2002; Astleitner, 2004, pp.128-147; Glowalla, Glowalla & Kohnert 2002; Euler, Seufert & Wirth, 2005, as well as the contributions in Sindler et al., 2006).

In essence, three pedagogical approaches to quality management have been synthesized for the following cycle: (1) the system theory inspired approach by Astleitner and Sindler (1999), (2) the chronologically structured phase model by Niegemann (2001), and (3) the stage model by Koring (2001), which is chronological and cyclic at the same time.[8]

Approach by Astleitner and Sindler 1999

Analyzing where quality assuring measures can start, according to Astleitner and Sindler (1999, p. 119; cp. also Astleitner, 2004, p. 128), three realms regarding the production and implementation of web-based learning offerings have to be differentiated:

- Inputs
- Management Processes
- Outputs

Inputs are the general framework in which a web-based learning environment is developed. These inputs, or requirements, are, for example, determined by political decisions or temporal, technical, and financial demands. They are not under control of the organization that intends to create and implement a learning environment.

---

7   Benchmarks are reference values, against which products, services, or even their single components can be measured. Benchmarks give content and goals for quality management measures, in which "Learning from the best" (best practices) is aspired to. Empirically tested benchmarks for the success of web-learning have been presented by the Institute for Higher Education Policy (2000). Quality seals and certifications for web-learning offerings can in some way perform the function of benchmarks, as proper criteria are specified, that an offering has to meet to be certified as high quality. Comparisons to quality seals and certifications in the area of e-learning are summarized in Euler, Seufert & Wirth (2005) and Balli, Krekel & Sauter (2005) and exemplarily in Abt, Ehlers & Pawlowski (2006), Bruder et al. (2006), Berger & Eilert-Ebke (2006) and Wirth, Euler & Seufert (2006).

8   These three models constitute the basis of our phase model, which is, however, compatible with other currently published phase models – e.g., with Ehler's "4-Phase-Cycle" (2006, pp. 40-50), Pächter's six stage "Quality Circle" (2006, pp. 58) and Bremer's "4-Level-Model" for quality assurance (2006, pp. 185-6.).

Outputs, in turn, are regarded as the consequences of the development, production and implementation of a web-based learning offering. This means that the actual Net-based course (its content-related, didactical, and technical realization) on the one hand, and its success on the other, both count as 'output.' Success includes all the changes regarding the knowledge and competencies of the course participants, the experiences the course organizers have gained, and the appreciation of the course by others.

Finally, the term 'management processes' embraces all measures that correspond to the implementation of learning systems, to the information flow within the (educational) institution and between project participants, and finally to the production process. Quality management is part of the management processes and tries to ensure an optimal output via mediation processes and continuous quality checks,.

This quite rudimentary differentiation is helpful to identify the focus of quality management: as inputs have to be seen as largely fixed parameters, they can hardly be influenced by measures of quality management. Thus, it is essential to analyze the inputs and then to produce high quality outputs through the use of existing organizational structures and the skills of involved individuals (Astleitner, 2002).

Starting Points and Contexts of Quality Management for Web-Learning

Inputs	Management Processes	Outputs
	Coordination of internal and external employees of organizations	
- Legal, contractual, etc. regulations - Budget - Timing - Technical equipment - Employee training - Customers/ target group - Teaching materials - Organizational structure	- Instruction designers - Media designers - Technicians - Tutors - Administrators - Programmers - Librarians - Evaluators	- Courses - Achievements of the students - Satisfaction of the students - Number of dropouts - Reputation/admission of the learning environment in international programs - Satisfaction of the employees - Transferability - Revenues/ Profits - Demand

Figure 1. Starting points and contexts of quality management for Web-learning (table according to Astleitner, 2002)

Phase Models

Niegemann (2001, p. 17) and Koring (2001, specified by Baeßler et al., 2003, pp. 15-6) have identified phases or steps that should be carried out chronologically during the development of web-based learning environments. Within each step, different strategies of quality management apply. If – starting from Astleitner's three components – Niegemann's four phases[9] and the eight stages of Koring's quality management cycle[10] are synthesized, the following exemplary process of the development and implementation of a web-based learning environment emerges:

1. Input analysis
2. Specification of didactics and learning contents
3. Specification of the technology to be used
4. Development of a test lesson
5. Pretest
6. Production of the learning environment
7. Implementation
8. Evaluation of the output and further advancement

These steps shall be specified in the following. In the process it is explicated where quality assuring measures can be employed.

4   Developing an Eight-Phase-Model of Quality Management

Phase I: Input Analysis

In a first step, the general framework for the development and implementation of the new learning environment has to be analyzed. We distinguish between six goals of analysis:

1. Knowledge, tasks and target analysis
2. Analysis of the resources
3. Analysis of the target group

---

9   Niegemann distinguishes between 1. Analysis, 2. Design, 3. Production, and 4. Implementation. In the first phase the general framework (or according to Astleitner the "Inputs") has to be analyzed. Niegemann here again differentiates between problem and target analyses respectively, needs assessments, target group analysis, analysis of the learning matter, analysis of available resources, and analysis of the application context (Niegemann, 2001, pp. 69-96).

10   Koring distinguishes between 1. Problem and task definition, 2. Survey of the relevant didactic information (learning contents), 3. Development of a lesson-like (receptive) and problem-oriented (creative) didactic design, 4. Development of a test lesson, 5. Pretest, 6. Production, 7. Implementation, and 8. Evaluation and advancement (Baeßler et al., 2003, pp. 15-6). Comparing Niegemann's and Koring's work stages, obviously – despite all parallelism of procedure – Koring's eight stage cycle puts a stronger emphasis on quality checks (especially in the form of the phases "Pretest" and "Evaluation").

4. Technology analysis
5. Analysis of the subsequent application context
6. Analysis of the legal and contractual regulations

The *knowledge, tasks, and target analysis* can be perceived as the central analysis task which should be performed first. The already existing contents (professional knowledge stocks and especially teaching materials) are contrasted with the aspired knowledge or competencies of the addressees. This analysis activity cannot be carried out independently of the overall mission statement of the educational institution, of the existing curriculum, nor of the embedding of professional competence in the form of human resources at the respective institute. This means that the (quality) goals of different administrative levels, from the university administration to the institute, should be incorporated into the analysis (Bremer, 2006, pp. 185-9).

Subsequently, the analysis of the available *resources* includes possibilities and limits, which are set by *budget* and *timing*, and also the technical accoutrement of the project or the involved organizational units. The specific *equipment with hard- and software* should be accurately collected (so e.g., the availability of devices for video recording and editing, but also the configuration of university computers, provided that the future web-learning user is supposed to work with them, and the personal equipment of future users with computers and mobile end devices), because only the knowledge about the available technical infrastructure allows the conception of a learning environment that can actually be realized by the project team and used by the students. Web-learning initiatives are generally cooperative projects. Usually, several institutions cooperate, and even within one institution there are often several organizational units involved – e.g., besides the project team, the institute, the department, the computer center, centers for teaching or examination offices, and – if existing – e-learning centers. Therefore, the *structure of the involved organizational units* should be carefully analyzed with respect to what support can be realistically expected. Last, but not least, the *employee situation* has to be clarified during the resource analysis. Which employees are available for the web-learning project? On how many people can the project count? Which knowledge, competencies, and personal characteristics will they bring in?

Besides the collection of these various resources, the *addressees* or the *target group* has to be *analyzed*. How much previous knowledge and which competencies does the targeted student group already possess? On what can be built, what has to be taught from scratch? When answering these questions, it matters, of course, on which semester level the potential students are, whether the subject is their major or minor, and whether a homogeneous or a heterogeneous group can be expected. Taking the didactics of microlearning into account, daily routines and possible time slots for using the learning environment should be analyzed.

Also, the students' technical competences and their technical equipment play an important role. Knowledge about that not only facilitates the conception of adequate introductory tutorials, but also enables the adjustment of the learning environment to be designed to the currently common computer and cell phone equipment of the target group. Obviously, the most sophisticated learning system makes no sense if the software does not run on the 'outdated' computers of the target group.

As stated in our introduction, a multitude of web-based learning programs already exists. Their solutions for the creation of a learning environment can sometimes be of help as an inspirational source – or through the purchase of a licence. During the analysis phase, thus, an *analysis of existing web-learning technologies* is necessary. What are their advantages and disadvantages? Can they be used – and above all, on what terms? Or is a new production on the basis of the collected analysis outcomes advised?

Web-learning projects are, however, not only bound to commitments that involve the purchase of licences. They equally have to consider *legal and contractual regulations* which their investor imposes on them. Depending on the project proposal and the financier, different regulations regarding the production, distribution, and patent rights may apply. The analysis of those regulations should take place early enough in order to design a learning environment which both fulfils all product requirements and whose application and (further) distribution is ensured in the long run, as well (Euler, Seufert & Zellweger 2006).

The *analysis of the subsequent application context* of the learning system also is of essential importance. Given the situation in most German study programs, teaching usually takes place in the traditional classroom setting and the courses are often crowded. The high number of students is, for the most part, disproportionate to the equipment of the institutes, whose human, but also (computer) technical resources are often insufficient.

From the outcomes of the application context analysis arise new questions about the conception of the learning environment. If web-learning is only employed complementary to the classroom teaching as "blended learning," it can typically be replaced by traditional courses at any time. That is why the question of how comprehensive and sustainable the application of web-learning is going to be needs to be clarified from the outset. Should merely one course (or even only a thematic complex within a course) be developed, or is a multi-course platform planned? Should the learning environment be applied once (only as an experiment), repeatedly or even continuously?

Phase II: Specification of Didactics and Learning Contents

Based on the results of the analysis, in particular on the findings from knowledge, tasks and target analysis, as well as the addressee analysis, the didactic design and the concrete learning contents are determined in a next step.

In principle, diverse didactic designs are imaginable. For the distribution of knowledge contents, e.g., a classical, 'direct' instruction design according to Gagné (1985) can be applied.[11] As introductory courses, first and foremost, convey basic knowledge, a traditional instruction design was chosen for the conception of the learning environment CLIC in Erfurt. For other courses, however, completely different instruction designs may be appropriate, depending on the knowledge to be conveyed and the aspired competencies. For example, a Goal-Based-Scenario (Niegemann, 2001, p. 57) was positively evaluated in an academic context. It aims at the advancement of skills by not only offering a participant factual knowledge in the context of possible applications, but also by giving them practical assignments. During the completion of these assignments, students are to deepen the conveyed knowledge in scenario-actions (Schank, 1998).[12]

Once a decision for an instructional design has been made, the learning contents can be specified. In the beginning of this task, as many academics of the relevant organization as possible should be integrated. Despite different understandings of the subject, the sustainable implementation of a learning system needs to represent the contents of the curriculum, based on a consensus within the organization that the learning environment covers central parts of the course of study.

Phase III: Specification of the Technology to be Used

Beyond didactics and content, a decision about the appropriate technology needs to be taken. The decision for a technology is deliberately placed third, because it should result from the decisions about didactics and learning contents. For certain instruction designs and subject matters (e.g., the simulation of scenarios) numerous technical options are required, while others get by with a more rudimentary technology. The outcomes of the analysis of existing web-learning technologies (phase I) should facilitate the decision about which authoring and/or course management systems can be used, and to which extent (partial) reprogrammings are necessary.

The conceptual considerations made in the previous three phases are initially to be placed on the so-called macro level, because the entire organizational requirements and content-related objectives on the part of the university, the faculty, the department and the institute are taken into account. The specification of contents, didactics, and technology leads to the development of an overall design for a learning environment. The development of this overall design is, according to Euler, Seufert & Wirth (2005,

---

11 The instruction design, according to Gagné, contains the teaching steps: attracting attention, informing about learning targets, activating previous knowledge, presentation of the learning matter with the characteristic features, guiding learning, letting perform, giving informative feedback, controlling and evaluating achievement, assuring retention and transfer (cp. Niegemann, 2001, pp. 25-32).

12 At this point it would be going too far to list and present the established instruction designs in detail. Hence, reference is made to the highly instructive summary outline by Niegemann (2001, pp. 21-68).

p. 518), already located on the so-called meso level, while Hug (2005, p. 3) still puts these activities on the macro level. It shall only be stated at this point, that not until the next step, the development of a test lesson, do principles of microlearning apply, as it is about developing modularized contents and testing their effects on the learning process.

Phase IV: Development of a Test Lesson

Following the most important conceptual decisions (didactics, content, technology), the entire learning system should not be immediately produced. Rather, a test lesson should be developed that represents the chosen didactic instruction design. At this point, considerations may influence the process of microlearning. For example, a (preliminary) decision is made about the extent to which the learning material is to be modularized, which can by all means affect the time periods of learning. The more modularized a learning material is, the more options are created for the learners to handle the learning matter in small portions and, at the same time, to access the contents of their choice.[13] Moreover, on the production side, experiences can be made during the creation of a test lesson that help to specify the expenditure of time, work, and costs more precisely.

Phase V: Pretest

Beyond testing the technical operability, a pretest can help to assess the evaluations of the potential users of the learning environment. For this purpose, students are usually confronted with the test lesson, then they have to work with it and are surveyed afterwards. The pretest results can lead to the conclusion that the first three work phases (input analysis, specification of didactics and contents, as well as technology specification) have to be carried out again. Obviously, our phase model includes a feedback loop: mainly data collected on the micro level (from survey results of learners about their learning processes) provide for conclusions with regard to problems on the meso level (didactic, content-related, and technological design), and with regard to the achievement of objectives on the macro level (i.e. specification of quality goals).

Some results of our pretest (which was conducted twice before implementation of the system) can be interpreted more precisely with the didactics of microlearning in mind. Clickstream records, for example, have shown that machine-interactive modules were predominantly used in the beginning. These modules, that complied to a great extent with the principles of microlearning, are apparently relevant for the determination of learning success, on the one hand, and could be handled in a short time, on the other

---

13 Although the choice of the learning module can apparently become a burden. At least the results from three evaluations of the Erfurt CLIC project indicate that indeed the modularization of the subject matter was very appreciated (every aspect as regards content is described with, at most, 400 words and one lesson is typically composed of 30 modules), the possibility, however, to determine ones-self the sequence of the modules, was rarely used.

hand. We developed interactive animations and so-called 'checks,' i.e. batteries of up to 10 test questions with automated feedback, whose processing took normally between two and five minutes. These small interactive learning bits were evaluated very positively in the beginning and were regarded to be very motivating to learning. Once the students, however, completed the entire learning course, they especially assessed the checks still as being motivating, though ultimately not as promoting knowledge. Rather, they evaluated the traditional 'guiding questions' (which generally corresponded to larger topical realms that were established through a multitude of modules or entire lessons) as very helpful. These results indicate a constructive information processing on the students' part which can be initiated by small motivating learning modules (or microlearning). The importance of the didactics of microlearning seems to decrease, however, with the increasing number and integration of knowledge stocks.

Phase VI: Production

After the pretest, the learning environment is produced. In this phase, many coordinating management tasks arise, especially if the technical realization of the learning system is produced within the organization, but programmed from externals, due to outsourcing.

Phase VII: Implementation

It would be illusionary to believe that a web-learning project is completed when the learning environment is readily produced. A sustainable learning environment on the web has to be temporally, factually, and socially incorporated into the entire teaching process. Otherwise, there is a risk that the extensively produced learning environment is never, or only once, applied. The implementation phase is thus crucial to the success and the sustainability of web-learning. Essentially, the four addressees of implementation activities need to be integrated carefully: the organization members, the computing personnel, the tutors, and the students.

1.   Implementation Tasks on the Part of the Institute and its Employees

Usually, only part of the academic staff of a university institute already has experiences with e-learning, while doubts about one's own technological competence, and scepticism about the new learning form, are widespread (cp. Issing, 2002, p. 14; Encarnação, 2002, p. 95). That is why it is all the more important to introduce the learning environment – with its advantages and disadvantages – to the members of the institute. For a sustained implementation of web-learning, institute-wide consensus to cover certain courses with web-learning and a close tie to the curriculum should already be established at the beginning of the project. In addition, a continuous implementation of a web-learning environment is supported if one institute member is assigned the responsibility for web-learning in the long run.

2.   Implementation Tasks on the Part of the Computing Personnel

For proper operation of the learning environment, several technological requirements have to be met. This can, for example, be the installation of the learning environment on the university server, the installation of additional programs (e.g., for the playback of videos and animations) on university computers, or the setup of a technology hotline for the users of the learning environment. Very often, these tasks are in the field of responsibility of university computer centers. They should be integrated into the development of the project from a very early point in time. After an initial inquiry concerning the extent to which resources can be made available, an active contact should be maintained during the implementation to coordinate solutions for technological concerns.

3.   Training of Tutors

An efficient communication – be it within the student body or between the students and instructors – is still a prerequisite for the acceptance of a learning system and the learning success (e.g., Astleitner & Baumgartner, 2000, pp. 167-69; Kinnebrock, Koschel & Rössler, 2004, p. 38). Therefore tutors need to be trained for their tasks and responsibilities. Tutorial responsibilities are, for example, the maintenance of discussion forums, the administration of chats, the support of the students via e-mails, as well as the explanation of learning checks and their results. To enhance the motivation of the students, it is extremely important to answer e-mails in a timely manner and to keep the feedback constructive (Astleitner, 2000, pp. 26-27). During the training of tutors this should be emphasized.

4.   Preparing the Students for Web-Learning

E-learning encounters reservations from students, as well (cp. exemplarily Baeßler, Wünsch & Kinnebrock 2004, p. 28-37; Kinnebrock, Koschel & Rössler 2004, p. 33-34). Therefore, the application of web-learning requires further justification. Furthermore, students have to be carefully introduced to the learning environment. Both electronic tutorials and introductory courses in university computer rooms are appropriate for this purpose. Within the scope of introductory courses, the handling of the technical tools of the learning environment should be practiced, and students should also be encouraged to use the possibilities for online communication inherent to the system. The extent of social contact – with instructors, but also with fellow students – remains the decisive factor that determines motivation and dropout for web-learning (Astleitner & Schinagl, 2000, p. 63).

Phase VIII: Evaluation and Advancement

After the output, the web-based learning course, has been run once, important findings for the improvement and advancement of the learning environment can be drawn from different evaluations. Basically, we may distinguish between *internal and external evaluations*.

A common form of internal evaluation is a *student survey*. In standardized surveys, or with the help of guided interviews, the satisfaction of the web-learning user, common usage patterns, and especially criticism on the learning offerings can be collected. These data allow inferences on how learning processes work on a micro level. Beyond the subjective satisfaction of students the learning success, measured by grades, is a central objective of teaching. Thus we strongly suggest including the *results of achievement inquiries* in the overall evaluation.

As the academic staff is confronted with the application of e-learning, too, a survey of those who designed the learning environment and conducted the learning course should be interviewed about their experiences. How satisfied were the *contributors* with the progression of the course, the virtual course administration, and with the achievements of the students? What is the proportion of results achieved and the effort that has been expended for the establishment of the learning environment? The contributors should make a *summary objective-outcome comparison* after the first completed application of the learning environment, whose starting point should be the results of the knowledge, task and target analysis (phase I).

In addition, other *data material* is available that can be used for internal evaluation: *indices* that help to describe the success of web-learning (e.g., dropout rates, grade point averages, etc.) can be calculated. *Messages of students*, that are accumulated during use of the learning environment (e.g., e-mails, entries on discussion forums), can also be collected and evaluated with a content analysis.

Apart from the results of internal evaluations, the outcomes of *external evaluations* are instructive, too. External evaluations can be carried out by experts, on the one hand, or through the collection of reference data, on the other hand. Expert judgments are, for example, relevant, when the content of the learning system has to be evaluated, or when the question of whether the latest subject matter has been displayed adequately has to be clarified. Here, *external academics* can be consulted and asked for their expertise. The didactic design, in turn, should be evaluated by *external pedagogues*.

Furthermore, a comparison with reference data is useful within the framework of the external evaluation, because the internally calculated indices (e.g., dropout rates) have few explanatory powers concerning the quality of the created learning environment as long as no reference data is given. Empirically tested *Benchmarks* for the success of web-learning or the establishment of *seals of quality*, as well as the passing through a *certification process* might be of relevance here. Through the participation at *competitions*, i.e. the direct comparison with competing learning environments, an evaluation of the quality of one's own product can be obtained. The reasons for the jury's judgments should provide important clues here (also for the improvement of the learning environment).

We want to emphasize that only a combination of different forms of evaluation allows a quality judgement about the created web-learning environment. Whether, for example, a learning matter is out of date, or contains factual mistakes might not be adequately judged by a student who is confronted with it for the first time. Here, the expertise of an accounted expert is needed. But only the students, in turn, can provide information about motivation problems during learning. The evaluation thus should be perceived as a process, in which sources of different origin are collected, evaluated and balanced.

After combining the different evaluation results, it might eventually be useful to get back to previous phases of the quality management cycle – e.g., to go back again to the first stage, the analysis, to modify the objectives. Consequently, a circular model of quality management for the implementation of web-based learning environments (see figure 2) can be developed from our experiences.

**Eight-Phase-Model of Quality Management For
Web-Learning**

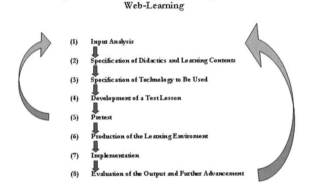

(1)   Input Analysis

(2)   Specification of Didactics and Learning Contents

(3)   Specification of Technology to Be Used

(4)   Development of a Test Lesson

(5)   Pretest

(6)   Production of the Learning Environment

(7)   Implementation

(8)   Evaluation of the Output and Further Advancement

Figure 2. Circular model of quality management for the implementation of web-based learning environments

5   Conclusion

Web-based learning environments are indeed used for university teaching, but up to now sustainable changes in teaching can only exceptionally be recognized. Often, the end of project promotion also means the end of efforts to establish web-based learning environments in the long term (Kerres, 2002, p. 58; Ehlers, 2006, p. 37). From our perspective, this is a distressing development, because not only resources are wasted, but also important potentials of web-learning are not used. The free choice of the place and time of learning, the self-determined study time, motivational multimedia-based and machine-interactive editing of contents, a comprehension-promoting modularization of the learning matter – all these are opportunities provided by web-learning, which – ideally – lead to a greater learning success.

The planning and realization of such learning environments, however, is a highly complex process. To structure the progress of web-learning projects and to establish continuous quality checks, an Eight-Phase-Model of quality management was suggested. The different levels on which learning or coordination processes take place were addressed during the elaboration of the individual phases.

A main characteristic of web-learning, and especially microlearning, is that it can be used independent of places. A learning environment is potentially available everywhere, through Internet/WWW or cellular phone networks. Moreover, the extreme modularization of content allows the students to determine not only the places where they learn, but also the time periods they dedicate to learning. Our evaluations indicate a dynamic interplay between small, motivating microlearning modules (that are especially important to initiate learning processes), on the one hand, and larger learning units that allow a deeper integration of knowledge stocks on the other. These dynamic relations should be further investigated – and this is particularly true from a quality management perspective. Among all the different goals that are to be defined and achieved within the process of quality management, the improvement of learning processes is still crucial – and to a great extent, controllable. As a consequence, quality management in the field of web-learning must respect the didactics of microlearning.

References

Abbey, B. (2000) *Instructional and Cognitive Iimpacts of Web-Based Education.* Hershey, PA: Idea Group Publishing.

Abt, M., Ehlers U-D. & Pawlowsiki, J. (2006) Qualitätssiegel E-Learning bei der RAG Aktiengesellschaft in Essen. In: Sindler, A., Bremer, C., Dittler, U., Hennecke, P., Sengstag, C. & Wedekind, J. ed. *Qualitätssicherung im E-Learning.* Münster: Waxmann, pp. 21–32.

Astleitner, H. (2000) Qualität von web-basierter Instruktion. Was wissen wir aus der experimentellen Forschung? In: Scheuermann, F. ed. *Campus 2000. Lernen in neuen Organisationsformen.* Münster: Waxmann, pp. 15–39.

Astleitner, H. (2002) *Qualitätsmanagement von E-Learning. Research Report.* Institut für Erziehungswissenschaft der Universität Salzburg. Available from: <http://www.sbg.ac.at/erz/as/AS_QUAL2.DOC > [Accessed 19 August 2004].

Astleitner, H. (2004) *Qualität des Lernens im Internet. Virtuelle Schulen und Universitäten auf dem Prüfstand.* 2nd ed. Frankfurt M.: Lang.

Astleitner, H. (2005) Principles of effective instruction. General standards for teachers and instructional designers. In: *Journal of Instructional Psychology*, 32, March, pp. 3–8.

Astleitner, H. (2006) Standard-basiertes E-Lehren und selbstreguliertes Lernen. Selbstreguliertes Lernen als Voraussetzung für Qualitätsinnovationen im E-Learning. In: Sindler, A. et al., eds. *Qualitätssicherung im E-Learning.* Münster: Waxmann, pp. 21-32.

Astleitner, H. & Baumgartner, A. (2000) Dropout bei web-basiertem Fernunterricht. In: Kammerl, R. & Astleitner, H. eds. *Computerunterstütztes Lernen.* München/Wien: Oldenbourg, pp. 166–187.

414 Susanne Kinnebrock, Berit Baeßler & Patrick Rössler

Astleitner, H. & Schinagl, W. (2000) *High-level Telelernen und Wissensmanagement.* Frankfurt a.m.: Peter Lang.

Astleitner, H. & Sindler, A. (1999) *Pädagogische Grundlagen virtueller Ausbildung. Telelernen im Fachhochschulbereich.* Wien: Universitätsverlag.

Baeßler, B. et al. (2003) E-Learning-Systeme. Theoriegeleitete Konzeption, Qualitätsmanagement, Implementierung. In: *Zeitschrift für Medienpsychologie,* 15 (1), pp. 13–23.

Baeßler, B., Wünsch, J. & Kinnebrock, S. (2004) Innovation in der kommunikationswissenschaftlichen Lehre? Evaluation eines internetbasierten Lernsystems zur Einführung in die Kommunikationswissenschaft. In: Neubert, K. & Scherer, H. eds. *Die Zukunft der Kommunikationsberufe – Ausbildung, Berufsfelder, Arbeitsweisen.* Konstanz: UVK medien, pp. 19–39.

Balli, C., Krekel E.M., Sauter, E. (2005) Qualitätsentwicklung in der Weiterbildung aus der Sicht von Bildungsanbietern – Diskussionsstand, Verfahren, Entwicklungstendenzen. In: Balli, C., Krekel E.M. & Sauter, E. eds. *Qualitätsentwicklung in der Weiterbildung. Zum Stand der Anwendung von Qualitätssicherungs- und Qualitätsmanagementsystemen bei Weiterbildungsanbietern.* Bonn: Schriftenreihe des Bundesinstituts für Berufsbildung [Wissenschaftliche Diskussionspapiere Heft 62], pp. 5–24.

Berger, N. & Eilert-Ebke, G. (2006) Corporate Communication and Language Trainer Certificate (CLTC) als Werkzeug zur Qualitätssicherung. In: Sindler, A. et al., eds. *Qualitätssicherung im E-Learning.* Münster: Waxmann, pp. 125–34.

Bremer, C. (2006) Qualitätssicherung und E-Learning. Implementierungsansätze für die Hochschule. In: Sindler, A. et al., eds. *Qualitätssicherung im E-Learning.* Münster: Waxmann, pp. 185–202.

Bruder, R. et al. (2006) Qualitätssicherung mit einem E-Learining-Label für universitäre Lehre und einem Gütesiegel. In: Sindler, A. et al., eds. *Qualitätssicherung im E-Learning.* Münster: Waxmann, pp. 87–98.

Bruhn, M. (2003) *Qualitätsmanagement für Dienstleistungen. Grundlagen, Konzepte, Methoden.* Berlin: Springer.

Carstensen, D. (2006) Studierende im Mittelpunkt. Qualitätsperspektiven in multimedialen Lehr- und Lernsettings an Hochschulen. In: Sindler, A. et al., eds. *Qualitätssicherung im E-Learning.* Münster: Waxmann, pp. 13–20.

Ehlers, U.-D. (2006) Bildungsrelevante Qualitätsentwicklung. Qualitätskompetenz als Grundlage für Partizipation im Qualitätsprozess. In: Sindler, A. et al. eds. *Qualitätssicherung im E-Learning.* Münster: Waxmann, pp. 33–54.

Encarnação, J.L. (2002) Entwicklung multimedialer Software für das Studium. In: Issing, L.J. & Stärk, G. eds. *Studieren mit Multimedia und Internet. Ende der traditionellen Hochschule oder Innovationsschub?* Münster: Waxmann, pp. 91–112.

Euler, D., Seufert, S. & Zellweger, F. (2006) Geschäftsmodelle zur nachhaltigen Implementierung von eLearning an Hochschulen. In: *Zeitschrift für Betriebswirtschaft.* Special Issue 2 [E-Learning Geschäftsmodelle und Einsatzkonzepte], pp. 85–104.

Euler, D., Seufert, S. & Wirth, M. (2005) Gestaltung des Qualitätsmanagements zur Zertifizierung von E-Learning-Programmen. In: Euler, D. & Seufert S. eds. *E-Learning in Hochschulen und Bildungszentren.* München/Wien: Oldenbourg, pp. 513–28.

Horton, W. (2000) *Designing Web-Based Training.* New York: Wiley.

Hug, T. (2005) *Microlearning and narration. Exploring possibilities of unitilization of narrations and storytelling for the designing of "micro units" and didactical microlearning arrangements.* Paper presented at the forth Media in Transition conference. May 6-8, Massachusetts Institute of Technology, Cambridge (MA), USA. Available from: <http://web.mit.edu/comm-forum/mit4/papers/hug.pdf> [Accessed 19 November 2005].

Gagné, R.M. (1985) *The Conditions of Learning and Theory of Instruction.* New York: Holt, Rinehart & Winston.

Garrett, R. (2005) *E-Learning in Tertiary Education. Where Do We stand?* Center of Educational Research and Innovation. Paris: OECD Publications.

Gerpott, T.J. & Schlegel, M. (2000) Online-Zeitungen. Charakteristika und Anwendungspotenziale eines neuen Medienangebotes. In: *Medien & Kommunikationswissenschaft*, 48 (3), pp. 335–353.

Glowalla, U., Glowalla, G. & Kohnert, A. (2002) Qualitätsmanagement interaktiver Studienangebote. In: Issing, L.J. & Stärk, G. eds. *Studieren mit Multimedia und Internet. Ende der traditionellen Hochschule oder Innovationsschub?* Münster: Waxmann, pp. 113–28.

Horton, W. (2000) *Designing Web-Based Training.* New York: Wiley.

Issing, L.J. (2002) Neue Medien – Herausforderung und Chance für die Hochschule. In: Issing, L.J. & Stärk, G. eds. *Studieren mit Multimedia und Internet. Ende der traditionellen Hochschule oder Innovationsschub?* Münster: Waxmann, pp. 9–17.

Kerres, M. (2002) Medien und Hochschule. Strategien zur Erneuerung der Hochschullehre. In: Issing, L.J. & Stärk, G. eds. *Studieren mit Multimedia und Internet. Ende der traditionellen Hochschule oder Innovationsschub?* Münster: Waxmann, pp. 57–70.

Kinnebrock, S. & Baeßler, B. (2004) Qualitätsmanagement bei der Implementierung von webbasierten Lernumgebungen in die kommunikationswissenschaftliche Lehre. In: Neubert, K. & Scherer, H. eds. *Die Zukunft der Kommunikationsberufe – Ausbildung, Berufsfelder, Arbeitsweisen.* Konstanz: UVK medien, pp. 41–60.

Kinnebrock, S., Koschel, F. & Rössler, P. (2004) Web-Learning. Konzeption und Evaluation des Lernsystems CLIC. In: *Medien Journal*, 28 (4), pp. 31–9.

Koring, B. (2001) *Qualitätsmanagement bei der Entwicklung von Tele-Learning-Kursen für die Universität.* Paper presented at the University of Erfurt. Feb. 4.

Niegemann, H.M. (2001) *Neue Lernmedien – Konzipieren, Entwickeln, Einsetzen.* Göttingen/ Bern: H. Huber.

Oess, A. (1993) *Total Quality Management. Die ganzheitliche Qualitätsstrategie.* Wiesbaden: Gabler.

Pächter, M. (2006) Von der didaktischen Vision zum messbaren Indikator. Entwicklung eines Qualitätssystems für medienbasierte Lehre. In: Sindler, A. et al., eds. *Qualitätssicherung im E-Learning.* Münster: Waxmann, pp. 55–72.

Schank, R.C. (1998) *Tell Me a Story. Narrative and intelligence.* 2nd ed.. Evanston: Northwestern University Press.

Sindler, A. et al., eds. (2006) *Qualitätssicherung im E-Learning.* Münster: Waxmann.

Wirth, M., Euler, D. & Seufert, S. (2006) Qualität von E-Learning beurteilen, sichern, verbessern. Herausforderungen in der Umsetzung und Erfahrungen mit dem neuen Qualitätszertifikat "CEL" von EFMD. In: Sindler, A. et al., eds. *Qualitätssicherung im E-Learning.* Münster: Waxmann, pp. 153–68.

Zollondz, H.-D. (2002) Grundlagen Qualitätsmanagement. Einführung in Geschichte, Begriffe, Systeme und Konzepte. München/Wien: Oldenbourg.

About the Contributors

Berit Baeßler is a PhD candidate at the Department of Media and Communication at the University of Erfurt. From 2001 until 2003 she was affiliated with this department as a research fellow in the CLIC project to develop the internet-based learning system CLIC (Computer-based Learning in Communications). She is currently finishing her dissertation about parasocial relationships to people in different media. Her research interests are media use and effects, e-learning development and evaluation and online communication.

Anthony 'Skip' Basiel is a senior lecturer at the Centre for Excellence in Work Based Learning, Middlesex University, UK. He is an Adobe International Educational Leader and was joint e-Tutor of the Year in 2004 for the UK Higher Education Academy. He is currently completing a professional Doctorate in e-pedagogy.

Sigrid Blömeke is a professor of General Education and Instructional Research at the Humboldt University of Berlin, Germany, an Associate Dean at its Faculty of Arts and Germany's National Research Coordinator of the IEA study "Teacher Education and Development: Learning to teach mathematics" (TEDS-M). Her area of specialization is empirical research on teaching and learning with ICT and on the effects of teacher education. She is the author of *Universität und Lehrerausbildung* (Klinkhardt 2002, 2nd ed. 2003), *Gestaltung von Unterricht. Eine Einführung in die Didaktik* (Klinkhardt 2004), the first editor of *Handbuch Lehrerbildung* (Klinkhardt & Westermann 2004) and one of the editors of the *journal für lehrerInnenbildung* (Studienverlag).

Matthias Bopp is research professor at the Centre for Advanced Imaging (CAI) at the University of Bremen, Germany. He studied educational science, German language and literature, sociology and philosophy at the Universities of Mainz and Frankfurt/Main, worked as a teacher at a German grammar school (Gymnasium) and as a research assistant in educational science at the Universities of Gießen and Nürnberg. Currently he finishes his post doctoral lecture qualification on "Computer games and digital learning games" and is Director of learning in the European Commission's sixth frame work program project ELEKTRA (Enhanced Learning Experience and Knowledge Transfer, contract No.: 027986) which has supported the completion of this article.

Raphael Commins is currently Project Manager at the National Centre for Work Based Learning Partnerships, Middlesex University, UK. His interests are in researching, developing and supporting learning technologies at university level. He is involved in web development, systems administration, and playing technical lead in projects including testing, piloting, and rolling out of new systems. He was joint e-Tutor of the Year in 2004 for the UK Higher Education Academy. He is commencing a Doctorate in Learning Contexts and Social Networking at the Centre for Informatics and Systems at the University of Coimbra, Portugal.

Thomas Eibl is responsible for the development of computer-based training devices for pilots and mechanics at the Eurocopter Group, a global helicopter manufacturing and support company. In periodical courses at the Universität der Bundeswehr in Munich, he teaches how to bridge the gap between the theory of didactics and instructional design and the realization of actual projects. He is the author of Hypertext. Geschichte und Formen sowie Einsatz als Lern- und Lehrmedium (kopaed 2004).

Bernhard Ertl is senior researcher at Bundeswehr University in Munich. His current research interests lie in the research on video-mediated learning, Internet collaboration and online-courses with a particular focus on the support of collaborative knowledge construction by structured communication interfaces. He earned his Diploma in computer science from the Ludwig Maximilian University Munich in 1998 and his Doctorate in education 2003. From 1999 to 2006, he was research assistant at the Department Psychology of Ludwig Maximilian University of Munich and working with Professor Heinz Mandl in DFG-funded research projects focusing on collaborative learning, e.g. *"Collaborative Learning in Graphics-enhanced Tele-learning Environments"* and *"Collaborative Knowledge Construction in Desktop Videoconferencing"*.

Norm Friesen has been developing and studying Web technologies in educational contexts since 1995. Norm is currently a SSHRC Postdoctoral Fellow at the School of Communication at Simon Fraser University, and is the principal investigator in the "learningspaces.org" project sponsored by SSHRC (the Social Sciences and Humanities Research Council of Canada). Norm is also an Adjunct Faculty member at Athabasca University, Canada's Open University, and has recently been a visiting scholar at the Faculty of Information Studies at the University of Toronto, and at the Leopold Franzens University, Innsbruck, Austria. In addition to authoring dozens of articles and reports, Norm has produced several editions of books on the instructional use of WebCT and on the implementation of the IEEE Learning Object Metadata standard. His recent articles include "'Ed Tech in Reverse': Information Technologies and the Cognitive Revolution," "Three Objections to Learning Objects," and "Communication Genres and the Mediatic Turn." His academic credentials include Master's degrees in Library and Information Studies from the University of Alberta and in German Literature and Philosophy from the Johns Hopkins University. Norm holds a PhD in Education from the University of Alberta.

Robert Grigg has spent years playing, designing and building games with the many changing technologies that have past by during the last 15 years. During this time he has founded and developed two successful gaming companies as well as worked with US based developers and publishers in the release of worldwide titles. Academically Robert seeks to bring the gaming edge to University research and education in new and exciting projects with close industry involvement. His research is in Game Design and Game Architectural areas through to projects such as the Interactive Online and Broadcast TV production "Come Ride With Me". Currently Robert is working at the

University of Portsmouth in his Senior Lecturer and Industry Liaison role at the Department of Creative Technology.

Wolfgang Hagleitner, born in 1966, studied educational sciences, evaluation and psychology at the Paris-Lodron-University of Salzburg. He worked in the field of therapeutic pedagogy for many years. In the context of his thesis, he evaluated the Austrian Centre for the Study of Giftedness and published selected research findings at the 9th ECHA Conference in Pamplona. During his studies, he collaborated in numerous evaluation projects, primarily in the field of schooling and education (e.g. PISA, IMST2). Since March 2006, he is the project manager for evaluation at the Studio eLearning Environments of the Research Studios Austria.

Stylianos Hatzipanagos is a lecturer in Higher Education and programme director on the Graduate Certificate in Academic Practice at King's Institute of Learning and Teaching, King's College, London, UK. His research interests are in innovation in learning and teaching, computer mediated communication and computer supported collaborative work.

Helmwart Hierdeis, born in 1937, taught educational sciences at the University of Bamberg, the University of Erlangen-Nurnberg, the University of Innsbruck, and the University of Bozen at Brixen. He is currently a practicing psychoanalyst. The focus of his scholarly interest includes the historiography of education, educational theory, the theory of educational institutions, and psychoanalytical pedagogics.

Theo Hug is a professor of educational sciences at the University of Innsbruck (Austria) and coordinator of the Innsbruck Media Studies research group. His areas of interest are media education and media literacy, e-education and microlearning, theory of knowledge and philosophy of science. He is particularly interested in interfaces of medialization and knowledge dynamics as well as learning processes. He is author of Diskursive Feldforschung (1996), Instantwissen und Bricolage (with J. Perger, 2000) and editor of Wie kommt Wissenschaft zu Wissen? (2001), Technologiekritik und Medienpädagogik (1998), Taschenbuch der Pädagogik (with H. Hierdeis, 1997), Phantom Wirklichkeit. Theoretische Annäherungen an Wirklichkeitsverständnisse (with H. J. Walter, 2002), and Media Communities (with B. Hipfl, 2006). Website: http://www.hug-web.at.

Nina Kahnwald is a research associate at the faculty of educational sciences at the Technical University of Dresden, Germany. She is working in the field of educational technology in research and implementation projects on virtual communities, e-learning and online research. She is the author of Netzkunst als Medienkritik (kopaed, 2006) and Mediennutzung im digitalen Leben: Aktive Content-Interfaces, Paid Content und integrierte Geschäftsmodelle (with L. Seidenfaden and C. Kaspar, Businessvillage, 2005).

Michael Kerres is a professor of educational sciences at the University of Duisburg-Essen, Germany, and head of Duisburg Learning Lab. He is currently working on instructional design of blended learning arrangements and strategies for e-learning in higher education.

Susanne Kinnebrock is a research fellow at the Department of Media and Communication at the University of Erfurt. From 2001 until 2002 she was a project coordinator at the University of Erfurt and developed the internet-based learning system CLIC (Computer-based Learning in Communications). She is currently working on women in journalism, women's magazines and their publics, and the effects of narrative patterns in media. She is the author of *Anita Augspurg (1857-1943). Feministin und Pazifistin zwischen Journalismus und Politik. Eine kommunikationshistorische Biographie* (Centaurus 2005) and the editor of *Media Cultures* (with William Uricchio, Universitätsverlag Winter 2006). Morevover she published numerous essays on gender and media as well as on the implementation and evaluation of e-learning.

Patrick Kranzlmüller is a designer and programmer. He studied communication studies and theatre, film and media studies at the University of Vienna (A) and the John Moores University of Liverpool (GB). He was leading the THE THING VIENNA (Association for supporting Culture, Theory, Research and Science in electronic media), together with Dr. Marc Ries. In 2000 he founded *vonautomatisch werkstaetten*, a laboratory for production and research in the fields of digital media. Patrick prepares his dissertation on "Cooperative Structures. The socio-technical architecture of information society".Website: www.vonautomatisch.at

Gunther Kress is Professor of English and Head of the School of Culture, Language, and Communication at the Institute of Education, University of London. Professor Kress' work addresses questions of meaning in their interrelations with social and cultural organization. In his professional location, the focus of his work is on learning and on the necessary shape of curricula and forms of pedagogy in a globalizing world. His conceptions around representation and communication include all the modes through which a culture represents itself and in which meanings are made, as well as the dominant media and their social effects. In this he has focused on the visual mode, for instance, as much as on language and literacy, within a broad, socially founded semiotics. His recent books include Multimodal Discourse, Before Writing: Rethinking Paths to Literacy, Literacy in the New Media Age, and Reading Images: The Grammar of Graphic Design.

Peter Krieg is a freelance filmmaker, producer and writer in Berlin. He made several documentaries on science, technology and radical constructivism (e.g. "Machine Dreams" 1988, "Suspicious Minds" 1991) and published and edited (together with Paul Watzlawick) "Das Auge des Betrachters" (1991). Since 1999 he is also active in the development of a new software technology ("Pile") that attempts to overcome the limitations of data based computing with a purely relational approach. His recent book

"Die paranoide Maschine" (2005) describes the background of this invention, as does his paper: "What Makes a Thinking Machine?" in "Semiotics and Intelligent Systems Development (ed. R. Gudwin & J. Queiroz, 2007).

Karl Leidlmair is a professor of psychologie at the University of Innsbruck (Austria). His areas of interest are Cognitive Science, philosophy of technology, media theory and media psychology (chat communication). He is the author of Künstliche Intelligenz und Heidegger. Über den Zwiespalt von Natur und Geist (1991) and editor of Wozu künstliche Intelligenz? (with O. Neumaier, 1988) and Martin Heidegger. Technik-Ethik-Politik (with R. Margreiter, 1991). Website: http://www.leidlmair.at.

Heinz Mandl is Professor of Education and Educational Psychology at Ludwig Maximilian University of Munich. From 1961–1967 he was a teacher at primary and secondary schools, 1967–1978 Assistance Professor at University of Augsburg, 1978–1990 Professor at University of Tuebingen, before he went to University of Munich (1990). He was President of the European Association for Research on Learning and Instruction (EARLI; 1989–1991). He got the Oeuvre Award for outstanding contributions to the Science of Learning & Instruction of the European Association for Research on Learning and Instruction. Main research areas are knowledge management, acquisition and use of knowledge, netbased knowledge communication, design of virtual learning environments. He was co-initiator of several research programmes of Deutsche Forschungsgemeinschaft (DFG): Knowledge Psychology; Knowledge and Action; Teaching-Learning-processes in Business Education; Netbased Cooperation in Groups. In research and development projects he cooperates with companies and organisations like Siemens, BMW, Telekom, ALTANA, Andersen Consulting, Bundesministerium für Bildung und Forschung, Bundesrechnungshof.

Tony Manninen, PhD, Assistant Professor, LudoCraft Game Design and Research Unit, University of Oulu. Tony is a computer games designer, researcher and teacher. His areas of research include design, analysis and production of multiplayer games and their diverse applications. In his PhD research he studied the issues related to interaction forms and their manifestations in multiplayer games. He has designed several experimental games and has published game related papers in academic forums, as well as, game reviews and game related articles in popular media. He is the leader of LudoCraft, which studies games and applies the theoretical knowledge into game design.

Pasi Mattila, MA Ed is a Project Manager in the City of Oulu. He is leading the mLearning Project in the Educational Office. The aim is to design and create a mLearning platform for mobile devices in the use of Primary School Education. His special research and teaching interests are ICT-technology and mobile solutions in learning process.

Jukka Miettunen, MA Ed, ICT-coordinator, educational, City Of Oulu. Jukka has both commercial and educational education. He has worked in both private and public sectors. His areas of interest are new learning technology and relationships to working culture and leadership.

Christiane Müller is a research fellow at the department of General Education and Instructional Research at the Humboldt University of Berlin, Germany. Her area of specialization is empirical research on teaching and learning with ICT. She is the author of *Chancen und Grenzen von Videostudien in der Unterrichtsforschung* (together with Dana Eichler and Sigrid Blömeke, in: Rahm, Mammes, Schratz (Eds.), Schulpädagogische Forschung – Unterrichtsforschung – Perspektiven innovativer Ansätze) and *Unterricht mit digitalen Medien – zwischen Innovation und Tradition?* (together with Sigrid Blömeke and Dana Eichler, in Zeitschrift für Erziehungswissenschaft).

Kendal Newman spent 10 years developing computer games and educational software as an animator, programmer, project manager and producer. He has produced many internationally successful titles including "Star Wars", "True Lies", and "Nightshade" for SNES game console and the award winning "Language Market" CDROM series. He has been the producer of a number of innovative online communities and interactive documentary projects including "ComeRideWithMe2002", "Albert Goes Latin" and most recently "Albert in the Land of the Vikings". Kendal is currently a researcher and Senior Lecturer at the University of Portsmouth in the UK.

Beverley Oliver is Senior Lecturer and Manager of the Teaching Development Unit at Curtin University of Technology in Australia. In her PhD she drew on her experience in teaching communication and information literacy skills to undergraduate students to research how technology might facilitate quality learning in these key areas. She recently led a transnational research project exploring undergraduates' use of mobile devices and Web 2.0 applications in developing information literacy. Beverley's current work is in change management in teaching and learning at the institutional and level, and she is particularly engaged in student evaluation of the quality of higher education teaching and learning, and in university curriculum reform. Her research and publications embrace all of these areas.

Norbert Pachler is a Reader in Education at the Institute of Education, University of London where is Co-Director of the Centre for Excellence in Work-based Learning for Education Professional. His research interests include foreign language pedagogy, teacher education and development, and (digital) technologies in education. He has published widely in these fields. He is currently co-editor of the Language Learning Journal (Routledge), associate editor of the London Review of Education (Routledge), editor of Reflecting Education (WLE Centre), and co-editor of German as a Foreign Language (in conjunction with the DAAD, the Goethe-Institut and the AMGS).

Markus F. Peschl is professor for Cognitive Science and Philosophy of Science at the Dept. of Philosophy, Research Group Philosophy of Science: Cultures and Technologies of Knowledge, University of Vienna, Austria. His focus of research is on the question of knowledge (creation/innovation, construction, and representation of knowledge) in various contexts: in natural and artificial cognitive (neural) systems, in science, in organizational and learning settings, in educational /knowledge transfer processes, as well as in the context of knowledge technologies and their embedding in social systems. The philosophical, epistemological, anthropological, and cognitive foundations of the human person and his/her knowledge are at the center of his attention. He follows a radically interdisciplinary approach integrating concepts from the natural sciences, philosophy (of science), from the humanities, as well as from (knowledge) technology. M. Peschl has published 6 books and more than 80 papers in international journals and collections. For further information see: http://www.univie.ac.at/wissenschaftstheorie/peschl/.

Klaus Puhl teaches Philosophy at the Universities of Innsbruck, Vienna and Graz. His research interests are Wittgenstein, Cultural Theory and Modernism. He is the editor of *Meaning Scepticism* and the author of *Subjekt und Körper* as well as of essays on Wittgenstein, Freud, Post-Structuralism and the Philosophy of Language.

Ravi Purushotma is a researcher in the MIT Education Arcade and New Media Literacies groups. A former English teacher in southern China, his interests are in how foreign language learning will need to be re conceptualized to take advantage of the instantaneous access to foreign culture and media available with today's technologies.

Joost Raessens is Associate Professor of New Media Studies at Utrecht University, the Netherlands, and head of the master programme New Media and Digital Culture. In 2003 he was conference chair of the inaugural Digital Games Research Conference 'Level Up,' organised by Utrecht University in collaboration with DiGRA. He co-edited Level Up. Digital Games Research Conference (Utrecht University, 2003) and the Handbook of Computer Game Studies (The MIT Press, 2005). He is a member of the editorial board of Games and Culture (Sage Publications). Joost Raessens' research interests include the playful construction of personal and cultural identity and serious gaming. In his study of serious gaming, he focuses in particular on the learning and design principles underlying educational games and on the use of games for political purposes. See www.raessens.nl.

Patrick Rössler is Chair of Communication Science/Empirical Research at the University of Erfurt, Germany. In 2006 he was elected for President of the German Communication Association (DGPuK). He is editor of the book series "Internet Research" and "medien + gesundheit", co-editor of the book series "Reihe Rezeptionsforschung" (all R. Fischer Verlag, Munich). His main fields of scholarly interest are media effects research, new media developments and online communication, audience research, health communication and the history of magazines.

Mirko Tobias Schäfer is a junior teacher and researcher at the Institute for Media and Re/presentation at Utrecht University (NL). He studied theatre, film and media studies and communication studies at Vienna University (A) and digital culture at Utrecht University (NL). He was organizer and co-curator of [d]vision – Vienna Festival for Digital Culture. Mirko received a magister in philosophy from the University of Vienna. Currently he is writing his dissertation on the impact of computer technology and users on the cultural industries. Website: www.mtschaefer.net

Franziska Scherer is a psychologist and behavioral therapist-in-training. She works at the psycho-oncological department of an oncological rehabilitation clinic. From 2002-2004, she was research fellow at the department of social psychology at the Helmut-Schmidt-University of the Armed Forces in Hamburg. Now, she works as a free researcher in association with the Department of General Practice at the University of Göttingen.

Martin Scherer is a research fellow in the Department of General Practice, University of Göttingen, and a half-time general practitioner. He is funded by the German Ministry of Education and Research (Young Investigators Award). His main research topics are guideline development and implementation, heart failure in primary care and psychosocial morbidity.

Christiane Schmidt (Dipl. Päd., Dr. Phil.) is currently researching and teaching on virtual teams at the University of Hildesheim. The main focuses of her work are quailtative interview and observation methods, learning by doing research, the evaluation of internet-based seminars and the subjective coping with experiences with (networks of) computers. She is the author of "The Analysis of Semi-Structured Interviews" in the "Companion to Qualitative Research" (Sage 2004) and also author or co-author of many publications about the findings of her research projects, qualitative methods and seminar conceptions.

Monika Seidl is Professor of Cultural Studies at the English Department of Vienna University. Her research interests are wide-ranging with a focus on visual texts, literary classics and popular culture. She is currently President of the AAUTE (Austrian Association of University Teachers of English) and Director of Studies at the English Department of Vienna University.

George Siemens is a prominent writer and researcher on learning, networks, technology and organizational effectiveness in digital environments. He is the author of Knowing Knowledge, an exploration of how the context and characteristics of knowledge have changed and what it means to organizations today. Siemens is also Associate Director, Research and Development, with the Learning Technologies Centre at University of Manitoba, and founder and President of Complexive Systems Inc., a learning lab focused on helping organizations develop integrated learning structures to meet the needs of global strategy execution. Siemens also maintains the websites www.elearnspace.org, www.connectivism.ca, and www.knowingknowledge.com.